Religion and Legitimation of Power

Religion and Legitimation of Power In Thailand, Laos, and Burma

Edited by Bardwell L. Smith

South and Southeast Asia Studies by
ANIMA Books

Library of Congress Cataloging in Publication Data

Main entry under title:

Religion and legitimation of power in Thailand, Laos, and Burma.

(Religion and legitimation of power)
Includes bibliographies.
1. Buddhism and state—Thailand—Addresses, essays, lectures.
2. Buddhism and state—Laos—Addresses, essays, lectures. 3. Buddhism and state—Burma—Addresses, essays, lectures. 4. Buddhism and politics—Addresses, essays, lectures. I. Smith, Bardwell L., 1925-   II. Series.
BQ554.R44   294.3'3'770959   77-7444
ISBN 0-89012-009-9

South and Southeast Asia Studies
by ANIMA Books

ANIMA Books are published by Conococheague Associates, Inc., 1053 Wilson Avenue, Chambersburg PA 17201.

LC Number 77-7444
ISBN 0-89012-009-9

The map on page xi is reprinted from G. William Skinner and A. Thomas Kirsch (eds.): *Change and Persistence in Thai Society: Essays in Honor of Lauriston Sharp.* © 1975 by Cornell University. Used by permission of Cornell University Press.

Foreword

Bardwell L. Smith

This volume is one of three collections of essays on the theme of religion and the legitimation of power in South and Southeast Asia. As a whole, they examine various aspects of Islam, the Hindu tradition and Theravada Buddhism in relationship to the social and political order in several cultural and historical contexts. One volume, entitled *Religion and Legitimation of Power in South Asia* and published by E. J. Brill (Leiden, 1978), deals principally with India, though it contains an essay on Pakistan and another on Sri Lanka. Originally, it was to have included ones on Bangladesh and on Nepal, but these essays were not completed as planned. A second volume is entitled *Religion and Legitimation of Power in Sri Lanka.* Because of its more limited scope, it is perhaps the most cohesive of the three collections, though it does include consideration of Ceylon's long-term relationship with South India. The present volume deals mainly with Burma and Thailand, especially the latter, though two of its essays devote attention to the Laotian context.

In 1973, when the idea for a set of essays on this topic was first considered, the plan called for a single volume, with essentially one chapter on most countries in South Asia and mainland Southeast Asia. At the 1975 annual meetings of the Canadian Association for South Asian Studies and the American Academy of Religion two symposia were held at which the larger share of the essays appearing in these three collections were first read. Both because it did not prove possible to obtain essays on certain countries and because several excellent ones were submitted on the same country (covering different historical periods and diverse aspects of the basic theme), the original plan was modified and the material fell into three groupings rather than one. Subsequent to the 1975 meetings of those two professional associations other papers were solicited from persons known to be working on comparable material, and it was also decided to reprint a few previously

Essentially the same Foreword serves to introduce each of these volumes. Given the complexity of the various languages involved, it has been impossible to maintain full consistency in the use of diacritical marks. Generally speaking, the usage of the individual authors has been retained. While consistency is sought within each essay, a fuller use of diacritics is found in those essays which deal with the pre-modern period than in the other essays. In those essays where diacritical marks are used more fully, a simplified transliteration system with Sanskrit and Pāli terms is employed and the omission of relatively unimportant diacritics in local languages (e.g., Dǫk has been changed to Dok). With regard to Sanskrit and Pāli we have followed the lead of A. L. Basham, editor, *A Cultural History of India* (1975), who employs a system in which, for the most part, only long vowel and palatal marks (ā, ī, ū, ñ and ś) are used except in quotations and in the Index. Ordinarily, terms which appear in *Webster's New International Dictionary* (e.g., Theravada, Mahayana, Brahmanism, etc.) are used without long vowel marks.

published articles, in most cases from journals not well known in this country.

In any collection of essays by several contributors it almost goes without saying, though no reviewer worth his or her salt fails to point this out, that certain chapters are of more enduring value than others and that the volume as a whole does not possess the same cohesiveness a single first-rate scholar could bring to the subject. Certainly, in these collections, there are not only important lacunae, but there is no systematic attempt to relate ideas in one chapter to those in another, let alone to relate one volume to either or both of the others. The attempt here is more modest. It is simply to present together several reflections on a common theme, with breadth of scope and diversity of analysis compensating in part for lack of cohesiveness. Such is the editor's *apologia pro libro suo* in each of these three cases. It is necessary, however, to say something about the theme itself and to indicate how the concept was presented to those who wrote expressly for one or another of these volumes.

On a very general level the theme served to help the contributors focus their attention on how political leaders or a politicized group within a specific religious tradition and its membership (*or* an ideological tradition, for example, Marxism, civil religion in its modern guises, secularism, etc.) made use of "religious" beliefs, practices and institutions to provide cohesiveness to the realm and legitimacy to the holding of power. Examples of this, of course, abound in history. Some of the more famous ones include Constantine in the fourth century A.D., Aśoka in the third century B.C., and Han Wu-ti in the early Han dynasty of the second century B.C.

In the examination of any particular context one needs to consider a number of factors. Obviously, in any short essay only a few considerations can be explored in depth, though one can allude to others which could be examined in a longer treatment. The following factors were suggested to each contributor, though they were not intended to be exhaustive. In fact, part of each symposium's intent was to go beyond the merely descriptive approach to the subject and to help sharpen theoretical tools, i.e., to perceive new ways of analyzing the ongoing relationship between various kinds of ideology and political, social and economic power.

First, some attention must be given to the context itself in an essentially chronological manner. What factors, events, circumstances give rise to a situation in which it becomes possible and/or important for political power to align itself with and make use of a specific ideology or tradition in order to gain credibility and empower its sanctions? One need not begin with this descriptive analysis, but some attention is obviously in order.

Second, beyond the particulars which evolve over time to create a new social context, analysis includes examination of factors of social change, social contact and conflict, forms of cultural and political pluralism, and other aspects of an essentially dynamic picture which prompt different approaches to the organizing and enhancing of power.

Third, other pertinent considerations are the process and forms of legitimation which take place as power seeks to authenticate itself in the minds of potential supporters. Except in circumstances where "naked" or autocratic power is used, one finds a whole spectrum of subtle manifestations of legitimation, e.g., patronage of the arts, the granting of political patronage, direct or indirect support to certain religious groups, etc. Part of the picture here includes exploring how legitimation is nurtured, both within the body politic and within religious communities themselves.

Fourth, in the process of this evolution what happens to the religious tradition (or the ideology) when used in these ways? What happens to the political process, its structures and its goals? One needs to consider the dangers of communalism and the effect upon social, ethnic and religious minorities within the society. Does one find an inevitable corruption of religious tradition and ideology, or may reform and the seeds of a genuine renaissance emerge from these sorts of circumstances? What forms of syncretism emerge and how are these continuous or discontinuous with past forms?

Fifth, part of any such analysis may reveal challenges to the very process of legitimation itself from other forces within the society when threatened by such a development and by members of the political or religious hierarchy who perceive this process as inimical to a healthy social order and/or a given religious tradition. Examining these kinds of factors highlight the complexities of any situation and question univocal interpretations of what may otherwise appear as clearcut and self-evident forces at work.

As implied above, the intent of this endeavor was not to discover one set of criteria by which to examine the relationship between social power and ideological legitimacy, but to open up the investigation in fresh ways. This entails examining critically and with intensity an immense variety of common factors which, while present in most situations of these kinds, assume different forms and possess their own unique dynamics. To identify as many common factors as possible was thus one purpose, but to perceive their idiosyncratic combinations was no less important.

The present collection focuses primarily on Thailand, though Burma and Laos are also examined. Both contemporary and earlier contexts are analysed, with considerable emphasis given to the relationship between them. Stress is upon the dynamics and the patterns of legitimation, with attention paid to the import of ritual and symbolism as well as to the supportive yet often conflicting relationship between religion and polity. The final essay by S. N. Eisenstadt deals with no particular period of history, nor with any specific religious tradition. It is included because of its exceedingly suggestive implications for the theme at hand. Its theoretical reflections are pertinent to further consideration of this theme.

While many published articles and books are germane to a study of this topic, two recent publications are of central importance. One is E. Michael Mendelson, *Sangha and State in Burma: A Study of Monastic Sectarianism and Leadership*, edited by John P. Ferguson (Ithaca and London: Cornell University Press, 1975); the other is S. J. Tambiah, *World Conqueror and World Renouncer: A Study of Buddhism and Polity in Thailand against a Historical Background* (Cambridge and New York: Cambridge University Press, 1976), from which his chapter in this volume is an adaptation of some themes he develops more fully in his own book.

Contents

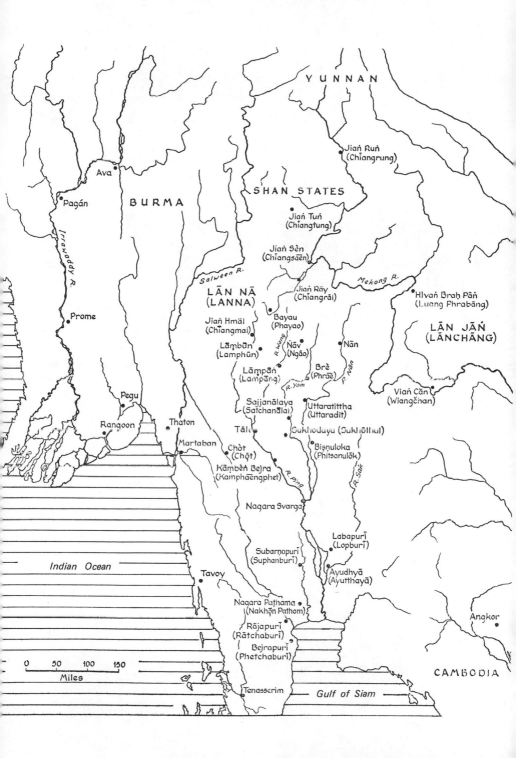

Part One

Sangha, Kingship, and Polity:
The Dynamics of Legitimation

Statecraft in the Reign of Lü Tai of Sukhodaya (ca. 1347-1374)*

Barbara Watson Andaya

Introduction

MUCH OF THE fascination of early Southeast Asian history lies in the frequent encounter with the unexpected. The deciphering of an obscure inscription, the discovery of an unsuspected text, or simply a fresh synthesis of known but neglected facts can lead to a complete reversal of accepted theories. Such has been the case in recent years with regard to the history of Sukhodaya, the precursor of modern Thailand. This is not to imply a denigration of the monumental compilations made by M. George Coedès, the doyen of orientalists.[1] His pioneer work of collecting, translating and annotating native sources has been fundamental in establishing a framework within which to construct the events and chronology of the period. Together with archaeological remains, these inscriptions form the bones and sinews of Sukhodayan history. Despite their tangibility, however, they are essentially incomplete historical documents. While posterity, lacking other evidence, must base its judgment on them, the historian should always be prepared to revise his opinion if new information appears.

For instance, Ram Kamheng (Lord Rāma, the Brave), lionized in the inscription from thirteenth-century Sukhodaya, is portrayed as a just, paternal monarch. It was he who "instructed the Thai" and gave them a script, who "courageously conquered" his enemies;[2] under him Sukhodaya reached its apogee. Modern historians have found no cause to quarrel with this verdict; in contrast, his grandson, Lü Tai (Lidaiya Mahādharmarāja I),[3] has met with somewhat less commendation in the literature. A theme can be traced through Western historical writing on Thailand, beginning with W.A.R. Wood's pioneer study,[4] which sees Lü Tai as a wise and virtuous king, but one who, by his "peaceful inclinations," encouraged and finally submitted to the might of Ayudhiā.[5] The standard text of Southeast Asian history depicts him as "a scholar who was completely pre-occupied with religion and eventually resigned

---

*I would like to acknowledge the advice and criticism of Professor A. Thomas Kirsch (Department of Anthropology, Cornell University) and Professor David Wyatt (Department of History, Cornell University) in the preparation of this paper.

Since this essay was written several important pieces of research have appeared which are relevant to this topic. Of particular value: A. B. Griswold and Prasert ṇa Nagara, "Epigraphic and Historical Studies No. 11, Part 1. The Epigraphy of Mahādharmarājā I of Sukhodaya," *JSS*, LXI (Jan. 1973), 71-182,and Part 2, *JSS* LXI (July 1973), 91-128; Craig J. Reynolds, "Buddhist Cosmography in Thai History, with Special Reference to Nineteenth Century Culture Change," *JAS*, XXXV (Feb. 1976), 203-220; Michael Vickery, "A Note on the Date of the Traibhūmikathā," *JSS*, LXII (July, 1974), 275-284; Charnvit Kasetsiri, *The Rise of Ayudhya* (Kuala Lampur and London, 1976).

his crown in 1361 in order to enter a monastery."[6] Another writer feels that
under this monarch an attempt was made to attain the Buddhist ethical maximum, an attempt which failed because it was not compatible with practical
politics; furthermore, he has suggested that Lü Tai submitted to Ayudhiā basically because of a pious anxiety to avoid warfare.[7] A prominent Thai historian does not discern any real development in this reign except in the sphere of
religion,[8] and even Professor Griswold, one of the foremost scholars in the
field, has on occasion judged Lü Tai in harsh terms.[9] However, the discovery
of fresh inscriptions during the last decade has necessitated a *volte face* in traditional attitudes towards this king and a revision of the widely held historical
verdict.[10] Professor Griswold, in a generous and sympathetic manner, has rewritten the chronology of Lü Tai's reign and retracted previous statements
made concerning his character.[11] According to this new interpretation, Lidaiya
Mahādharmarāja was

> an able statesman and a competent soldier. By attracting a number of the vassals
> who had broken away and by subduing others, he recovered a territory stretching
> from above Uttaratittha on the north to Nagara Svarga on the south, from the val-
> ley of the Ping on the west to that of the Sak on the east. If his gains were modest
> compared with those of Ram Kamheng, they were nonetheless impressive, for he
> was faced with a limiting factor which did not exist in Ram Kamheng's time: the
> territory south of Nagara Svarga now belonged to so powerful a ruler that Lidaiya
> had to dismiss all hope of recovering it. Instead he cultivated friendly relations
> with him.[12]

A re-examination of an account given by the Chinese merchant Wang Ta-
yüen has led Professor Griswold to conclude that Sukhodaya did not submit
to Ayudhiā until well after Lü Tai's death.[13] In other words, this monarch has
been misjudged by history; his reign did not serve to emasculate the state, and
in exercising authority he did not sublimate religion to the exclusion of practical politics.

In light of this new evidence it is incumbent on the historian to re-consider
Lü Tai both as a king and as a man, to ask critical and penetrating questions
about the nature of his rule. What problems confronted him? What were the
resources, the political tools on which he could draw? To what extent was his
Buddhism simply the vision of a pious religious? Does the tenor of Sukhodaya
in the mid-fourteenth century mark it off as an aberration, or are there parallel developments in other burgeoning states of the same period? In short,
what factors strengthened monarchical control to the extent that Sukhodaya
was for so long able to maintain its independence *vis-à-vis* its more powerful
neighbor?

Lü Tai came to the throne of Sukhodaya in 1347 in less happy circumstances than his predecessors. He had seen under his father's rule the insid-
ious erosion of the state built up by Ram Kamheng, a state which had covered
virtually all the present kingdom of Thailand.[14] Allies such as Lān Nā and
Rāmaññadesa had broken away, gaining territory at Sukhodaya's expense,
while vassals in the Malay Peninsula and eastern Thailand, incorporated into
the Ayudhian mandala, no longer paid fealty to their former suzerain.[15] Probably the only area which remained under Lü Tai's jurisdiction at his *abhiseka*
was the Sukhodaya-Sajjanālaya heartland itself.[16] As a final indication of the
deterioration of centralized authority, palace factionalism erupted into armed
conflict and the throne was seized by a usurper.[17] Lü Tai, then governing in

Sajjanālaya as *Uparāja* was not slow to act; apprized of the usurpation, he "went quickly in order to organize an expedition of all his troops outside the sacred territory," and at the very moment he commanded his forces to surround the capital, break down all the doors and seize control, "the axe smote all his enemies."[18]

Thus, in a manner reminiscent of Jayavarman VII of Cambodia, Lü Tai was forced to employ force in order to gain his birthright, and was immediately confronted with the problem of reconstructing the administrative and political framework, of salvaging the alliance structure which had collapsed during his father's reign, of recovering for Sukhodaya some of the prestige which had been lost. Yet one must avoid imputing to Lü Tai the priorities and values of a twentieth-century historian; for him, believing as he did that every event has a natural cause, this dysnomy was simply the sign and symptom of something far more serious – the decline of the Buddhist religion itself. So concerned had he been that while *Uparāja* he had written a treatise, the *Traibhūmikathā* (1345), which spelled out his views on precisely this subject. Its interest for later historians is enhanced by the fact that it represents the first work dealing with Buddhist cosmology in a systematic fashion.[19] He culled his information from various sources, acknowledging a debt to the various monks of Sukhodaya and Sajjanālaya; undoubtedly, he would have consulted Mahāthera Anōmadassī who, coming to Sajjanālaya reordained in the Sinhalese rites, had been installed in Wat Bā Deng (Red Forest Monastery) just south of the city.[20] Much textual material was taken directly from Pāli sources; Lü Tai leaned heavily on the work of the great commentator Buddhaghosa who, expanding the replies of the monk Nāgasena to the questions of King Menander,[21] had listed five stages by which the decline of Buddhism would be noted. Stretching over five thousand years, this deterioration would be marked by the successive disappearance of, firstly, the acquisition of the degrees of sanctity; secondly, the observation of the precepts; thirdly, the knowledge of the scriptures; fourthly, the exterior signs of Buddhism; and, lastly, by the disappearance of the corporeal relics.

It must not be imagined that this concern with the decline of Buddhism was simply a foible or obsession of Lü Tai; various Buddhist commentators had expressed anxiety for the future of the faith, and this anxiety increased as 1456 – the date set for the disappearance of the Tripitaka – approached. It is interesting that a similar text, composed sixty years later in far-off Tibet and likewise entitled *Tray Phum*, manifests this same apprehension concerning the ultimate fate of Buddhism.[22]

While the *Traibhūmikathā* is a treatise on cosmology in its discussion of the universe and man's place therein, it also played a hortatory and pedagogic role. Lü Tai uses this method to explicate the attributes of a good ruler and the principles of good government; the legendary Buddhist king, Dharmāsokarāja, is cited as the ideal example of a Cakravartin who practised meritorious works and eased the lot of his people so that they could devote more time to spiritual matters. Moral injunction to ruler and ruled are lent added weight by graphic descriptions of the torments which await evil doers, in a manner calculated to impress the common man. For example, adaptations of the original Pāli texts are indicated by reference to *ngui* trees, which proliferate in the Siamese forest and, with their brilliant orange flowers, provided a perfect analogy for the flames of hell.[23]

The Nagara Jum inscription of 1357 furnishes evidence that these fears were not dissipated by time. Insisting that this is "our own personal work," Lü Tai delineates step by step the manner in which Buddhism will disappear; finally, after all knowledge of sacred texts has vanished, after the *sangha* is no more, the holy relics will rise from all quarters of the globe and fly to Ceylon. Here they will disappear into the sacred Bodhi tree, disintegrating in a great conflagration which will mark both the end of the Buddhist faith and the unleashing of malevolent forces over the face of the earth. It therefore behooves each individual to practice the Buddhist precepts assiduously, to pay homage to the stūpas and Buddhist relics, symbols of the Buddha himself, and to benefit from the fact that he is alive at a stage when the Doctrine still flourishes. According to Lü Tai's calculations, although the scriptures would disappear less than a century after this date, there would still remain one thousand years before the precepts would show signs of deterioration.[24]

This concern with the state of Buddhism is linked to another theme which can be traced through Lü Tai's reign — that of moral restoration, by which the level of merit in the country could be raised. By the natural law of karma, this would lead to success and prosperity, bringing greater prestige for Sukhodaya in the Buddhist world and rendering it a desirable friend and ally. But no people could undertake this course of action without direction; the scriptures and treatises in which Lü Tai was well versed are quite explicit in their definition of the king as teacher and leader. The classical Hindu view of the ruler was emphasized in the Mon *Dharmaśāstra*, a source well known to the Thai.[25] The ideal monarch

> abides steadfast in the ten kingly virtues, constantly upholding the five common precepts and on holy days the set of eight precepts, living in kindness and goodwill to all beings. He takes pains to study the Thammasat and to keep the four principles of justice, namely: to assess the right or wrong of all service or disservice rendered by him, to uphold the righteous and truthful through none but just means and to maintain the prosperity of his state through none but just means.[26]

In Buddhist terms, the domination of one man over his fellows cannot be justified unless he endeavours to smooth the path towards Nirvāna for all his people in return for their loyalty. This theory of social contract, of reciprocal relationship between king and people was reinforced by reference to ideal monarchs who exemplified all the Buddhist virtues and were thus a universal model whom any ruler should strive to emulate. Strongly entrenched in Southeast Asian tradition was the legend of Aśoka; Lü Tai's reference to him in the *Traibhūmikathā* is pregnant with implication, for the myth of the "Aśokan ideal" had become an integral part of the kingly ethos. Stories of his paternalism and concern for the welfare of his subjects were legion; underscoring this traditional ideal was the example of Lü Tai's own grandfather, brave, merciful, learned, a sincere Buddhist and a just ruler under whom "this Sukhodaya (fared) well."[27] It was axiomatic that the moral standard of the king and the happiness of his subjects were inextricably linked. A virtuous ruler ensures the prosperity of his country, but "an unrighteous king destroys his kingdom ... and is a scourge to his country. He hereafter must suffer in Tapanna Hell."[28]

There could thus be no doubt in the mind of Lü Tai as to what was expected of him, and considering the context in which he came to the throne, the accretion of national strength, his own personal fears about the moral state of the realm, it is not fanciful to conceive of this king as a "man with a mission," whose purpose was to assert his authority in both temporal and spiritual spheres, using whatever resources were at his command.

In an age of emerging Thai kingdoms, "young people in a state of active expansion,"[29] when every petty principality had the potential of absorbing its neighbours, it was natural that allies should be desirable. But what should attract them? Nothing less than obvious power and blatant achievement; this is precisely what aided Sukhodaya to re-emerge as a leading state in the Menam Basin. For Sukhodaya was not without resources, and despite the vicissitudes of the previous thirty years, it still possessed the characteristics of the well-equipped state. Firstly, although Lü Tai avoided warfare where possible, in contrast to his grandfather, he could not be dismissed as a military commander. Had he not manifested his strength of arms (*bāhu-balam*) by capturing the capital, the centre of the cosmos, from an usurper? By the middle of his reign he was able to act the role of king-maker by evicting a pretender from the throne of *Nān*, replacing him with the legitimate heir. During the same period (1362-3) he advanced east of the Sak Valley, increasing in military strength as he was able to call on more vassals to supply manpower for his army.[30]

In traditional terms, Sukhodaya also possessed strength of wealth (*bhoga-balam*); situated at the crossroad of Thai and Khmer commerce, with access to several river systems, the country was in a favoured geographic position. During Ram Kamheng's reign trade had been brisk, stimulated by the absence of royal monopolies and tolls.[31] Bazaars and covered markets within the city precincts offered lucrative trading prospects to outside visitors and this thriving commercial centre was maintained even during the less happy days of Lo Tai's reign.[32] One can imagine that the traditional Southeast Asian hospitality was readily extended to all vendors and merchants in Sukhodaya, where the people could go "by barge to trade and by horse to sell their merchandise."[33] Indeed, the proliferation of wats, the extent of image-making, and the large quantities of alms and costly offerings tendered to the *sangha* together attest to a prosperity which the Thai themselves would have seen not as fortuitous, but as the result of great merit accumulated by both ruler and ruled.

Although this continued wealth itself implied a wise and just king, there were other means of glorification which demonstrated Lü Tai's fitness to reign, and the good fortune which would, *ipso facto*, devolve on to all his subjects. Strength of high birth (*abhijācca-balam*) had always been a potent way of enhancing royal glory; indeed, it has been argued that legitimisation through genealogy can be regarded as a major theme in Southeast Asian history.[34] Lü Tai may have felt an added incentive to emphasise his ancestry, since he had been forced to overthrow an usurper and there may still have been some nascent dissidence. In the trilingual inscriptions which commemorate the installation of a Buddha image in 1361, Lü Tai harks back to his pedigree, but glosses over the somewhat inglorious reign of his father. Instead, he stresses the achievements of Ram Kamheng, whom he refers to as "His Majesty Kamraten Añ Rāmarāja." Lü Tai himself had been granted this title by "the rulers at the four cardinal points," a title originally conferred on the founder of Sukhodaya by the God-King at Angkor.[35] Lü Tai is clearly portrayed as the legitimate successor to the throne, of whose ancestry and illustrious genealogy there could be no doubt.

Another source of glorification was the possession of the capital itself, the centre of the cosmos, the symbol of Mount Meru. Sukhodaya possessed a certain uniqueness in that there were not one, but two cities which were regarded as sacred, and from which all power emanated. About 55 kilometres apart, Sukhodaya (Production of Happiness) and Sajjanālaya (Paradise) had originally been small army outposts, but after the Khmer withdrawal were combined by the Thais into a duality. It became customary for the monarch to have his seat at Sukhodaya, while the *Uparāja* governed in Sajjanālaya. Linked by a good road which remained well above flood level, there was constant intercourse between them, and throughout the inscriptions the two cities are treated as a unit. Certainly there was little distinction in the number of monasteries, relics, or frequency of miracles, although the precedence of Sukhodaya is indicated by the fact that it was here that the actual *abhiseka* was confirmed, that this was regarded as the convergence of the four cardinal points, that it was carefully laid out in the foursquare plan, and that it imparted its name to the country.

Further evidence of Lü Tai's indisputable right to rule and his irrefutable claim to special powers lay in his possession of the regalia, especially the crown, the white parasol and the sacred sword, Jayasrī. [36] All these tangible objects underscored his connection with the still-revered Angkorian dynasty, since they had been conferred together with the title Kamraten Añ. Perhaps, too, the support of the Queen Mother was influential in giving added weight to Lü Tai's position. There was obviously a close relationship between them, for the *Traibhūmikathā* was dedicated to her, and to her would be transferred all merit acquired by the preaching of Dharma. In some sense, the approbation of, and alliance with, the dowager queen can be seen as an additional part of the royal trappings, albeit in abstract terms. [37]

To these essentially Hindu appendages of royal power can be added those pertaining to Buddhism, which fulfilled much the same function of adding lustre to the king's position and uplifting the status of the country *vis-à-vis* those less well endowed. H. L. Shorto, when writing of the Mons, has made a useful distinction between the power and charisma obtained from the possession of magical objects such as the regalia and that derived from spiritual attainments. [38] Ever since Aśoka's legendary dispatch of Buddha relics to Southeast Asia, the possession of such sacred artifacts had been a prime aim of every Buddhist monarch, for to have incontrovertible evidence of the Buddha's favor gave a kingdom both an aura of moral excellence and a source of supernatural power. Thus the wars ostensibly fought over white elephants, the machinations employed to acquire a Buddha image, were efforts, from a Buddhist viewpoint, to obtain some portion of a neighbor's strength. Naturally, the most prized relics came from the Buddha's homeland and from the island of Lankā (Ceylon), where gnosticism and scholarly learning flourished. It was thence that the monarchs of the neophyte Buddhist states sent to acquire these sacred objects. Some years earlier, when a famous *thera* had returned to Sukhodaya with the *Kesadhātu* (Hair relic) and the *Gīvādhātu* (neck-bone relic), Lü Tai's father had been overjoyed. All the kingdom had combined in a common ritual of veneration and the occasion was marked by a series of supernatural events which were interpreted as evidence that the king would attain "the status of a Buddha." [39] In the same reign a relic was discovered, supposedly left by King Aśoka, and this timely event must have given some touch of glory to a regime which was in all other respects far inferior to its predecessor. Lü Tai, as *Uparāja*, was surrounded by this atmosphere of religious fervor, when the court, bereft of opportunity for territorial expansion, withdrew into itself and found release in purely religious activity. He himself for a time bathed in the reflected glory of ruling a city which sheltered the Aśokan relic, until he reluctantly surrendered it to his father. A precedent had thus been established; at the time of his *abhiseka*, Lü Tai brought from Ceylon a Great Relic and a sprig from the very Bodhi tree under which the Buddha had gained enlightenment. This was no ordinary relic, he assured his people, but a truly authentic one, and whosoever revered it would gain merit tantamount to that gained by rendering homage to the Master himself.[40] Buddha images were likewise an important acquisition for any kingdom, and from the time of Ram Kamheng, the kings of Sukhodaya had publicly recorded their pious satisfaction at the numbers of statues in the country. While these images represent a distinctive style, it was imperative that they resemble an original portrait of the Buddha, in order to acquire some of its potency. Naturally, some images had greater power than others; what was important was not innovation, but a relationship, a proven connection between this portrait and another famous one.[41]

There are many stories of Buddha images which were taken from kingdom to kingdom, and which were regarded as the palladia of the realm itself. Some

> became famous in warding off human enemies and wicked demons, by protecting cities and winning battles, by calling down the life-giving rain to ensure good crops. The Prince who succeeds, by diplomacy or warfare, in getting hold of one of these choice objects, can feel confidence that his state will be safe and prosperous.[42]

Two early Dvāravatī-style statues found at Sukhodaya were not locally produced, but were probably transported there precisely because they possessed this supernatural power.[43] The palladium of Sukhodaya itself appears to have been the Sīhala (Ceylon) Buddha, but Lü Tai, like his predecessors, was indefatigable in acquiring even more images which were imbued with magical potency by special rites. Held in public, such rites united both ruler and subjects in a common act of veneration.[44]

Part of the prestige of, and reverence surrounding, the island of Lankā lay in the fact that it boasted indisputable evidence of the Buddha's presence, such as the famous Footprint on Adam's Peak. This was a source of wonderment and envy to all Buddhists, but in lieu of an original, Sukhodaya had to be content with a replica. Lü Tai had caused an impression to be made of the one in Ceylon, and then had had copies made which could be placed throughout the kingdom. His son went even further, paying so much veneration to the Buddha Footprint that its cult had become firmly established by the end of the fourteenth century.[45] Another Footprint was installed on Froghill sometime before 1357, bearing the 108 supernatural signs. These represented the cosmos, which, since they were beneath the Buddha's foot, both supported him and were subordinate to him. The presence of the Footprint demonstrated irrefutably that this land was stamped with the Master's own symbol and was blessed by him in an extraordinary way.[46]

> This mountain is named Sumanakūṭaparvata (Sanskrit for Adam's Peak) because it has upon its summit a copy made from the footprint left by our Lord Buddha on the top of Mount Sumanakūṭaparvata in Ceylon. It was put here so that divinities

and men might come to salute it, respect it and pay it homage. Whosoever climbs to the top of this mountain to salute the Footprint of our Lord Buddha will surely gain the Three Prosperities.[47]

When the king visited the footprint, he caused the road to be cleared and decorated.

> On both sides of the road ceremonial trees had been planted and garlands of flowers hung up. Torches and candles and lamps were lighted and fragrant incense was burning. There were flags and banners everywhere. On both sides of the road there were trays of areca nut and betel leaves. After doing obeisance, the people made merry, dancing, leaping and amusing themselves in a thousand ways. They sang songs of pious deeds, and again they did obeisance, accompanied by the music of wind instruments and strings, gongs and drums, of such loudness one might have thought the earth would burst.[48]

But these sacred objects, as well as reinforcing the Buddhist religion, raising the level of merit and manifesting the king's piety, served more practical purposes. Such nation-wide cults formed the basis of a common ritual which cut across regional differences, binding the people together.[49] Again, because they canalized spiritual forces to the benefit of the recipient, the gift of an image bespoke great goodwill on the part of the donor. In a sense, they can be regarded as part of the diplomatic equipage of the period; the monks who accompanied a sacred relic on its passage through the country helped strengthen the nexus between outlying centres and the capital, while visits to neighboring states assured brother kings of amicable feelings. When the King of Nān, for instance, helped Lü Tai to design a wat in Sukhodaya, the latter was so pleased with the result that he presented his friend with a number of holy relics and votive tablets, which were accorded special veneration by the people of Nān. A city was built close by the shrine where the relics were, so that the king could live in close proximity to such holiness.[50] In 1369 the Aśokan relics were sent to Chieng Mai under the charge of several prominent theras. They moved "from place to place," impressing the countryside, one would imagine, with stories of the wonderful miracles which were so frequent in the great city of Sukhodaya-Sajjanālaya.[51]

With the threat of Ayudhiā in the south, these ostensibly religious missions fulfilled a critical role in building up the network of alliances necessary to maintain a viable state. It is indicative that whereas fifty years earlier Mangrai of Lān Nā had gone to Monland as the source of Buddhist scholarship, his successors turned to Sukhodaya.[52] This may well have been influenced by the fervor of Buddhism in the south, and by Lü Tai's ominous predictions concerning the decline of the holy precepts. While Lü Tai, for his part, was anxious to see Buddhism propagated, this was a politic way of re-establishing alliances which had been allowed to lapse since the reign of Ram Kamheng. This re-forging of old ties was symbolized by the erection of Lotus-bud towers, unique to Sukhodayan architecture, in Chieng Mai and other outlying areas. They were a tangible sign of the spiritual links binding capital, province and vassal,[53] like the Buddha images of Angkor's Jayavarman VII.

Added weight was lent to Lü Tai's claim to authority by emphasizing the less tangible sources of power, his spiritual attainments and moral excellence. By portraying the monarch as wise and all-knowing, by describing him as the father of his people and sponsor of the sangha, there is a constant parallel drawn between Lü Tai and the ideal ruler. All these qualities are carefully delineated in the inscriptions which were installed throughout the country. Most important to the Buddhist concept of monarchy was the possession of intelligence and wisdom (pañña-balam), for a true king should be both philosopher and teacher, versed not only in religion but also in secular matters. Lü Tai inherited a tradition of scholarship, which had long held an honored place in Sukhodaya. There were frequent public recitations of scriptures held under the king's auspices, and the scholarly ranks were swelled by visitors from Ceylon and Monland, invited by the king himself. Lü Tai had expressed regret at the passing of the influence of the Brahmin astrologers and physicians, men versed in Hindu literature and scientific skills, which had been an indirect result of the withdrawal of Khmer influence from the area.[54] Yet it must not be imagined that the court was bereft of Hindu learning; even the sages of Angkor, famous for their knowledge, came to study science at Sukhodaya.[55] During Lü Tai's reign there was an increased interest in all things Hindu, and he was able to claim with justifiable pride that he had studied the Vedas as well as the Vinaya and the Abhidharma, "according to the traditional methods," that is, beginning with the Brahmins and ascetics. This was the time-honored pattern of instruction in ancient India, where a Brahmin guru, often an ascetic, would instruct his pupil in the sacred texts. Lü Tai had devoted particular attention to mathematics and astrology, for in the inscriptions he insists that it was he alone who made the necessary calculations for the stages of the decline of Buddhism; furthermore, "using his authority," he was able to reform the calendar. Prince Damrong has suggested that the mention in the northern annals of "a change in the era of reckoning" may refer to Lü Tai, who knew "the short years and the years with intercalary months, the days, the lunar calendar . . . His knowledge is unequalled. He knows the treatises and traditions, the law and maxims, beginning with the treatises on astronomy . . . that is only an abbreviated version of his knowledge."[56]

Besides being versed in these more secular matters, Lü Tai was an authority on all matters pertaining to Buddhism, for he was the mentor of "all the monks" who "observed his wisdom," he who "deserved to be honored by the wise ones."[57] He established a precedent for later Thai kings by sponsoring within the confines of his palace a hall of learning where bhikkhus and Brahmins alike engaged in learned discussion and casuistic debate.[58]

Like his grandfather, Lü Tai emphasized his own charity and goodness as an inducement for people to place themselves under his rule, for whereas "without royal morality, the people suffer, the harvests decline," it was axiomatic that wise and just rule would, by the very nature of things, result in happiness for all subjects.[59] It is not irrelevant to point out once again that in early Southeast Asia, it was manpower, not land, which was the ultimate source of wealth, especially in an underpopulated country such as Sukhodaya. This was an age when the spoils of battle were not only booty, but prisoners. Entire city populations were frequently removed wholesale, and resettled in the conquering kingdom, usually as slaves. But Lü Tai disavowed any desire to enslave his captives; he was a lover of peace, and on the few occasions when he did take up arms, he won renown less for his military victories than for the humanity with which he treated his prisoners.[60] "If he captures soldiers or enemy warriors, he does not kill them or wound them, but tends and nourishes them in order to avert their destruction."[61] One is tempted to believe that this is an effort to disassociate himself from the massive wars of the late thirteenth century which had ravaged much of the Menam Basin and Cambodia, with their consequent indifference to human misery.

One rendition of an inscription indicates that there were no slaves in Sukhodaya. Although slavery in its worst form probably did not exist, there is evidence of assigned temple servants, given "without reserve until their death,"[62] and in Monland, from whence Sukhodaya derived much of its tradition, temple slavery was a social institution. Again, this must be qualified; the people thus assigned did not apparently suffer any loss in status, and in many cases it was considered a great honor. Certainly, monasteries of Sukhodaya would have required upkeep, and personnel were necessary to tend to the needs of the monks. In Monland, too, there was some hereditary slavery, although slave-owners were generally benevolent.[63] In any event, the condition of the common man was much better in Lü Tai's realm than in that of his neighbor, Rama T'bodi: witness a law passed in Ayudhiā in 1356 which refers to frequent attempts by slaves to escape to Sukhodaya.[64]

There may be another reason for the lack of encouragement given to slavery. In later Ayudhiā, all free men were required to render some service to the king or to a noble; this may have existed in some incipient form in Sukhodaya, providing manpower for the tremendous building program.[65] Furthermore, recruits were also needed for the army; an inscription refers to army leaders as "each returning to his own place," which indicates that they were regional commanders each responsible for supplying fighting forces.[66] Thus it was in the king's own interest to protect the village and encourage agriculture, since this would mean peasants would be contented, there would be no threat of their leaving, and the source of manpower would be guaranteed. Right of inheritance and property are respected. "When a father dies, the king lets the children have his possessions; when an elder brother dies, he lets the younger brother have them . . . If the king sees the rice of others, he does not covet it, if he sees the wealth of others, he is not annoyed by it."[67] For the charity and mercy of Lü Tai were "as boundless as water of the ocean, he loves his people like his own children."[68]

Both in his inscriptions and in the *Traibhūmikathā* Lü Tai set forth limits on his own power; whilst by issuing stern moral and legal injunctions to vassal princes and regional lords, he demonstrated plainly that he required an honest and fair administration. By tradition, the king was entitled to one-tenth of the harvest (*sassamedha*), but Lü Tai emphasized that his officials should collect nothing from those people whose harvest had failed; a king could only exact moderate corvée from his subjects, and should not demand more than they were able to give, while old people should be completely exempt; the king should make available loans from the royal treasury, but could not, like private citizens, charge either tax or interest.[69]

The keynote of these inscriptions, set up at the various administrative centres such as Nagara Svarga, Bang Pan, Sukhodaya and Sajjanālaya, is universal justice and kindness. A ruler must give thought to his descendants, for it is they who will suffer if he metes out excessive impositions; they should do meritorious works and respect religion, for "all chiefs who govern well will govern a long time."[70] But Lü Tai's eulogizing of his utopian kingdom must not be seen as unique, but rather as a means adopted by many Buddhist rulers of rallying and maintaining support. Lü Tai himself takes some of his descriptions almost verbatim from those of his father, while farther north, Fah Ngum of Lan Chang, in virtually identical terms, describes the halcyon state of his own kingdom.

There shall be no thieves and no acts of banditry in our territory. There shall be no fighting and no unnecessary blood shed among us all. Disputes shall be thoroughly examined and fairly judged. Life sentence shall be pronounced only as a last resort. Those found guilty shall be gaoled and released only after they have served their time in prison so they can resume their normal activities. [71]

Like Fah Ngum, Lü Tai might have emphasized that there must be people in the land "before we can produce the things we need," for he himself customarily pardoned criminals, "giving them the wherewithal to make restitution for their crimes, and sent them home." [72] Moreover, "if he catches people guilty of deceit and insolence, people who put poison in his rice in order to cause him sickness and death, he never kills or beats them, but he pardons all who behave wickedly towards him." [73] If a King dealt thus with his enemies, how much better would he treat his friends! But this seemingly enlightened and merciful rule cannot be attributed solely to religious piety and the mitigating influence of Theravada Buddhism. In 1292 Chou Ta Kuan, while attesting the primacy of Theravada Buddhism in Angkor, noticed tortures, live burials, trial by ordeal. These may perhaps be imputed to the Hindu tradition yet strong in Cambodia, for the judicial system of India used stern measures to ascertain guilt, and often tortured in order to elicit a confession. [74] The lessened Hindu tradition in Sukhodaya which allowed for the development of a paternal monarchy was, in addition, stimulated by the exigencies of the moment and the great need to keep the population at a level comparable or superior to that of surrounding states.

Although Lü Tai was a king "without equal," who reigned "according to the precepts," "gifted with the ten royal virtues," "as liberal as Vessantara," [75] his prestige and power were reinforced by his claim to supernatural and magical skills. The inscriptions point out that not only is the king able to make machines, but is proficient in playing dice and chess. Both games combined skill and luck, dice being a favorite sport in ancient India; its inclusion in a royal proclamation would have recalled the great gambling tournament in the *Mahābhārata* epic, while stories such as the *Anubhata Jātaka* portrayed the Bodhisattva as an accomplished player. Without doubt, the ability to perceive whether the dice were falling in the right manner demanded uncommon intuition and shrewdness, and demonstrated the magical good fortune of the winner. [76] Furthermore, the inscriptions describe the king's prowess in riding and hunting elephants, which required not only complete mastery and control of the great beasts, but also denoted a religious discipline and inordinate exercise of royal authority. This may have been because the elephant occupied such an important place in Buddhist teachings, and also because the hunt itself was carried out in the jungle, the domain of the omniscient and omnipotent spirits. [77]

Lü Tai's great merit was manifested in a more tangible way in the building program which included not only *vihāras* and *cetiyas* for the monks, but roads and irrigation works for his people. The planting of areca palm trees, mango groves, jackfruit trees encouraged agriculture, as did the clearing of the forest undergrowth in areas like Song Kwe. In the Angkorian tradition, rice fields were laid out fed by Barays and canal systems. And why did he do all this?

Not, he assured his people, because he wanted power, but because he desired to become a Buddha, and to lead all people across the ocean of the three sorrows of transmigration.[78] He disclaims any pretensions to *cakravartin* status, probably to allay the fears of those erstwhile rebellious vassals who had been forgiven and welcomed back into the fold.[79]

This emergence of the Bodhisattva ideal, the saintly leader who remains with men to aid them to Nirvāna is more strongly developed in Mahayana Buddhism, but is not alien to Theravada thinking. Although Lü Tai made no attempt to proclaim himself a Buddha, the inferences are pointed. At his ordination in 1361, miracles, associated with extraordinary piety occurred; the earth, incapable of supporting the weight of such kingly virtue, trembled and quaked; this phenomenon was followed by "all kinds of other supernatural events, as is the ordinary course of happenings in the career of a Bodhisattva."[80]

It must not be supposed that Buddhist doctrine as defined in the Pāli Canon was the only belief system on which statecraft in Sukhodaya rested. Despite the assertion of Ram Kamheng that all his subjects "believe in Buddhism," it is obvious that the syncretism so characteristic of Buddhism generally was not absent in thirteenth century Thailand. An inscription from the reign of Ram Kamheng refers to Phra Kapung, "superior to any other spirit,"[81] attesting the existence of a strong animist cult. The fact that this deity is not mentioned in Lü Tai's inscriptions does not indicate that the cult was no longer important. Although it may not have received the same official support, Lü Tai himself is careful to show due deference to "the guardians and spirits" who were of prime importance in maintaining the country's prosperity.[82] The non-Buddhistic elements present in Thai Buddhism today — the elements which may in part account for its continued viability as a belief system — are also apparent in the religion of Sukhodaya. For example, Lü Tai notes nostalgically the waning of Brahmanic influence from 1218, and it appears that during his reign the Brahmins, mentioned frequently in the inscriptions, acquired an enhanced prestige. They must have played a valuable role in strengthening the central administration, acting as advisors on all matters pertaining to statecraft and legal administration, besides presiding over such magic religious rites as the coronation, annual ploughing, and Swinging Festival.[83] It was the Brahmins, too, who were an indispensable part of the *devarāja* cult as it had been practiced in Angkor, and in Sukhodaya this concept becomes fused with the Bodhisattva ideal; the Śiva and Vishnu statues erected by Lü Tai bear such distinctive features that Professor Griswold has suggested that they are portraits of Lü Tai himself.[84] These were installed in the *Devatāyamahāksetra* (Brahmanic Temple), which was probably built by Lü Tai and before them the Brahmins and ascetics rendered "a cult in perpetuity."[85] No doubt this served to recapture some of the mystical and awful aspects surrounding kingship which had been mitigated by the royal practice of *vacapeyyan* (friendly conversation) between the Sukhodayan king and people. For, while Buddhism in its social ethic certainly supports political stability, it is "singularly lacking in doctrine to regulate the institution of monarchy" because of its "repudiation of caste and consequent neutrality towards status systems generally."[86] Furthermore, cult worship would have ensured the continued and unceasing acquisition of royal merit which could then be shared among all and used for the good of the kingdom.

Thus, then as now, Buddhism provided a wide umbrella under which many could find shelter. To Lü Tai, the Brahmins, the *śramanas*, the ascetics and the anchorities were as one; he compares himself to Janaka, an ancient philosopher-king of 7th century India, noted for his patronage of religion and general toler-ance.[87] Yet it must not be forgotten that the ideal Buddhist king was the spon-sor of the *sangha*; the lengthy account of the reception accorded a visiting *thera*, and that of his own ordination, must not be dismissed. These events were recorded for very specific reasons, and the fact that such learned monks would deign to journey from far-off places was tangible proof of Sukhodaya's prestige as a patron of religion. Like the relics and the Buddha images, these scholarly and pious men lent an aura of sanctity to the realm in which all in-habitants shared. This public rejoicing is recorded in an inscription which vivid-ly mirrors the panoply and pageantry of the welcome given to the Mahāswāmi Sangharāja, who had come from Pan at the request of Lü Tai.

> When the monk was on his way, the king sent workmen to prepare the building of *kutis* and a *vihāra* (preaching hall) to the west of Sukhodaya, in the Mango Grove, which he levelled out, smoothed, banked up with sand, and on all sides, made it as beautiful as a work conceived by Vishnu . . . He ordered his ministers, officials, and members of his family to go and receive the monk and pay homage to him.
>
> Immediately the king ordered the sweeping and cleaning of the royal road going from the eastern door to the western door, and to the Mango Grove where *kutis* and a *vihāra* had been built. He ordered veils of all colours to be hung everywhere, in order to stop the burning rays of the sun, then he had draperies and garlands of flowers attached, and spread lengths of materials in five different colours out on the ground so that the Buddha's feet would not touch the ground in any spot. He made so many preparations to honour the monk that it is impossible to enumerate them. If one wished to make a comparison, one could say that the royal road was as beau-tiful as the entrance to Heaven.[88]

The implications of the king's ordination, following shortly after this, also merit attention. This "rite of passage" served to enhance his spiritual powers still further by endowing his person and infusing his reputation with a magico-religious quality. In Buddhist thinking it was not kings who held the most revered place in society; theoretically, at least, the lowest *bhikkhu* was super-ior to the wealthiest *day* (noble). The way of the world and the way of the monk were quite distinct. There was no doubt in the mind of the common man who was closer to Nirvāna. It was almost predictable, then, that Lü Tai should emulate his father and enter the monastery. What is interesting is the timing. Why did he wait until 1361, more than a decade after his *abhiseka*, before donning the yellow robe? Probably it was a matter of politics; by this juncture the kingdom of Sukhodaya had been virtually reconstructed, and per-haps he felt that he could safely leave the reigns of government in other hands. There was some kind of *modus vivendi* with Ayudhiā; the cities along the Ping had returned as vassals; Nān had been friendly since 1351; Chieng Mai was showing no signs of enmity. He may have felt, too, that this was an auspicious moment to endow both the kingdom and himself with greater spiritual po-tency.

> As never before, this momentous occasion is a time for doing good works, the ben-eficial results of which can be realised by listening to the preaching of the Law . . . As a sign of his changed status, he was given a new name, and in honour of the occasion Pali verses were composed by the *Mahāthera*.[89]

Perhaps Lü Tai saw this as the culmination of his royal career, a spiritual re-juvenation, but there is no evidence he intended to abrogate royal responsibility completely. In any case, events outside his control made the continuation of this meditative life impossible. The throne of Nān was seized by an usurper; it is possible that an appeal was made to the king to come out of retirement and lead his people again. To mark his return to secular life, his chief monk, acting on behalf of the civil and military officers, bestowed on him two new titles. There is no record, and indeed, it seems unlikely, that Lü Tai entered the monkhood again. By 1370 Rama T'bodi of Ayudhiā was dead, and his successor had begun harassing Sukhodaya's borders. But Lü Tai must have looked back with satisfaction at his ordination; he had consecrated himself, and the very earth itself, proclaimed the inscriptions, acknowledged the oath. In so doing, his success as a ruler was re-affirmed both for his contemporaries and for posterity.

Conclusion

The recently published inscriptions edited by Professor Griswold and Dr. Prasert ṇa Nagara in a sense extend Sukhodayan history for another century, and cast a new light on the role played by Lü Tai. It appears that the 1378 "oath of allegiance" was of so nominal a nature that the pattern of government in Sukhodaya was hardly altered. Far from becoming an abject vassal of Ayudhiā, the kingdom had sufficient strength in 1388 to gain a victory over Chieng Rai, and when Ayudhiā was rent by civil wars, it was still seen as an ally worth cultivating. An inscription of 1390, in a buoyant mood, gives no hint of vassal status, and proudly records a treaty concluded between Sukhodaya and Nān. By 1400, its forces had rallied to the extent of recovering Nagara Svarga, the linch pin of the riverine communications system, and its king proclaimed that Sukhodaya had "succeeded to the enjoyment of supreme sovereignty."[90]

From this evidence, it does not appear that Lü Tai's reign was instrumental in bringing about the decline of the kingdom. On the contrary, his rule imparted to Sukhodaya a momentum which was to carry it forward for half a century after his death. Two hundred years enabled the kings of Sukhodaya to establish and develop principles of government attuned both to wise diplomacy and Buddhist ethics. If the chronology of Lü Tai inscriptions is traced, it can be seen that the major ones appeared before he entered the monastery in 1361. Thus this strong public emphasis on the Buddhist nature of the state was most pronounced when he was consolidating his power. While his genuine piety cannot be questioned, it must also be emphasized that Lü Tai fully exploited a most efficacious political tool. Rather than being "completely pre-occupied with religion," Lü Tai was equally concerned with practical politics. During the thirty years of his reign, Sukhodaya grew and prospered, maintained friendly relations with its neighbors, and established itself as an important locus of Buddhist activity. Lü Tai himself perpetuated a model of paternal rule that was later incorporated into the very conception of Thai kingship.

Abbreviations: BEFEO   Bulletin de l'École Française d'Extrême Orient (Hanoi)
                JSS   Journal of the Siam Society (Bangkok)
                JBRS   Journal of the Burma Research Society (Rangoon)

Notes

1. Especially *Recueil des Inscriptions du Siam*, Bangkok 1924 and "Documents sur l'histoire religieux et politique du Laos Occidental," *BEFEO*, XXV, 1925, 1-200.

2. Coedès, *Recueil*, Insc. I, pp. 44-48.

3. For the sake of convenience, the usual system of numbering the Sukhodaya kings has been followed. In actual fact, Lü Tai's father was also called Dharmarāja. Coedès, *Recueil*, Insc. II, p. 64.

4. W. A. R. Wood, *A History of Siam*, Bangkok, 1924.

5. G. Coedès, *The Indianised States of Southeast Asia*, trans. by Susan Brown Cowing, edited by Walter Vella, Honolulu, 1968, p. 221.

6. D. G. E. Hall, *A. History of Southeast Asia*, London, 1964, p. 164.

7. E. Sarkisyanz, *Buddhist Backgrounds of the Burmese Revolution*, The Hague, 1965, p. 47 and a personal conversation with the writer.

8. Prince Dhaninivat, *A History of Buddhism in Thailand*, Bangkok, 1961, p. 10.

9. A. B. Griswold, "New Evidence for the Dating of Sukhodaya Art," *Artibus Asiae*, XIX (3/4, 1956), 243 ff; "The Buddhas of Sukhodaya," *Chinese Art Archives of America*, VII (1953), 32.

10. Prajum, *Collected Stone Inscriptions*, Part I, Bangkok, 1957, and Part III, 1965 (in Thai).

11. A. B. Griswold, *Towards a History of Sukhodaya Art*, Bangkok, 1967, pp. 30-42 and n. 83.

12. A. B. Griswold and Prasert ṇa Nagara, "A Declaration of Independence and its Consequences," *JSS*. LVI (July, 1968), 208-9.

13. I am aware that there is still some debate as to the actual date of the assertion of Ayudhiā's control over Sukhodaya, and also concerning the date of Lü Tai's death. On both counts I have accepted Professor Griswold's conclusions, which are partially based on research done by Professor O. W. Wolters. Griswold, *Towards a History*, p. 39 n. 108.

14. Coedès, *Recueil*, Insc. I, p. 48; Griswold, *Towards a History*, p. 6.

15. Ayudhiā was founded about the middle of the fourteenth century by Rāmādhipati (Prince U Tong), incorporating the province of Lavo (Lopburi) and territory around the Gulf of Siam, together with Subarnapurī, Rājapurī, Bejrapurī and the northern Malay Peninsula. Griswold, *Towards a History*, p. 31.

16. Griswold, *Towards a History*, pp. 15, 31.

17. An inscription discovered in 1956 near Sukhodaya gives a list of Kings which inserts the name of Ngua Nam Tom between that of Lo Tai and Lü Tai. Griswold, *Towards a History*, p. 29.

18. Coedès, *Recueil*, Insc. IV, p. 97.

19. As the *Tray Phum* (Three Worlds), it is still used in Thailand today, and forms much of the basis of popular Buddhist beliefs. The bulk of the following remarks are drawn from George Coedès, "The *Traibhumikathā*. Buddhist Cosmology and Treaty on Ethics," *East and West*, VII (April, 1956), 349-353.

20. The *Jinakālamāli*, written in 1517 at Chieng Mai, relates the events which led to the establishment of the Sinhalese sect (*Sīhalabhikkhus*) in Sukhodaya. Forest dwelling *Sīhalabhikkhus* had come to Monland in the early fourteenth century and two monks from Sukhodaya, Sumana and Anōmadassī, had gone to study there in order to be reordained as Forest Dwellers. After a consequent visit, and a further period of study, they were given the title of Mahāthera. Together with eight other monks, they were sent back to Sukhodaya at Lo Tai's request, to introduce the Sīhalabhikkhu sect there. Coedès, *Documents*, p. 95.

21. The Greek King Milinda, or Menander, (c. 200 B.C.) who ruled over northwestern India, was converted to Buddhism by Nāgasena. "The Questions of King Menander" were written down in the early centuries of the Christian Era.

22. P. Schweisguth, *Étude sur la Litterature Siamoise*, Paris, 1951, pp. 3608. Compare *Le Dict de Padma*, translated from the Tibetan by Charles Toussaint, Paris, 1933, pp. 400-6 with Lü Tai's inscription at Nagara Jum (Coedès, *Recueil*, Inscr. III, pp. 85-7) and the descriptions of hell from the *Traibhūmikathā*.

23. Coedès, "Buddhist Cosmology," 350; Schweisguth, *Étude*, pp. 36-8.

24. Coedès, *Recueil*, Insc. III, pp. 84-6; Coedès, "Buddhist Cosmology," 352.

25. Wareru, the King of Rāmaññadesa, who had compiled the collection of Laws, was a son-

in-law of Ram Kamheng. It was from here that much religious stimulation came to Sukhodaya, and also from whence Lü Tai obtained many sacred texts.

26. Prince Dhani, "The Old Siamese conception of the monarchy," Siam Society Fiftieth Anniversary, Bangkok, 1954.

27. Coedès, *Recueil*, Insc. I, p. 44.

28. Tapanna is one of the eight Buddhist hells. Naung Tin, "Rajadhiraja Vilasini. The Manifestation of the King of Kings," *JBRS*. IV (April, 1914), 20-1. This aspect can also be noted in Hindu writings. See Kautilya's *Arthaśāstra*, abridged as *Essentials of Indian Statecraft*, T. Ramaswamy, London, 1962, p. 30.

29. George Coedès, "Siamese Votive Tablets," *Siam Society, Fiftieth Anniversary*, I, 1904-1929, 163.

30. Griswold, "A Declaration," 209 n. 6; Coedès, *Recueil*, Inscr. VIII, pp. 128-9.

31. Coedès, *Recueil*, Insc. I, p. 44.

32. Coedès, *Recueil*, Insc. II, p. 69.

33. Coedès, *Recueil*, Insc. III, p. 89.

34. H. L. Shorto, "A Mon Genealogy of Kings," in *Historians of Southeast Asia*, ed. D. G. E. Hall, London, 1961, p. 67. In an unpublished manuscript, Professor T. Kirsch of Cornell University has suggested that the listing of ancestors and kinsmen can also be regarded as a display of allies and friends who could be called upon for support. A. Thomas Kirsch, "A Note on 'Concentric Conformity' in Ancient Khmer Kinship Organization," Mimeo. February, 1967, p. 9.

35. Coedès, *Recueil*, Insc. IV and V. As Griswold points out, it is unlikely that the representatives of "the four cardinal points" were anything more than the governors of four cities, since so much territory was lost to Sukhodaya under Lo Tai. *Towards a History*, p. 30.

36. In the seventeenth century Ayudhiā, de la Loubère noted that the Siamese placed great emphasis on the possession of the Seal and the Treasury as a means of legitimizing a claimant to the throne. S. de la Loubère, *A New Historical Relation of the Kingdom of Siam by M. de la Loubère, Envoy Extraordinary from the French King to the King of Siam in the years 1687 and 1688*. London, 1693, 1969. The symbols of royalty – the sword, diadem, slippers, and fan – which comprised the royal regalia, would have played a similar role in earlier Thai history.

37. The Queen Mother obviously played an important role in Sukhodaya; In 1399, the widow of Mahādharmarāja II founded a monastery called the Asokārama, and composed a dedicatory inscription. In 1400, together with her son, she led an army in a campaign to recover territory held by Ayudhiā. (Griswold, "A Declaration," 213, 226.) Six years later, she helped decide on the head of the *sangha*. Coedès, *Recueil*, Insc. IX, p. 138.
In 1449, the dowager queen of Chieng Mai helped her son in a military campaign and combined with him in accomplishing meritorious works. Camille Notton, *Annales du Siam*, III, Paris, 1932, 110 ff; Coedès, "Documents," pp. 130-132. In fifteenth century Angkor, the alliance of the Siamese dowager queen with her grandson against her own son was instrumental in bringing about the latter's downfall. O. W. Wolters, "The Khmer King at Basan," *Asia Major*, XII (I, 1966), 74-75.

38. Shorto, "A Mon Genealogy," p. 67.

39. Coedès, *Recueil*, II, pp. 70-4; Griswold, *Towards a History*, p. 19.

40. Coedès, *Recueil*, Insc. III, p. 84.

41. A. B. Griswold, "Imported Images and the Nature of Copying in the Art of Siam," in *Essays Presented to G. H. Luce, Artibus Asiae*, Supplement XXII, II, 37.

42. Griswold, "The Buddhas of Sukhodaya," 18.

43. Jean Boisselier, "Récentes Recherches archeologiques en Thailande," *Arts Asiatiques*.

44. See, for example, the rite described in Insc. IV, Coedès, *Recueil*, p. 100.

45. In 1426, Mahādharmarāja IV caused a double footprint to be installed "similar and conforming in measure to the Holy Footprint manifested by the Supreme Lord of the World on Adam's Peak." Coedès, *Recueil*, Insc. XII, p. 155.

46. Griswold, *Towards a History*, p. 39, n. 105; Griswold, "The Buddhas of Sukhodaya," 29.

47. Coedès, *Recueil*, Insc. VIII, p. 127.

48. Coedès, *Recueil*, Insc. VIII.

49. Suggested by Noel Battye in an unpublished paper in the possession of Professor O. W. Wolters, Cornell University, p. 20.

50. *The Nan Chronicle*, translated by Prasoet Churatana, ed. by David K. Wyatt. Cornell Southeast Asia Data Paper, No. 59, Ithaca, 1966, p. 10.

51. Coedès, "Documents," pp. 95-97.

52. Notton *Annales*, III, 47.

53. Griswold, *Towards a History*, pp. 33, 41.

54. Coedès, *Recueil*, III, p. 84.

55. Coedès, *Recueil*, I, p. 47; II, p. 64.

56. Coedès, *Recueil*, IV, pp. 98-9; Prince Damrong, "Siamese History prior to the founding of Ayudhiā," *Selected Articles from the Siam Society Journal*, III, Bangkok, 1959, 83. Kautilya, in the Hindu tradition, would have heartily approved of this training, for in his view, "the ruler who is educated well and taught the sciences governs his subjects well, and all people will enjoy the earth unchallenged." Kautilya, *Arthaśāstra*, p. 50.

57. Coedès, *Recueil*, Insc. III, p. 87; Insc. VI, p. 115; Insc. VII, p. 120.

58. Coedès, *Recueil*, Insc. IV, p. 98.

59. Maung Tin, "The Manifestation," 18. As anthropology has shown, this concept is by no means limited to Buddhism, but is common to many societies.

60. Wood, *A History of Siam*, p. 60.

61. Coedès, *Recueil*, V, p. 107.

62. The proscription on slavery is taken from an inscription translated during the nineteenth century, which has since crumbled. The accuracy is therefore suspect. Wood, *A History*, p. 60. See also Coedès, *Recueil*, Insc. XIV, p. 168.

63. Than Tun, "Social Life in Burma, A.D. 1044-1287," *JBRS*. XLI (Dec., 1958), 42-6.

64. Wood, *A History*, pp. 67, 71.

65. See Akin Rahibhadana, *The Organisation of Thai Society and the Process of Change in the Early Bangkok Period*, Unpublished M. A. Thesis, Cornell University 1968, for an illuminating discussion of the *sakdi na* system as it was to emerge in later Thai history.

66. Coedès, *Recueil*, Insc. II, p. 64.

67. Coedès, *Recueil*, Insc. V, p. 107.

68. Coedès, *Recueil*, Insc. V, p. 107. This image of the king as father is a common theme throughout Buddhist inscriptions.

69. George Coedès, "L'art Siamois de l' epoque de Sukhodaya," *Arts Asiatiques*, I (4, 1954), 295.

70. Coedès, *Recueil*, Insc. III, p. 89.

71. Maha Sila Viravong, *History of Laos*, Vientiane, 1957, p. 36. (U. S. Joint Publications Research Service, Photocopy, 1958, N. Y. & Washington).

72. Wood, *A History*, p. 60.

73. Coedès, *Recueil*, Insc. V. p. 107. This magnanimity, although rare in practical politics, conforms with the doctrine of *ahimsā* contained in Buddhist teachings.

74. Chou Ta Kuan, *Notes on Cambodia*, pp. 30-1; A. L. Basham, *The Wonder that was India*, London, 1954, p. 117.

75. Coedès, *Recueil*, Insc. IV, p. 97; Insc. III, p. 84; Insc. VI, p. VI. Vessantara, the last Jātaka, epitomizes the Bodhisattva ideal, the king who was prepared to give up everything to gain Nirvāna.

76. C. W. Dunn, "Dice in the Vidhura Jātaka," *JBRS*, XXXIII (April, 1950), 10-14. Also see E. B. Cowell, ed. *The Jātakas or Stories of the Buddha's former births*, translated from the Pāli by various hands. London, 1957, V, 151: VI, 221.

77. King Kuna of Chieng Mai was also reputed to be skilled in the art of elephant hunting (*gajjaśāstra*) Notton, *Annales*, III, 85. Francis H. Giles has described these hunts in twentieth century Thailand, and includes collections of mantras used to invoke the aid of spiritual beings. "An account of the rites and ceremonies observed at elephant driving operations in the seaboard province of Lang Suan," *JSS*, XXV (July, 1932), 153-215; "Adverseria of Elephant Hunting," *JSS*, XXIII (Dec. 1929), 59-97.

78. That is, sensual existence, bodily existence, and spiritual existence. Coedès, *Recueil*, Insc. IV, p. 101; Insc. V, p. 107.

79. Coedès, *Recueil*, Insc. III, pp. 88, 89. Griswold suggests that the representation of Buddha subduing the pride of his rebellious relatives on a *mandapa* built by Lü Tai recalled for his subjects the king's own "near-miracle in bringing the disaffected vassals back under his suzerainty." *Towards a History*, p. 45.

80. Coedès, *Recueil*, Insc. VI, p. 115.

81. Coedès, *Recueil*, Insc. I, p. 46.

82. Coedès, *Recueil*, Insc. XI, p. 148.

83. See H. G. Quaritch Wales, *Siamese State Ceremonies*, London, 1931, for a description of the role these rites played in administration and court protocol. For the importance of Brahmins in Sukhodaya, see David K. Wyatt, *The Politics of Reform in Thailand*, Yale University Press, New Haven, 1969, pp. 4-7.

84. The sculptors concerned may well have taken note of the tradition that when a person of virtuous character commissions an image, its features will magically assume a likeness of his own. Griswold, *Towards a History*, pp. 5, 32.

85. Coedès, *Recueil*, Insc. IV, p. 98.

86. Shorto, "A Mon Genealogy," p. 67.

87. Basham, *The Wonder that was India*, p. 40; Coedès, *Recueil*, Insc. VI, p. 115.

88. Coedès, *Recueil*, Insc. IV, pp. 99-100.

89. Coedès, *Recueil*, Insc. IV, p. 102.

90. Griswold and Prasert ṇa Nagara, "A Declaration of Independence," 212-242.

The Relationship Between the Religious and Political Orders in Northern Thailand (14th-16th Centuries)

Donald K. Swearer and Sommai Premchit

ACCORDING TO THE northern Thai chronicles, Buddhism was established in northern Thailand by Queen Cāmadevī who was brought from Lāvapurī (modern Lopburī) to rule in Haripuñjaya (modern Lamphūn) in the seventh or eighth century A.D. Even though Buddhism was present in the region by the seventh century or earlier, evidence from the chronicles implies that Buddhism did not become widely accepted at Haripuñjaya until the reign of Ādittarāja in the eleventh century.[1] The chronicles portray Ādittarāja as a *cakkavattiñ* fore-ordained to discover a sacred relic of the Buddha buried under the site of the future king's palace. The chronicler traces the relic to a prediction made by the Blessed One during his miraculous visit to Haripuñjaya. Fifteen hundred years later Ādittarāja finds the relic and builds a *cetiya* (Thai: *cedī*) to enshrine it. He thereby actualizes or makes manifest the power of the Buddha only symbolically present in the form of the relic until his reign. As *cakkavattin* he establishes the law of the Buddha (*Buddhadhamma*) as the foundation of Haripuñjaya. Thereby, Ādittarāja legitimates his reign by making Haripuñjaya a Holy Kingdom, i.e., a *Buddhadesa*.

From the eleventh century until the present, Buddhism has been an important factor in the political history of northern Thailand. It has symbolized the transcendental unity of a moral community — not always manifested in reality — and has functioned to legitimate political authority especially in times of transition and expansion. Historically, the relationship between the religious order (*sāsanacakra*) and secular order (*āṇācakra*) has not been without its tensions. In order to provide a better understanding of the relationship between Buddhism and the State in Lānnā ("a million rice fields," i.e., northern Thailand) from the founding of the Thai dynasty at Chiang Mai at the end of the thirteenth century to its subjugation by the Burmese in 1578, this paper proposes to discuss the development of Buddhism from the reign of King Kuenā (1367-1388) through Phra Mu'ang Kaew(1495-1528).[2] A particular focus will be the nature of the symbiotic relationship between the religious and political spheres during the reign of the most famous monarch of Lānnā, Tilokarāja (1442-1487). At the outset, however, a few comments are in order about the nature of our sources and the difficulty of interpreting them.

The religious history of Lānnā has yet to be written. Archaeological materials discovered up to this point in time are scant, and analyses of the northern Thai chronicles — where they exist — have not put together a comprehensive story of Buddhism in northern Thailand. Our modest effort relies almost entirely on several northern Thai chronicles. Consequently, this essay may rightfully be considered an attempt to provide a viable interpretation of a particular segment of the religious history of the chronicles of Lānnā.

20

Of the chronicles used one has been translated into English and French (*Jinakālamālīpakaraṇam*), another was a compilation written in Thai but based on chronicles in Thai Yüan or Northern Thai (*Phongsāwadān Yōnok*), and the remainder are in Northern Thai (*Tamnān Mūlasāsanā Wat Pā Daeng, Tamnān Mūlasāsanā Wat Suan Dok*, and *Tamnān Muang Chiang Mai*).[3] The chronicles of northern Thailand are difficult to analyze. Factual disparities and differences in chronology plague the investigator. In some cases the garbled nature of the text at our disposal could only mean errors in copy transmission. Our research pointed to the necessity of using multiple copies of the same text; yet, even then linguistic archaisms and uncertain structure may confuse the meaning. We had neither the opportunity nor the resources at our disposal to resolve successfully all of these problems, or, in some cases, even to be able to identify them. Hopefully, the time will come when a team of scholars sufficiently conversant in Pāli, Sanskrit, Thai Yüan, and Central Thai will work together to arrive at definitive editions and interpretations of these texts.

Lānnā, that area of northern Thailand defined by the modern provinces of Mae Sariang, Fāng, Chiang Saen, Chiang Rai, Nān, Prae, Lamphūn, Lampāng, Tāk, and Chiang Mai had a history distinct from the central Thai kingdoms of Sukhōthai and Ayudhyā until the beginning of the nineteenth century. This area was one of petty Thai states often allied by marriages and generally dominated by the Mengrai dynastic line with its capital at Chiang Mai. At the height of its power under Tilokarāja, Lānnā extended west into the Shan States of northern Burma and east toward Luang Prabāng in Laos. In order to understand and interpret the religious situation in northern Thailand we must first survey the development of Buddhism during the time of Kuenā (1367-1388), the seventh ruler of Chiang Mai, through the succeeding reigns of Saen Mu'ang Mā (1388-1411) and Sām Fang Kaen (1411-1442) before going on to the period of Tilokarāja (1442-1487) and his most important successor, Phra Mu'ang Kaew (1495-1528). This period of roughly one hundred and fifty years witnessed the richest cultural and religious development of Lānnā. Shortly thereafter, in 1578, much of northern Thailand came under the suzerainty of Burma until the defeat of the Burmese by the central Thai general, Phra Chao Tāksin nearly two hundred years later. While Lānnā Thai Buddhism retained much of its independence during the next century, it never reached its former glory; and since the later part of the nineteenth century, the Buddhism of Lānnā has gradually lost its cultural distinctiveness.

After we have investigated the nature of Buddhism in Chiang Mai as it developed during the period from 1367 to 1442, we shall then turn to a more detailed analysis of the reign of Tilokarāja. In this section of the paper both secular and religious history will be utilized, for the nature of the relationship between Buddhism and the political order is decisively conditioned by Tilokarāja's expansionist policies. The entire discussion addresses four dimensions of the symbiosis between the religious and secular spheres: (1) during the reign of Kuenā one sect of Buddhism functions as a cultural mediator serving to integrate Haripuñjaya religious culture into a distinctive tradition identified with the Thai rather than the Mon-Lāva; (2) under Sām Fang Kaen political interference into religious disputes becomes a key factor in justifying a shift of political power; (3) with Tilokarāja a coalescence of the religious and political orders reaches unprecedented heights and is manifested both symbolically and historically; (4) the extensive political and religious harmony of the Tilokarāja era then provides the context for a florescence of significant Buddhist scholarship in Pāli and Northern Thai climaxed during the reign of Phra Mu'ang Kaew. While each of these dimensions of the inter-relationship between the Buddhist and the political spheres is peculiar to Lānnā, they can also be seen as instances of a more universal typology. This study will show the crucial role of religion as a cultural mediator when one ethnic group assumes dominance over another; the role a religious institution can play in abetting political change; the integrating power of commonly held religious symbols and ideology embodied in a religious institution supportive of and supported by the State; and, the possibilities for the development of significant religious scholarship in a politically favorable climate.

Buddhism in Lānnā from Kuenā to Sām Fang Kaen

In its most general terms Buddhism in Lānnā appears to consist of three traditions: one associated with the pre-Thai Haripuñjaya period (pre-thirteenth century), the other two being introduced during the reigns of Kuenā and Saen Mu'ang Mā or Sām Fang Kaen.[4] Pre-Thai Buddhism in northern Thailand has most often been labeled as Mon-Theravada. Indeed, many Thai historians associate King Aśoka's missionaries, Sona and Uttara, with the Mon of Suvannabhūmi (central Thailand and lower Burma). It has been generally assumed that Cāmadevī brought this tradition with her to Haripuñjaya from Lāvapurī, which may have been a Mon center at that time. Unfortunately, we know very little about the nature of pre-Thai Buddhism and the assumption of a continuous Pāli tradition has been challenged by Piriya Krairiksh who argues that one of the earliest Buddhist sites in central Thailand was probably rooted in a Sanskritic rather than a Pāli tradition.[5] Although this finding obviously does not obviate the early Mon Buddhist tradition in Thailand, it warns against an easy assumption about its nature. Following Dr. Piriya's lead, we would suggest that current evidence makes it difficult to type the earliest Buddhist tradition in northern Thailand and we would be advised at this juncture to refer to it simply as Haripuñjaya Buddhism or Mon-Lāva Buddhism in recognition of the ethnic significance of the Lāva in the north during the Cāmadevī period. Certainly there was a pre-Thai northern Thai Buddhism. This very tradition was probably intended by the reference in the chronicles to the *nagaravāsī* or chapter of town-dwelling monks. Beyond that we can say very little other than to assume that Haripuñjaya Buddhism was of a Hīnayāna orientation with clear evidence of Pāli only by the eleventh or twelfth century, and that in all probability it was highly syncretized with Brahmanical and animistic elements.

The other two traditions of northern Thai Buddhism have a less ambiguous origin and a more clearly differentiated historical development. Each comes from Śrī Lankā, the dominant Buddhist influence in Thailand from the latter part of the fourteenth to the sixteenth century. As the fountainhead of classical Theravada Buddhism, Śrī Lankā succeeded India of the Maurya, Gupta, Pallava, and Pāla-Sena periods as the major Buddhist influence in Southeast Asia. Countries like Burma and Thailand which had an earlier contact with Indian Buddhism quite naturally looked to Śrī Lankā for support. It represented the obvious center of high culture most compatible with the religious heritages of these countries. In northern Thailand two streams of Sinhalese Buddhism competed with one another, the first mediated through Burma and the second brought directly from Śrī Lankā by Thai and Sīhala monks. The earlier tradition

was brought during the reign of Kuenā by the Sukhōthai monk, Sumana Mahāthera; the latter tradition was established by the Chiang Mai monk, Ñāṇagambhīra,
during the reign of Sām Fang Kaen. The chronicles relate the establishment of
Sinhalese Buddhism in Lānnā principally through the story of these two monks.
We turn now to an analysis of these two narratives.

Sumana Mahāthera and his friend and associate, Anōmadassī were disciples
of Mahāpabbata, the Sangharāja of Sukhōthai.[6] The two were exceptional monks.
They had gone to study the Buddhist scriptures in Ayudhyā (founded by the
Prince of U Thong) and, later, hearing of a Sinhalese trained monk who had
established a new order in Mu'ang Pan (Martaban) they journeyed there.
This monk, Anumati by name, along with eleven others returned to Burma from
Śrī Lankā in 1331. During their stay in the island kingdom they studied with
the abbot of the Udumbaragiri monastery from whom they received reordina-
tion. Upon their return to Martaban they established this "forest dwelling" order
there. The founding of a Sīhala (Sinhalese) order in Burma was nothing new.
According to the Kalyāṇī Inscription, by the thirteenth century four Theravada
sects had been established in Burma, one related to the old Mon tradition and
the other three developing from sectarian divisions within the order of Sīhala
monks established in Pagan in 1180.[7]

Sumana and Anōmadassī studied with Udumbarapupphā Mahāswāmi, the head
of the Martaban chapter of the Udumbaragiri order, for five years, a sufficient
period of time to enable them to teach on their own authority but not to ordain
into the Order. After the requisite ten years, they were elevated to the status of
upajjāya giving them the right to ordain. With this rank they returned to Sukhōthai along with eight other Sukhōthai monks and proceeded to establish the
Udumbaragiri order in Thailand. The *Chronicle of the Founding of the Religion
(Mūlasāsanā)* of Wat Suan Dok makes the return of the Sukhōthai monks an
outstanding moment for the development of this Order. The Udumbarapupphā
Mahāswāmi predicts that, "The Buddhism I brought from Śrī Lankā was not
firmly established in the Mon country but will be firmly established in your
country for five thousand years."[8] The Chronicle, furthermore, makes these
monks the major instrument in the spread of the Order to Ayudhyā, Pitsanulōk,
Nān, Chiang Mai, and Luang Prabāng.

Sumana and Anōmadassī were received royally by King Mahādhammarāja I
(Līthai, 1347-c.1370) of Sukhōthai. Sumana was ensconced in the Mango Grove
Monastery (Wat Pā Mamuang) at Sukhōthai and Anōmadassī in the Red Forest
Monastery (Wat Pā Daeng) at neighboring Sajjanālaya. Both proceeded to teach
and ordain, providing the impetus for the Order's growth and development.
Sumana's special role as the chief missioner of the Udumbaragiri Order to
northern Thailand finds a particular connection with a Buddha relic reportedly
consecrated by King Aśoka and sent to the Sukhōthai area. The Chronicle's
description of the portentous appearance of the relic follows a conventional
form, i.e., characterized by dazzling light and miraculous flight. Sumana calls
on the relic to display its powers for the rulers of both Sajjanālaya and
Sukhōthai. When lustrated by Sumana for the ruler of Sajjanālaya, the relic
sprang up above the surface of the water like a dancing *hamsa* bird and shot
forth rays of six colors, thereby dispelling any doubt among the people about
the relic's genuineness.[9] The King of Sukhōthai was less fortunate. When first
lustrated, the relic performed no miracles "because that city was not the place

where the Lord Buddha's relic was to remain."[10] In this way the *Chronicle of the Founding of the Religion* (Wat Suan Dok) provides a rationale for Sumana's later journey with the relic to Chiang Mai.

The story of Sumana and the relic has an analog with Ādittarāja's discovery of the Buddha relic in connection with the founding of Haripuñjaya. In the two cases, however, the roles of the religious and secular actors are reversed. Ādittarāja, the secular ruler, discovers the Buddha relic attributed to the Blessed One, himself; Sumana, the founder of the Udumbaragiri Order in Thailand, discovers a Buddha relic consecrated by the secular ruler, King Aśoka. The contextual significance of the role reversal only serves to enhance the symbolic measure of Buddha relics as a mediator between the religious and secular spheres (*sāsanacakra/āṇācakra*).

In Chiang Mai King Kuenā, hearing of the fame of the Udumbarapupphā Mahāswāmi, sent a representative to Martaban requesting that he establish his forest-dwelling Sinhalese sect there. The Mahāswāmi declined, sending in his stead Ānanda, a Mon monk who had studied in Śrī Laṅkā under the same Order. Ānanda's preaching pleased Kuenā; however, lacking the *upajjāya* status necessary to perform the acts of the Order (*upasampadākamma*), he was unable to perform the ordination ceremony. To establish and perpetuate the Udumbaragiri Order in northern Thailand, Ānanda suggested that King Kuenā invite Sumana to come from Sukhōthai. Sumana, like his own teacher before him, declines the invitation sending his colleague, Saddhatissa, in his place. For reasons not made clear in the Chronicle Saddhatissa, who we would assume could perform the *sanghakamma*, chooses not to do the *upasampadā*. Again frustrated in his desire to found the new Sīhala Order of monks in Chiang Mai, Kuenā sends envoys to Līthai King of Sukhōthai and also to Sumana making his request for the third time. Sumana finally relents, the time-honored tradition of three requests having been met, and goes to Chiang Mai taking the Buddha relic and a copy of the *Tripiṭaka*.

According to an inscription at Wat Phra Yün in Lamphūn (Haripuñjaya), Sumana and his followers set forth for Lānnā in 1369.[11] This monastery was constructed for Sumana by King Kuenā at the major pre-Thai city of the north. One wonders why the king chose Haripuñjaya rather than the new Thai capital of Chiang Mai in which to build a monastery for this important religious emissary. The chronicles provide no specific answer, but we can speculate that only fifty years after the death of Mengrai, the founder of the Thai dynasty in Chiang Mai, there was still the sense that Haripuñjaya remained as the cultural and spiritual center of the north. Consequentially, it would make perfectly good sense for Kuenā to build Wat Phra Yün outside of Haripuñjaya rather than Chiang Mai. By doing so he would have served both to establish a continuity between the Buddhism of the Mon-Lāva and the new Sinhalese variety brought by Sumana, as well as indicate through royal favor the supremacy of the Sumana-Udumbaragiri Order. We would argue, consequently, that the coming of Sumana to Chiang Mai acts as a means by which the Mengrai dynastic line furthers its own distinctive identity and authority over the heart of the northern region they had occupied, i.e., Chiang Mai-Lamphūn.

The above rationale for locating Wat Phra Yün near Lamphūn does not appear in the chronicles. The *Chronicle of the Founding of the Religion* of Wat Suan Dok states that Sumana, himself, chose the site. According to the chron-

icle, in reply to Kuenā's inquiry about where the Mahāthera would like to reside, he replies, "Take heed, your majesty! All men of wisdom, beginning with
the Omniscient Lord Buddha, whenever they came to a market town to lead
the townspeople and villagers to salvation, have been accustomed since ancient
times to settle at a measured distance of five hundred bow lengths from the
gatepost of the town."[12] It can be no coincidence that such a location accords
with the place where the Buddha, himself, stood when, according to numerous
northern Thai chronicles, he visited this area. It was also the same spot where
a former ruler of Haripuñjaya, Dhammikarāja (flourished, end of twelfth century), reputedly commemorated this event by building a Buddha image eighteen
cubits (8.50 meters) high, the legendary height of the Buddha.[13] In short, establishing Sumana at Wat Phra Yün symbolizes the continuity of the Order he
established with the pre-Thai historical past *and* the mythical-legendary foundations of northern Thailand.

Wat Phra Yün was a complete religious center. It contained an assembly or
worship hall (*vihāra*), an ordination hall (*uposathāgāra*), monks residences
(*kuṭi*), and various covered areas for lay people to carry out merit-making activities on behalf of the monks. There Sumana conducted the ordination rites
of the Udumbaragiri Order, firmly establishing this Sinhalese sect in Lānnā.
The *Chronicle of the Founding of the Religion* of Wat Suan Dok spares little
hyperbole in describing the virtues of Sumana, the excellence of his preaching,
the miraculous displays of the relic, and the progress of this branch of Buddhism. It may even have been that Sumana began to usurp the popularity of
the king. Hence, the chronicler finds it necessary to record that the king had
a dream in which Indra appeared saying, "Take heed, Your Majesty! I am not
an ordinary person, I am King Indra; and I have descended to the earth in this
vision to help you increase your store of merit. The Mahāthera (Sumana) is
neither boastful or exacting. He has made great merit in past lives, and is des-
tined to become a Buddha himself after Metteyya. And you, Your Majesty,
will become his righthand disciple at that time."[14] Indra's prediction may
have assuaged the king's apprehension about his chief monk; on the other
hand, his formal status is made subservient to the future Buddha!

In 1373 Sumana and the relic moved to a monastery on the outskirts of
Chiang Mai which formerly had been the king's own pleasure garden. Perhaps
this move was an attempt to keep Sumana's popularity in close surveillance or
was simply Kuenā's generous response to Sumana's request.[15] On the other
hand, the move may have reflected a second phase of a mutually beneficial
collaboration between the religious and secular orders. From this point of
view, establishing Sumana initially at Wat Phra Yün in Lamphūn provides
continuity with the pre-Thai mythical, legendary, and historical traditions of
Haripuñjaya. Moving him to Wat Suan Dok, a new monastery built on the
king's own property in Chiang Mai, symbolizes the transition to a new cultural
and religious center. Building Wat Suan Dok for Sumana would only be natural
since Chiang Mai was Kuenā's political capital. Kuenā provides support for the
new Order in several ways: builds Wat Suan Dok as the center of the Sumana-
Udumbaragiri Order; donates revenue-producing lands to maintain the monks;
and confers the title of *rājaguru* on Sumana, an office Wat Suan Dok abbots
may have held until 1441.[16] What benefits did the king receive? In general, he
creates a new religious institution essentially identified with the Chiang Mai-

Thai dynastic order. The relic enshrined at Wat Suan Dok symbolizes the symbiosis between the two. In addition, however, we cannot help but speculate
whether Sumana's place as *rājaguru* did not relate to particular alliances between Chiang Mai and other Thai city states. In this regard we must keep in
mind that Sumana was sent to Chiang Mai with the blessing of the king of
Sukhōthai, and that Sumana's cousin was made the ruler of Tāk. It would appear, therefore, that Kuenā gained much more than religious merit by establishing the charismatic monk, Sumana, and his miraculous relic as the official
religion of the Chiang Mai kingdom!

The story of the Mahāthera Sumana and King Kuenā has served to illustrate
that facet of the relationship between religion and the state where religion
functions as a mediator of cultural assimilation thus facilitating the eventual
dominance of one ethnic group over another. The Udumbaragiri Order eventually becomes the most prominent tradition in Chiang Mai. We have observed
that ensconcing Sumana at Wat Phra Yün at least makes a symbolic connection with the indigenous Mon-Lāva Buddhist traditions and served to establish
a continuity between them and the newly dominant Thai. We cannot determine
the exact nature of the Udumbaragiri's teachings or discipline, although religious controversy during succeeding reigns reveals an outline of their form.

We can also assume some continuity with its parent sect in Śrī Lankā. In
summary, this episode in the history of the development of Buddhism in
northern Thailand shows how a sect of Sinhalese Buddhism mediated through
Martaban becomes the established tradition in Chiang Mai through the favor of
a Thai monarch. In doing so we have taken the position that it provided continuity with the past, for the Buddhism of Sumana apparently does not reject
or come into conflict with the Mon-Lāva traditions. The tradition, however,
also represents a break with the past. A new religious institution is created
which prospers under royal favor. Hence, under Kuenā, religion plays a crucial
role in establishing the authority of the Chiang Mai Thai in northern Thailand.

We now turn to a second facet of the inter-relationship between Buddhism
and the State in Lānnā, namely, where religious controversy serves as a catalyst
to political change. This aspect emerges during the reign of Sām Fang Kaen
(1411-1442) when Buddhist sectarian squabbles are interpreted in the chronicles
as part of the reason for Sām Fang Kaen's political demise. From the standpoint
of those holding secular power such a development must be perceived as a breakdown of the relationship between the religious and political spheres. From the
standpoint of those exploiting religious controversy for their own political gain,
however, it merely re-establishes the symbiosis in their favor. It might be claimed
that in such a situation a religious institution is merely a pawn in a political
power struggle. We would rather argue for the more general point of view that
in such cases a religious institution plays a crucial role in political change. This
aspect of the problem is important, for all too often religion is cast in the role
of always preserving the *status quo*. Obviously such a stereotype does not do
justice to the complexity of the relationship between the religious and secular
spheres in every historical or cultural circumstance.

As noted earlier (see note 4), the historical details illustrating this aspect of
our study are very confusing. The heart of the problem is whether the account
of the controversy recorded in the *Chronicle of the Founding of the Religion*
of Wat Suan Dok during the reign of Saen Mu'ang Mā (1388-1411) actually

took place during his reign or that of his successor, Sām Fang Kaen. Either the controversy began during the reign of Saen Mu'ang Mā and accelerated during the time of Sām Fang Kaen, or must have taken place during the latter's reign. Given the facts that the account in the Wat Suan Dok Chronicle appears to be garbled, that the account as we have it in the *Epochs of the Conqueror* favors the reign of Sām Fang Kaen, and that placing the controversy during the reign of Saen Mu'ang Mā creates problems in accounting for the reasons for the succession of Tilokarāja to the throne, we have opted for the theory that the controversy belongs to the era of Sām Fang Kaen. We shall now examine the account first as we have it in the *Chronicle of the Founding of the Religion* of Wat Suan Dok and then as related in *Epochs of the Conqueror*. Finally, we shall offer our own deductions.

When Saen Mu'ang Mā came to power, Sumana Thera was still alive and the abbot of Wat Suan Dok. The religion prospered and the relationship between the Sangha and the state progressed to the mutual benefit of both parties. When Sumana's third successor, Buddhapaññā, was designated as *sanghanāyaka*, however, the felicitious marriage between the religious and political orders began to sour. The Chronicle reports conflicts on two levels, individual and institutional. On the individual level, the conflict emerged because of personality differences or, as the Chronicle states, Saen Mu'ang Mā thought Buddhapaññā (or Buddhaññāna) was rapacious.[17] Whatever the reasons for the personal pique, the king had him transferred to Wat Jetubana in Haripuñjaya. On the Sangha level, the report offers more difficulties of interpretation. It focuses on the introduction of a new, reformist sect of Sinhalese Buddhism, presumably of the Mahāvihāra tradition. This group had apparently established itself at Ayudhyā during the reign of Boromarāja and from there proceeded to Chiang Mai. This Order followed a different *vinaya* than the Wat Suan Dok Order of Sumana. They did not cover their alms bowls with their robes, nor did they carry statts. They also objected to the practice of accepting money, owning property and rice lands.[18] Controversy between the two groups became heated and the king was called upon to resolve the dispute. The Chronicle suggests two differing resolutions: either the king favored the old group probably because they represented traditional, vested religious interests, and drove the new group from Chiang Mai; or Saen Mu'ang Mā refused to settle the dispute until finally the rancor between the two Orders became so divisive that he drove all of them from Chiang Mai.

The account in the Wat Suan Dok Chronicle contains a serious internal dating problem. The abbot of Wat Suan Dok, Ñānarangsī, who favored the new group from Śrī Lankā, succeeded to his position well after the reign of Saen Mu'ang Mā. Furthermore, when we examine the *Epochs of the Conqueror*, we find that the introduction of the new Sinhalese tradition to Chiang Mai is unequivocally placed during the reign of Sām Fang Kaen. We might infer, therefore, that Saen Mu'ang Mā did, indeed, have a falling out with one of the abbots of Wat Suan Dok and had him removed from office, but that the sectarian controversy which provides a necessary background to Tilokarāja's assumption of power occurred during the era of his father, Sām Fang Kaen.

Even though the *Epochs of the Conqueror* does not provide us with an account of the inter-sectarian controversy in Chiang Mai, it contains considerable detail about the founding of the new Sinhalese Order in Thailand. A group of thirty-nine monks from Chiang Mai, Lopburī, and lower Burma go to Śrī Lankā in 1423 (during the reign of Parākramabāhu VI of Kotte). They learned the Sīhala script and Sinhalese style of recitation, made pilgrimage to the famous tooth relic in Kandy, visited the Buddha's footprint and the sixteen traditional Buddhist pilgrimage sites on the island, and were reordained into the Mahāvihāra Order in 1424. Then they returned to Thailand with two Sinhalese monks as *upajjāya*. Of this group the *Chronicle of the Founding of the Religion* of Wat Pā Daeng makes Ñāṇagambhīra the spokesman, while the *Epochs of the Conqueror* portrays Medhaṅkara as the leader of the group.

Returning to Ayudhyā, they reside there for four rains retreats (*vassā*). Ñāṇagambhīra has the king abolish the old religion and establish the Sīhala Nikāya as the orthodox sect.[20] With this official beginning the Chronicle proceeds to record the spectacular growth of the new Order: six hundred temples in Ayudhyā, three thousand monks in Pitsanulōk, seven thousand five hundred and twenty at Sukhōthai, and so on. The new Order arrives in Chiang Mai in 1430. They are established in Wat Pā Daeng (the Red Forest Monastery) for two *vassā* but for some unspecified reason then spend most of their time outside of Chiang Mai in Lamphūn (Haripuñjaya), Lampāng, and Chiang Saen. The *Epochs of the Conqueror* provides no details about the sectarian controversy in Chiang Mai, nor does it mention Sām Fang Kaen's intervention in Sangha quarrels. However, in addition to the usual formulaic praise of royal support for the Sangha, it makes this criticism of the King: "He who was of little faith in the Dispensation but possessed much faith in external systems, without betaking himself to the virtuous, greatly honored the votaries of demons."[21] It goes on to say that he worshiped wooded groves, trees, heaped mounds, rocks, and forests with offerings of cattle and buffalo. This kind of criticism is unusual. We would probably correctly assume that the kings of Chiang Mai all offered sacrifices to the guardian spirits of the city. Why single out Sām Fang Kaen for special criticism? Perhaps he was excessively attentive to this non-Buddhist religion; or, might there be some connection between this criticism and the fact that he backed the losing side in the Buddhist sectarian controversy? In any event, Sām Fang Kaen falls out of favor and is deposed by his son, Tilokarāja. There can be little doubt that the Buddhist sectarian controversy and Sām Fang Kaen's role in it was an important factor in his overthrow.

We can make some reasonable deductions on the basis of our analysis of the chronicles. The new Sīhala Order came to Chiang Mai during the reign of Sām Fang Kaen and not his predecessor, Saen Mu'ang Mā. During Saen Mu'ang Mā's reign the dispute between the secular and religious spheres was largely personal in nature and was resolved by the king through the removal of the abbot of Wat Suan Dok. The controversy during the time of Sām Fang Kaen was probably a bitter sectarian fight that focused on *vinaya* rules. Both the chronicles and the existence of double *sīmā* boundary markers around *uposatha* halls of this period testify to the fact that the new order both reordained monks and also reconsecrated sacred monastery precincts. We do not know the exact nature of the relationship between the reformist religious group and the aristocracy that supported Tilokarāja against his father. It may well be that the religious controversy merely provided a convenient excuse for those who opposed Sām Fang Kaen to seize power. Whatever the particular historic circumstances, the new Sīhala Order provided a basis within the religious sphere (*sāsanacakra*) for change within the political sphere (*āṇācakra*).

Our analysis of the coming of a new Sīhala Order to Chiang Mai in 1430 has brought out a second dimension of the inter-relationship between Buddhism and the State in Lānnā; namely, the way in which the dynamics of the relationship may serve to support or even justify political change. Political change having been successfully engineered, Lānnā now enters a period of expansion and solidification under its most able political ruler, Tilokarāja (1442-1487). It is also an era of intense efforts to build a single moral community unified by a single religio-political symbol system. At no time in the history of Lānnā is the mutual inter-relationship between Sangha and State so close. This era precedes the greatest page in the history of the development of Buddhist scholarship in Thailand climaxed during the reign of Muʼang Kaew (1495-1528). We turn now to this period of growth, development, stabilization, and unification.

Tilokarāja and Muʼang Kaew

Those who sought to overthrow Sām Fang Kaen needed a leader, a son of the royal family, who would be willing to supersede his father. They found their leader in Tilokarāja, the tenth son of the king, who had been removed by his father as the vice-regent of Payao and sent to Mae Sarieng, a relatively insignificant town to the south and west of Chiang Mai. Tilokarāja must have been offended by this demotion, and therefore receptive to the invitation to take the throne. Indeed, it may even have been the case that his removal from Payao came as a consequence of his political ambitions. Tilokarāja also had his uncle, the ruler of Lampāng, as his ally. It is worth remembering that Lampāng was one of the major centers of the Sīhala Order, and that this group focused its sphere of activity outside of Chiang Mai after spending two *vassā* there. These facts lend support to the inference that the new reformist group supported Tilokarāja, especially if Sām Fang Kaen had sided with the Sumana tradition and had expelled the new Order from Chiang Mai.

Tilokarāja comes to power in 1442 presumably with the military support of the army of Lampāng, and the moral and spiritual backing of the Sīhala Nikāya. The new king immediately rewards Nāṇagambhīra by building a royal chapel (*rājamaṇḍina*) for him. Royal support leads to dramatic growth of the new Order. Indeed, the chronicle reports that so many monks were reordained that the city did not have sufficient accommodations for them.[22] Tilokarāja's mother has Wat Pā Tān constructed. This monastery later becomes one of the most famous centers of the Sīhala Nikāya in Chiang Mai. The king has Wat Pā Daeng expanded and improved. The Chronicle claims that Tilokarāja built twenty to fifty *wats* every year until Chiang Mai had upwards of five hundred monasteries. In addition to solidifying the Sīhala Nikāya as the dominant Order in Chiang Mai, it was extended to many other major northern towns including Payao, Chiang Saen, and Chiang Tung in the Shan States. As Tilokarāja pushed out the borders of his northern kingdom, the Sīhala Nikāya continued to grow and expand. The Chronicle of Wat Pā Daeng relates episode after episode of reordinations in one town after another until the Sīhala Nikāya becomes co-extensive with Tilokarāja's hegemony over northern Thailand.

Tilokarāja carries out a dual religious policy: the advancement of the Sīhala Nikāya, and the propagation of religious tolerance and harmony. The first expresses itself in his strong support of centers of the new Order, e.g., Wat Pā Daeng, Wat Pā Tān. He appoints the Mahāswāmi Medhaṅkara as the "*atula-*

sakyadhikārana-mahāswāmi, The Great Sage of the Incomparable Powers of Justice"; builds a special *prāsād* for him at Wat Cedī Luang in Chiang Mai; and creates the office of *sangharāja* which is controlled by the new Sīhala Order. The king, himself, is ordained at Wat Pā Daeng with Medhankara as the *rājaguru*. In the Chronicle of Wat Pā Daeng Tilokarāja's ordination in 1448 is justified by historical precedent — he is following in the footsteps of King Līthai of Sukhō-thai — and on the grounds of his desire to become a Buddha in the future.[23] In the *Epochs of the Conqueror* the decision is rationalized as the king's wish "to be an heir of the Dispensation" and as "an expression of gratitude towards his parents."[24]

The king's support of the Sīhala Nikāya headquartered at Wat Pā Daeng cannot be contested. However, we would be misled to conclude that he also persecuted other Buddhist groups, in particular the Wat Suan Dok-Sumana tradition. In addition to favoring the new reformist order, he also followed a policy of religious tolerance, trying to minimize sectarian differences without forcing conformity. In pursuit of this policy the chronicles attest to the fact that Tilokarāja called a general council in 1477 (B.E. 2120) at Wat Cedī Cet Yot (The Temple Monastery of the Cetiya with Seven Towers), also known as Wat Bodharāma, for the purpose of producing a new recension of the Pāli canon. Thai Buddhists consider this meeting to be the eighth official Buddhist council but, unfortunately, the chronicles tell us practically nothing about it. Given the significance attributed to the council, it is amazing that no account is found in the northern Thai chronicles. While we must admit the possibility that a crucial missing chapter from the *Epochs of the Conqueror* might be a discussion of the council, on the basis of present evidence we might also infer that it did not occur as generally assumed. In order to suggest an answer to this perplexing problem, we look to the *Chronicle of the Founding of the Religion* of Wat Pā Daeng.

In this Chronicle we find a relatively detailed account of a council to resolve a sectarian controversy between the Wat Pā Daeng Order and a group of monks from Chiang Tung who followed the Wat Suan Dok-Sumana tradition. This council is put in the reign of Tilokarāja although the date given, 1507, is during the time of Phra Mu'ang Kaew. Whether the council took place under Tilokarāja or Mu'ang Kaew is not the main point at issue. Our primary interest focuses on the possibility that the resolution of a relatively modest sectarian quarrel might have been transposed into more grandiose proportions at the hands of chroniclers interested in adding to Tilokarāja's luster as the Aśoka of northern Thailand. We shall suggest such an alternative after discussing the nature of the dispute and its resolution.

The grounds of the dispute are presented in the Chronicle of Wat Pā Daeng as a break between Ñāṇagambhīra and his teacher, Dhammakitti, the abbot of Wat Suan Dok. Ñāṇagambhīra, in pursuit of higher wisdom, had gone to study in Śrī Lankā. There he learned a stricter tradition, bringing back with him Sīhala monks, the Pāli canon, and relics. Upon his return he objected to several vinaya practices of the Sumana tradition such as owning rice land and handling money as well as the way in which Pāli was studied and chanted. Therefore, he insisted that the ordination of the old Order was invalid. Ñāṇagambhīra's stand antagonized a group of monks from Chiang Tung who argued that Ñāṇagambhīra had shown disdain and disrespect to his teacher, Dhammakitti. The king, called upon to resolve the problem, called a meeting of the two parties presided over by the Mahāsangharāja of Wat Phra Singh. He decides the issue by holding two palm leaves, one inscribed with Nāṇagambhīra's name and the other with Dhammakitti's, over a fire. Dhammakitti's burned, thereby attesting to the justice of Nāṇagambhīra's action. As a consequence, the Chiang Tung group of monks was reordained into the new Order.

Numerous possible interpretations of this episode exist. One, however, is that this meeting or another similar to it was the historical basis for the so-called Eighth Council. We realize that such a suggestion is highly speculative. However, we make it on the grounds that none of the major northern Thai chronicles with which we are familiar provide any detail about the Eighth Council; and, furthermore, the attribution of such a general council to Tilokarāja would serve to enhance the Aśoka-*cakkavattin* status he assumes in the chronicles. In short, we would argue that accompanying Tilokarāja's efforts to unify the most extensive kingdom in the history of Lānnā was an attempt to break down the parochialistic loyalties of Buddhist sectarianism. Hence, while tolerating diversity he strongly favored the new reformist order from Srī Lankā, willingly supporting meetings where potential sectarian controversy was resolved in favor of the new Order. Was the Eighth Council such a meeting? The evidence suggests the possibility of such an interpretation.

Both historically and symbolically Tilokarāja exemplifies the *cakkavattin* ideal. The Wat Pā Daeng monks extol him: "renowned in all quarters as the Universal Monarch Sridhamma, the Emperor Tiloka" who is endowed with "heroism, valour, prowess, and splendor, was capable of discerning what is beneficient to one's self and others, was prudent, faithful, and pious, and was possessed of profound wisdom."[25] The king builds Wat Bodharāmā or Wat Cedī Cet Yot (The Temple-Monastery of the Seven Spires) after the model of Bodh Gaya to symbolize the seven sacred places the Buddha stayed at after his enlightenment. He brought seedlings from the Bodhi tree at Anurādhapura, "and when he had it planted he caused the construction of a scaffolding resembling that around the Great Bodhi under which Māra was conquered."[26] He rebuilds the great cetiya at Wat Cedī Luang which the Chronicle describes as crowning Chiang Mai like the Culamaṇī Cetiya where Sakka enshrined the future Buddha's hair and crest gem on the summit of Mt. Sumeru in Tāvatimsa heaven. Finally, we should also mention Tilokarāja's association with the Jewel Image or Emerald Buddha (see the essay by Frank Reynolds) whose miraculous power serves the purpose of establishing a *Buddhadesa* ruled over by a *cakkavattin.*

Tilokarāja is the great unifier of northern Thailand. Historically, the increasing dominance of the Sīhala Nikāya facilitates this role. Furthermore, the king is surrounded by the symbols of a Universal Monarch which enhance both the sacrality and magical power of his territory. The Buddha and the gods support his reign. Of all the monarchs of Lānnā Tilokarāja best exemplifies efforts to build a single moral community unified on the sociological level by a common religious institution, and symbolically by his own person as *cakkavattin.* His reign, then, embodies a third model of the symbiosis between the religious and political spheres, and lays the groundwork for the golden age of Buddhist scholarship in Lānnā during the reign of Phra Muang Kaew (1495-1528).

Mu'ang Kaew continues and amplifies the support of Buddhism, especially the Sīhala Nikāya, begun by his grandfather, Tilokarāja. The *Epochs of the*

Conqueror describes him as ". . . endowed with the highest religious devotion, like the great ocean which is agitated by the limitless flow of mighty currents of water . . . constantly pervaded with thoughts of making hundred-fold gifts of the four requisites and of making the four sacrifices."[27] He was a great builder of religious edifices and, like his predecessors, propagated the unity of the Sangha. The Chronicle reports that when he consecrated a new *uposatha* hall at Wat Cedī Cet Yot monks came from the three *nikāyas* — Sīhala, Nagara (the pre-Thai order), and Pupphārāma (the Sumana-Suan Dok Order) — and from the towns of Chiang Rai (Jamrāya), Chiang Saen (Jayasena), Phayao (Buyāva), Lampāng (Khelānga), and Nān (Nandapura).[28]

From the standpoint of our analysis of the varied aspects of the inter-relationship between religion and the state, the era of Phra Mu'ang Kaew reaps the fruit of the power and fame of Lānnā which attracted and sustained a rela-tively unified *bhikkhusangha* and trained an unusual group of scholars. This period represents a climax to the development of Buddhist Pāli scholarship which began under Tilokarāja. Of the numerous outstanding commentaries, chronicles, and treatises we can only mention a few: 1) the *Cāmadevīvamsa*, or the chronicle of the reign of Queen Cāmadevī in Haripuñjaya, composed by Bodhiramsi the author of the *Sihinganidāna*, a story of the miraculous Sihinga Buddha image; 2) the *Samanta-pāsādika-atthayojanā*, a commentary by Ñānakitti on the *Samantapāsadikā* written at the end of the fifteenth century; 3) the *Vessantaradīpanī*, an exposition of the *Vessantarajātaka* composed by Siriman-galācariya in 1517; 4) the *Mangalatthadīpanī* written in 1524 by the same author; 5) the *Jinakālamāli*, one of the most important of the northern Thai chronicles, was written by Ratanapañña in 1517.[29] Of these works the *Mangalatthadīpanī*, or commentary on the *Mangala Sutta*, stands as the most famous Pāli work written in Thailand. It is well known throughout the Thera-vada world and continues to be used as a major part of the Pāli degree program of the Thai Sangha.

The inter-relationship or symbiosis between religious and political orders cannot be characterized in a univocal manner. Our study of the relationship between Buddhism and the state in northern Thailand during the one hundred and fifty year period from Kuenā through Phra Mu'ang Kaew has attempted to bring out selected historical and symbolic aspects of this interesting problem. On the one hand, we have seen the pervasive significance of the *cakkavattin* ideal on the symbolic level; on the other, we have also been able to construct three or four types of relationships through our analysis of historical materials. We believe that while on one level those dimensions are peculiar to the northern Thai situation, on another they are applicable to other historical and cultural environments as well. In the latter sense, what we have loosely characterized as aspects or dimensions of the relationship between the religious and political orders in Lānnā Thai can also be thought of as ideal types. Hence, although we believe that our study of this particular problem during this crucial period of northern Thai history makes a contribution to an understanding of Thailand's religious history, we also believe that our investigation has a more general ap-plicability to the problem of religion and political legitimation.

Notes
1. See Donald K. Swearer, *Wat Haripuñjaya. The Royal Temple of the Buddha's Relic,*

Lamphun, Thailand. AAR Studies in Religion, 10. (Missoula: The Scholars Press, 1976), ch. 1, for substantiation of this claim.

2. There is some disagreement on the dates of the Chiang Mai dynasties among the various chronicles. See G. H. Luce and Ba Shin, "A Chiangmai Mahathera Visits Pagan (1393 A.D.)," *Artibus Asiae. George Coedès Felicitation Volume*, ed. A. B. Griswold and Jean Boisselier (Ascona: Artibus Asiae, 1961), pp. 330-337. We have chosen to follow the *Phongsāwadān Yōnok*, along with Dr. Likhit Likhitānanta, *Yuk Thong Haeng Wannakamma Buddhasāsanā Khong Lānnā Thai* (Chiang Mai: n.d.), pp. 3-4. Western scholars after Coedès have tended to favor the *Jinakālamālipakaranam* as more reliable.

3. Ratannapanna Thera, *The Sheaf of Garlands of the Epochs of the Conqueror*, trans. N. A. Jayawickrama. PTS Translation Series, 36. (London: Luzac & Co., 1968); G. Coedès, "Documents sur l'histoire politique du Laos Occidental," *Bulletin de l'École Française d'Extrême-Orient*, 25:1-2 (1925), pp. 1-202; *Tamnān Mūlasāsanā* (Bangkok: Dept. of Fine Arts, B.E. 2513); *Phongsāwadān Yōnok* (Bangkok: Klang Witaya, B.E. 2503); *Tamnān Pu'n Mu'ang Chiang Mai* (Bangkok, 2514). The *Mūlasāsanā (Wat Pā Daeng)* is currently available in a mimeographed form done under the aegis of the Lānnā Thai Research Center, Chiang Mai University.

4. The three traditions are briefly described by Dr. Saeng Manavidura in the introduction to *Epochs of the Conqueror*, (p. xliv). The historical problem of whether the Sīhala Nikāya was introduced during the reign of Saen Mu'ang Mā or Sām Fang Kaen is taken up later in the paper.

5. Piriya Krairiksh, *Buddhist Folk Tales Depicted at Chula Pathon Cedi* (Bangkok: Prachandra Press, 1974).

6. Here our account is based mainly on the *Mūlasāsanā* (Wat Suan Dok). It should be noted that the northern Thai chronicles used in this paper reflect sectarian biases. In this paper we have addressed the sectarian problem only as it has impinged on our major theme.

7. A. B. Griswold, *Wat Pra Yün Reconsidered* (Bangkok: The Siam Society, 1975), pp. 7-8.

8. *Mūlasāsanā* (Wat Suan Dok), p. 227.

9. *Ibid.*, p. 230.

10. *Mūlasāsanā* (Wat Suan Dok), quoted in A. B. Griswold, *op. cit.*, p. 14.

11. A. B. Griswold, *op. cit.*, p. 22.

12. *Mūlasāsanā* (Wat Suan Dok), p. 239.

13. A. B. Griswold, *op. cit.*, p. 24.

14. *Mūlasāsanā* (Wat Suan Dok), p. 242.

15. See Griswold, *op. cit.*, pp. 39ff, for support of the former point.

16. The title of *rājaguru* was later to pass to the Sīhala Order. See *Epochs of the Conqueror*, p. xxviii.

17. *Mūlasāsanā* (Wat Suan Dok), p. 251.

18. *Ibid.*, p. 253.

19. *Ibid.*

20. *Mūlasāsanā* (Wat Pā Daeng), p. 17.

21. *Epochs of the Conqueror*, p. 128.

22. *Mūlasāsanā* (Wat Pā Daeng), p. 19. Italics ours.

23. *Epochs of the Conqueror*, p. 136.

24. *Ibid.*

25. *Ibid.*, p. 134.

26. *Ibid.*, p. 139.

27. *Ibid.*, p. 148.

28. *Ibid.*, p. 149.

29. Dr. Likhit Lihitānanta will soon be publishing his extensive study of Pāli literature in Thailand. For a shorter treatment currently available, see H. Saddhatissa, "Pāli Literature of Thailand" in *Buddhist Studies in Honour of I. B. Horner*, edited by L. Cousins et al. (Dordrecht-Holland: Reidel Publishing Co., 1974), pp. 211-225.

Thai Kingship and Religious Reform (18th-19th Centuries)

John W. Butt

HUMAN LIFE IS a dynamic process of change and development. Because religion is not an abstract entity but is inextricably linked to human life, it shares in this process. Individuals and societies are perpetually changing, and so their religious faith and its various expressions must be continually refashioned and adapted to ever new and different circumstances. Throughout human history such reformulations have been a universal and necessary feature of living religious faith and traditions. Together with other aspects of culture and like life itself, the forms of religion are characterized by birth and growth, death and decay, renewal and transformation.

The reform of religion is not unrelated to the changes taking place in other spheres of human life and society.[1] Indeed, religious reforms are frequently made in response to these changes. Shifts in political or economic patterns or in prevailing social customs, for example, may make it necessary to reformulate one's religious faith and its expressions so that they will become meaningful to new social conditions. In other instances the impetus for religious reform may come from within the religious system itself. In such cases the reforms made in the religious sector may affect other areas and necessitate changes being made there as well. In either case religious reforms should be viewed not as isolated and independent events, having only religious causes and consequences, but rather as part of a broader and more complex process of personal and socio-cultural change.[2]

The study that follows is concerned with one aspect of this interrelationship between religion and other areas and dimensions of human life. It focuses in particular on interaction between the religious and political sectors, especially on the role of political leaders in stimulating and fostering religious reforms. Encouragement and support by government officials have often contributed decisively to the success of a particular religious reform. At the same time participation in religious affairs by government leaders has frequently served to legitimate and strengthen the political power of those leaders. This has not always been the result of such involvement, however. Becoming identified with a new form of religiousness can have the opposite effect; it may serve to delegitimate a ruler or potential ruler's authority and thereby contribute to his or her political downfall. In the study that follows reference will be made to just such a case. We shall also examine another case in which a political leader sought and gained legitimacy in part through his active participation in the religious reform of his country.

Our study focuses on events that took place in Thailand at the end of the eighteenth century. This was an unusually difficult period in Thai history, dur-

34

ing which many important and significant changes, including major religious reforms, took place in Thai society. After surveying the background and nature of some of these reforms, we shall discuss the role of the Thai king and other members of the royal family in helping to bring about religious change. Our discussion will conclude with some comments on present-day religious reform in Thailand and the significance of government involvement in such reforms.

The Disruption of Thai Traditions: The Fall of Ayuthia

The capture and destruction of Ayuthia by the Burmese in April 1767 threatened not only the continued existence of an independent Thai state in Southeast Asia but also the survival of many of the cultural and religious traditions that had characterized previous Thai kingdoms in the area.[3] The Thai king, symbol of national unity and identity, was dead, and the most prominent surviving member of the royal family, together with other important government officials, had been taken captive. Ayuthia, once a magnificent city, lay in ruins. During the prolonged siege and fierce fighting that preceded its capture and the extensive looting that followed, many national treasures and works of art had been badly damaged or stolen. Numerous manuscripts, many of them irreplaceable, were destroyed or permanently lost. The main center of Thai cultural activity, the royal court, was no longer existent, and there appeared little likelihood of its being soon reestablished. Given these losses and the existing political and military situation, both the future of the Thai state and the continuation of Thai culture seemed at best uncertain and problematic.

The chaotic conditions prevailing in and around the capital had a very adverse affect on Thai religious life in general and the Buddhist monastic community in particular. Many monasteries had been partially or totally demolished in the fighting and looting; as a result some monks had been forced to seek new places of residence. Others had left their monasteries because of inadequate lay support. Finding new residences and support was not easy, however. Large areas of the city had become virtually deserted, and the drastically reduced size of the lay population coupled with a severe shortage of food made it almost impossible for all the monks to obtain enough food to survive. Faced with this situation, some elected to disrobe and leave the Sangha rather than break their monastic regulations. Others, less scrupulous, foraged for themselves and survived as best they could on their own. Those separated from their former monasteries and customary routines were deprived of much of the religious and disciplinary oversight and support they would have normally received. In many cases their behavior soon began to degenerate, and their example in turn had a debilitating and demoralizing effect on the rest of the monks and populace.

The Sangha has always represented a vital and necessary element in the religious faith and practices of the Buddhist laity. Thus, an increasing lack of respect for the monks, as a result of visibly lowered standards of conduct, and the chaotic disorganization of the Sangha directly affected the quality of lay religious life. Many normal religious activities traditionally provided to the laity by the monastic community were neglected or necessarily curtailed. The amount of religious and moral instruction, for instance, decreased sharply, as did the number of opportunities for merit-making. In summary, the religious situation among both monks and laity had seriously deteriorated, and the need for positive reforms and improvements had become alarmingly obvious. Until the military and political situation changed, however, there was little that could be done to stem the decline in Thai religious life.

The Alteration of Thai Traditions: The Reign of King Taksin (1767-1782)

The political void created by the loss of the capital and the death of the Thai king turned out to be of short duration. Even though Ayuthia was occupied by the Burmese, some parts of the kingdom were still controlled by the Thai, and a number of persons assembled military forces in these areas to continue the fight against the invaders. No single leader immediately emerged to unite these groups and claim the allegiance of the whole Thai people, but by far the most successful commander was Phraya Taksin.[4] Only six months after the fall of Ayuthia, Taksin and his followers succeeded in defeating the small army of occupation that had been left behind by the Burmese.[5] Having retaken Ayuthia, Taksin returned to his main base of operations at Thonburi where he was crowned king. His position was far from secure, however. Not only was there the ever-present danger of a new invasion from Burma (the Burmese continued to attack Thailand almost yearly for the next nine years); there was also the threat posed by rival Thai leaders.[6]

One of the most interesting of these rivals was a Buddhist monk by the name of Ruan. He is especially significant because he reveals how degenerate the religious situation had become throughout much of the country. Ruan's popularity and rise to power were probably linked to Buddhist messianic notions, and he was viewed by his followers as possessing magical or supernatural powers. Although his conduct and life-style were far removed from the traditional way of life of a Buddhist monk, he continued to wear his monastic robes. Similar robes were worn also by his military and political officers. Ruan's power was based in the north, in the area near Uttaradit where he established a "religious" state called the Kingdom of Fang. For a while this kingdom included a large portion of northern Thailand and reached as far south as Phitsanulok, but in 1770 Ruan's troops were defeated by the armies of Taksin, and the King of Fang fled to the north where he disappeared.

Taksin, having won the north, immediately took steps to solidify and secure his control of that area. Probably for political as much as religious reasons, he sought to discover which monks had actively supported Ruan and been associated with him.[7] All such monks were removed from the Sangha and punished. Monks from the south were then sent to the north in an effort to raise the standards of monastic life there and to ensure that the northern monks did not again become involved in political activities opposing Taksin.

The example of Ruan and his followers indicates the type of religious ideas and behavior that was current and the appeal that errant forms of religion apparently had. In Buddhist history, as well as in the history of religion generally, periods of social crisis and disruption frequently promote radical departures from traditional forms. Often these new movements are characterized by eschatological and messianic notions that sometimes involve the participants either directly or indirectly in subversive political activities.[8] Ruan and his followers illustrate that such aberrations were present and probably widespread in Thailand at this time. We shall see that Taksin himself later participated in religious activities that were in some ways like those espoused by the monk-ruler of Fang.

Taksin's undoing seems to have been caused partially by his own insecurity in being king. As time went by, this insecurity became expressed in increasingly irresponsible and eccentric ways. Taksin's fears were not without basis, for, theoretically, he had no rightful claim to the throne. His ancestry was not of royal blood, and he had not been in the recognized line of succession. His political power and authority had been gained through fortuitous circumstances and the use of military force. But force alone does not provide an enduring foundation upon which to base political leadership. To be maintained successfully political power must in some way become legitimated. Although power legitimates itself to an extent, there are obvious disadvantages to relying exclusively upon force for one's authority. Coercion can be an extremely effective form of control, but it also creates opposition, and tyrannies based on power alone are notoriously short-lived.[9]

Taksin appears to have been well aware of the importance of legitimating his political power. Further, he recognized that his own claims to the Thai throne were tenuous and problematic. One of his primary concerns, therefore, was to establish the legitimacy of his new position, and thereby gain popular acceptance not only of his actual leadership but also of his *right* to lead. Soon after his initial military victories he began to seek ways by which to accomplish this goal. His decision to be crowned king at Thonburi and to establish his capital there rather than at Ayuthia may have been prompted in part by this objective.[10] By moving the capital to a new site, he would avoid the political incongruity and embarrassment of occupying a seat of government for which he had no legitimate claim. Whereas in Ayuthia he would look suspiciously like an usurper, in Thonburi he could present himself as the founder of a new kingdom and as a legitimate ruler. Thonburi and its throne would be identified exclusively with him, and he would thus be able to side-step the embarrassing problem of having no royal prerequisites or credentials.[11]

One of the important legitimating acts of former Thai kings had been the building of many splendid palaces and temples. Such edifices were a visible sign of a king's authority and greatness, and they served to impress upon the king's subjects the validity of his position as ruler. Taksin, no doubt, desired to emulate his predecessors and in time to transform Thonburi into an impressive center and symbol of political power. A glorious new capital would have served to validate his position and that of his descendants in the same way that Ayuthia's grandeur and magnificence had helped to legitimate the power of its rulers. The dream of making Thonburi into a "new Ayuthia" was never realized, however. Social conditions remained turbulent throughout most of Taksin's reign, and he was therefore prevented from ever embarking upon the extensive building program that might have transformed the new capital into an imposing symbol of power.[12] In comparison to Ayuthia's past splendor, Thonburi remained modest and unimpressive.

Taksin tried to establish the legitimacy of his rule in other ways as well. Traditionally, one recognized means of legitimating political power was for the Thai king to support the Buddhist Sangha, as a demonstration of his virtue and hence of his right to rule. Almost without exception the great Thai rulers of the past were those who had built large monastic establishments and who encouraged high moral and religious standards among the monks. Such actions gained respect and loyalty from the people, thus helping to ensure submission and assent to political authority even when a particular decision or policy might be unpopular. Although the military and political situation prevented Taksin from sponsoring any large-scale construction of religious buildings and monuments, he demonstrated interest in and support of the Buddhist community in other ways.

Mention has already been made of the religious reforms that Taksin initiated in the northern provinces following the defeat of the King of Fang. His concern about the organizational strength and purity of the Sangha was also demonstrated by his appointment of a highly respected monk from Nakhon Si Thammarat to the position of Supreme Patriarch in 1769. Prior to that he had taken other steps to improve the quality and purity of Thai religious life by rewarding study of the Buddhist scriptures. In 1768 a government official was assigned to determine which members of the Sangha were most advanced in religious knowledge and scholarship. Taksin then formally recognized the scholarly achievements of those deemed most knowledgeable by presenting them with new robes. He also ordered that Buddhist manuscripts not available in the capital but found elsewhere in the land be brought to Thonburi and copied. In addition, instructions were given that religious texts in friendly neighboring countries be duplicated and the copies brought to the Thai capital to be used in revising the scriptures already there.[13]

This fostering of Buddhist education and scholarship and the purification of the Sangha were traditional expressions of a king's religious piety and devotion; for that very reason they represented effective means of legitimating royal power. Although Taksin's support of such activities may have been prompted by a sincere religious faith, he was doubtlessly aware of the political benefits of such actions. Some of Taksin's activities in the religious sphere did not, however, bring such benefits. Especially during the latter part of his reign, he became increasingly involved in forms of religious behavior that represented a departure from norms established by former Thai kings. His espousal of aberrant religious ideas and practices eventually brought him into conflict with the Sangha, contributing significantly to the process of political delegitimation which culminated in his overthrow.

Taksin's clash with the Sangha was apparently caused by excessive religious claims and demands on his part, resulting partly from his obsession with meditation. In 1777 the Supreme Patriarch and several other leading Buddhist monks presented Taksin with some Pali texts dealing with Buddhist meditation. At about the same time he also received some non-Buddhist writings in which other forms of meditation were discussed. The reading of these materials apparently stimulated his interest to the point that he began to experiment personally with various meditational techniques and practices. Coinciding with the beginning of these experiments or shortly thereafter, Taksin began to make extravagant religious claims about himself and to exhibit noticeable signs of erratic behavior. He became convinced, for example, that through his meditation he would eventually be transformed into a divine or divine-like being. This transformation would be evidenced by his ability to fly through the air. In addition, his blood would turn white like that of the gods. Apparently, Taksin believed not only that these superhuman feats and metamorphoses would be possible but also that he was already in the process of achieving such results. He claimed that certain physical resemblances existed between his own body and that of a Buddha, and he interpreted these marks as signifying that he had become a "Stream-enterer" (sotāpanna) into the Path of Enlightenment. He also maintained that because of his elevation to this exalted spiritual status he should be accorded homage by both laity and monks, that monks as well as lay persons should bow before him. It was this latter demand that brought the king into conflict with the Sangha and created major dissensions within the Buddhist community.[14]

The majority of monks were evidently willing to accept the king's demand, but a minority of about five hundred led by the Supreme Patriarch and two other high-ranking members of the Sangha refused. Their protest was based not on a denial of the king's sotāpanna status but rather on the affirmation that even if Taksin did have such status it would still be improper for the monks to bow before him. No true Buddhist monk, they maintained, should pay homage to any lay person regardless of that person's spiritual status. The king responded by replacing the Supreme Patriarch and demoting the other two high-ranking Sangha officials involved in the protest. The remaining dissenters were removed from their monasteries, flogged, and sentenced to perform menial labor at the monastery of the new Supreme Patriarch.[15]

Taksin's handling of this whole affair amounted to a very serious political blunder. The Sangha was then and still is the single most respected group within Thai society. Without its unanimous or near unanimous support and endorsement no Thai leader could or can hope to legitimate his political position and power. A harmonious and cooperative relationship between the Sangha and the government, or at least the appearance of such harmony, is an absolute necessity for long-term political success.[16] Thus, Taksin's fostering of dissension and division within the Sangha and his visible estrangement from some of the leading monks constituted a major political liability. Furthermore, the disrespect and subsequent harsh treatment shown towards dissenting monks made a very unfavorable impression on many of the Thai people and helped to create in their minds a strong sense of the king's impiety. Such misadventures in the religious sphere were certain to have negative political repercussions. For Taksin the repercussions were indeed serious and quick in coming. In 1782, the year following his confrontation with the Sangha, he was forceably deposed.

The religious behavior of Taksin during the latter part of his reign has been characterized as the excesses of a deranged and tormented mind.[17] There may be some truth to such accusations, but, on the other hand, the religious ideas and practices that he embraced during this period of his life, although not exactly typical, were by no means without precedent in Buddhist and Thai history. Indeed, they appear to have been widely held especially during this particular period. For the most part, Taksin's so-called aberrant religious behavior was a rather bizarre outgrowth of longstanding and popular beliefs and traditions, and it should not in itself be considered conclusive evidence of madness or heresy. Taksin's preoccupation with the supernatural, for example, was commonly shared by most Thai Buddhists. Apparently, even some of the leading monks who advised the king and were themselves considered experts in meditation encouraged and supported Taksin in his pursuit of superhuman goals. Further, the Pali texts, while warning that a desire to perform supernatural feats could be detrimental to one's quest for ultimate salvation, stated that such powers do exist and that they are obtainable through the practice of meditation.[18]

As for the idea that a ruler could become divine, this too was not the creation of Taksin's disturbed mind but was drawn from indigenous Southeast Asian beliefs and Indian conceptions of sacred kingship. Usually when Buddhism prevailed, as was the case in Thailand, these beliefs were modified so that the ruler was viewed as a Bodhisatta or "Future Buddha" rather than a god.[19] These traditions formed the basis for Taksin's quest to obtain divine status and his claim of having acquired the physical marks of a Buddha. They also help to explain why he was motivated to seek these goals. The possession of superhuman qualities and powers and his transformation into a divine being or Buddha would have provided clear and indisputable proof of his kingly stature and his legitimate right to rule.

Taksin's confrontation with the monks stemmed not from his aberrant spiritual practices or religious beliefs as such, most of which were rooted in recognizable Thai Buddhist traditions, but from his claims of spiritual superiority over the monks. Had this issue of authority not arisen, the conflict with the monks might never have occurred. As it was, the dissenting monks did not object directly to Taksin's personal religious practices and beliefs. Instead, their protest focused on the issue of spiritual authority symbolized by whether or not they should bow before the king. This demand, not doctrinal matters or spiritual practices, was the basis for the dispute. In claiming spiritual authority over the monks, Taksin had departed from traditional patterns of interaction between the king and the monks. Although he was not the first Buddhist or Thai king to overextend his authority in this way, the blatant manner in which he made his claims and then tried to enforce them represented a major affront to the spiritual leadership of the Sangha and made conflict with the monks inevitable. This conflict in turn ensured the failure of Taksin's efforts to validate his political power through religious means. Instead of serving to legitimate his rule, as he had hoped, his excessive involvement in the religious sphere became the path to his undoing.

The Restoration of Thai Traditions: The Reign of King Rama I (1782-1809)

The revolt against Taksin began in March 1782. The king's support had by that time sunk so low that he was able to offer no effective resistance to the rebels. When it became clear that the situation was hopeless, Taksin agreed to abdicate the throne on the condition that his life would be spared and that he would be allowed to retire to a Buddhist monastery. The abdication was followed by a brief period of political confusion after which Chao Phraya Chakri, one of Taksin's most respected generals, emerged as the new leader of the Thai nation.[20]

The new king does not appear to have been involved directly in the plans to overthrow Taksin; nor did he participate in the rebellion itself. At the time when the fighting broke out, he was away from the capital preparing his troops for a military campaign against the Cambodians. When word arrived of the insurrection, he hurried back to Thonburi but did not reach the capital until after Taksin had been deposed. As he approached the city, he was met by the rebel leaders who were in control of the capital and was asked to become the new king. On April 6, 1782 Chao Phraya Chakri accepted this invitation and became the first ruler of the dynasty that presently occupies the Thai throne.[21]

An abbreviated and relatively small ceremony of investiture for the new monarch was held on June 13, 1782. This was followed three years later by a more elaborate and impressive coronation based on the model of those formerly held at Ayuthia.[22] As we shall see, the new king was concerned throughout his reign to identify himself and his kingdom with the heritage of Ayuthia and to restore that kingdom's traditions to the Thai nation. It is significant that one of the royal titles bestowed on the new ruler at his initial coronation in 1782 was Rama Tibodi, an appellation also given to the first king of Ayuthia. The royal name by which Chao Phraya Chakri is best known, however, is Rama I, a designation given to him posthumously by his great-great-grandson.[23]

Although Rama I was now officially in charge of the Thai government, he was faced with a situation that made his position far from secure. The most immediate problem was what to do with the former king. The continued presence of Taksin represented both an embarrassment and a potential danger to the new ruler. Rama I resolved this problem by following, apparently with great reluctance, the advice of his chief counselors and ordering his former commander's execution.[24] Another imminent danger was the threat of renewed military aggression by the Burmese. In order to defend against a possible attack on the capital, Rama I put into effect plans apparently already in existence to move the capital to the more defensible area across the river from Thonburi.[25] The construction of the new capital at Bangkok was also related to another major concern of King Rama I: the legitimation of his newly acquired political position and power.

Rama I, like his predecessor, had no convincing hereditary claims with which to justify his elevation to the office of king.[26] The decisive factors in his being chosen and accepted as Taksin's replacement were his military skill and his popularity with the army. Had he not been accompanied and supported by his troops when he returned to Thonburi, it is unlikely that the other Thai leaders would have offered him the throne so readily and unanimously. That they did so was in fact an acknowledgment of his military advantage and superiority. Thus, like Taksin before him, Rama I had gained the leadership of the nation on the basis of his military strength, and, like Taksin, he was faced with the challenge of finding additional ways in which to justify that leadership so that his hold on the throne might become more secure.

Although Rama I had not been directly involved in the rebellion against Taksin, he was nevertheless vulnerable to charges of treason and usurpation. By failing to restore Taksin to power and willingly agreeing to sit upon the throne in his stead, Rama I seemed to place himself on the side of those who had opposed the former king and favored his overthrow. Further, the ordering of Taksin's execution made the new king susceptible to the additional charge of regicide. In order to counteract these accusations, Rama I needed to disassociate himself from the rebellion as much as possible. This was accomplished in part by declaring the rebel leader guilty of treason and ordering his execution. (This action also served to eliminate an ambitious rival, who probably had royal aspirations of his own.) Further, Rama I was able to point out that, unlike the rebels, he had not seized the throne away from its rightful occupant but had agreed to become king only after Taksin had already been deposed and the throne was, at least theoretically, vacant. In excusing his failure to try to restore Taksin to power, he could argue, probably with justification, that Taksin's behavior and mental condition prior to his overthrow had shown him to be unfit to continue as ruler. As for the execution of Taksin, this was defended on the grounds that the former king's continued presence would have represented a severe threat to the nation's stability and security.[27]

The above arguments were aimed at justifying Rama I's part in removing Taksin from office, but further evidence was needed to establish the new king's own right to the throne and show why he rather than someone else was entitled to be Taksin's successor. Of course, the primary justification for Rama I's having taken over political control of the nation was the fact that he had been asked to do so by other prominent leaders in the Thai government. This request did not provide, however, a secure base upon which to establish the legitimacy of his rule. The invitation itself could be viewed as illegitimate because of its having been issued by those who had rebelled against or ignored the authority of King Taksin. Further, as we have mentioned, the primary reason for the offer's having been made was Chao Phraya Chakri's military superiority. If that advantage were not maintained, few of the new king's rivals would find the invitation itself to be adequate evidence of his right to govern or a compelling reason why they should not rise against him and claim the throne for themselves. Additional evidence of legitimacy was needed in order to ensure against such an eventuality.

In trying to establish this evidence, Rama I was careful to avoid the mistakes of his predecessor. Whereas Taksin had erred in sometimes acting contrary to the norms and expectations associated with Thai kingship, Rama I returned to more customary patterns of behavior and legitimation. He recognized that successfully restoring and upholding the traditions of the past would not only benefit and strengthen the nation but also validate his own political leadership and authority. His primary objective, therefore, was to recreate a strong and secure Thai kingdom, one that was patterned after and similar to that of Ayuthia.

The establishing of a new capital at Bangkok was an important step in this direction. In addition to improving the nation's defenses, the building of Bangkok was a conscious and deliberate attempt to create a "new Ayuthia." The city itself was modeled as far as possible after the former capital to impress visibly upon the people the similarity between the two kingdoms. An obvious implication was to show that a parallel likeness also existed between the new ruler of Bangkok and the great kings who had once ruled over Ayuthia.

It was not enough merely to rebuild a physical replica of Ayuthia. In order for Bangkok to become a "new Ayuthia," it would have to share creatively in the previous kingdom's cultural traditions and heritage. When Rama I came to the throne, this was still far from being the case. Although the nation had progressed both militarily and politically under Taksin, many cultural traditions remained disrupted and the society itself continued to be badly disordered and divided. Unless this situation were altered, Rama I would never be able to present himself successfuly as a ruler equal to the former honored kings of Ayuthia. One of his major challenges and tasks, therefore, was to restore Thai society and culture to a state comparable to that which had characterized Ayuthia during its heyday.

One of the divisions of Thai society that was especially disrupted, hence in need of immediate attention and repair, was the religious sector. The Buddhist Sangha in particular needed extensive reform and purification. Monastic organization and discipline had never fully recovered from the havoc caused by the destruction of Ayuthia, and the religious irregularities of Taksin's reign had contributed still further to the disorder and degeneracy of the monks. Rama I recognized the seriousness of this decline and the negative affect that it was having on Thai society. Early in his reign he took steps to reform the Sangha and improve the quality of religious life generally. These actions were seen by the Thai people as demonstrations of the king's religious interest and concern and as proof of his own virtue and merit. Hence, they not only benefited the Buddhist community and the society as a whole but also contributed to the king's personal quest for political legitimation.[28]

The first step of religious reform was to reinstate the monks whom Taksin had ousted from the Sangha because of their objections to his claims of religious superiority. At the same time Rama I also expelled or demoted those monks who had been given high-ranking monastic appointments during the preceding reign but whom he considered unqualified or unworthy. In addition, during the first two years of his rule, the new king issued a total of seven royal edicts pertaining directly to religious affairs. The main purpose of these decrees was to restore popular respect for the Thai Sangha by improving the moral and religious behavior of the monks.[29] The decree issued on May 8, 1783, for example, imposed stricter disciplinary and organizational controls over individual monks. It stated that each monk must be attached to a particular monastery and be under the direct supervision of a qualified monk who would act as his preceptor. Each monk was also required to carry identification papers showing the monastery with which he was associated, and each monastery in turn was ordered to keep a list of all the monks under its jurisdiction.[30]

Other royal decrees issued during this period dealt with ways in which the laity could assist the monks in maintaining higher standards of ethical and religious conduct. Civil authorities and lay persons were ordered to report any forbidden or unseemly behavior by monks to the proper religious officials. The laity was also instructed and encouraged to provide properly for the material needs of the Sangha. We have seen that inadequate lay support contributed directly to monastic disorder and degeneracy following the fall of Ayuthia, but on other occasions the support had been too lavish, and this also had had a corrupting influence. Lay persons had frequently lost sight of the distinction between their own life-style and that of the monks and had presented the monks with inappropriately expensive and luxurious gifts. The possession of such items conflicted, of course, with the Buddhist monastic ideals of renunciation and poverty; this failure to adhere strictly to their ascetic standards had been a major reason for the decline in the monks' reputation. In order to change this situation the king prohibited the giving of extravagant presents to the monks and reminded his subjects that the purity of the Sangha was essential for acquiring religious merit. By thus reestablishing the distinction between

the life-styles of householders and monks and by fostering a proper relationship between the two groups, the king hoped to restore respect and purity to
the Thai religious community.[31]

One feature of the religious situation that threatened to interfere with attaining this goal was the widespread involvement of the monks in animistic
and magical practices.[32] This involvement had a detracting and debilitating influence on the religious life of both monks and laity. Also, such beliefs and
practices could easily become linked with political activities and be manipulated for political purposes. The King of Fang, for example, had apparently
used the claim of special supernatural powers to attract followers, and Taksin
had made similar claims in hopes of fostering his political ambitions and
achieving political legitimacy. Another example that showed the potentially
subversive use of magical beliefs and practices was the brief rebellion that had
taken place in the capital in April 1783. This rebellion, which was supported
by some of the nobility, had been instigated by two ex-monks claiming that
they possessed various supernatural powers. Rama I wanted to ensure that
similar uprisings would not occur again in the future and that the religious
sector would not contribute to their outbreak. This fear was one of the reasons for his having already instituted tighter disciplinary controls over the
monks. As a further prevention, the king instructed the people not to depend
upon supernatural beings and powers, nor to be led astray by those who did;
instead, they should cultivate religious merit through acts of liberality and
morality. The monks, for their part, were encouraged to refrain from all activities not pertaining directly to their religious profession as followers of the
Buddha.[33]

In 1789, 1794, and 1801 additional religious edicts were issued by the
king. The tenth and final decree of 1801 represented in many respects the culmination of his efforts to improve the Thai religious situation and rid the
Buddhist monastic communities of unworthy and degenerate elements. It ordered that one hundred and twenty-eight monks be expelled from the Sangha
and sentenced to hard labor. These monks were accused of various forms of
immorality and misconduct, including drinking intoxicants, wandering out at
night to see entertainments, rubbing shoulders with women, engaging in loose
talk, obtaining fanciful objects of merchandise, flirting with women excur-
sionists, practicing the life of a highwayman, and attending low and undigni-
fied amusements. This list of offences is instructive, for it reveals the disreput-
able state into which some of the Sangha's members had fallen and shows how
far they had departed from their ascetic ideals. The expulsion of guilty monks
and the public announcement by the king of his disapproval of their actions
were important steps toward reforming and rectifying monastic conduct. The
reform of the Sangha had the effect of improving Thai religious life in general,
and this improvement contributed to the betterment of Thai society as a
whole.[34]

Prior to promulgating the final three edicts on religion mentioned above,
Rama I had undertaken another project of religious reform that also was of
great importance and significance to the Thai Buddhist community. In 1788
he convened a Council of leading Buddhist monks and scholars at Wat
Mahathat in Bangkok for the purpose of revising the Thai version of the Buddhist scriptures. This revision was greatly needed since many of the most re-

liable and authoritative Thai manuscripts had been lost or destroyed during the war with Burma and the extant texts contained many discrepancies and errors. The variant readings in the available texts could at times become a source of considerable confusion, and they raised doubts as to which reading was the authentic "Buddha-word." They also hindered the progress of religious reform since there was uncertainty about what was scripturally correct and therefore normative. In order to remove this uncertainty, Rama I convened the Council at Wat Mahathat and commissioned the participants to produce a revised text that would serve as a definitive version of the Buddhist scriptures and as a normative guide for religious reform.[35]

The work of the Council was carried out by two hundred fifty scholars and took about five months to complete. The revised texts were then transcribed onto palm-leaf manuscripts, which were guilded and placed in a building constructed specifically for that purpose. Throughout the entire proceedings the king played a very important role. He was present at the opening ceremony and continued to show much interest in the Council's work and progress during the days and months that followed. Also, he provided for the needs and expenses of all the participants. Sponsoring a Buddhist assembly of this magnitude had political as well as religious significance for Rama I. It identified him with the pious rulers of Thailand's past and with the great and devout kings of Buddhist history, kings such as Asoka and Vattagamini, who also had convened Councils for the purpose of reforming the Sangha and revising the scriptures.[36] Further, the Council and its work served as public demonstration of his concern for the restoration of the true "Buddha-word" and his allegiance to the Dhamma or Teaching of the Buddha, providing another indication of Rama I's legitimacy as a political ruler.

In addition to its assigned task of revising the scriptures, the Council also served another important function. It brought together representatives of the main factions which had developed among the monks and involved them in a common endeavor of great historical and religious importance. Their joint participation in this solemn and sacred work helped to heal some of the divisions within the Buddhist community and thus contributed not only to the purification of the Dhamma but also to the unification of the Sangha. By helping to foster religious unity, the Council also contributed to the restoration of a harmonious and unified Thai society, which was among Rama I's primary political objectives.[37]

A further reason for Rama I's interest in the Council and its work was perhaps the belief that a direct and corresponding relationship exists between the state of the Buddhist scriptures and the condition of the society. According to the Buddhist world view, history follows a regressive course of devolution characterized in part by the deterioration of the social order. This decay is in turn linked to a decline of the Dhamma. One way of halting and reversing this process, therefore, would be to revise and restore the Dhamma as represented in the scriptures to its supposedly true and original form. Rama I may have seen the work of the Council as important for this reason. Not only would the Council produce an improved version of the scriptures, its work would also help to bring about a corresponding improvement in Thai society. This improvement would, of course, have had the additonal effect of strengthening Rama I's own personal political position as king and head of state.[38]

The efforts of Rama I to reform Thai religion and improve the conditions of Thai society were highly successful. This was also true of his attempts to gain political legitimation for himself and his descendants. When he died in 1809, the succession to the throne passed peacefully and orderly to his son, Rama II, and the royal line has remained in the Chakri family ever since. (The present King of Thailand is the ninth ruler of the dynasty.) The accomplishments of Rama I during the seventeen years that he ruled over the Thai nation were many. Politically and militarily, he continued to build upon what King Taksin had begun. Although troubled by renewed attacks from the Burmese during much of his reign, he succeeded in increasing his kingdom's military strength and political influence and in expanding its territory till at the time of his death Thailand was once again the most powerful country in Southeast Asia. But even more significant than these achievements were his accomplishments in the sphere of cultural and religious reform and restoration. During his reign many of the traditions that had been disrupted and were in danger of being lost were reestablished and preserved for future generations. Indeed, without his efforts much of Thailand's traditional heritage might not have survived.

Thus, in the end Rama I succeeded in accomplishing both of his major goals. He formed again ("reformed") a Thai kingdom that was in many ways modeled after and similar to the glorious and powerful one that had existed at Ayuthia, and he established himself and his family as legitimate holders of political power and as rightful occupants of the Thai throne. These two goals were not unrelated, and, as we have tried to show, the reform of Thai religion was central to the achievement of both.

The Continuation of Reform: Concluding Comments

The religious reforms of King Rama I reestablished a pattern of religious reform that was followed in succeeding reigns. Whereas Taksin had made a significant break with past Thai traditions on the question of religious authority and the relationship between the monarchy and the Sangha, Rama I consciously attempted to recreate and return to patterns of religious life found in Thailand's past. The intention of his reform was not to produce radical innovations in Thai religion but to restore the beliefs and practices characteristic of the former Kingdom of Ayuthia prior to its decline and fall. Thus, his religious reforms were basically of a very traditional and conservative nature, and for that very reason they proved to be more successful, and more acceptable to the Sangha and the Thai people, than had been those of Taksin. This aim of recreating an ideal religious past continued to be the dominant theme and motivation behind Thai religious reform in the years that followed.

The most important religious reformer in Thailand during the nineteenth century was Prince (later King) Mongkut, a grandson of Rama I. His reforms, like those of his grandfather, were an attempt to reestablish in their pure and pristine forms the religious practices and beliefs which he believed to be part of the original Buddhist tradition. What made his reforms appear more radical and controversial than those of his grandfather was that his model for "pure" or "true" Buddhist religion went back even farther into history than had the one used by Rama I. Whereas Rama I had used the traditions of Ayuthia as the main model for his reforms, Mongkut was inspired and guided by other traditions, some of which he had learned from Mon Buddhists and which he considered to be older and therefore purer and truer than those held by the Thai. He was influenced and informed also by his personal study and interpretation of the Pali texts. Because the ideas he derived from these sources sometimes clashed with practices and beliefs which over the years had come to be accepted as orthodox by most Thai, Mongkut was frequently accused of supporting radically innovative changes in Buddhist faith and life. In fact, many changes he sought to bring about were based upon religious traditions that were more ancient than those then being followed in Thailand. Thus, although Rama I and Mongkut differed in using different models of reform, they were similar in looking to the past as a guide to what the religious situation should be and in striving to return to an older and therefore, in their opinion, more authentic form of Buddhist religion.[39]

This orientation towards the past has been shared by most, if not all, of the major Thai religious thinkers and reformers since the end of the eighteenth century. Although stimulated by changes taking place in the modern world and though sometimes incorporating elements of these changes, Thai religious reforms have continued to have as their central thrust the restoration and conservation of earlier traditions. Even the contemporary Thai Buddhist monk, Buddhadasa Bhikkhu, whom many now see as an important new religious innovator and reformer, is to a very great extent calling for a return to a form of faith and a style of life that are representative of the past.[40]

One must ask at this point whether religious reforms growing out of such an orientation can still adequately meet the challenges now facing Thai religion and Thai society. During the time of Rama I reforms with an orientation towards the past were clearly needed. They enabled the Thai Buddhist community and the Thai nation to regain a sense of identity and continuity with its own history following the disruptions occasioned by the destruction of Ayuthia and the turbulence of Taksin's reign. This sense of historical continuity was a valuable asset to the Thai people in the nineteenth and twentieth centuries, when it provided Thailand with a stability that was often missing in other Southeast Asian countries. This stability enabled Thailand to cope more successfully than most of its neighbors with the problems and challenges posed by modernization and increasing contacts with Europe and America. The question remains, however, whether this religious orientation towards the past will be capable of producing forms of Buddhist faith that will be viable for modern Thai society and life, or whether the Buddhist community in Thailand has reached a time when reforms of a more innovative and future-oriented nature are appropriate and necessary.

The examples of Taksin and Rama I can perhaps be instructive to those charting the course of religious reform in Thailand today. Taksin's attempted reform of Thai religion was certainly in some respects innovative; yet, it failed. Part of the reason for this failure was that Taksin ignored important historical precedents and did not always maintain adequate continuity with Thailand's past religious traditions. Contemporary Thai Buddhists making this same mistake will almost certainly suffer similar consequences. Successful religious reform today must take into account and be responsible to the historical nature of the faith and tradition being reformed. At the same time it will not be enough simply to try to restore or return to the past. The situation today requires a combination of innovation and historical responsibility. It is the task of contemporary Thai Buddhists to discover and work out what the innovative limits of responsible religious reform presently are. In many ways this is a more difficult challenge than that faced by Rama I, for it demands not a re-creation of the past but an innovative and responsible venture into the future.

The examples of Taksin and Rama I also illustrate the important role that the Thai government has traditionally played and can still play in bringing about religious reform. In the latter part of the eighteenth century the Thai king was both symbolically and in reality the head of the government, and, as we have seen, both King Taksin and King Rama I actively involved themselves in the religious affairs of the nation. Both officially initiated or attempted to initiate significant changes in Thai religion, and both relied on their participation in the religious sector and their support of its activities to strengthen and legitimate their political power.

The central role played by the Thai king and the royal family in the process of religious reform continued through the nineteenth century. Although Mongkut was a Buddhist monk and therefore not officially a part of the government when he began his reforms of the Buddhist community, he was nevertheless an important member of the royal family, a legitimate heir to the throne, and in the eyes of at least some Thai the rightful king.[41] It is very doubtful that his reforms would have had the impact they eventually did or even have succeeded at all if they had been attempted by someone not in his position. Also in the twentieth century the ties between religious reform and the royal family have been maintained. The most significant religious reformer of the early twentieth century, and probably of modern times, was Prince-Patriarch Wachirayan (Vajirañāna), King Mongkut's son and a half-brother of King Rama V (Chulalongkorn). Under Prince-Patriarch Wachirayan's leadership and guidance and with the support and encouragement of King Chulalongkorn many of the reforms begun by Mongkut were continued and institutionalized. Prince-Patriarch Wachirayan directed, for example, a thorough reorganization of the Sangha and instituted a completely new program of monastic education throughout the country. These reforms, which very much affected the entire Thai Buddhist community, helped to bring the Sangha into step with the movements towards modernization that were taking place in the rest of the society.[42]

Thus, for almost two hundred years either the king or an heir-apparent to the throne or some other close relative of the king usually acting with the king's support was instrumental in bringing about the major successful reforms of Thai religion. This involvement by the king and his relatives was in many cases apparently quite sincere and inspired by genuinely religious motives. (Certainly this seems to have been true of the royal examples we have mentioned thus far.) At the same time the king and his family were aware of the political benefits to be gained from their involvement in the religious sphere. By demonstrating publicly their religious piety and virtue, they gave evidence of their right to rule the nation and sit upon the throne. The sponsoring and fostering of religious reforms was a very successful way of accomplishing this political goal. Moreover, such reforms usually contributed directly to the improvement and well-being of the society, which in turn, of course, strengthened the ruler's political position.

The assistance of the Thai government has been extremely important and necessary for the success of Thai religious reforms. This aid has traditionally come from the king or other members of the royal family. In the past the king and his family possessed real political power and institutional control, and they could exercise this power and control in support of a particular reform, thereby almost ensuring its success.[43] Today, of course, this situation has radically changed. Since 1932 the Thai king has not been an absolute monarch with absolute powers. Although he has retained symbolic leadership of the nation, real political power and control are now found elsewhere — often with the military. Under these circumstances the support of the king is no longer adequate to guarantee that a particular religious reform will be successful. For any real chance of lasting success support must come from those holding real power in the government.

The support of the king and the royal family is still vitally important, however. The effectiveness of the king as a religious reformer was always based on more than just his political power; it was also a result of his spiritual authority.[44] Although since 1932 the king has been without real political power or institutional control, he has retained this spiritual authority, and with it the popular respect and reverence of the Thai people. For this reason, if any major religious reform is to succeed today, it must have the support not only of those actually in charge of running the government but also of the king.

Religious reform is as needed today in Thailand as it was during the reigns of Taksin and Rama I, but the contemporary Thai situation calls for a reform that is innovative without being irresponsible and forward-looking without being blind to the past. But this kind of reformation is unlikely to occur or be very successful unless the Thai king and the Thai government actively and enthusiastically support and encourage it. The giving of such support and encouragement would in turn bring the benefit of greater political legitimacy and security to the government and the king. It would also provide them with the personal knowledge and satisfaction that they had contributed to the religious development and well-being of the Thai Buddhist community and the Thai nation.

Notes

1. The term *reform* is used throughout the paper to refer to religious change in the most general sense. It is possible to delineate different types of reform according to the various agents, aims, causes, etc., that characterize these changes. For example, some reforms may be conscious attempts to alter a religious tradition and form of faith in a certain way that has been thought out beforehand; other reforms may occur more or less without the intent or even the conscious awareness of the members whose community is being changed. In this latter case the reforms may be simply a result of natural evolution within the tradition or due to subtle changes caused by acculturation.

2. A classic study of the dynamics of religious change and of the possible effects that it may have on other areas of society is Max Weber's *The Protestant Ethic and the Spirit of Capitalism* (New York: Charles Scribner's Sons, 1958). Weber's thesis has been developed and refined by later scholars to show that rather than one sector or dimension of life and society influencing and affecting another, it is more correct to see the situation as one of mutual influence or confluence and interdependence.

3. English language accounts of the capture and destruction of Ayuthia can be found in D. G. E. Hall, *A History of South-East Asia* (2nd ed.; London: MacMillan & Co. Ltd., 1964), pp. 426 ff.; W. A. R. Wood, *A History of Siam* (Bangkok: n.p., 1924?), pp. 231-50; and Craig James Reynolds, "The Buddhist Monkhood in Nineteenth Century Thailand" (unpublished Ph.D. dissertation, Cornell University, 1972). Reynolds deals especially with

the effects of the Burmese war on the Thai religious community.

4. For a discussion of the background and reign of King Taksin, see Prince Chula Chakrabongse, *Lords of Life* (London: Alvin Redman, 1960), pp. 70-79; cf. also Wood, *History*, pp. 252-72. See Reynolds, "Buddhist Monkhood," pp. 30-35, for a discussion of the Buddhist community during Taksin's reign.

5. The Thai's recovery of their land from the Burmese was assisted by a series of Chinese attacks on Burma's northern borders at this time. Although the Burmese repelled the attack, this distraction gave the Thai an opportunity to strengthen their forces and take the initiative. Cf. Prince Chula, *Lords*, p. 71.

6. For a list of the five main rivals, see Wood, *History*, p. 254. Among these rivals for the throne there were relatives of the last king of Ayuthia.

7. Cf. Wood, *History*, p. 259.

8. On messianic notions in Buddhism, see Melford E. Spiro, *Buddhism and Society* (New York: Harper & Row, Publishers, 1970), pp. 171-87. As Spiro points out, the idea of a future king is still found among Burmese Buddhists and has played a prominent role in Burmese politics in recent times.

9. For a discussion of the legitimation of political power from a social science perspective, see Claus Mueller, *The Politics of Communication: A Study in the Political Sociology of Language, Socialization, and Legitimation* (New York: Oxford University Press, 1973).

10. The usual explanations given for the decision to shift the capital to Thonburi are that it was strategically more favorably situated and that astrological evidence indicated that the shift should be made.

11. One of Taksin's rivals was a son of a former king of Ayuthia.

12. Craig Reynolds has suggested that the rapidity with which Rama I was able to move the capital to the Bangkok side of the river indicates that plans for this shift may have already been made by Taksin.

13. Cf. Reynolds, "Buddhist Monkhood," pp. 34-35.

14. The accounts accusing Taksin of insanity should be read with caution. Statements by European observers claiming that the king was mad can hardly be considered unbiased. In fact, there was a tendency to view religious beliefs or practices as superstitious or crazy unless they were Christian. As for the Thai accounts, they had a vested interest in justifying the kingship of Rama I. In assessing Taksin's tyrannical behavior, one must remember that Rama IV (King Mongkut) was known at times to have angry outbursts and become enraged, but he was hardly considered insane. Cf. Reynolds, "Buddhist Monkhood," pp. 31-34.

15. *Ibid.*, pp. 33-34.

16. This respect is demonstrated by the deference given to the Buddhist monks and to Buddhist symbols by the "radical" Thai university students who not long ago overthrew the government of Prime Minister Thanom Kittikachorn (1973).

17. Cf. note 14 above.

18. Cf. the discussion by Spiro referred to above in Note 8. Also cf. Reynolds, "Buddhist Monkhood," pp. 31-32.

19. Cf. John F. Cady, *Southeast Asia: Its Historical Development* (New York: McGraw-Hill Book Company, 1964), pp. 35, 37-38, and 44-49.

20. On the last days of Taksin, cf. Prince Chula, *Lords*, pp. 78-79; and Wood, *History*, pp. 270-72.

21. The present Thai king, Bhumibol Adulyadej, King Rama IX, is the ninth reigning member of the Chakri dynasty founded by Rama I.

22. See Reynolds, "Buddhist Monkhood," pp. 35-37.

23. See Prince Chula, *Lords*, p. 80.

24. *Ibid.*, pp. 78-79.

25. Cf. note 12 above.

26. Cf. Prince Chula, *Lords*, pp. 80-81, where he speculates that the Chakri family might be descended from the royal lines of both Sukhothai and Ayuthia. He admits that there is no satisfactory evidence documenting these claims, however.

27. Cf. *ibid.*, pp. 78 and 84.

28. In addition to trying to create a "new Ayuthia" architecturally and reform Thai religion, Rama I performed other traditionally accepted acts in order to establish the legitimacy of his rule. He sought and gained, for example, official recognition from the Chinese Emperor of his right to rule over the Thai kingdom. He also reestablished control over Ayuthia's former vassal states and obtained from their leaders further acknowledgement of his authority. In addition, he ordered that several white elephants, special symbols of blessing and prosperity which had recently been discovered be brought to the capital as visible proof that the kingdom was prospering under his rule. In other efforts to impress visibly upon the people his power and thereby gain recognition of it, he devoted considerable attention to various royal ceremonies, often of a religious nature.

29. On the religious reforms of King Rama I, see Prince Dhani Nivat, *A History of Buddhism in Siam* (Bangkok: The Siam Society, 1965), pp. 21-30; Klaus Wenk, *The Restoration of Thailand under Rama I, 1782-1809* (Tucson: Published for the Association for Asian Studies by the University of Arizona Press, 1968), pp. 38-42; and Reynolds, "Buddhist Monkhood," pp. 35-62.

30. Reynolds, "Buddhist Monkhood," pp. 38-49.

31. *Ibid.*

32. In order to earn money or simply because of personal interest some monks had begun to serve as dealers in herbal medicines, astrologers, masseurs, etc.

33. Reynolds, "Buddhist Monkhood," pp. 38-49.

34. Cf. Wenk, *Restoration*, pp. 38-42.

35. *Ibid.* Also cf. Reynolds, "Buddhist Monkhood," pp. 50-55, and Prince Dhani, *History*, pp. 22-23.

36. *Ibid.* According to Thai reckoning, the Council held in Bangkok in 1788 was the Ninth Buddhist Council.

37. Cf. Reynolds, "Buddhist Monkhood," pp. 50-55.

38. *Ibid.*

39. For a discussion of the religious career of Prince Mongkut and his reforms and their significance, see Abbot Low Moffat, *Mongkut, the King of Siam* (Ithaca: Cornell University Press, 1961), pp. 11-22; Reynolds, "Buddhist Monkhood," pp. 63-119. Compare also the commemorative publication *His Majesty King Rama the Fourth, Mongkut*, printed in Bangkok in 1968; and Prince Dhani, *History*, pp. 30-36.

40. For a discussion of Buddhadasa Bhikkhu and a translation of some of his writings, see *Buddhadāsa, Toward the Truth*, ed. by Donald K. Swearer (Philadelphia: Westminster Press, 1971).

41. Because of his age and lack of experience Mongkut had been passed over when the selection was made with regard to who should succeed to the throne after the death of his father, King Rama II. A considerable amount of intrigue and suspicion seems to have existed between Mongkut and his half-brother, King Rama III, throughout most of the Third Reign.

42. On Prince-Patriarch Wachirayan, see Reynolds, "Buddhist Monkhood," pp. 137-152.

43. The example of Taksin shows that this was not always the case and that there were limits to what even the king could do.

44. A large part of the king's spiritual authority derived from the belief that he was a Chakravartin. Since the Buddhist tradition states that Gotama might have become a Chakravartin instead of a Buddha, it was believed that the two were composed of the same sacred substance. This link between the Chakravartin and the Buddha gave the king great spiritual and religious as well as political authority, and it provided a theoretical basis for his leadership in religious affairs. It also carried the seeds of potential conflict between the monks and the king over religious authority. Cf. Reynolds, "Buddhist Monkhood," p. 35.

Modernizing Implications of Nineteenth Century Reforms in the Thai Sangha

A. Thomas Kirsch

MOST ANTHROPOLOGICAL studies of Thai religion have concentrated on the rural scene and village religion. By contrast, historians interested in Thai society have largely concentrated on urban elites. Though the anthropologists and historians involved have each benefitted from the contributions of the others, a kind of academic "division of labor" has existed. Happily, this division of labor seems to be breaking down as anthropologists have concerned themselves more with historical questions and the Thai urban milieu, while historians have come to focus on the impact of urban cultural and social changes on the Thai hinterlands. E. H. Carr's dictum that "the more sociological history becomes, and the more historical sociology becomes, the better for both" seems close to realization in Thai studies at least.[1] Despite this apparent convergence of interest amongst anthropologists and historians of Thailand, with a few notable exceptions, little effort has been made to integrate the two disciplines with a more psychological perspective which seeks to understand historical and anthropological phenomena in relation to the structure of the aspirations, values and goals of the Thai people themselves.

In this paper I will concentrate on a particular historical phenomenon which was initiated in nineteenth century Thailand: a series of monastic "reforms" instigated by a monk of royal parentage who later left the monkhood to become King Rama IV, better known to westerners as King Mongkut.[2] Though the division is somewhat artificial I want to sketch out the impact of these reforms "historically," i.e., in the nineteenth and early twentieth centuries, and also in terms of their more "contemporary" implications. The theme I wish to explore is the implications of these reforms for the modernization of Thai society. My division of these implications into "historical" and "contemporary" dimensions is simply a convenient device for exploring two aspects of these reforms which might otherwise be masked.

Two general observations may help set a frame in which to consider the modernizing implication of Mongkut's monastic reforms. One observation has to do with the form that "sectarian" disputes have frequently taken in Theravada Buddhism; the other has to do with what we might expect the purportedly "Other Worldly" emphasis of Buddhism to imply with respect to secular modernization. Also, in order to highlight the changes which Mongkut's re-

---

Originally published in *The Psychological Study of Theravada Societies* (Leiden: E. J. Brill, 1975), edited by Steven Piker. This was Volume 8 of *Contributions to Asian Studies*. Reprinted with permission.

forms supported, it will be necessary to sketch out certain aspects of Thai history.

"Sectarianism" in Theravada Buddhism

Theravada Buddhism seems to contrast with western religions, particularly Christianity, in the form which religious disputes have taken. In Christianity religious disputes have frequently focused on questions of doctrine and belief. The disputes have involved the problem of "heresy" and its resolution. Such disputes have occasionally resulted in radical religious change and the formation of religious sects, with important implications for the non-religious sphere. The most notable example of this in the western tradition would be the Protestant Reformation as viewed from the perspective of the Weber thesis.[3]

By contrast, since the foundation of the Pali Canon disputes within the Theravada Buddhist tradition have rarely focused on doctrinal questions. More commonly, disputes have taken place *within* the Sangha and have centered on questions of monastic discipline. The history of Buddhism in Burma and Ceylon is particularly rich in instances of such disciplinary disputes.[4] To the western observer these monastic disputes frequently seem to concern rather formal and even superficial questions, e.g., the style of monastic dress and/or how the monks' robes should be worn or the proper boundaries within which legitimate ordination could take place. Despite the seeming formalism or triviality of the issues involved such disciplinary dispute could engender considerable passion on the part of the various contenders, threatening schism within the monastic community. Indeed, the disagreement within the Sangha could become so heated that it might spill out of the Sangha proper to involve the Buddhist laity as well.

One problem with the resolution of these disputes about monastic discipline was that although Buddhist monks were symbolically united into a single Sangha, in most Theravada Buddhist societies the Sangha was not organizationally united. Nor were there any well defined internal mechanisms within the Sangha for the resolution of these disputes. It was commonly the practice for a Buddhist king in his role of "Defender of the Faith" to seek some sort of resolution of these monastic disagreements. But, because the disputes frequently involved mutually exclusive interpretation of proper monastic discipline a compromise solution was frequently impossible. The king – guided by senior monastic counsellors, some of whom could be active participants in the dispute – might be forced to opt for the suppression of one side or the other. For example, the king might officially deny the legitimacy of one group's ordination practice, requiring them to be reordained according to the orthodox pattern designated by the king as correct.

Though these matters of disciplinary argument within the Buddhist Sangha were extremely complicated, they show one common form that sectarianism takes in Theravada Buddhism. Buddhist sects may form around divergent interpretations of proper monastic discipline, interpretations which cannot always be resolved within the Sangha itself. I would propose further that despite the seeming triviality of the surface issues involved in these disciplinary matters, they may actually have masked far more fundamental questions about the role of the monk and his relationship to Buddhist society, questions which might have important implications far outside the boundaries of the Sangha itself.

Buddhist "Other Worldliness" and Secular Modernization

Formally, Buddhism characterizes the phenomenal world of everyday experience as one of "ignorance" and "illusion." To be involved in this everyday world is to be caught up in desires and thirsts which inevitably produce a karmic response leading to a cycle of rebirths. The Buddhist religious goal is to escape from the clutches of *karma* and the cycle of rebirths by separating oneself from the world of ignorance and illusion; thereby gaining wisdom and insight into the karmically conditioned world which underlies the phenomenal world, and ultimately gaining Nirvana. Such conceptions and attitudes have led to the characterization of Buddhism as "Other Worldly" in its focus. And, insofar as this characterization has any validity at all, the primary locus of Buddhist Other Worldliness lies in the role of the monk and the Sangha. It is peculiarly the role of the monk to separate himself from the temptations of everyday life, to seek enlightenment and freedom from rebirth.

Despite these religious conceptions and attitudes toward the everyday world, Buddhism has been institutionalized into the very fabric of Thai society and the separation of the monk from lay society is not absolute. For one thing, the monk is dependent on lay support to maintain his separation from society, and the monk ordinarily performs a number of "pastoral" duties for the layman.[5] However, we might expect that insofar as Buddhist orthodoxy is emphasized by the monk, the more withdrawn from ordinary secular concerns he would be and, the less likely it is that the monk's role would have any positive significance for secular modernization. Indeed, some argue that the primary thrust of Buddhist values and beliefs poses a barrier to secular modernization.[6]

If the foregoing remarks have any validity at all, then the sectarian developments which took place in the Thai Sangha in the late nineteenth century and which persist to the present seem to be anomalous. That is, a wing of the Thai Sangha which represents a trend to a more rigorous monastic ideal and to a higher level of orthodox religious commitment on the part of the monk has also been influential in encouraging the modernization of Thai society. Historically, this has occurred at an overt level, and continues to operate perhaps at a more covert level today. To elaborate the way in which these sectarian developments have influenced Thai modernization I must first sketch out certain aspects of Thai history.

Aspects of Thai History

When discussing Southeast Asian history in general it has commonly been the practice to speak in terms of the "emergence," the "rise" and the "decline" of a number of groups identified in terms of ethnic and/or linguistic labels. Hence, we speak of the Mon, the Khmer, the Burmese, the Cham, the Thai, the Shan, the Lao, the Vietnamese, etc. While this has clearly been a useful practice, it has served to mask the common form of polity in which many of these groups were historically organized. Basically, these groups were organized in the form of city-states of varying degrees of size, elaboration and stability. All these groups (with a few exceptions such as the early Cham and Khmer and the Vietnamese) shared a common political form which was grounded in Theravada Buddhist conceptions of kingship which were further elaborated and specified by Brahmanistic and indigenous religious conceptions. Each polity was ruled by a king who modeled his rule after the Buddhist ideal of the *chakravartin* "The Wheel-Turning Universal Monarch."[7] The core of each polity was a capital city which dominated a rural hinterland.

The Thai emerged in history in the late thirteenth century with the establishment of a number of such city-states (e.g., Sukothai, Chiengrai, Lamphun, etc.) in the area that is now north Thailand. Early inscriptions such as that of Ramkamhaeng (ca. 1292) suggest a close correlation between the foundation of these city-states and the Thai adoption of Theravada Buddhism.[8] As Heine-Geldern has observed, such early Southeast Asian states were commonly microcosmic reproductions of macrocosmic conceptions of the universe.[9] The physical and geographic layout of these kingdoms and the legitimation of their authority were grounded in religious beliefs such as those manifested in such works as the Traiphum ("The Three Worlds"), a copy of which was compiled by Ly Thai who ruled the kingdom of Sukhothai in the early fourteenth century.[10]

In the Traiphum the universe was represented as consisting of an infinite number of solar systems, each depending on a central mountain, Mt. Meru. Around Mt. Meru there were belts of mountains and oceans littered with islands. The cosmos included numerous levels of heavens which existed above the world of man, each level occupied by gods (*devas*) of differing attributes and qualities up to the very purest of being (*brahmas*) without form or desire. And there were numerous levels of hells below the world of man, occupied by spirits (*phi*) and demons (*pret*) of various sorts. These cosmological notions were spelled out in great detail and with great precision and became a part of popular knowledge through such media as temple paintings. They were not only taken to be an accurate representation of the universe but each state sought to precisely replicate this macrocosmic structure in a worldly microcosm. For example, an artificial mountain might be constructed to represent Mt. Meru in the center of a capital city situated in a flat area. And capital cities were laid out in concentric circles modeled on the vision of the structure of the Hindu-Buddhist pantheon, frequently Siva. In sum, the structure and institutions of these early Theravada Buddhist states were pervaded with and shaped by religious sentiments and beliefs.

From the fourteenth to the eighteenth century the area of the Caophraja river basin was dominated by Ayutthaya, a Thai city-state which was founded in 1350. Ayutthaya had succeeded in expanding its boundaries and incorporating a number of formerly autonomous states into its central jurisdiction while maintaining a series of quasi-autonomous vassal states on its borders.[11] The Ayutthayan kingdom was continually contending for a position of paramount authority with similar kingdoms in Burma, the Shan area, Laos and Cambodia. One factor in this continuing contention was the Chakravartin ideal of Buddhist kingship. The periodic warfare of the region could be seen as an effort to establish a kind of Buddhist-defined "peck-order" amongst the various contending states by creating tributary relations with an important symbolic aspect. The religious dimension of these wars is indicated by the prominent role which possession of Buddha images, white elephants (symbols of Buddhist kingship), or sets of Buddhist Scriptures played.

In 1767 the Burmese launched a devastating attack on Ayutthaya. The capital was utterly sacked, its records were destroyed, and the defeated royal family along with leading monks and officials were transported to Burma. The area that had been dominated by Ayutthaya for so long simply fell apart into a number of regions headed by leaders who sought to fill the power vacuum created by the downfall of the capital and the loss of the king. After years of bitter struggle order was restored by the forces led by a former official of Ayutthaya of Chinese ancestry. This man, Tak Sin, established his capital at Thonburi in 1768, many miles south of Ayutthaya. The devastation of the Ayutthayan kingdom was so complete that, in essence, Tak Sin was faced with a blank slate. That is, since the old records and law codes were so scattered he might have chosen to reconstitute the Thai kingdom in a variety of ways unencumbered by traditional constraints. However, he chose to precisely emulate the pattern of the traditional Ayutthayan social order, including the model of the Buddhist macrocosm provided by the Traiphum.

Tak Sin was particularly concerned with religious matters and with reestablishing Buddhism and the Sangha, as well as a stable government. Indeed, the two went hand in hand. However, Tak Sin's reign was cut short when he displayed symptoms of "madness" which threatened the traditional order of society. Apparently Tak Sin claimed that he was a "stream-winner" (*sotapanna*) with such miraculous powers that Buddhist monks should reverence him, rather than the reverse.[12] Although some monks acquiesced, others refused and were demoted or unfrocked. While it seems likely that other factors were involved as well, Tak Sin's claims to special religious status played an important role in his being deposed and eventually executed. He was succeeded by one of his proteges, an exceptionally able general who was the founder of the presently reigning Chakkri dynasty.

On assuming the kingship Rama I moved his capital across the river from Thonburi to Bangkok. He followed the same procedure as Tak Sin had in attempting to reconstruct the Thai kingdom precisely along the lines of the Ayutthayan regime.[13] And like Tak Sin he maintained a special interest in Buddhism. Though Tak Sin had ordered a complete retranscription of the Tripitaka during his reign, Rama I scrapped this version and ordered another. He also investigated the status of the monkhood and found it wanting. He had monks whose practice was beyond the pale unfrocked, others reordained, and reinstated and promoted those monks who had resisted Tak Sin's claims to special religious status.

Like all previous Thai kings Rama I subscribed to the cosmological notions of the Traiphum. Hence he decreed in precise detail the appropriate ordering of the elements of Thai religion with Buddhism at the apex, worship of gods (*thewada*) and spirits (*phi*) in a subordinate position.[14] The king's role was that of a Buddhist monarch invested with the attributes of a Brahmanistic god. His person could not be touched nor could he even be looked at by ordinary men under penalty of death. Astrological considerations determined the activities of the court and the kingdom. Brahmanistic ceremonies such as the First Plowing ceremony and the ceremony of the Giant Swing regulated the seasons while various stages of the life cycle or of natural functions were marked by such ceremonies as the tonsure ceremony or the "roasting" of women after childbirth. Rama I also attempted to microcosmically recapitulate the macrocosm in the physical structure of his capital and kingdom. An artificial mountain representing Mt. Meru was constructed in Bangkok which was laid out in a series of concentric circles symbolically identifying cosmos and kingdom.

The condition of Buddhism in their kingdom was an important concern of all the Chakkri kings. Special government departments were set up to facilitate the support of the Sangha, supervising temple lands and providing subsidies to individual monks. A government department provided scholar-teachers for Pali study and supervised the Pali examinations held periodically to provide ecclesiastical ranks for successful monks. The king took a special interest in these examinations, attending them personally and rewarding especially expert monks with badges of rank and high monastic titles. The Chakkri kings also underwrote the construction of numerous temples and maintained a large number of royal temples at their own expense. And, their commitment to Buddhism might even be used by the Chakkri kings to justify warfare. For example, in the mid-19th century Rama III sent Thai armies into Cambodia to protect Buddhism from the encroaching Vietnamese.[15] From their various activities it is clear then that the Thai kings felt that Buddhism and Buddhist institutions were an integral and indeed a vital part of the Thai social order. But this social order was also simultaneously pervaded with a variety of "magical" elements derived from Brahmanistic and indigenous belief which had been grafted on or supplemented to Buddhist beliefs and practices. It is in the context of this general commitment to the perpetuation of a social order grounded in Buddhist belief and practice intimately linked with Brahmanistic and animistic elements that we can examine the activities of a Chakkri prince who spent twenty-seven years in the monkhood and subsequently became king Rama IV. He is best known as Mongkut, the king of "The King and I."

Mongkut and His Reforms

Mongkut was the eldest son of Rama II by a royal wife and by most criteria could be considered the leading heir of the king.[16] As a youth Mongkut had served for a time as a novice but had returned to secular life and was being trained as a prince who would most likely become king. In 1824 his father Rama II became ill and Mongkut's planned ordination as a monk was speeded up somewhat so that the merit could be applied to his ill father. But, a few weeks after his ordination Rama II died and one of Mongkut's older half-brothers, a son of Rama II by a non-royal wife, was crowned as Rama III. It seems clear that a power play had occurred in the palace, and there is reason to believe that Mongkut might very well have considered leaving the monkhood to contend with his half-brother for the crown. Apparently, however, he saw that this would involve a bloody fratricidal fight with a problematic outcome. At any rate, Mongkut seems to have made a conscious decision to remove himself from contention and threw himself into his monastic role.

Initially he was located at Wat Mahathat, a royal temple which specialized in meditation but disdained Pali studies. Apparently, Mongkut became adept at meditation but he also became concerned with understanding the reasons behind meditational practice. He turned to a study of the Pali Canon. He was a gifted linguist and made himself one of the leading Thai Pali scholars, as well as learning Latin and English from western missionaries somewhat later. He became so adept in Pali that his half-brother the king made him chief examiner for the Pali examinations in Bangkok, rewarding him with a high ecclesiastical rank.

Apparently, it was the study of the Pali Canon that led Mongkut to see serious discrepancies between Buddhist Scriptures and the actual practice of Thai monks. He was so anguished about this discrepancy he vowed that he would disrobe if he did not receive some sign that the monastic line of succession back to the Buddha had not been broken in Thailand.

As it happened, shortly after making this vow Mongkut met with a monk of Mon extraction living in a temple near Bangkok. (The Thai Sangha was not organizationally unified and this monk was the head of the monks who followed Mon monastic practice which differed from that followed by the majority of Thai monks.) Studying this Mon monastic practice, Mongkut became convinced that this discipline was closer to the original Buddhist practice as set out in the Vinaya. He adopted this discipline as his own and gathered a number of Thai monks of similar persuasion around him. When Mongkut was subsequently appointed abbot of Wat Bowonniwet by Rama III this group settled there and formed the nucleus of what was to become a new "sect" (nikai) within the Thai Sangha.[17] Mongkut called his group of monks Thammayut, "those adhering to the doctrine" which he contrasted with the Mahanikai majority whom he deemed "those adhering to long standing habit."[18]

Some of the distinctive practices adopted by Mongkut were rather technical matters in the Vinaya. One matter involved the ordination ceremony. Legitimate ordination must take place on unencumbered land, but Mongkut felt that it was impossible to be absolutely sure that any in the Bangkok area was completely unencumbered. Hence, strictly speaking, any ordination carried out in Bangkok might be questionable. He had himself reordained under what he took to be impeccable conditions — in his case on a raft moored in a river — and insisted his followers do likewise.[19] Another technical matter involved the manner of wearing the monastic robe. Mongkut took the Vinaya to prescribe that the monk should wear his robe in such a way that both shoulders were covered, though the majority of Thai monks wore their robes to leave one shoulder bare. Apparently, this issue was especially touchy, perhaps because it was one which made visible the differences in views between the Thammayut and Mahanikai practice. Though Rama III had given Mongkut considerable support in his various monastic endeavors, it was this issue which troubled the king the most about Mongkut's reforms. It was on the grounds that Mongkut might impose this "Mon" style of dress on the entire Sangha that Rama III on his deathbed rejected Mongkut's candidacy as his successor to the kingship.

There were other reforms which Mongkut instituted amongst his followers of a less technical but no less important sort. Mahanikai monks ordinarily ate two meals a day and some, particularly in large urban temples, neglected their daily round collecting alms. Thammayut monks ate only one meal a day, and were expected to eat only food that was placed in their alms-bowls. Mahanikai monks accepted side-dishes offered separately from the rice placed in their alms-bowls; the Thammayut practice produced an unappetizing mixure of foods. Thammayut monks were also expected to attain some proficiency in both meditation and scholarship, whereas the standards among Mahanikai were more lax. And, in contrast to Mahanikai monks, the Thammayut monks were encouraged to preach extemporaneously in the vernacular, rather than to recite memorized sermons filled with Pali words which laymen (and many monks) could not understand.

Though Mongkut's reforms were directed at upgrading monastic discipline, this went hand in hand with certain ideological commitments as well. For one thing, Mongkut rejected a great many traditional beliefs and practices as superstitious interpolations into Buddhism. He rejected the cosmology and cosmogony represented in the Traiphum, arguing that cosmology had to accord with empirical knowledge, and particularly with scientific views that he learned in his contact with westerners. A voluminous reader and insatiably curious, Mongkut became familiar with a considerable body of western scientific knowledge both while in the monkhood and later as king. He took particular pride in his knowledge of astronomy, widely publicizing his prediction of an eclipse in 1868 and ridiculing traditional beliefs that eclipses occurred because a dragon swallowed the moon and later disgorged it. (In fact, Mongkut contracted his fatal illness while on a scientific expedition to observe an eclipse.) Mongkut's monastic reform involved then, not only an effort to upgrade monastic practice and make it more orthodox, but also included an attempt, in western terms, to demythologize the world.[21] The implications of Mongkut's monastic reforms can be seen not only in his own activities as king, but in the activities of his subsequent followers both monk and laymen.

Historical Implications of Mongkut's Reforms

Mongkut left the Sangha and assumed the kingship on the death of Rama III in 1851. He ruled for eighteen years. His efforts at demythologizing the world were continued as he encouraged the introduction of printing presses and western knowledge. He modified a number of royal coronation ceremonies which were heavily Brahmanistic to emphasize the role of the king as a Buddhist monarch morally subordinate to the Sangha.[22] He re-channeled Thai relations with the west, modifying the structure of Thai society so that it was more in line with western practice. Corvee labor was gradually done away with and replaced by taxes and wage labor, and Mongkut laid the groundwork for the abolition of "slavery" (typically a form of debt bondage) which occurred in the following reign of his son Chulalongkorn.

With respect to the Sangha Mongkut did not, as Rama III had feared, impose the Thammayut discipline on the entire Sangha. Rather he seems to have walked a very narrow line, providing encouragement and facilitating his Thammayut followers without going so far as to seem to be denigrating the Mahanikai. Insofar as he was able Mongkut discouraged men from leaving the monkhood.[23] Monastic education had frequently been used a vehicle for upward mobility in the secular world. Highly trained monks would unfrock and gain positions of great power. Mongkut strongly discouraged the disrobing of long term monks and limited the offices which such men could enter to those which were least powerful or most closely connected with religious affairs. Though as king he had over twenty wives and numerous concubines, he viewed the sexuality of women as a threat to the monkhood. He decried those women who, in his terms, looked on monks as "fattened hogs" who were "likely to be driven crazy" by these women and seduced into leaving the monkhood.[24]

The implications of Mongkut's views concerning Buddhism and secular belief and activity are seen clearly in the works of one of his closest followers while king. Thiphakorawong (Kham Bunnak) was Mongkut's "Foreign Minister" (Phra Klang) and by duty as well as inclination he had considerable contacts both with Mongkut and with westerners. Thiphakorawong wrote a book titled *Kitchanukit*, "a book explaining many things," which was designed by him to be used as a kind of textbook for the instruction of modern Thai.[25] About half the book is devoted to debunking the traditional cosmological beliefs against empirical western science. For example, Thiphakorawong expounds on the scientific explanation for rain, contrasting it with the cosmological explanation and rejects the latter in favor of the western views. A substantial amount of the book is devoted to expounding the essence of Buddhist doctrine which he grounded in the doctrines of *karma* and multiple rebirth and the notion that varying degrees of religious merit can account for the variations in the social order. Underlying his view of religion is the belief that the world operates on a law of perfect justice which he uses to confound and refute western missionaries. Thiphakorawong also makes a strong distinction between worldly matters and religious matters. But, what obviously counts most for him is the religious, for adherence to Buddhist principles determines a man's future, whereas any misperception of the natural world would simply be a temporary inconvenience. Whether Thiphakorawong's views were derived directly from Mongkut is not clear, but in any case they were clearly consistent with the thrust of Mongkut's monastic reforms. But, in emphasizing Buddhist orthodoxy and undermining the traditional cosmology, Mongkut's monastic reforms had freed the Thai institutional order of at least some of its magical underpinnings, opening the way for a variety of social innovations.

The impact of Mongkut's monastic reforms did not cease on his death in 1868. Mongkut was succeeded by his son Chulalongkorn who ruled until 1910. It was during this long reign that many of the modernizing implications of Mongkut's reforms were carried out. Formerly, government departments had been multifunctional with overlapping jurisdictions and functions. They were replaced by functionally specialized departments with relatively non-overlapping jurisdictions. The provincial administration was rationalized and brought more fully under central control. Foreign experts were brought in to help reorganize the police, legal and court systems, as well as to advise on economic policy, the improvement and expansion of agriculture, water control projects and communications and transportation networks throughout the kingdom. The recruitment and training of officials was standardized and several universities were established in Bangkok to serve this end. Western medical practices were widely adopted and the importance of western knowledge and technology was clearly recognized. Over the years a number of deserving and able "King's Scholars" as well as members of the Royal family were sent abroad to obtain western training.[26] And, a national "secular" educational system was inaugurated which was designed to teach both Buddhist moral principles and a modern academic curriculum adapted to the situation of Thai society. It is worth noting that King Chulalongkorn put his younger brother Prince Wachirayan, the head of the Thammayut *nikai* in charge of setting up the national school system and initially at least made use of existing temple schools and monk teachers.[27]

A number of changes in traditional Thai religion also seem to have begun in Chulalongkorn's reign. The role of Court Brahmans in determining auspicious times for official events was muted and ultimately downgraded. A number of Brahmanistic and animistic ceremonies such as the tonsure ceremony, the Giant Swing ceremony and the roasting of women after childbirth virtually disappeared. The First Plowing ceremony was retained, but more as a spectacle than a basic national ritual. It is performed even today, largely as a tourist attraction. Hence, many non-Buddhist religious elements were deeply eroded and Buddhism was upgraded as a result of Thammayut demythologizing.

Although Chulalongkorn followed the same balanced treatment of both Thammayut and Mahanikai monks that Mongkut had, the Thammayut monks achieved full status as a legitimate "sect" (*nikai*) within the Sangha during his reign. At the same time Chulalongkorn was rationalizing and centralizing his government, the organization of the Sangha was also centralized. Formerly autonomous groupings of monks in the provinces were brought into a unified Sangha structure paralleling the structure of the government. Monastic standards were made more uniform and, in an effort to upgrade the quality of the monkhood two Buddhist universities were established in Bangkok, one for each of the two *nikai*. The practice of naming a Thammayut monk as Supreme Patriarch (Sangkharat) of the entire Thai Sangha was unbroken until 1938 and indicates the continuing close relationship between the royal rulers and the reform order of monks.[28]

Viewed in broadest terms Mongkut's religious reforms were aimed at upgrading the religious standards of the Thai Sangha in an effort to more closely approximate a pure Buddhist orthodoxy. Mongkut's view was that the monk must strive to adhere as closely as possible to the monastic standards contained in the Vinaya, while avoiding any interpolations which were contrary to empirical knowledge. Thus, Mongkut's reforms also encouraged the demythologizing of the natural world and the erosion of various elements of traditional religious belief and practice. This demythologizing freed both monk and lay supporters to view the secular world in a new way and opened the possibility of real social innovation. For Mongkut and his followers, Buddhism was a religion which accorded perfectly with empirical reality, but that reality had both a moral dimension and a natural one. Orthodox Buddhist belief and practice defined the moral dimension, and the natural dimension was susceptible to empirical study and verification. There was no contradiction for a Buddhist in coming to grips with the world, though he might have to do so in a distinctively Buddhist fashion. Despite the increasing orthodoxy which Mongkut's reforms encouraged, it posed no intrinsic barriers to modernizing various facets of traditional Thai society, and to some extent actually encouraged this process. This "elective affinity" between Mongkut's monastic reforms and modernizing trends is indicated overtly by the linkage between the Thammayut religious orientation and the activities of those religious and secular leaders who historically helped to alter the traditional structure of Thai society. But, the modernizing significance of Mongkut's reforms is not restricted exclusively to the historical period. In a more covert way they are operative today as well.

Contemporary Implications of Mongkut's Reforms

Although the modern Thai State guarantees religious liberty, it still retains its official Buddhist character. Constitutionally, the Thai king must be a Buddhist to perform his traditional role as Defender of the Buddhist Faith, and government agencies still provide various forms of support for Buddhist institutions. And virtually all Thai, of high estate or low, urban or rural, are firmly committed to Buddhist values and tries, each in his own way, to order his life in a manner that is congruent with Buddhist morality. The monk serves as a proximate exemplar of Buddhist values and the highest state that a Buddhist can aspire to is to live the life of the monk. Many Thai men do spend at least a small portion of their lives in the Sangha, and a smaller number make the monkhood their lifelong career.

The initial impact of Mongkut's reforms was felt most strongly by a relatively small group of religious and secular leaders drawn from the urban elite. But subsequently the Thammayut *nikai* was made a part of the fabric of the national Thai Sangha (and spread to the Sanghas of Laos and Cambodia as well). Though Thammayut monks form only a small part of the Thai Sangha, their influence has penetrated to the countryside. They are often found in "forest" temples located on the outskirts of provincial centers and rural villages where they follow their ascetic regime and carry out their exemplary role distinct from the village monks of the Mahanikai.

In his efforts to upgrade the standards of monastic practice Mongkut, in essence, made the task of being a monk more rigorous and demanding than it had once been. To be a Thammayut monk requires a conscious commitment and a higher level personal involvement than is necessary for the Mahanikai monk.[29] This situation holds implications not only for the monk but the dedicated layman as well. Since the Thammayut monk's role is so demanding, the layman who is most strongly committed to Buddhist values and to Buddhist orthodoxy may also feel that his personal qualities are such that he cannot meet the high standards expected of the Thammayut monk. Such dedicated laymen are then forced to live and achieve in the secular world and to harness their Buddhist commitments to their secular roles. It is notable that in the countryside where Thammayut monks are found, their strongest lay supporters are drawn from among the group of local leaders, schoolteachers, storekeepers, and a nascent group of local traders who are also oriented to national concerns and are the innovators and modernizers of village society.[30] This situation suggests that there is a social and psychological "fit" between a modernizing and national orientation among local leaders and the Buddhist orientation fostered by Mongkut's monastic reforms. The aspirations, goals and self-images of these local leaders apparently mesh well with support of the Thammayut monks. Hence, it appears that the elective affinity between Mongkut's Buddhist reform movement and a modernizing attitude is still operative today.

Conclusions

Several points might be drawn from this consideration of the modernizing implications of Mongkut's efforts to reform the Thai Buddhist Sangha in the nineteenth century. For one thing, though the contemporary social scientist is most likely to be interested in tracing out any social or psychological correlates of these reforms, he should beware of the temptation to "reduce" Mongkut's reforms to a simple-minded sociologism. That is, the available evidence indicates Mongkut was not simply reacting to existing social strains in Thai society, nor was he seeking to harmonize Buddhism with an impinging modern world.

The primary impetus for his reforms seems clearly to have been purely religious. Indeed, his reforms were consistent with a long standing tradition within Theravada Buddhism in seeking to harmonize the actual practice of monks with Vinaya standards.

It is also important to consider the matter of historical contingency and beware of a retrospective view of historical events as having been in some sense "inevitable." If the instigator of these reforms had been anyone other than Mongkut, the course of their effects on Thai society might well have been very different. At least, it seems likely that it was the combination of a number of factors (Mongkut's high rank, the fact that he later became king, and that he was succeeded by his son Chulalongkorn) which must be considered together in understanding the impact of these reforms on Thai society. It seems that none of these events or their combination was at all "inevitable."

Mongkut's reforms are of special interest to the student of Theravada Buddhism, for they suggest that there is no intrinsic opposition between a strongly orthodox Buddhism and various facets of modernization. At least, one can make a case that Mongkut's efforts to upgrade the Thai Sangha facilitated subsequent efforts to modernize the nonreligious spheres of Thai society, and that these efforts have some influence on the aspirations and values of contemporary Thai.

Social scientists are no longer surprised to learn that acts and events may have hidden or unintended consequences. Nor are they surprised to discover that past events can have present consequences. But, Mongkut's efforts to upgrade the Thai monkhood and to modernize Thai society may not only provide some insight into the present, they may also provide a model for the future as well. In recent years there has been a movement in Thailand, encouraged by a number of westerners among others, to make Buddhism and the monkhood "more relevant" to the daily lives and problems of the Thai people and nation. Monks have been encouraged to take on tasks of "community development" and to serve as "religious ambassadors" to the non-Buddhist hill peoples.[31] Perhaps a lesson that could be learned from Mongkut's religious reforms is that the Buddhist monk is most relevant to Thai society when he lives a more orthodox monastic life, a life which does not intrude too deeply into the everyday cares of secular society.

Notes

1. Edward H. Carr, *What is History?* (New York: Alfred A. Knopf, 1964), p. 84.
2. Preliminary versions of this paper were read at the annual meetings of the Society for the Scientific Study of Religion in Boston (October, 1972) and of the American Anthropological Association in New Orleans (November, 1973), as well as at a meeting of the Thailand Council of the Asia Society in New York (April, 1973). In preparing this paper I must acknowledge a special debt to Craig Reynolds, *The Buddhist Monkhood in 19th Century Thailand*, a doctoral dissertation in History submitted to the Graduate School of Cornell University in 1972. Many of the issues relating to the historical impact of Mongkut's monastic reforms which are touched on in this paper are treated definitively in Reynolds' dissertation.
3. Max Weber, *The Protestant Ethic and the Spirit of Capitalism* (New York: Scribners, 1958).
4. Such sectarian disputes within the Sinhalese tradition are treated by Walpola Rahula, *The History of Buddhism in Ceylon: The Anuradhapura Period* (Colombo, 1956). For Burma, see Nihar-Ranji Ray, *An Introduction to the Study of Theravada Buddhism in Burma* (Calcutta, University of Calcutta Press, 1943).

5. For a description of the contemporary Thai monk's pastoral duties, see Jane Bunnag, *Buddhist Monk: Buddhist Layman* (Cambridge: Cambridge University Press, 1973), esp. Ch. 2.

6. For example, see Eliezer Ayal, "Value systems and economic development in Japan and Thailand," *Journal of Social Issues*, 19 (1963), pp. 35-51.

7. The most general source on Buddhist kingship is Charles Drekmeier, *Kingship and Community in Early India* (Stanford: Stanford University Press, 1962). See also Frank Reynolds, "The Two Wheels of Dhamma: A Study of Early Buddhism," in Bardwell Smith (ed.), *The Two Wheels of Dhamma* (American Academy of Religion, Studies in Religion, 3, 1972), pp. 6-30, and B. G. Gokhale, "Early Buddhist Kingship," *Journal of Asian Studies*, 26 (1966), pp. 15-22. Prince Dhani, "The old Siamese conception of the Monarchy," *Journal of the Siam Society*, 36 (1948), discusses the religious underpinnings of Siamese kingship.

8. For relevant inscriptions see George Coedès, *Receuil des Inscriptions du Siam* (Bangkok, 1924-1929). Ramkamhaeng's inscription is also translated in Bradley, "The oldest writing in Siamese," *Journal of the Siam Society*, 6 (1909), pp. 1-64.

9. Robert Heine-Geldern, *Conceptions of State and Kingship in Southeast Asia* (Ithaca: Cornell University Southeast Asia Program, Data Paper 18, 1956). See also Fred Riggs, *Thailand: The Modernization of a Bureaucratic Polity* (Honolulu: East-West Center Press, 1966), Ch. 2, for the ways in which cosmological notions served to structure the physical layout of the Thai kingdom.

10. On the Thai Traiphum, see George Coedès, "The Traibhumikatha, Buddhist Cosmology and Treaty on Ethics," *East and West*, VII (1957).

11. A comprehensive description of Ayutthaya's administrative structure is provided by H. Quartich Wales, *Ancient Siamese Government and Administration* (London: Bernard Quartich Ltd., 1934). Though referring to a much later period, Akin Rabibhadana, *The Organization of Thai Society in the Early Bangkok Period, 1782-1873* (Ithaca: Cornell University Southeast Asia Program, Data Paper, 74, 1969) is also useful.

12. See C. Reynolds, *op. cit.*, pp. 32-33.

13. Several sources discuss the efforts of Rama I to reconstitute the Thai kingdom after the fall of Ayutthaya and the downfall of Taksin. See, for example, Klaus Wenk, *The Restoration of Thailand Under Rama I: 1782-1803* (Tucson, 1968); H. R. H. Dhani, "The reconstruction of Rama I of the Chakkri Dynasty," *Journal of the Siam Society*, 43 (1955); H. R. H. Chula, *Lords of Life: The Paternal Monarchy of Bangkok, 1782-1932* (London: Remans, 1960), Ch. 1.

14. This decree is referred to in H. R. H. Chula, *ibid.*, p. 89. The decree is dated 21 August 1782 and can be found in the last volume of *The Three Seals Law* of 1805. Since violating the ordering of religious elements set out in the decree was to be punished by death we might suspect that this was a very important issue in the eyes of Rama I.

15. See Walter Vella, *Siam Under Rama III: 1824-1851* (Locust Valley, N.Y., 1957), p. 107.

16. Of all Thai kings of the modern era Mongkut has particularly fascinated western scholars and there is an extensive literature on him. See Alexander Griswold, *King Mongkut of Siam* (N.Y., 1961); Abbot L. Moffat, *Mongkut, The King of Siam* (Ithaca, 1961); Seni Pramoj, "King Mongkut as Legislator," in *Selected Articles From The Journal of the Siam Society* (Bangkok 1960), Vol. 4; and H. R. H. Chula, *op. cit.*, Ch. 4. Of special relevance to Mongkut's religious life are Robert Lingat, "La vie religieuses du roi Mongkut," *Journal of the Siam Society*, 20 (1926) and "La double crise l'église Bouddhique au Siam," *Journal of World History*, 4 (1958). C. Reynolds, *op. cit.*, contains the most complete discussion of Mongkut's religious life and reforms.

17. The formation of the Thammayut nikai followed the historic pattern of "sect" formation characteristic of Theravada Buddhism as sketched out above, and it is conventional to translate the Thai term *nikai* as "sect." However, in contemporary Thailand the distinction between the Thammayutnikai and the Mahanikai monks is more comparable to that between different religious "orders" (e.g., Jesuits *vs.* Franciscans) within the Christian tradition.

18. See C. Reynolds, *op. cit.*, p. 95.

19. *Ibid.*, p. 83.

20. *Ibid.*, p. 99.

21. See C. Reynolds, *op. cit.*, p. 128ff., for a discussion of the demythologizing efforts of a number of Thai elite during this period.

22. See H. Quartich Wales, *Siamese State Ceremonies* (London, 1931), Ch. 4.

23. For a discussion of the role of the monkhood as a channel of mobility, see David Wyatt, "The Buddhist Monkhood as an Avenue of Social Mobility in Traditional Thai Society," *Sinlapakron* (Fine Arts), 10, (1966).

24. See Pramoj, *op. cit.*, for Mongkut's attitudes towards women as a threat to the integrity of the Monkhood.

25. Substantial portions of Thiphakorawong's book have been translated and published by Henry Alabaster under the title *The Modern Buddhist* (London, 1871). See also the discussion of Thiphakorawong in C. Reynolds, *op. cit.*, pp. 129ff.

26. It is interesting to note that it was from the group of King's Scholars that those who carried out the coup of 1932, which toppled the absolute monarchy, were recruited.

27. On the development of the modern Thai educational system, see David Wyatt, *The Politics of Reform: Education in the Reign of King Chulalongkorn* (New Haven, 1969). Also see the discussion of Prince Wachirayan in C. Reynolds, *op. cit.*, p. 137ff.

28. See C. Reynolds, *op. cit.*, pp. 123-124.

29. Indeed, it is tempting to liken the sense of personal commitment required of the Thammayut monk with the Protestant sense of "calling." However, it should be noted that a comparable level of personal commitment is not precluded to the Mahanikai monk, but it is a requisite for the Thammayut monk.

30. This observation is based on fieldwork carried out in Northeast Thailand in 1962-1964, which was supported by an NIMH predoctoral fellowship and research grant supplement. See A. Thomas Kirsch, *Phu Thai Religious Syncretism*, unpublished doctoral dissertation in Social Anthropology submitted to the Graduate School of Harvard University, 1967, Ch. 8. The linkage between local elites and support of Thammayut monks is also reported in Cambodia by May Ebihara, "Interrelations between Buddhism and Social Systems in Cambodian Peasant Culture," in Manning Nash (ed.), *Anthropological Studies in Theravada Buddhism* (Yale Southeast Asia Cultural Report Series, 13, 1966), pp. 175-196.

31. Some of these developments are discussed in Donald Swearer, "Some Observations on New Directions in Thai Buddhism," *Sangkhomsat Paritat* (Social Science Review), 6 (1968), and *Buddhism in Transition* (Philadelphia, 1970). See also Our Correspondent, "The Sangha and Social Activities," *Sangkhomsat Paritat*, 2 (1963), and Charles Keyes, "Buddhism and National Integration in Thailand," *Journal of Asian Studies*, 30 (1971), pp. 551-568.

The Quest for Legitimation by Burmese Monks and Kings: The Case of the Shwegyin Sect (19th-20th Centuries)

John P. Ferguson

IN MANY CULTURES one can notice how men of prowess tend to be fascinated by severe ascetics.[1] The interest of powerful leaders in those who renounce worldly attachment is particularly strong in Southeast Asia. More specifically, in Theravada Buddhist countries there seems to be an important symbolic bond between king and monk; in Burma it is possible to document such relationships over a thousand years of history. The basic pattern of religious and secular bonding seems clear enough, but why men of prowess are so fascinated with severe ascetics is a difficult question to answer. In this paper it will be argued that the main reason for such bonding is the mutual need for the special legitimation that each can give the other. Furthermore, the quest for legitimation is involved in the formation of the modern sects found in Burma today, particularly the Shwegyin Sect.

Understanding the source of this legitimation depends first upon a realization of the basic symbolism involving the Buddha and the world emperor. As Reynolds (1971:23) has so clearly demonstrated, the two basic symbols of the Buddha and the powerful king (the *cakravartin*) have been closely related to each other since the early days of Buddhist history. In essence, the Buddha is said to have had the choice of becoming the enlightened one or the world emperor, and thus he combined in one person the potential for maximum fulfillment of secular or spiritual dreams of power. The stories of the life of the Buddha make it very clear that one of the most important worldly attachments renounced by Prince Siddhartha was the kingship itself as it was offered by his father. The Buddha, after winning the right to sit on the "throne" of enlightenment, sets in motion the "wheel" of the dhamma or the teachings, instead of the wheel or the weapon of the world emperor. At his death, his remains are honored with the same type of stupa or funerary mound as that used for a world emperor. Such symbolic parallelism between royal and monastic roles in Buddhist literature is maintained throughout Burmese history and in their literature as well.

The archetypal exemplars of the king-monk bonding for Burma are the Indian King Asoka and his chosen monk, Moggali Putta Tissa. King Asoka is conceived not only as the great conqueror of the continents but also as the man of prowess who promotes Buddhism, particularly in the sense of purifying the monkhood and validating its superior monks, who then attempt to impose unity upon any incipient sectarians. Kings in Asoka's position can convene a council or sangayana of leading monks to purify the texts and define

A preliminary version of this paper was read for a panel on Religious Traditions in Transition in South and Southeast Asia at the New York State Conference for Asian Studies at Colgate University, October 12, 1975.

orthodoxy. Moggali Putta Tissa is seen as the purifying leader of the Asoka council. The message is clear. A strong king can use his secular power to honor and support those monks deemed to be the most legitimate inheritors and transmitters of the Buddha's teachings, banishing the unorthodox to the hinterlands. By itself, the monkhood tends toward fission because all successful pupils of the same important teacher can claim equal orthodoxy, but only one will ultimately be the monk whom monastic history selects as the main transmitter of orthodoxy in the vitally important monastic lineages that link today's monks directly to the Buddha.[2] Even more important is the fact that in Burma monastic historians have consistently included as key lineage leaders those very monks selected by kings as the royal favorite, such as Moggali Putta Tissa. Thus it is clear that the kingship is used by the Sangha to legitimatize its own claim to carry orthodoxy down through the ages. The more the power of the king in the Asoka tradition, the more the power of the monk he honors to insist upon obedience and conformity. Such monastic leadership as we can find has been developed mainly through the combination of royal appointment and the maintenance of a sense of lineage that links the living monks to the Buddha.

The monk-king bonding benefits not only the Sangha: the kings have their own needs that the monkhood can meet. Even Asoka, fresh from the battlefield, had only the raw legitimation of military conquest to support him. It would seem most plausible that he felt the need for moral and spiritual strength, and his enthusiastic support of Buddhism can be reasonably interpreted as a quest for a source of personal validation and a place for his kingdom in a cosmic order. A disciplined, respected, and admired body of monks distributed as exemplars and teachers amidst the emperor's domains could only reflect favorably upon the fitness of the man of prowess at the center of the political mandala. A favorite Burmese metaphor is that the great king shines like the resplendent golden sun and he should be matched by a pure and radiant moon of a monkhood living by the orthodox teachings of the Buddha. When both heavenly bodies shine brightly, all is well. Also important to the Buddhist king was his charismatic ability to attract to his capital for royal support those leading scholars and forest ascetics most respected by the people. The presence of learned monks and strict disciplinarians at or near the court gave the impression that there was stability and peace in the realm. The king traditionally built monasteries for such monks, supplied them with food and necessities, gave them long titles of honor, and often put them in charge of monks in provinces and districts outside the capital. Of course, not all monks were willing to be so involved, and many in the history of Burma refused the royal invitation and the possible corruption from attachment to court life and its obligations. Weaker kings particularly found it difficult to attract or keep such illustrious monks near them to validate, however indirectly, their often tenuous claim to the throne.

One can therefore see the monks of Burma as having a symbolic role to play, should they wish, in the legitimation of the kingship, although it was apparently never as strong a role as that played by Sinhalese monks, who on occasion actually selected royalty (Ariyapala, 1956:55). While most Burmese kings were educated by their father's royal monk, their actual ascension to the throne was more often the outcome of palace intrigue against brothers and fathers than the result of monastic influence. In Burmese history, however, strong kings and great monks are believed to be bonded as a natural and logical consequence of their previous merit and rebirths that bring them together for the benefit of the realm, as in the case of King Anawrahta of Pagan and his royal monastic leader and reformer, Shin Arahan. Such bonding seems to be conceived as vital to Burmese culture in a complex fashion.

At one level, of course, the roles of monk and king present sharp symbolic contrasts. The king thrives on aggression; the monk abhors it. The king owns all by right and lavishly displays his wealth; the monk ideally renounces all but a few simple necessities for survival. The king enjoys his many wives and concubines and is respected for his powers to control as many women as possible and keep them happy; the monk is to avoid even touching women, talking to them alone, or having anything to do with marriage or sex. The king takes anything he wants by right; the monk must not use anything that is not given. The king displays his long hair; the monk shaves his head bare. The king wears rich robes and crown, both studded with jewels; the monk wears a simple robe made formerly of grave windings and he goes bareheaded. The king rides his royal elephant under his tiered white umbrella; the monk walks, often barefoot and without parasol. The contrasts are numerous and very sharp. One is tempted to see them as foils, each helping by inversion to define the other. In that sense each definitely needs the other to be seen in the full splendor of his cultural role. Such symbolic usefulness is a vital aspect of mutual legitimation. But they are more than foils or binary opposites in the Levi-Strauss sense.

It is the nature of the interrelationship between monk and king that is most important, not just their symbolic opposition. In terms of Burmese culture, it is the monk who is clearly the most respected exemplar. It is the king who must ultimately bow down to the monk, and historically the orthodox monks of Burma, including royally favored monks, never allowed any Burmese king to collapse the symbolic bonding and claim to be both the world monarch and the future or next Buddha at the same time. The classic case was King Bodawpaya, who, despite his dramatic but brief retreat to his forest court of simplicity, could not force or persuade his monks to call him *the* Buddha. They allowed him to be a Paccekabuddha who comes between major Buddhas (Fytche, 1871I:76-78). Previous kings who had made the same bid were sometimes allowed to think of themselves as Bodhisattas working toward being Buddhas someday.[3] The argument was not an idle theological debate but a spirited defense by the monkhood of the superiority of the monk's role over the royal one. At the ultimate symbolic level, monk and king may be one, as was true in the being who became the Buddha, but the behavioral separation of monk from king since then is the core of Burmese culture — a threshold beyond which the religion will not pass.[4] There were pressures, however, for both monks and kings to attempt to borrow the splendor of each other's symbols.

One way in which the symbolic system was strained was by the development of the crowned Buddha image, which portrayed the Buddha dressed as a world emperor, as illustrated by the most popular statue in Burma: the Mahamuni Buddha at Mandalay. It is significant that King Bodawpaya himself installed that image in Upper Burma after he captured it from Arakan, and his fascination with it would be a natural outcome of his desire to be both the world emperor and the Maitreya or coming Buddha. The image of the crowned

Buddha portrays in icon a collapse of the symbolic bonding that no living king was allowed to proclaim. Yet the image itself is mute testimony to the temptation and the fascination.

Just as there were kings who would be the future Buddha, so there were monks who would be king or coopt their symbols. Many monks quit the Sangha to become king, as did the famous Mon Dhammaceti. Such was no strain upon the symbolic system. The tension came when monks appointed by the king as head of the Sangha imitated royal symbolic behavior: sitting on thrones, travelling under white umbrellas, living in golden, many-roofed monasteries more like palaces than hermitages, supervising great landholdings, and dabbling in politics. Such monastic rulers, called the *thathanabaing* (THA THA.NA PAIN[5]), are not authorized by the Vinaya, the orthodox rules for the Theravada monkhood. They represent compromises with the ideal of a democratic Sangha in perpetual unity without an ecclesiastical hierarchy. For that very reason many monks resisted the concept of the thathanabaing, and it is doubtful that more than a few kings of prowess were able to impose one upon the Burmese Sangha. That the head of the Sangha borrowed his paraphernalia of legitimation from the royal sphere illustrates how tempting it was for either side of the king-monk bonding to want to monopolize all the available symbols from both sides. The basic nature of the bonding required instead that they be kept apart in actual life but conceived as unified in the terms of their ultimate source — related but behaviorally separate always.

In reality there were few kings in history who ruled enough of the Burmese countryside to claim they were world emperors, and it is extremely doubtful that heads of the Sangha, entitled thathanabaing or not, had much control at a distance from the capital. Historical records reveal that the monk chosen by most kings was simply called a *thathanapyu* (THA THA.NA PYU) or purifier (*pyu*) of the religion (*thathana*). That title leads us closer to a diachronic view of the actual nature of the Sangha.

A careful analysis of Burmese monastic history reveals that the Sangha has always contained a number of factions, any one of which may be strengthened by the king's selecting as his royal monk the leader of any particular faction. The royally sponsored leader then "purifies" the rest, usually making it necessary for those "shameless" monks not purified to leave the capital. The Burmese system, however, has been so tolerant of these factions that those who are banished simply bide their time nearby and are available for the next king to recognize, should he wish to legitimate his reign by backing a faction different from that of his predecessor. Very seldom were the victims of purification disrobed and turned into laymen; instead, the Sangha contained a group of historically recognized rivals who, locked in bonded relationships, gave a certain dynamic resiliency to the monkhood at all times.

These rival factions are best conceived as bonded symbolic dimensions of the Sangha itself rather than as autonomous sects in the western sense.[6] It is useful to conceive of four of these pairs of ancient rivals. Most important is the rivalry between forest and town monks. The forest monks typically renounce living close to their lay supporters and take up a strict ascetic regimen in the jungle. They see themselves as applying the Vinaya rules more determinedly to themselves than do most village or town monks. The latter, however, see the forest monks as too weak to resist temptation in the village or town and thus as escapists. The forest monks retort that village monks are too weak to renounce their over-dependence on luxuries lavished upon them by the faithful. The argument is classic and unresolvable in Burma as it is also in other Theravada countries, yet both types of monks contribute much to the capacity of the Sangha to navigate through social upheavals. The forest monks particularly represent a reserve of talent that can be tapped for revitalization when war and other changes enervate the town and village monks. In normal times each side of the bonded dimension of the Sangha keeps the other alert in a fashion that creates a dynamic and healthy rivalry.

The second most important bonded dimension is that between the meditating and the educating monks. The former stress the primacy of meditation over all other means of attaining total non-attachment or Nirvana; the latter stress the importance of memorizing, reading, and teaching the sacred Buddhist texts, as well as writing grammars, commentaries, and other scholarly works. The meditating monks tend to prefer the solitude of the forest and cave, but in modern times, many are to be found in urban meditation centers as well. The scholarly monks tend to cluster in large teaching monasteries that are much like western universities or colleges. The two aspects of this bonded dimension of the Sangha are not always mutually exclusive, but by and large they have gone their separate ways. Both have long been recognized as valid and legitimate Buddhist paths.

The third and fourth rivalries center about ethnic and geographic groups that claim supreme orthodoxy by virtue of the alleged purity of their linkage to the teachings of the Buddha himself. The oldest of these tensions is between the Upper Burmese and the Mons of Lower Burma. This competition is the essence of the argument over the type of Buddhism brought back to Pagan by King Anawrahta when he conquered the Mon city of Thaton. Many Burmese believe that "pure" Buddhism from Lower Burma thereby entered a less than orthodox northern Sangha. Others believe the Upper Burmese monks had maintained orthodoxy which compared exactly with that of the conquered Mons. The bitter political rivalry between these two groups has only added fuel to the religious contentions between northern and southern rival Sangha factions that have vied with each other for almost a millennia.

The final dimension to Sangha dynamics is provided by the Burma-Ceylon rivalry. Soon after the rise of Pagan in the eleventh century, missionary monks from Ceylon established both forest and town monasteries that claimed a lineage through Asoka missionaries to Ceylon that was reputed to be more legitimate than any extant Burmese line. They convinced many kings of the validity of their position, and before long Ceylon to many Burmese became a fabled land where Burmese monks might go for pilgrimages or revitalization through re-ordination. This attitude was countered by those Burmese who felt their own traditions were better, and it was noted that things in Ceylon had sometimes been so desperate that Burmese monks had to be imported to keep Buddhism alive at all. The reformist Sinhalese monks have provided a constant source of internal pressure toward Vinaya-based behavior that has inspired Burmese monks to work harder toward their ideals. Each side of the bonding has, in a sense, contributed to the improvement of the other.

All four rivalries involve a similar vital tension that locks the factions into culturally bonded dimensions which give great resiliency to the Sangha from within, enabling the monkhood as a symbolic system to adopt new directions and emphases during periods of change. Yet this very flexibility opens up areas for the kings to use if they wish. When a king seeks monks to honor, he can pick monks from any of these bonded dimensions to legitimate his reign, but he must also face the fact that whatever side he chooses will be opposed by its traditional rival. The legitimation, consequently, has no ultimacy. The potential for challenge to legitimacy always exists. To back one side is to alienate the other. Such is the eternal problem for any king of prowess who seeks to unify or purify the Burmese Sangha.[7]

With these basic patterns now set forth, we can turn to the case of the birth and development of the Shwegyin (HYWEI CIN) Sect in Burma, for the advent of this sect in the nineteenth century and its subsequent growth provides us with examples of the classic attempt of monarch and monk to use each other to promote the political and religious destiny of the society.

The roots of the Shwegyin movement can be traced to the reign of King Pagan (1846-1853), who appointed the second Bagaya Sayadaw (BA:KA.YA HSA.YA TO) as head monk or thathanapyu for the Sangha.[8] The Bagaya was a strong-willed Vinaya expert who brooked no disagreements with his rulings on monastic law. He, therefore, banished from the capital and all important monastic centers the Shangalegyun (HYAN:KA LEI:CUN:) Sayadaw for the latter's reformist, forest-monk notions of Vinaya strictness. The Shangalegyun, in turn, established a forest following in a remote monastery at Kawtaw (HKO:TO:), a village south of Shwebo. He was a Manipuri captive from India, as was his sister Me Kin (ME KIN), a greatly respected nun.[9] Both he and his sister were highly self-disciplined ascetics in the forest tradition who were fearlessly critical of luxury and self-indulgence wherever found, but the focus of their attack was upon the town monks.

By the late 1840s a young monk from nearby Shwegyin village came under the influence of the Shangalegyun Sayadaw; and this younger disciple later became the Shwegyin Sayadaw, the founder of the sect named after him. National events in this period influenced the reformist spirit so characteristic of the times. The Burmese had lost their maritime provinces twenty years earlier to the British colonial forces, and the Burmese kings were having to face the grim fact that in their attempts to model themselves after the Asoka world emperor pattern their efforts were somewhat pathetic in terms of the strength of British military power. The Sangha leaned toward more self-denial, greater self-discipline, and a zeal for purification as a counterbalance to a diminished kingship. At least one can wonder whether this is a possible explanation for the religious developments which followed. Kings, in turn, blocked militarily from fulfilling their Asoka dreams of power by the realities of colonial guns, turned all the more determinedly to Asoka purification efforts, such as King Pagan and Mindon's Sangayanas to cleanse the scriptures and Mindon's fascination with the Shangalegyun Sayadaw when Mindon assumed power in 1853, a year after the second war with the British, when Lower Burma became permanently lost to the colonialist armies.

King Mindon, like Mongkut (his Sangha-reforming counterpart in Thailand), had spent much time in monasteries himself, during which time he met the Shwegyin Sayadaw and developed his conviction that the monks he would pick for his dreams of reform would be of such caliber.[10] Once on the throne previously held by his brother, Mindon made his father's favorite monk the head of the Sangha and adopted the policy of inviting back to the capital for honor the very monk his brother's head monk had banished, that is, the Shangalegyun Sayadaw from his forest retreat. By the mid 1850s Mindon was supporting the latter monk in a two-pronged campaign: first, to banish from Upper Burma those monks who had fled the British in Lower Burma but did not live by the Vinaya and, second, to reform the remaining Upper Burmese monks to a strict standard that prohibited, among many other things, the wearing of sandals and the using of umbrellas.

Mindon played a complex role in this process. On one hand, he backed his officially appointed head of the Sangha, the second Maungdaung (MAUN: HTAUN) Sayadaw, and the council of senior monks who worked with him, the entire body known as the Thudhamma (THU.DAN MA). These were to be the most highly honored monks in the nation, and their verdicts in council on matters of Vinaya and other aspects of Buddhist law knew no appeal. Mindon, nevertheless, seems deliberately to have decided to honor the forest side of the forest-town bonded dimension by building the Shangalegyun Sayadaw a monastery in 1855 and by asking him to draw up a new version of monastic rules which were presented to the Thudhamma Council for approval and implementation.[11] By this time both the Shwegyin Sayadaw and the Gupyu Tawya (GU HPYU TO:YA.) Sayadaw had joined under the leadership of the Shangalegyun to form a reformist group centered at an island monastery named the Shangalegyun Kyaungtaik (CAUN:TAI') on the west side of Mandalay.[12] This group of forest monks represented Mindon's bellwether favorites, and there is evidence that the urbane monks on the Council were persuaded by royal pressure to go along with the new stringent monastic rules that grew directly out of the forest tradition of their rivals.

A most vocal representative of the opposition, however, appeared in the form of the witty, handsome, poet-monk, the Bhamo (BAN:MO) Sayadaw, who launched a satirical attack on the Council (which he saw as spineless), the Shangalegyun Sayadaw (whom he saw as a presumptuous, meddling foreigner), forest monks in general (whom he taunted by saying they escaped to the woods to flee temptation), and even the nun Me Kin (the sister of the Shangalegyun).[13] After the poetic attacks on the latter degenerated into sexual insults and the head of the Sangha was outraged, Mindon himself became involved and finally banished the outspoken Bhamo Sayadaw to the north.[14] Amidst all this furor, the Bhamo Sayadaw made two very serious accusations against Mindon. The Bhamo was a learned and respected Vinaya scholar who collected the decisions of the second Bagaya Sayadaw and his opinions were based upon deep knowledge of Sangha law.

First, the Bhamo Sayadaw warned Mindon that using his bellwether group to purify the Sangha was dangerous because the opinions of the Shangalegyun Sayadaw were private, personal interpretations representing unreasonable interpolations of Vinaya law. If Mindon wanted to purify according to the proposed new rules, he should convene a full-fledged Sangayana which would compare in scholarly fashion the new rules with the old. If the assembly of the Sangayana approved the new rules, then, and only then, could the king use his royal secular power to enforce them. Second, the Bhamo Sayadaw warned the king not to encourage the laity to become judges of monastic behavior so that they would, in effect, bring about an Asokan purification by refusing to honor with food and material support those they considered "bad" monks. For the laity to criticize the Sangha, he said, was to open the way to hell.

The Bhamo Sayadaw stated openly what was felt by many. Resistance to the new reforms among the town monks was extensive, and only the death of the Shangalegyun Sayadaw in 1858 seems to have prevented severe dissension and fissioning in the Sangha. Mindon, however, began to honor specially the Shwegyin Sayadaw from that point on, particularly after the new capital at Mandalay was built in 1859. In 1860 Mindon built five monasteries for the Shwegyin Sayadaw near Mandalay Hill, and he then had the Shwegyin become the teacher of his son-princes.[15] The nun Me Kin was also persuaded to come to the capital and do what she could educationally about the frivolity and light-headedness of the princesses.[16] This emphasis by the king produced a fairly quick Thudhamma response from the town monks at the capital.

The head of the Sangha appointed by Mindon, the second Maungdaung Sayadaw, and the Shwegyin Sayadaw came to a serious impasse that brought Mindon's policies to a point where he had to make a critical decision. As in every argument there are two sides, accounts in Burma exist from both the Thudhamma and Shwegyin points of view: in essence, the Shwegyin Sayadaw was either insulted and demeaned, or he was arrogant toward and disdainful of the Maungdaung.[17] The Shwegyin Sayadaw apparently went to Mindon and asked for royal approval to leave the city for the forest, rather than submit to the authority of the royally appointed head of the Sangha. Mindon, in a historically crucial decision, told the Shwegyin Sayadaw that he and his followers henceforth were independent and no longer under the authority of the Thudhamma leadership. Thus the Shwegyin Sect was officially, and, of course, royally sponsored, and its birth can be traced to that moment.

At this point, one has to investigate more closely what is meant by the English term *sect*, as the word most frequently used by the Burmese is *gaing* (GAIN:) — a fluid concept that is difficult to define. The Burmese word gaing is derived from the Pāli term *gana*, which means a meeting or chapter of monks, as differentiated from the Sangha as a whole or the individual monks, or it can refer to an assemblage of any kind, including one of monks. In Pāli the word *nikāya* can be used to mean a group, sect, class, or collection, and also can denote a collection of Buddhist texts.[18] Burmese monks seem to use the Pāli term *nikāya* when they wish to stress separateness in a sectarian fashion. Gaing can mean "sect" at times, but on other occasions it denotes simply a loosely organized monastic following of a given charismatic leader. Gaing can also be used in a geographic sense to indicate an area covered by the authority of a monastic official appointed by royal or sectarian leaders. Furthermore, the word can be used to describe any number of esoteric cult groups on the fringes of orthodox Buddhism, such as those connected with what Mendelson has called Messianic Buddhism.[19] The term *gaing*, therefore, covers the exact area of extreme sensitivity where a group of monks might stop considering themselves a part of the Sangha like everyone else and start to consider themselves a distinct sect. In the latter case, we usually find the following tell-tale sectarian characteristics: a sense of distinct monastic lineage; a written history of the sect's formation and the lives of its leaders; separate rules based on their particular interpretation of the Vinaya; a hierarchical chain of command under a leader; some attempt at national coverage in terms of member monasteries; insistence upon separate ordination rituals, distinctive interpretations of scripture, sometimes the refusal to eat, study, or associate closely with other monks in the Sangha; and, most importantly, official recognition in some fashion of their distinctiveness by royalty or some branch of modern government. It was the royal declaration by King Mindon that established the separate identity of the Shwegyin Sect and gave it the legitimacy of freedom from control of the Thudhamma Council.

One can only speculate as to Mindon's motivations. Clearly Mindon was a dedicated and intense Buddhist, and he deeply respected the Shwegyin Sayadaw as an exemplar for the entire Sangha. Perhaps Mindon perceived at some level of consciousness that the end of royal Burma was nigh, and he launched his royal sect to carry on into an uncertain future the teachings he so strongly believed, much the same as Mongkut did with the Thammayut Sect in Thailand at roughly the same time.[20] A highly disciplined and organized sect like the Shwegyin creates its own autonomous administrative system that reforms and purifies itself. It needs no outside Thathanapyu purifier, Thathanabaing patriarch, nor even a would-be Asoka. As such, it could have appealed strongly to a Buddhist king already facing the cultural degeneration of the Burmese laity and monks in Lower Burma under a heathen regime.

It is a well-known fact that King Mindon was no Asoka (THEIN: 1958:43-45). He could not summon royal secular power to enforce Sangha unity and purity, and he obviously turned to other means to influence the monkhood. While the monk he had chosen as official thathanabaing was from the scholarly and town side of the bonded dimensions, his new official blessing for the Shwegyin Sect represented support for the meditation and forest rivals. The king apparently sought to bolster his status by backing both sides at once, a strategy not unknown in Burmese history, but a dangerous policy nevertheless because it more often signaled weakness rather than strength. The Shwegyin Sayadaw, on the other hand, could use the royal blessing as a claim to legitimacy for his movement.

At the death of the second Maungdaung thathanabaing in 1865, Mindon left the post vacant, unwilling to appoint the Shwegyin Sayadaw as head of the Sangha and significantly reluctant to select a senior Thudhamma successor either. Apparently the chief queen played a part in blocking the appointment of the Shwegyin Sayadaw.[21] Nevertheless, for the rest of Mindon's reign the Shwegyin was able to develop his sect with considerable independence, and the balance of power between monk and monarch developed so that the Shwegyin Sayadaw frequently lectured or scolded Mindon, particularly when the Shwegyin thought the king was over-playing his defender of the faith role in disciplining monks.[22] But Mindon faithfully supported the five Shwegyin monasteries so that the thousand or so students were fed by royal grants and did not have to make daily walks to receive food alms (HYWEI HIN THA HSA.YA TO, 1963:153). He even supported liberally the parents of the Shwegyin Sayadaw, whom he had asked to move to Mandalay (HYWEI HIN THA HSA.YA TO, 1963:153, 300). A significant insight to the monk-king relationship is a reputed dream of the Shwegyin Sayadaw in which he wanted to place a piece of cloth above a statue of the Buddha to honor it, but he was too short to put it there. At that time King Mindon happened to come by and offered to let the Shwegyin Sayadaw stand on his back. The king's humble aid was accepted, and thereby the religious offering to the Buddha was completed. This highly symbolic dream, true or not, sums up nicely the role of the king in terms of the development of the sect (HYWEI HIN THA HSA.YA TO, 1963:138).

Only three years after the death of the second Maungdaung, Mindon gave the Shwegyin Sayadaw the responsibility to act as thathanapyu in the Alon area, up the Chindwin River. The assignment was to purify the Sangha there of such traditional evils as catering to the material needs of the laity, involvement with buying and selling, practicing medicine, telling fortunes, riding in bullock carts, farming, renting property, making coffins, wearing sandals, using umbrellas, and taking tobacco and betel in the afternoon.[23] It is not at all clear if the Shwegyin had authority in the Alon area over only his own gaing followers or was a royal emissary to purify all the monks in the area, but clearly the Shwegyin was cooperating in an administrative capacity with the king. For a forest monk, such involvement has its dangers in terms of one's self-definition. It is not surprising, therefore, that when Mindon in 1871 tried to offer the Shwegyin a traditional honorary title for having been in the monkhood for thirty years, the king was repulsed (HYWEI HIN THA HSA.YA TO, 1963:107). By means of such denials a forest monk retains the necessary distance from the laity and maintains his position in the bonded dimension with his town-monk rivals.

King Mindon, not to be discouraged, offered in 1871 twelve monasteries to the Shwegyin Sayadaw, including the famous Mahawithudarama (MA.HA WI.THOU' DA YA MA.) Taik; they were accepted but were immediately turned over to chosen disciples to administer (HYWEI HIN THA HSA.YA TO,1963:107). The Shwegyin Sayadaw in so doing was acting out a very important pattern that sets an example for his sect. In essence, a very holy monk by his exemplary self-denial and non-attachment to material things inspires the laity to honor him by generous donations of land and property. The honored recipient, however, to preserve his position, turns over all donations to his followers. The unintended consequence, in a Weberian sense, of all of this is to stimulate the growth of the monk's following, and the sect develops rapidly as more and more gifts pour in and are redistributed among an increasing number of disciples. Significantly, the Mahawithudarama Taik became the residence of the monk who would lead the sect after the death of the Shwegyin

Mindon, in 1871, was also busy holding his famous "Fifth" Sangayana or Buddhist Council to purify the scriptures, almost as if he had at last hearkened to the warnings of the Bhamo Sayadaw years before. But this royal effort to unify the Sangha failed, just as U Nu's similar attempts in the 1950s could not bring about the end of gaing separatism and divisive Sangha factionalism. Mindon's Sangayana seems to have been predominantly a Thudhamma affair, and I have found no evidence that the Shwegyin or other reformist gaing leaders such as the Okpo (QOU'HPOU') Sayadaw took any part in it. Actually, it would seem that the grand occasion of the convening of 2,400 monks for the Sangayana at Mandalay only drove the Shwegyin and others of a like mind still further from the fold. Four years later the Shwegyin Sayadaw retired from all his official thathanapyu duties and began to spend increasing amounts of time away from the capital at forest retreats. When not in the forest, he turned his eyes toward Rangoon in British Lower Burma (he preached there in 1876) and toward the holy sites and relics of Ceylon (Mindon refused him permission to go, but he went anyway).[24]

By the time of Mindon's death in 1878, the Shwegyin had, in effect, rejected Mandalay to promote his interests elsewhere. In Lower Burma a number of critical laity had taken their cue from Mindon's policies and were actively condemning lax monks. The situation degenerated into street fights between lay Buddhist groups known as Sulagandi (SU LA.GAN HTI.) and Mahagandi (MA.HA GAN HTI.).[25] The former supported the forest monk and meditation side of the bonded dimensions, often identifying themselves with the Dwaya (DWA YA) Gaing of the Okpo Sayadaw. The Shwegyin and the Okpo had a falling out in 1878 in Rangoon over publication of a text to help resolve the lay disputes, and from that point on the Dwaya Gaing seems to have gone its own way in Lower Burma.[26] The division of Burma itself because of colonial conquest only gave further impetus to the ancient rivalry locked into the Upper and Lower Burma bonded dimension. These tensions affected the Shwegyin Sect as well, as will be evident later.

By 1881 Mindon's son and successor, King Thibaw, had attempted a unique solution to the sectarian problem by nominating *both* the Shwegyin Sayadaw and the Taungdaw (TAUN TO) Sayadaw as joint Sangha heads, or thathanabaing. The latter Thudhamma monk, slightly senior to the Shwegyin Sayadaw, had been selected by the Shwegyin to take over the education responsibilities for the princes at the palace, and thus he was the teacher of Thibaw when the prince was a very promising Pāli scholar.[27] According to most accounts, the Shwegyin Sayadaw refused the office of thathanabaing but did come back from the forest for a few years to help administer nine ecclesiastical departments in Upper Burma. Shwegyin missionary monks with royal backing were sent out to the key centers of Myadaung, Kyaukse, Pyinmana, Taungdwingyi, Minhla, Alon (where the Shwegyin himself had gone for Mindon), Shwebo, and Bhamo. The ninth department, the Shan states, was deemed not ready yet for a mission (HYWEI HIN THA HSA.YA TO, 1963:110, 386). Quite definitely, Thibaw was, in effect, giving the Shwegyin monks as much or more royal backing than his father had given them. By 1884, however, the Shwegyin Sayadaw had returned to the forest life, this time to Mingun,[28] and he remained there in what can be seen as a significant symbolic statement of protest about his society as the monarchy came to an end in 1885, with Thibaw quickly defeated, deposed, and deported to India and the whole of Burma suddenly in heathen hands. Upper Burma for at least a decade was torn by rebellions and general disorder in the society, and little is known of the activities of the Shwegyin during that chaotic period.[29]

The kings of Burma were suddenly destroyed. The Sangha lost its symbolic counterpart, and the British refused, under the guise of neutrality toward religious matters, to take up Buddhist responsibilities as the new rulers. As a consequence, the monastic factions normally produced by the rivalries in the bonded dimensions were free to develop without any regard to political surveillance or control. Only the Shwegyin Sect entered the colonial period with the vital legitimization from royalty. In its sectarian histories it stresses constantly its royal origins. The other monastic groups, lacking royal sponsorship, are best seen as gaings rather than sects, since their legitimacy is self-defined, not given by royalty. The Shwegyin Sayadaw did his best to maximize the boon of the original royal approval in terms of promoting his organization.

The Shwegyin died in 1893, but during his last year he effected the merger of the Tawya (TO:YA.) Gaing in Pegu (Lower Burma) with the Shwegyin Sect. The Tawya (forest) Gaing was a group of Lower Burmese reformists led by the highly respected Tawya Sayadaw, U Thila (QU: THI LA.). Born in Pegu, U Thila began his forest activities in 1860 and by 1871 developed his following into a forest monk gaing with a very strong Vinaya emphasis. He urged Lower Burmese monks in the Mon country to give up their comfortable monasteries and the security of their lay supporters for the purer ascetic life in the woods. Before long he was said to have developed meditational disciplines to the point where he was thought by many to have the supra-normal powers of an arahant.[30] He came under the influence of the Shwegyin Sayadaw during a trip to Mandalay, and both monks began to work together upon a common cause — the reformation of the lax Sangha majority as the society began to feel the full demoralizing impact of a colonial regime. The merger of the two organizations in 1893 gave the Shwegyin its first real influence upon the Mon side of that bonded dimension, but it was an act of considerable diplomacy to get the ancient Upper and Lower Burmese rivals working together. At the death of the Shwegyin Sayadaw, however, the next leader of the amalgamated sect was significantly an Upper Burmese.

In retrospect, the Shwegyin Sayadaw can be evaluated as a monk who on the eve of the twentieth century represented a traditionalist's response to the challenges of colonialism, Christianity, and modernization. He was a dignified, disciplined, independent, perceptive monk who had considerable talents as a leader, preacher, teacher, and writer. The main thrust of his message was to put more symbolic distance between monk and laity so that the ideal of the monk could be more visible in troubled times. As a royal monk he strove to act for his principles without being overwhelmed with the power, wealth, and honors thrust upon him by the royal household and wealthy patrons. At moments of crisis he would reject the laity and turn to the more ascetic bonded dimensions, such as the forest austerities (one meal a day, not lying down to sleep, simple robes, no sandals or umbrellas, and so on), the discipline of meditation upon the impermanence of this world, and, later in his career, the worship of relics at the accepted founts of orthodoxy, as in Ceylon. At his death he left behind an organization held together by respect for him, respect and love for one's teachers, an acceptance of hierarchical monastic authority, a willingness to accept austere rules, and a country-wide network of reformist monasteries looking to Mandalay for leadership. At his funeral the rites were characteristically simple and reserved, without the fanfare so dear to the Thudhamma laity.

His place was filled by one of his closest pupils, the Mahawithudarama (MA.HA WI.THOU'DA YA MA.) Sayadaw.[31] This monk came from an upper class family of great wealth that really did not want their son to remain in the Sangha, but the boy showed both a determination to be a monk and a considerable bent for scholarship from the age of eight. After studying under the Shwegyin Sayadaw, he rose rapidly in the Mandalay hierarchy and became a lecturer at the central Shwegyin monastery. He was a strict leader, a good preacher with natural presence, an attentive listener to those below him, a tireless scholar and writer, and an ascetic much like the Shwegyin himself. He also avoided betel and medicines after noon, used neither slippers nor umbrella, honored the Buddha daily as would any novice with candles, water, and flowers, went occasionally to the forest for the rainy season, and totally renounced his family's wealth at the death of his father in 1870, cancelling all debts owed to his family, freeing all bonded servants, and giving the rest to his elder brother's children. By 1872 he had come to the attention of both Mindon and Queen Sinpyumashin, the latter donating a monastery to him and the king naming it the Mahawithudarama Taik,[32] which later was to become the Sect's central headquarters.

The Mahawithudarama Sayadaw, while stressing traditional Sangha verities, also faced the twentieth century squarely. He refused ox carts but would travel on trains and steamboats. He rejected the donation of newly minted peacock coins as modern substitutes for traditional gifts of food and other necessities. He went to India in 1903 by ship to visit the historic sites of the Buddha, where he was shocked by the poverty and beggars. He taught for a while in Lower Burma at Rangoon at the Kyaikkassan Taik, founded by U Thila of the original Tawya Gaing. As part of his wide correspondence with Buddhist scholars abroad, he wrote letters to Mrs. Davids, the Pāli scholar, in England. Near the end of his life he was awarded the honorary A.M.P. title by the colonial government. At his death in 1916 a simple cremation in the Shwegyin style was held, with a modern touch added by the igniting of the coffin with a dry cell battery.[33]

Toward the end in 1915 he sensed his failing faculties and appointed eight monks as his assistants, one of whom was to become head of the Sect in 1950, the Sankin (SAN KIN:) Sayadaw. Two others, the Abayarama (QA.BA.YA YA MA) and the Si Shin (SI HYIN), carried extensive responsibilities at the central headquarters until their deaths in the 1940s. The Mahawithudarama Sayadaw was known to his followers as the "Shwegyin Second Thathanabaing," almost as if the sect had assembled itself to select him as a king formerly would have done. He and other heads of the sect were also known as sammuti (THAN MU.TI) thathanabaing, sammuti (good judge) being a reference to the king of the gods or spirits Thakyamin (THA.CA:MIN:) who watched over the religion and, in particular, guided the kings of Burma as defenders of the faith. In essence, then, the sect used the very title to honor its head monk that the founder of the sect had rejected from King Thibaw, but their title was in reference to a heavenly king, presumably to be a more successful protector of the religion than were the last kings of Burma.

Beneath the sect's thathanabaing in rank were officials known as the Taik-ok (TAI'QOU') and Taik-kyat (TAI'CA'), but neither of these two was selected as successor to the Mahawithudarama after his death, when there was a general meeting of the sect in 1916. Instead, the Dipeyin (DI PE:YIN:) and Kyaikkasan Sayadaws were appointed as joint leaders, thus combining symbolically the Upper and Lower Burma bonded dimensions as the Shwegyin himself had done in 1893.

The Kyaikkasan Sayadaw was born in Pegu and was ordained by the Mogaung (MOU:KOUN:) Sayadaw in Mandalay.[34] He later came under the influence of the Tawya Gaing and spent eight years in the forest. In 1901 he received the Kyaikkasan Monastery in Rangoon from the Mahawithudarama

Sayadaw and from that base worked as a unifying force in the Shwegyin organization, going back every year to Pegu for the traditional Vinaya Sapyan Pwe (WINI:SA PYAN PWE:), or ritual recital of the Vinaya and confession of faults. The Kyaikkasan Sayadaw unfortunately died in 1917, only a year after becoming joint head of the Shwegyin Sect.[35] Unity through joint leadership was thus achieved only briefly.

The sect was then led by the surviving Dipeyin Sayadaw, and no attempt seems to have been made to find a Lower Burma monk to govern with him. For ten years, until 1927, the Dipeyin directed the sect alone. He, like the Mahawithudarama Sayadaw, had come from a very wealthy family, in the Mounywa area, and had renounced material wealth, turning over everything that was ever given to him to the welfare of the sect. His uncle, a forest monk, had ordained him, and he studied under both the Mahawithudarama and the Salin (SA.LIN:) Sayadaws, the latter a Thudhamma Council monk who was very sympathetic to the Shwegyin cause. He eventually became leader of the Salin Monastery in Mandalay and then the first lecturer at the sect headquarters at the Mahawithudarama Monastery (HYWEI HIN THA HSA.YA TO, 1963:281-289). He is clearly an Upper Burmese monk identified with the centralized power base at Mandalay, and as such he set a pattern that has been followed, as far as I can determine, to the present day. All the sect's leaders since 1917 have been Upper Burmese.

In 1927, after the death of the Dipeyin, the Shwegyin representatives met again at Mandalay and selected, according to the ancient Vinaya principle of seniority, the eighty-two-year-old Pattamaya (PA'TA MYA:) Sayadaw from Mandalay. He reported to the assembly that his spirit was willing to lead but that his body was too weak. Therefore, he stepped down for a "younger" man, the Alon (QA.LOUN) Sayadaw, who was seventy-eight. The Alon Sayadaw, like the Dipeyin, was from the Mounywa area and likewise had studied under the Mahawithudarama (HYWEI HIN THA HSA.YA TO, 1963: 293-294). Thus the sect's leaders were continuing not only to be Upper Burmese monks but also to be members of a teacher-pupil "lineage" chain that linked them to the Shwegyin Sayadaw himself. The Alon Sayadaw lived only a year; consequently, the sect had to meet again in 1929, this time at Moulmein in Lower Burma, presumably as a symbolic gesture of country-wide unity after all the Mandalay meetings.

By this time, the sect had concluded that organizational stability was not best served through placing all responsibility in the hands of aged leaders, and in 1927 six monks were appointed to carry on most of the day-by-day administrative functions. Three were called *wunhsaung* (WUN HSAUN) or officials who carry responsibilities: (1) the Abayarama, (2) Sankin, and (3) Si Shin — all three to have a strong influence on sectarian policy for many years to come with No. 2 becoming head of the sect in 1950. They also selected as Gana [GA.NA. (Gain:)] Palaka [PA LA.KA (protector)] Thathanapyu (purifiers) three others who presumably were disciplinary officers: (1) Gugyimaw (GU CI:MO), (2) Kyaungkon (CAUN:KOUN:), and (3) Pissimayon (PI'HSI.MA YOUN), the latter monk becoming head in 1935 (HYWEI HIN THA HSA.YA TO, 1963:294). By creating these offices, the sect in effect established a reserve of experienced and trained elder monks who could be tapped for future leadership to steady the organization as it passed through the frequent changes at the top. At the same time control was established over the sect's appointments at the district levels, which had previously been locally determined. The development of the sect at this point was clearly toward consolidation and centralization.

At the meeting at Moulmein in 1929 the sect selected the Chanthagyi (HCAN:THA CI:) Sayadaw as head. He was eighty-seven at the time and had actually been ordained by the Shwegyin Sayadaw himself in 1862, coming originally from the Shwebo area, as had the Shwegyin. For two years he had studied under the Okpo Sayadaw and thus was well exposed to the reformist tradition, later moving to Mandalay under the Mahawithudarama Sayadaw at sect headquarters (HYWEI HIN THA HSA.YA TO, 1963:296). He only lived for three years after being selected, and the sect met at Mandalay in 1932 to select the Hlataw (HLA.TO:) as his successor.

The Hlataw, at eighty-one years of age, represented symbolically the roots of the sect itself. He was a nephew of the Shwegyin and had been ordained by him. But, because of his age, he appointed four assistant leaders to do the actual work of administration. It became a matter of official new sectarian policy that these assistant monks would become serially the next leaders in turn from then on. Selected under this new policy were the following: (1) Pissimayon, (2) Taik-ok, (3) Sankin, and (4) the Abayarama (HYWEI HIN THA HSA.YA TO, 1963:298-299). The latter died in 1943 and thus never became head as did all of the others. The Hlataw Sayadaw himself only lived for two more years so that the Pissimayon took over according to the new serial plan in 1934 and was head of the sect at its sixth meeting at Rangoon.[36]

The Pissimayon Sayadaw, from Sagaing District, continued the Upper Burma emphasis in leadership, and he also had studied under the Mahawithudarama Sayadaw, becoming a lecturer at the central monastery. He traveled widely, going to Ceylon in 1913 and later to Bangkok. On the way home from Bangkok in 1932 he became the first Burmese monk to fly in an airplane. Once again, there is the pattern of a willingness to accept *part* of the modern world, although the same monk may refuse to ride in an ox cart. He was head of the sect during World War II when many monks fled to the holy hills of Sagaing to escape the bombing of Mandalay, and it was not until 1946 at Taunggyi that conditions in Burma were stable enough so that he was able to convene the sect's delegates again. At that meeting his leadership was confirmed, as were four assistants in line for future high office: (1) the Taik-ok, (2) Sankin, (3) Sankyaung (SAN CAUN:), and the Si Shin. The last two died before they could be appointed; and at the death of the Pissimayon in 1949, the Taik-ok took over.[37]

During these years of active nationalist politics and war-time experiments in Sangha organization many Thudhamma monks joined political organizations and thereby exerted much power upon events, but the Shwegyin Sect took a strong stand against such monastic interest groups. Their position was that there was no need for the Shwegyin Sect to seek unity through new country-wide Sangha political organizations. The Shwegyin were already country-wide and unified. Furthermore, politics were said to be affairs of the laity that monks should avoid to maintain their dignity. In other words, the sect's leadership did not approve of Sangha participation in nationalist movements such as those espoused or initiated by famous monks such as U

Ottama (QU: QOU'TA.MA).[38] It consequently separated itself even more from the active members of the Thudhamma majority.

Leadership of the sect changed rapidly again during the late forties as the Taik-ok Sayadaw from the central monastery in Mandalay lived only a year in office, dying in 1950, when he was succeeded by the next in line, the Sankin Sayadaw.[39] The latter monk therefore headed the sect during most of the tumultuous days of Burma's experiments with independence and democracy.

If the Shwegyin Sect is thought of as basically a traditionalist element in the continuum of the modern Sangha, the Sankin Sayadaw can be said to have been the ideal leader for the Cold War period. Like his predecessors, he was an Upper Burman (born near Sagaing) and a student of the Mahawithudarama. A dedicated forest monk, he specialized in Vipassana (WI.PA.THA NA) meditation at the famous Mahagandayon (MA.HA GAN DA YOUN) Monastery at Sagaing, the center of Burmese forest and meditation monks for centuries. He was a composed and peaceful proponent of a respected combination of the forest life and insightful meditation. He also spent many years in Mandalay as administrative assistant to various heads of the sect from 1915 on. Even though he was given the Rattaguru(YA.TA.GU.YU)title by the U Nu government in 1953 and was greatly honored, he did not participate in either the government programs for the Sangha or the Sixth Sangayana. He kept himself and most members of his sect free from political involvement.[40] He lived well into the Ne Win era and died only recently in his nineties, having been succeeded by the Myaungmya (MYAUN:MYA.) Sayadaw, who had been his assistant at central headquarters since 1952.[41] I was told in 1974 that the Myaungmya Sayadaw was leading the sect at that time.

Such is a brief history of the birth and development of the Shwegyin Sect from the days of the monarchs down to modern times. Several main themes have been stressed that can now be reviewed here. Most importantly, the Shwegyin Sect was given legitimation by a king, and I would argue that it formed its tight organizational structure after the colonial destruction of the monarchy to protect itself and its ideals from the interference, first, of colonial government and, then after independence, the politicians of modern Burma. In its evolution it developed its own forms of self-legitimation. From being a traditional Burmese gaing loosely organized by respect for a charismatic leader, the Shwegyin monks evolved into a sect that, in effect, recreated in the modern world their version of the ideal Sangha under an ideal king (albeit a heavenly one), complete with the office of a thathanabaing. Symbolically, it is a traditionalist defense of the old legitimate culture against colonialism, modern notions of government, and a heathen outside world.

Also important in understanding the sect is the realization that it represents a definite attempt to balance possibly unsettling movements of the four bonded dimensions. From its founder on down to the Sankin Sayadaw, there has been a clear forest monk emphasis, with the accompanying stress upon Vinaya purity as a counterpoint to modern materialism. At the same time, the sect's leaders have been willing to come in from the forest and assume administrative tasks at Mandalay. While meditation has been a vital discipline for many leaders and subordinates, scholarship and textual excellence have been more heavily stressed through emphasis upon teaching. In terms of the Upper Burma-

Ceylon bonded dimension, there are two versions of the sect's origins. One tradition traces their lineage teachers back through the saintly Thilon (THI: LOUN:) Sayadaw in the Upper Burma northeast, and another version claims descent through monks at Pakangyi who are descendants of the Sinhalese missionaries. Trips to Ceylon and a branch of the sect established there contribute to this latter emphasis. As we have seen, Mon-Upper Burmese rivalries are involved in the initial union of the northern Shwegyin and Pegu-based Tawya Gaing, the attempt at joint leadership, and the custom of holding some of the sect's meetings in the south. Despite all these efforts to achieve a golden mean, one can notice that, all things considered, the sect leans toward the forest, scholarly, Upper Burmese sides of the four bonded dimensions, that is, the most conservative ones.

Quite clearly, on the other hand, the sect has been affected by modern ideas to some degree. Its leaders have been the first monks to use airplanes; they have modified the festival atmosphere at monastic cremations to meet foreign sensitivities; and they have created semblances of Western notions of committees, assemblies, elections, written reports, and other paraphernalia of bureaucracy. But these examples are outweighed, I feel, by their basic traditionalist beginnings and development. A number of their leaders have been conservative sons of wealthy families. The sect has avoided modern politics by and large. They retain the ancient cosmology with its heavens, gods, and hells. Most importantly, they seem more comfortable with hierarchy than with democracy. Even though the kings are gone, thus removing the monks' symbolic counterparts, the sect seems to remain faithful to what it considers ideal for both Buddhism and Burma. It has survived the cultural and social changes of its first century of existence with these ideals remarkably intact.

Finally, it should be noted that the Shwegyin Sect seems to be a permanent sociological entity within the Sangha. It is not likely to be reabsorbed in the foreseeable future as part of a unified Sangha totality. It is my belief that only strong kings could reabsorb such organizations into one Sangha. The dethroning of Thibaw by the British and the subsequent refusal of the colonial government to give real power to the office of the thathanabaing only strengthened the Shwegyin Sect after it had been given royal legitimacy by King Mindon. No man of prowess since then has had the Asokan strength to unify the Burmese monkhood.

Instead, a number of gaings, such as the Dwaya, Hngetwin (HNGE'TWIN:), Pakokku (PA.HKOU'KU.), and Weluwun (WEI LU.WUN) have claimed equal status with the Shwegyin Sect, tracing their legitimacy to founder monks in the Mindon and Thibaw reigns. One sectarian leader in 1974 over-optimistically told me, "You see, now that there are no more kings, there can be no more new gaings – only those here today." Evidence coming out of Burma, however, reports that, as Mendelson's work would suggest, new gaings are a constant product of Burmese Buddhism. The Shwegyin may be the only historically legitimate sect to have specific royal blessing, but many other monastic groups are competing strongly with them today. It is interesting that U Ne Win, whom many Burmese see as a man of prowess, is reported recently (1975) as apparently fascinated by the Shwegyin Sect. Whether fascination leads to any attempt to unify or purify, using the Shwegyin Sect as Mindon tried to do, remains to be seen. In Burma, it may be that no leaders since the kings have been able to claim convincingly a sufficient cultural legitimacy to play a strong leadership role in dealing with the Sangha. Until such a leader develops, one can expect continuing fragmentation of the Burmese monkhood into factions composed of the traditional bonded dimensions of the Sangha and by the new charismatic gaings and older sects that trace their origins to the royal days.

Notes

1. I am indebted to Professor O. W. Wolters for drawing attention to the phenomenon in one of his classes. The wording of this sentence also reflects his phrasing as I remember it.

2. The process of creating and maintaining these lineages is complex. For details, see Mendelson (1975) and Ferguson (1975).

3. For details on how the Sangha allowed some kings a Bodhisatta status, see Ferguson (1975:86;183-184). The exalted Mahayanist ideal was thereby reduced to the representation of a mere Burmese king of great ambition. For the case of King Bodawpaya, see Albert Fytche, *Burma, Past and Present*, 2 vols. (London: C. Kegan Paul, 1878).

4. The useful concept of limiting thresholds of belief beyond which even the most deviant of members of a culture will not be tolerant is developed by Smith (1974).

5. In this paper Burmese will be romanized first according to the British government system because such spellings are more familiar to most readers and also will agree with the work done by Mendelson (1975). For those trained under the American system, Burmese words will also, on first mention, be romanized on the basis of a literal (as opposed to aural) transcription of *written* Burmese according to the Cornyn and Roop system. Bibliographic references for works not previously translated will be made in terms of the American system. For discussion of the technicalities involved, see Appendix A in Ferguson (1975).

6. For a more complete discussion of the four bonded dimensions, see Ferguson (1975).

7. For other observations on Theravada kingship, see F. Reynolds (1972), Bechert (1970), and Gokhale (1966). For the Thai situation, see C. Reynolds (1973). For the Burmese monarchy, see Mendelson (1975).

8. See MAUN MAUN TIN (1967III:104,106,133). Some sources (HYWEI HIN THA HSA.YA TO 1963:97) refer to him as *thathanabaing*, or ruler of the Sangha. Both titles can be found during this period of Burmese history.
   Interestingly, the Bagaya also taught the Okpo (QOU'HPOU') Sayadaw, the leader of the Dwaya (DWA YA) Gaing (GAIN:), which became a rival of the Shwegyin Sect. See below for explanation of the word *gaing*.

9. For the Shwegyin version of these events, see HYWEI HIN THA HSA.YA TO (1963:97, 451-452).

10. See the biography of the Shwegyin Sayadaw in HTUN:MYIN. (1954a:411-413).

11. The Shwegyin version of these events is in HYWEI HIN THA HSA.YA TO (1963:97-98, 451-452). The Thudhamma version is found in THEIN: (1958:102,294,408ff.).

12. The Gupyu Tawya (Tawya = forest) was the former head of the Pakan (PA.HKAN) Gaing. He had studied under the second Bagaya, the head of the Sangha under King Pagan, but he supported the monk his teacher banished. The Gupyu Tawya Sayadaw subsequently taught many of the leading monks of the Shwegyin Sect (HYWEI HIN THA HSA.YA TO 1963:450ff.). Details on monastery location are in YA.WEI HTUN: (1965:166).

13. Details on the Bhamo Sayadaw are found in THEIN: (1958:382ff.) and Anonymous (1954VIII:195-198).

14. Under pressure from Mindon's chief queen, the Bhamo Sayadaw was allowed to return, but, characteristically, he refused to come to the capital and stayed at Sagaing, where henceforth he was a thorn in Mindon's side.

15. For details, see HYWEI HIN THA HSA.YA TO (1963:106) and MAUN MAUN TIN (1967III:287).

16. Nuns (THI LA.HYIN) were particularly honored during Mindon's reign. Very interesting

data is found in YA.WEI HTUN: (1965:153-185). I am greatly indebted to Paul J. Bennett for the use of his notes on this work.

17. Mendelson (1975:96-98) discusses the different versions of the event. The official Shwegyin position is found in HYWEI HIN THA HSA.YA TO (1963:139-140).

18. For *gana*, see Davids and Stede (1921-25, II:70). For *nikāya*, see Davids and Stede (1921-25, II:188) and Buddhadatta (1969:138). For *gaing*, see Judson (1953:318-319).

19. See particularly Mendelson (1961a; 1962b; 1963; 1975). See also Spiro (1970:315-320) for his gloss of "branch" for *gaing*.

20. See C. Reynolds (1973) and Kirsch (1975) for the significance of King Mongkut's sectarian reforms, which parallel those of King Mindon in many ways.

21. The HYWEI HIN THA HSA.YA TO (1963:137) is critical of Mindon for not making the Shwegyin the *thathanabaing* and for raising QEIN TO PA (Nanmadaw?) to be his chief queen, who presumably was against the Shwegyin Sayadaw.

22. Details of how the Shwegyin Sayadaw scolded the king and at another time won the freedom of jailed monks and took them under his own custody are given in HYWEI HIN THA HSA.YA TO (1963:137,184). I was told a similar story in 1974 at Mandalay by a Shwegyin leader who said four rescued monks then went to Rangoon to start a Shwegyin monastery there.

23. See HYWEI HIN THA HSA.YA TO (1963:107,117,532) and HTUN MYIN (1954a:412).

24. See HTUN MYIN. (1954XI:412) and HYWEI HIN THA HSA.YA TO (1963:110,186-187, 202-203). The BU.YA:HPYU (Peyapyu) HSA.YA TO (1928:79) suggests that the Thudhamma Council again tried to make the Shwegyin Sayadaw submit to its authority. The retreat to the forest at Minla (MIN:HLA.) may be related to Mindon's characteristic inability to decide between two warring parties.

25. For a review of the complex issues involved, see Mendelson (1975:87-92) and Ferguson (1975:242-246).

26. The falling out is discussed in HYWEI HIN THA HSA.YA TO (1963:175), but I have not completed my research on the Dwaya Gaing history to obtain a full understanding of their side of the matter. It is clear that the Shwegyin Sayadaw had studied under the Okpo, who was senior to him, and the two monks were fellow reformists in a similar tradition. The lineage of the Okpo, however, traces back to the second Bagaya, whereas the main thrust of the lineage of the Shwegyin traces to the opponents of the Bagaya or to the much revered forest monk, the Thilon (THI:LOUN:) Sayadaw. Lineage always plays a critical role in monastic rivalry in Burma.

27. The Taungdaw had studied under the Okpo, Shwegyin, and Thilon Sayadaws and thus represented a reformist wing of the Thudhamma very much in harmony with the Shwegyin Sect. For details, see HYWEI HIN THA HSA.YA TO (1963:104,117,236-237) and MAUN MAUN TIN (1967III:413,416,490).

28. He is said to have been there in 1884 and 1885 (HYWEI HIN THA HSA.YA TO, 1963: 222,301).

29. In 1890 he established the Maungdaung (MAUN:HTAUN) Taik with the fourth Maungdaung Sayadaw, the latter in the lineage of the Thudhamma *thathanabaing* of King Mindon! The fourth Maungdaung was one of the close scholars of both the Shwegyin and the second Maungdaung. He consequently represents a Shwegyin convert from the Alon area who worked as an administrator in the Bassein district of Lower Burma. See HLA. THA.MEIN (1961:121) and HYWEI HIN THA HSA.YA TO (1963:233,238,523).

30. Details on the merger and on U Thila can be found in HLA.THA.MEIN (1961:113-114, 168) and HYWEI HIN THA HSA.YA TO (1963:126-135,455,506). For discussion of the disciplined way of life at a famous monastery he started, the Shwehintha Tawya (HYWEI HIN THA TO:YA.) Taik, see Mendelson (1975:129-130,147-149).

31. He is also known as the Mahawithudayon (MA.HA WI.THOU'DA YOUN) Sayadaw because from 1903 on he stayed at a monastery of that name. Biographies can be found in HYWEI HIN THA HSA.YA TO (1963:241-281), HLA.THA.MEIN (1961:115), and HTUN MYIN. (1954b:467-468).

32. Queen Sinpyumashin, in contrast to the chief queen Nanmadaw (who is said to have blocked the appointment of the Shwegyin as *thathanabaing* seven years earlier), was apparently a Shwegyin supporter. As the famous mother of Thibaw's queen, she, of course, later exerted much political influence. Sinpyumashin and the chief queen were bitter

rivals, and their backing of opposing Sangha factions is a good example of the complex interrelationship of church and state in Burma.

33. The HYWEI HIN THA HSA.YA TO (1963:281) notes that the simplicity of the funerals was due to a desire to avoid criticism by "foreigners," presumably the British.

34. The Mogaung Sayadaw may be the same monk discussed by Smith (1965:49), who claimed a right to be considered the *thathanabaing* after the death of the Taungdaw in 1894. He was exiled by the Thudhamma Council to Henzada and thus became part of the growing number of monastic leaders in Lower Burma who were in defiance of Thudhamma control.

35. Biographical details are found in HYWEI HIN THA HSA.YA TO (1963:234,267,290-292).

36. Mendelson acquired a Burmese version of a 1936 Shwegyin report that describes the sect's meeting at Rangoon. The cover had been ripped off, and thus no bibliographic information can be given.

37. The Pissimayon was also known as the Kyaiklat (CAI'LA) Pissimayon. For his biography, see HYWEI HIN THA HSA.YA TO (1963:305-311).

38. This position was clearly stated by the Dipeyin Sayadaw as early as 1921 (HYWEI HIN THA HSA.YA TO, 1963: 328-329). For considerable detail on U Ottama, see Mendelson (1975:199-206, 221-224).

39. The Taik-ok, eighty-four at the time, was the third head to come from the Mounywa District. He, like all the leaders since 1917, had studied under the Mahawithudarama Sayadaw. Since 1930 he had carried administrative responsibilities for the entire sect at the Mahawithudarama Taik (HYWEI HIN THA HSA.YA TO, 1963:310-312,348).

40. For details on his life, see HYWEI HIN THA HSA.YA TO (1963:311,312-319). For a full portrait of the involvement of the Sangha sects in the U Nu government's programs, see Mendelson (1975:236-355).

41. The Myaungmya Sayadaw is an Upper Burman monk from Myinmu (near Sagaing) who has a reputation for firm leadership, strictness with his many Pāli pupils, abruptness with the laity, and much administrative experience as an administrator at Mandalay (HYWEI HIN THA HSA.YA TO, 1963:370,373-380,416,470).

References Cited

Anonymous
1954 BAN:MO HSA.YA TO. *In* MYAN MA.SWE SOUN CAN:, Vol. VIII:195-198. Rangoon: Burma Translation Society.

Ariyapala, M. B.
1956 *Society in Mediaeval Ceylon*. Columbo, Ceylon: Dept. of Cultural Affairs.

Bechert, Heinz
1970 "Theravada Buddhist Sangha: Some General Observations on Historical and Political Factors in its Development," *Journal of Asian Studies*, 29:761-778.

Buddhadatta, A. P.
1969 *Pali-English Dictionary*. New York: Saphrograph.

BU.YA:HPYU HSA.YA TO
1928 THA THA.NA.BA.HU.THU.TA'PA.KA THA.NI CAN:. Rangoon: Deedock Press. Press.

Davids, T. W. Rhys, and Stede, William, eds.
    The Pali Text Society's Pali-English Dictionary. London: Pali Text Society, 1921-25.

Gokhale, Balkrishna G.
1966 "Early Buddhist Kingship," *Journal of Asian Studies*, 26:15-22.

Ferguson, John P.
1975 "The Symbolic Dimensions of the Burmese Sangha." Ph.D. diss., Cornell University.

Foucar, Emile C. V.
1946 *They Reigned in Mandalay*. London: D. Dobson.

HLA.THA.MEIN
1961 GAN HTA.WIN POU'GOU'CO MYA: QA'HTOU'PA'TI. Rangoon: Hanthawaddy Press.

HTUN:MYIN.
1954a HYWEI CIN HSA.YA TO. *In* MYAN MA.SWE SOUN CAN:, Vol. XI:411-413.
Rangoon: Burma Translation Society.
1954b MA.HA WI.THOU'DA YOUN HSA.YA TO. *In* MYAN MA.SWE SOUN CAN:,
Vol. VIII:467-468. Rangoon: Burma Translation Society.
HYWEI HIN THA HSA.YA TO
1963 HYWEI CIN NI.KA YA THA THA.NA WIN. [No further details given].

Judson, Adoniram
1953 *Judson's Burmese-English Dictionary*. Rangoon: Baptist Board of Publications.

Kirsch, A. Thomas
1975 "Modernizing Implications of 19th Century Reforms in the Thai Sangha," in
Contributions to Asian Studies, Vol. VIII:8-23.

MAUN MAUN TIN
1967 KOUN:BOUN HSE' MA.HA YA.ZA.WIN TO CI:, Vol. I-III. Rangoon: LE TI
MAN TAIN, POUN NEI'TAI'.

Mendelson, E. Michael
1960 "Religion and Authority in Modern Burma," *World Today*, 16:110-118.

1961a "A Messianic Buddhist Association in Upper Burma," *Bulletin of the School of
Oriental and African Studies*, University of London, 24:560-580.

1961b "The King of the Weaving Mountain," *Royal Central Asian Journal*, 48:229-237.

1963 "Observations on a Tour in the Region of Mount Popa, Central Burma," *France-
Asie*, 179:786-807.

1975 *Sangha and State in Burma: A Study of Monastic Sectarianism and Leadership*, ed.
John P. Ferguson. Ithaca, N.Y.: Cornell University Press.

Reynolds, Craig J.
1973 "The Buddhist Monkhood in Nineteenth Century Thailand." Ph.D. diss., Cornell
University.

Reynolds, Frank E.
1971 "Buddhism and Sacral Kingship: A Study in the History of Thai Religion." Ph.D.
diss., University of Chicago.

1972 "The Two Wheels of Dhamma: A Study of Early Buddhism," in *The Two Wheels
of Dhamma*, ed., Bardwell L. Smith. Chambersburg, Pa.: American Academy of
Religion, Studies in Religion, No. 3, pp. 6-30.

Smith, Donald E.
1965 *Religion and Politics in Burma*. Princeton, N.J.: Princeton University Press.

Smith, Robert J.
1974 "Afterward," in *Religion and Ritual in Chinese Society*, ed., Arthur P. Wolf.
Stanford: Stanford University Press. Pp. 337-348.

Spiro, Melford E.
1970 *Buddhism and Society: A Great Tradition and Its Burmese Vicissitudes*. New
York: Harper & Row.

THEIN:, HSA.YA (THEIN:HAN,QU:)
1958 THIN GA.ZA SA.KA:POUN. Rangoon: Hanthawaddy Press.

YA.WEI HTUN:
1965 THI LA.HYIN THA.MAIN. [Rangoon]: Pyinnya Alinbya Bookstore.

Buddhist Backgrounds of Burmese Socialism

E. Sarkisyanz

BURMA IS THE only Theravāda Buddhist country to reach independence through a revolutionary mass movement during an acute crisis of traditional culture. Among her striking acculturation phenomena is Buddhist-Marxist syncretism. Its intellectual history has been obscured by a one-sided image of "Hīnayāna" Buddhism in terms of the other-worldly monastic tradition of the Pāli Canon with the resulting notion that, as it depreciates the world and society, Buddhism could not possibly produce a social or political ethos.[1] It is true that the Buddhist Order was apolitical. But lay rulers since the third century B.C. have proclaimed aspirations to base their charisma on a Buddhist political ethos. That "Aśokan" historical lay Buddhism is more relevant for Buddhist political thought than the monastic Buddhism of the Canon is rarely considered.

Burma's Buddhist historiography ascribes prophecies about the Buddhist destinies of the country to the Buddha himself. From his lineage it derived the Burmese dynasties, including that of Pagan (1044-1287),[2] the classical formation period of Burmese culture. History was to illustrate the impermanence of all existence, the cyclical regularity and causality of endless change. Events tended to be assimilated to happenings of the distant or legendary past and, indeed, to those of the future.[3] Even Burma's last dynasty claimed descent from the First Ruler,[4] whom men had chosen when the primeval utopia of common property (over crops growing without labor) had vanished, when the aberration of selfishness produced private property.[5] Such a "social contract" theory of kingship has been called a Buddhist contribution to Indian political theory. Republican politics of early Buddhist India probably stimulated the canonic republican structure of the Buddhist Order[6] before it came under control of monarchies like Aśoka's. In an inscription Aśoka proclaimed:

> On the roads I have planted banyan trees. They will offer shade to men and beast. I have grown mango-orchards. I have caused wells to be dug; . . . and I have rest houses [built] . . . *I have done this with the intent* that men may practise practices of Dhamma.[7]

Apparently, such welfare measures were meant by Aśoka to facilitate the observation of the Dhamma, Buddhism's moral Law — if not to provide leisure opportunities for meditation towards the pursuit of nirvāna. Subsequent Theravāda Buddhist rulers have again and again proclaimed such Buddhist principles of government. Though Aśoka's inscriptions were forgotten, Buddhist legend transmitted his vision of a Buddhist welfare state. It is echoed in the Chronicle of Ceylon, reporting, for example, about King Mahinda II (772-792): "The poor who were shamed to beg he supported in secret, and there were none in the island who were not supported by him. . . ." Mahinda IV (956-972 or 1026-1042)

> built an alms hall and gave to beggars alms and couches. In all hospitals he distributed medicine and beds, and he had food given regularly to criminals in prison. . . . The King had rows of rice laid down in heaps with the injunction that the poor should take of it as much as they wanted.[8]

An examination of *historical* (as distinguished from *canonical*) Buddhism does not bear out Max Weber's contention that there is no bridge between the Buddhist ideal and active social endeavor.[9] It is true that the Buddhist scriptures emphasize that

> all things perish, that all things are grief and pain, that all forms are unreal. He who knows and sees this becomes passive in pain; Woe upon life in this world. . . . Having left son and wife, father and mother, wealth, and corn and relatives, the different objects of desire, let one wander alone like a rhinoceros.[10]

Buddhism denies reality to the concept of "mineness"(*mamatā*). The basic notions of "my," "this is I," "this is myself" are seen as devoid of reality. Attachment to attributes of mineness is to be overcome. Consciousness of the self as actor of a deed is considered an illusion.[11] Therefore, power of an individual over others could not be fully rationalized in Buddhist terms. If it proved, nevertheless, possible to derive the *ideal* of political power from Buddhist ethics, it was precisely because "non-substantiality of mineness" implied an aspiration to realize the basic oneness of "self" and "other selves." Such non-distinction between the happiness and sorrow of "others" and of "one's self" is called *karunā*.[12] It means the widening of consciousness in a mystical sense to a point where it embraces all living beings, just as the Enlightened Being, the Bodhisattva, a potential Buddha, was to renounce his salvation until all beings had been saved. It was largely through such a Bodhisattva ethos that "Buddhism developed . . . into one of the politically most effective systems in the world," wrote Paul Mus. By the boundlessness of his abnegation, the Bodhisattva's kingly powers over others were to merge with the quest for their salvation from fetters of illusory "mineness."

Though the Bodhisattva ideal developed mainly in Mahāyāna Buddhism, it entered the Theravāda Buddhism of Ceylon and Burma too — since the sixth century as a royal cult and to the present on the level of folk religion.[13] An inscription of Ceylon's Mahinda IV declares that "*none but Bodhisattvas would become kings of Lanka* [Ceylon] ," a belief surviving up to the British conquest.[14]

The future Buddha and only Bodhisattva of Theravāda Buddhism is Metteya (Maitreya). At his advent sevenfold crops are again to ripen without labor; the ill are to become healthy and the poor rich.[15] Burma's King Kyanzitthu of Pagan (1084-1112) proclaimed that he had tanks built and groves planted "only that all beings might escape out of Samsāra . . .

> King Sri Tribhūwanādityadhammarāja [Kyanzitthu] . . . the omniscient one, the Bodhisattva . . . that saves and redeems all beings. . . . All the people . . . shall eat plenty of food, they shall enjoy happiness . . . the barns and granaries shall be full.[16]

Good harvests were to be assured through the king's (pre-Buddhist) fertility magic.[17] This in turn contributed to state control over the agricultural economy; Burma's kings, lords of the "rain producing" White Elephant, were, at least formally, owners of a large part of all arable land.[18] The Buddhist rulers were to feed the people every six months (*purushamedha*) and to lend funds to insolvent debtors or even to remit their debts.[19] The ideal state of Aśokan

Buddhism was to insure such economic welfare as would permit the leisure
necessary for meditation to pursue nirvāna, a welfare state, at least to the extent of enabling everybody who wanted to withdraw from materially productive activities.[20]

To the Buddha is attributed the following description of the ideal kingdom:

... so was the royal city provided with all kinds of food. ... The Great King of Glory
established a perpetual grant ... to wit, food for the hungry, drink for the thirsty,
raiment for the naked, means of conveyance for those who needed it, couches for the
tired ... gold for the poor, and money for those who were in want. ... .[21]

Buddha is said to have postponed preaching about the impermanence of material satisfactions until his listener was fed:

"If I preach the Law while he is suffering from the pangs of hunger, he will not be able
to comprehend ..." as soon as the poor man's physical suffering became relieved, his
mind became tranquil. Then the Teacher preached the Law ... The poor man established in the truth of conversion.[22]

Thus could Kyanzitthu, one of the most renowned Burmese kings, proclaim in
the 1090s:

As by the Lord Buddha was foretold, so it has all come to pass ... The bar of the gate
of heaven ... by wisdom ... [the] king shall draw open for [all mankind]. The tears
... by his course of benevolence shall the king ... wipe away ... Even the poor old
women who sell pots ... shall become rich, ... those who lack cattle shall have plenty
of cattle. ... Even poor people who have difficulty in getting food and clothes ... [the
king] shall enrich them all. ... With his right hand he shall give boilt rice and bread to
all the people, with his left hand he shall give ornaments and wearing apparel to all
men. ... When the King of the Law shall preach the Law, the sound of applause of all
men [shall be] like the sound of rainstorm at the end of the year.[23]

Though professing such Buddhist aspirations, many of Burma's rulers conquered by methods of blood and iron. Thus, the empire builder Buyin Naung
(1551-1581) wanted to burn alive his defeated officers and rebels; intervention
of Buddhist monks saved many of them.[24] And, if the arbitrary brutality of
power in pre-colonial Burma surpassed its counterpart in the pre-totalitarian
Occident, Burma's Buddhist monkhood also went further in the protection of
human life than did the historical churches of Christendom — who rarely resisted and on the whole tacitly recognized the claim of the temporal powers to in-
flict death.[25] A Burmese proverb includes rulers among the Five Enemies (yan-
dhu-myou: nga: pa:), together with Fire, Thieves and Pestilence.[26] Theravāda
Buddhism has failed to rationalize the superhuman position of Indic kings; an
outright "anarchic spirit" has been attributed to it, writes Paul Mus. Actually,
in past life the subsequent Buddha took upon himself suffering upon suffering
only to avoid becoming king. The famous Ānanda Pagoda of Pagan is decorated
with illustrations from that Jātaka legend in which he reflected: "If I become
king, I shall be born in hell. ... My father through being a king is becoming
guilty of grievous action which brings men to hell."[27] That the pragma of power
with its political expediency worked as an obstacle to Buddhist renunciation
and detachment was a historical experience of the Burmese people. Therefore,
in practice, it failed to be fully justified in Buddhist terms. Amid the ruthless
power practices of rulers, the Bodhisattva ideal proved an insufficient ideology
for the state. Even in Theravāda Buddhist Burma kingship remained based on
Hinduist concepts. Hinduism's relativistic ethics provided more effective principles for the pragma of power than could the Buddhist ethos of overcoming
universal suffering. "Forgiveness shown to friend or foe, is an ornament in the

case of hermits, while the same shown to offenders by kings is a blemish," says such a Hindu maxim influential among Burma's rulers.[28]

It was through a "withering away" of the state that Buddhist social ideals were expected to find ultimate fulfillment. In a previous life the subsequent Buddha's message induced the king with a multitude of his subjects to abandon the kingdom and to become monks in the forest. Invaders, who overran the country to seize its treasures, joined the subsequent Buddha and the king in the renunciation of power and wealth. He "caused . . . his treasury to be thrown open . . . [so that] his treasure . . . would be exposed . . . that all who pleased might take of them . . . ." The ideal Buddhist world ruler of the future, the Cakkavatti-Samkha, is to renounce status and wealth to the poor, the homeless and destitute, and is himself to wander into homelessness. He and his army, with gigantic crowds accompanying them, shall become monks.[29] The Cakkavatti is to usher in the age of Metteya, the Future Buddha. Yet self-identification with him by the Burmese conqueror Bodawpaya (1781-1819)[30] may have contributed to Burma's westward expansion ending in the first Anglo-Burmese War (1824-1826).[31] At a time when the resulting territorial losses and indemnity payments were putting considerable burdens upon the Burmese peasant was first recorded a popularization of the canonic Pāli Cakkavatti prophecies into the folklore about Setkya-Min Buddha-Yaza ("Lord of the Weapon and Buddha-Ruler") of present-day Burma. When the reversion of the ethical and social order shall have reached its deepest point, he is to restore the observances of the Buddhist Dhamma, so that

> the totality of Burma's people shall be made happy through an abundance of gold and silver gems [and the] people of the entire world shall equally become Buddhists.

And all the countries in the world are then to be ordered according to the Dhamma Law.[32] Since 1839, peasants have in the name of Setkya Min again and again revolted both against Burmese kings and British conquerors (in 1839, 1855, 1858, and 1860).[33] Around Setkya Min claimants centered Burmese guerrilla resistance against the British conquest in 1886-1889;[34] the attempted peasant rising of 1922;[35] and, particularly, Saya San's ("Galon") peasant war of 1930-1931 which spread into twelve of Burma's forty districts and which required two British Indian divisions to crush it.[36] The "Galons' invulnerability" proved of no avail. Saya San's traditionalist revolt attempted a withdrawal from the technological power realities, a search for security in pre-colonial values, a desperate attempt to restore the old symbols of cosmic and social harmony. Saya San was executed. But his estate went to finance popularizations of Marxist literature in Burma. Although this nativistic response against the overwhelming impacts of an alien civilization developed in a militant folk-Buddhist and animistic context, it overlapped with modernistic Burmese revolutionary nationalism, which likewise developed out of the crisis of Burma's Buddhist society under British colonial rule.

British rule abandoned the state sponsorship of Buddhism, in the name of "liberalism," but not without influence from Victorian missionary Protestantism. Thus the missionary scholar Spence Hardy insisted that such

> nations have been placed under our authority, that we might carry on with better effect . . . the world's conversion from darkness to light and from the power of Satan unto God.[37]

Against such attacks the lay Buddhism of the English-educated Burmese came to invoke testimonies of modern western critics of historical Christianity. The beginning of this century was in Europe a time of disappointment in modern civilization, progress and Christendom, a time when Europe developed self-doubts about her civilization and mission. Theosophic idealizations of Indic religion, Nietzschean attacks on Christian professions, the Social Gospel's challenge to orthodoxy, and Marxian attacks on the economics of empire-building, all stimulated the apologetics of a modernistic Buddhism adjusting itself to the twentieth century. Among the Englishmen converted to Buddhism was Gordon Douglas, "son of an Earl . . . said to have come to the East . . . owing to his being an out and out radical with socialistic tendencies." As a Buddhist monk under the name Aśoka, he died in 1900 in Bassein, in southern Burma.

Modernist Buddhism began to project the traditional quest for deliverance from cosmic suffering into the direction of a quest for deliverance from social suffering. The Ceylonese Dharmapala, its main spokesman, talked by 1913 about "Buddha's Social Gospel," undertook social work and advocated social reform. His "Maha-Bodhi Journal" vehemently challenged the religious, cultural and economic arguments for British rule by challenging Protestantism, capitalism, and "progress."[38] Liberal England justified its domination and economic advantages in Asian countries by claiming to act as "a trustee for civilization in order to build up those conditions of liberty and opportunity for the individual in which the people can *learn* to govern themselves."[39] Since Edwardian times such claims that the peoples of Indic civilization had yet to be trained for self-government came to meet militant contradiction, first in terms of Occidental borrowings of liberal slogans of self-determination and subsequently by reinterpretations of old Indic culture, now claimed to contain indigenous democratic traditions, counterclaims about democracy being part of Buddhist tradition. After the British captivity of Burma's last king, Buddhist modernists contributed the monastic community's republican principles to the political ideologies of modern Burma.

As tradition had attributed to the omniscient Buddha "all the remedies that are current in the world for the benefit and welfare of man . . . all the expedients for the service of man," so the revolutionary watchwords of Fraternity, Equality, and Social Justice likewise came to be attributed to the Buddha under requirements of twentieth century situations. Thus the thesis of a Buddhist socialism antedates the First World War. Lakshmi Narasu's book, *The Essence of Buddhism* (published in 1907),[40] already contains Buddhist anticapitalism, anticipating in sharpness subsequent Communist slogans. Buddhism's canonic community of monastic property was called "a communistic negation of private property . . . very similar to the philosophy of modern socialism and communism."[41] Dharmapala declared that Buddhism's message is to soften British imperialism.[42] In the words of a Burmese abbot:

> And . . . without being free from bondage, which stems from the fact that one nation is subject to the rule of another, one can hardly find peace in one's heart or in one's environment, the environment in which the Buddhist way of life may be practiced or the compassionate love of a true Buddhist disseminated to humanity at large.[43]

A considerable part of Burma's modernistic Buddhists became associated with the independence movement. Its economic motivations had in the Burmese cultural context a Buddhist meaning:

> to be able to give alms [to the nirvāna seeking monks] one must first make provisions for one's own well-being before parting with what one has to give to another. . . .

wrote the same abbot, Zeyawadi U Thilasara, in 1923. This modernistic reinterpretation projected the Buddhist quest for deliverance from universal suffering into a quest for social deliverance from political and economic evils. Thereby, the concept of a nirvāna *within* life was endowed with revolutionary meaning. Sayadaw Zeyawadi U Thilasara described the stages of political struggle towards Independence as parallels to the stages of Buddhist deliverance – from the state of an ordinary human to final release by means of supreme enlightenment. Independence for Burma was to mean "nirvāna-within-this-world," according to the poet Thakin Kudaw Hmain.[44] Not only outward freedom, but even ultimate liberation into nirvāna was to be reached through the independence struggle, declared Sayadaw U Nye Ya, a popular preacher, active in Burma's Buddhist revival.[45] Most prominent among these political monks was U Ottama, who provided modernistic elite aspirations for independence with roots in traditional folk Buddhism. As a mass basis for political minority aspirations, folk Buddhism was attracted by the "new" emphasis on *political* conditions for the pursuit of "nirvāna-within-this-world." This symbol reflected folkloric memories of medieval Burmese state ideals and popular prophecies about the perfect Buddhist society of the future.

From "good government" as upholder of Buddhism was customarily expected an ethical harmony in nature which would make crops grow without labor. The government that the traditionalist majority of the Burmese desired was to be a cornucopia, an inexhaustible source of plenty. In the traditional lore the ideal Buddhist state was to be a source of material welfare and a prerequisite for leisure and meditation towards nirvāna. Its fulfillment was to follow the Age of Decline. Decline seemed manifest in Buddhist Burma by the time of the World Depression. Between 1870 and 1930 agricultural real wages in Lower Burma may have fallen by 20 percent. The Burmans' consumption of rice apparently fell by nearly 25 percent between 1921 and 1941.[46] The Burmese failed to benefit in proportion to the development of their economy by Britain. Their Buddhist social ethics showed little adaptation to a business society. The Theravada Buddhist ethos has little place for economic virtues like saving, calculating and investing. In Burma, Buddhist values remained an obstacle to rational accumulation, investment and profit.[47] During the fall of rice prices in the World Depression Burmese rice cultivators were dispossessed by foreclosure of mortgages. By 1933 the agriculturalists of Lower Burma had already lost 41 percent of their land to moneylenders.[48]

Marxism entered Burmese politics, since 1931, through the Thakin group of the Dobama Asiayon Party – which was to produce the main statesmen of post-war Burma. Their mentor was Thakin Kudaw Hmain. As a ten-year-old monastery pupil, in 1885, he had wept bitter tears when Burma's last king was led away into British captivity. Thakin Kudaw Hmain did not learn English; he is hardly mentioned in the standard books about Burma. Yet he provided a living link between the Burmese revolution and pre-British Burmese traditions. By the late 1930s he is said to have become something like "the real ideologist" of the Thakin group.[49] From Thakin Kudaw Hmain seem to stem some of the main symbols of Burma's post-war Buddhist socialism. In his book *Thakin Tīkā* (published in 1938) he reminded his readers that, according to the *Dīgha Nikāya* Buddhist scripture, men had voluntarily elected their first ruler, voluntarily taxing themselves to provide for him, to maintain lawfulness and government.[50] The subsequent Burmese Communist chieftain

Thakin Than Tun later cited the same Buddhist tradition about the primeval utopia of common property existing before the aberration of selfishness produced private property and made governments necessary.[51] The Buddhist scriptural account about the origin of government coincided with basic ideas of the Social Contract theory of early liberalism as well as with Marxist notions that the rise of private property gave origin to the state. The most orthodox theorist of Burmese Leninism, Thakin Soe, used Buddhist philosophical terminology to explain Marxist concepts. It would hardly have been possible to explain the unfamiliar new ideology otherwise than in terms of the familiar ancient religion. The only philosophical terms established in the Burmese language are designations for Buddhist concepts. Therefore, only Buddhist terminology was available to expound Marxism to Burma — if Marxism were to be widely understood. Thus, in Thakin Soe's exposition of Marxism-Leninism, the Buddhist term for cyclical generation and destruction of worlds was used to designate the eternal flux of matter in "dialectical materialism."[52] The terminology for strike (*thabeit hmauk*) and strikers (*thabeit hmauk-thu*) were borrowed from a traditional term for a refusal of Buddhist monks to accept alms (by inverting their bowls as protest against the givers).[53] Of Marxist origin is allegedly the term *Lokka Nibbān*, the worldly nirvāna.[54] Actually, the un-westernized Thakin Kudaw Hmain took this for granted by 1938.[55] This concept seems to have developed as an offshoot of secularizing trends in Burma's Buddhist modernism of the 1920s.

Such applications of Buddhism remained not unopposed as early as the 1930s. To counter anti-socialistic objections with Buddhist arguments U Nu wrote ("around 1935 or 1936") his essay "Kyan-to Buthama," presenting socialism within the context of a lay Buddhist ethos. As greed, hate, and delusion caused suffering, socialism of Buddhist modernists emphasized that among the reasons for greed, hate, and delusion are economic inequities; economic reform was to eliminate these aberrations. U Nu wrote that capitalistic concentration of wealth reduced the number of those economically capable of performing works of Buddhist piety. Thus he made the impact of capitalism on Burma responsible for people turning away from religion. He stressed that people must have assured economic support to be able to meditate about the impermanence of material things. As the struggle for self-preservation was to be reduced, so was Buddhist piety meant to increase. According to U Nu, neither social reforms, nor elimination of economic inequities, nor the enrichment of the poor should be ends in themselves. They were to be but economic methods for the achievement of a Buddhist religious goal.[56] A pamphlet of U Nu's colleague Thakin Tin identified in 1936 the traditional Buddhist monastic community of property with Socialism.[57] The unofficial anthem of his old Thakin Party, the Red Dragon Song, announced that the people would be freed from poverty *to enable them* to perform charities and to build monasteries. This revolutionary song reminded one of the gold and silver rains that were reputed to have fallen under the virtuous rulers of medieval Burma, announcing the approach of a comparable era of abundance and wealth.[58]

The constitution adopted by Burma after its independence was restored contains socialistic features. The Land Nationalization Law of 1948 was advocated by U Nu on Buddhist grounds. He declared that property has only a functional place as a means for the pursuit of nirvāna (through meditation) and that the class struggle has arisen out of the illusion about the inherent values of property, that this illusion has caused bloodshed throughout history, so that its overcoming would usher in a perfect society.[59] In 1949 and again in 1950 U Nu reminded that "when the world began," the material needs of all peoples were satisfied by nature without human effort, until greed had moved men to take more than their necessities, until the introduction of private property has caused want and misery ever since. He presented socialism as the teaching which can bring humanity back to that blissful perfection of the past.[60] This was a political application of the *Aggañña Sutta* of the Buddhist Canon.

Though democracy and socialism were adapted by Burma from Britain, they were accepted within the context of a Buddhist social ethos. In Burma the degree of Anglicization, even of the elite, was never as great as in Ceylon or even India. Therefore, ideological syncretism was inevitable. Independence from England increased the dependence of Burma's politicians upon the traditionalist majority for which the unfamiliar abstractions of "democracy" and "socialism" could become comprehensible only in the familiar Buddhist context. Thus Buddhism had to leave deep imprints on the absorption of borrowed Western political concepts by the Burmese public. This produced syncretistic rationalizations of socialism in Burma's English press. U Ba Yin, a former Minister of Education, wrote that Marx must have "directly or indirectly been influenced by Buddha."[61] Modernists claimed that the Buddhist message calls for a break with the alien business society's materialist values more radically than does any platform of social revolution. Marxism was meant to provide an economic methodology for Buddhist goals. Ba Swe, leader of the Burmese Socialist Party, in 1950 called Marxism a lower truth that could facilitate the achievement of the Buddhist higher truth, since "reflections about Ageing, Disease and Death cannot be clearly answered by the Marxist Abhidhamma" (philosophy). Ba Swe's Marxism was to give

> material satisfaction, while at the present time men, being lost in concerns about nourishment, concerns about clothing, and concerns about shelter cannot meditate about the phenomena of impermanence . . . they cannot free themselves from the fact of Death. But having obtained satisfaction for the corporal frame through material well-being, they shall be able to meditate over Ageing, Disease and the fact of Death,

finding in the Buddhist philosophy clear answers about release and liberation.[62]

But the Burmese Communists were not content to have Marxism accepted merely as one methodology of liberation from economic suffering within the far more universal Buddhist methodology of liberation from universal suffering. They refused to be content with the acceptance of Marxism as a limited economic truth within U Nu's Buddhist socialism, just as they refused to be content with coalition partnership in the Anti-Fascist People's Freedom League government. In vain did U Nu offer to step down in favor of the Communist *if* they could achieve a majority in free elections.[63] They started a civil war in 1949. A Communist victory would have transformed Marxism from an economic sub-structure for the Buddhist quest into an ideology monopolizing power and would have endangered Burma's Buddhist traditions and independence. Against this background U Nu abandoned "Marxism" in 1958. This meant the explicit rejection of Marxist *political and ideological* doctrines of Proletarian Dictatorship and Materialism, dogmas which had never been accepted by U Nu, even in his "Marxist" period. But, rejecting "Marxism," he and the Anti-Fascist People's Freedom League did not thereby reject the Marxist *economic* concepts.[64] This was evident since the split of 1958 between the followers of U Nu and Ba Swe with Kyaw Nyein. The latter continued to be influenced by Revisionist Marxism. *Politically*, their program hardly differed from U Nu's socialistic platform. When U Nu triumphed overwhelmingly in Burma's last free election in 1960, it was largely through the popularly Buddhist emphasis of his socialism. (U Nu was popularly taken for a future Buddha.)

In his elaborate pre-election speech of November 16, 1959, U Nu referred to the traditional ideal of the perfect Buddhist ruler. Describing his Buddhist socialism, he reiterated (as in 1935-1936) that acquisition economy had developed out of that illusion of the self which Buddhism aims to overcome. And, U Nu emphasized that acquisitive competition obstructs a social order that would make meditation economically possible for all, thereby permitting universal liberation from impermanence and suffering.[65] This frame of reference was not so much a pragmatic improvization as a modernized political application of a Buddhist state ethos professed in the inscriptions of Burma's old kings and partly preserved in popular folklore of the Burmese.

That the freely elected U Nu could be overthrown in 1962 by his army without significant mass protest may stem from Burmese pre-Buddhist and non-Buddhist attitudes toward physical force as authority: habits of dread and propitiation of Nat animism that are so strong in Burmese culture in which they satisfy the human needs for dependence, needs not provided for by Theravāda Buddhism.

Notes

Largely based on material collected in Burma under a grant from the Guggenheim Foundation. The author has treated the topic in greater detail in a book, *Buddhist Backgrounds of the Burmese Revolution*, which appeared with M. Nijhoff Co., The Hague, 1965.

1. Sarkisyanz, "On the place of U Nu's Buddhist Socialism in Burma's History of Ideas," in R. Sakai (Editor), *Studies on Asia, 1961* (Lincoln, Nebraska, U.S.A., 1961), p. 61.

2. *Lik Smin Asah, the story of the founding of Pegu* . . . With English translations and notes. Edited by R. Halliday (Rangoon, 1923), p. 69; *Hman nan: Maha Yazawin-togyi:*, CII (Mandalay, 1318/1956), p. 175ff.

3. Cf. A. K. Warder, "The Pāli Canon and its Commentaries as a historical record," in C. H. Philips, *Historians of India, Pakistan and Ceylon* (London, 1961), p. 51.

4. Cf. Shway Yoe, p. 96; *Nanabhivamsadhamma*, p. 17; U Tin, "Myanma Min Okchak-pon Sadan," II, §171, cited in Dr. Thaung, "Burmese Kingship in theory and practice during the reign of Mindon," in *JBRS,.XLII*, ii (December, 1959), pp. 175f.; Henry Yule, *A narrative of the mission . . . to Ava* (London, 1858), p. 107.

5. *Hman nan: Maha Yazawin-to-gyi:*, Pahtama, two, XII, p. 32; Badda-kaba maha-kappa u: asa Mahathamma ta-min: le' -hte mwa: caun: tha: Manu ama' si yin yei: tha: tho, *Manu-ce Dhammathat* (Rangoon, 1903), p. 3.

6. D. Gokuldas, *Democracy in Early Buddhist Samgha* (Calcutta, 1955), p. ix.

7. Pillar Edict, VII: D. R. Bhandarkar, *Asoka* (Calcutta, 1925), pp. 318, 319, author's italics throughout.

8. *Cūlavamsa*, XXXVII, 182; XLVIII, 146-147; LIV, 30-33: transl. Geiger, Part I, pp. 17f., 124; Part II, p. 181; cf. Archaeological Survey of Ceylon, *Epigraphia Zeylanica*, Vol. II (London, 1928), pp. 90, 81, 175f., 178.

9. Max Weber, *Gesammelte Aufsätze zur Religionssoziologie* (Tubingen, 1920-1921), Vol. II, pp. 229f.

10. *Dhammapada*, 277-279: transl. F. Max Müller, in *SBE*, Vol. X (1881), Part i, p. 67f.; *Sutta-Nipāta*, III, ii, 16; I, iii, 26-28: transl. by V. Fausböll, in *SBE*, Vol. X, Part ii, pp. 71, 9.
11. *Majjhima Nikāya* I (*Sallekha Sutta*), cited in B. C. Law, *History of Pāli Literature* (London, 1933), Vol. I, p. 120; *Sutta Nipāta*, 951: transl. by Fausböll, in *SBE*, X, ii, p. 179; Kacchapa-Jātaka (*Jātaka*, II, 81): transl. by Cowell, *Jātaka*, Vol. II (1957), p. 56; *Mahāvastu*, II, 142: transl., Jones, in *Sacred Books of the Buddhists*, Vol. XVII (London, 1949), p. 137.
12. H. Nakamura, *Ways of Thinking of Eastern Peoples* (Tokyo, 1960), pp. 75, 81, 84; *Mahāyāna Sūtrālankāra*, 19, 17; 176.27 (edition of S. Levi - Paris, 1911); *Bodhi-caryavatara*, viii, 110, 131, 136, 140 (I. Minaev's edition, 1889) cited by Har Dayal, *The Bodhisattva Doctrine in Buddhist Sanskrit Literature* (London, 1932), p. 179.
13. J. Przyluski, *La Légende de l' empereur Açoka (Açoka Avādana)*: Annales du Musée Guimet, *Bibliotheque d'Études*, Vol. XXXII (Paris, 1923), p. 171; S. Paranavitana, "Mahayanism in Ceylon," *Ceylon Journal of Science*, Section G, Vol. II (December, 1928/February, 1933), p. 52.
14. Archaeological Survey of Ceylon, *Epigraphia Zeylanica* (London, 1912), Vol. I, p. 240; Vol. III, p. 87.
15. Przyluski, *La Légende, p. 226*.
16. *Epigraphia Birmanica*, Vol. I, Part ii, pp. 126, 122, 166, 146.
17. Vessantara Jātaka, Kurudhamma-Jātaka: Cowell, *Jātaka*, Vol. II, p. 254; Vol. VI (157), p. 251f.; *Hastyayurveda*, IV, 22, quoted by H. Zimmer, *Myths and Symbols in Indian Art and Civilization* (New York, 1946); A. Bastian, "Reisen in Birma in den Jahren 1861-1862," *Die Völker des östlichen Asien*, Vol. II (Lepizig, 1866), p. 105.
18. R. von Heine-Geldern, "State and Kingship in Southeast Asia," *Far Eastern Quarterly*, Vol. II (1942), p. 26; Nai Thien, in *Siam Society Selected Articles from the Siam Society Journal*, Vol. V, Part i (Bangkok, 1959), p. 73; Howard Malcom, *Travels in South Eastern Asia embracing . . . a full account of the Burmese Empire*, Vol. I (Boston, 1839), p. 221.
19. *Nanabhivamsadhamma*, p. 21; Maung Htin Aung, *Burmese Law Tales: The Legal Element in Burmese Folklore* (London, 1962), p. 34.
20. E. Sarkisyanz, *Russland und der Messianismus des Orients* (Tubingen, 1955).
21. *Mahā-Sudassanā-Sutta*, I, 3; I, 63: transl. T. W. Rhys Davids, in *SBE*, Vol. XI (1881), pp. 248, 264.
22. *Buddhist Legends*, transl. from the original Pāli text of the Dhammapada Commentary by Eugene Watson Burlingame: *Harvard Oriental Series*, Vol. XXX (Cambridge, U.S.A., 1921), pp. 75, 76.
23. Kyanzittha's Myakan Inscription: *Epigraphia Birmanica*, Vol. II, Part i (1921), pp. 142, 117, 141F.; Vol. I, ii, p. 166.
24. *Hman-nan: Maha Yazawin-togyi:*, Duti-twe (Mandalay, 1319/1957), p. 404.
25. Sangermano, p. 95; H. Cordier, "Les Français en Birmanie au XVIIIe Siècle. Notes et Documents," *T'oung Pao*, Vol. II (1891), p. 13.
26. Tharrawaddy U: Nye Ya Ashin Mya', *Sasana lu-zun: gaun* (Rangoon, 1319/1957), p. 5; J. Gray, *Ancient Proverbs and Maxims from Burmese Sources: or, the Niti Literature of Burma* (London, 1886), pp. 28, 31; Shway Yoe, p. 207.
27. *Epigraphia Birmanica*, Vol. II, Part i, p. 3; Mūga-Pakkha Jātaka: Cowell, *Jātaka*, Vol. VI (London, 1957), pp. 3, 11.
28. *Hitopadeśa of Na'ra'yana*, edited with a Sanskrit commentary, transl. and notes in English by M. R. Ka'le (Bombay, 1924), p. 70; cf. J. Gray, *ibid.*, p. 141, Footnote 46.
29. Mūga-Pakkha Jātaka: Cowell, *Jātaka*, pp. 17, 18; *Anāgatavamsa* ("History of the Future"), text published by J. Minayeff, in *Journal of the Pāli Text Society*, 1886, pp. 41-53, summarized and cited in E. Abegg, *Der Buddha Maitreya*, p. 14f.
30. Sangermano, pp. 56, 59; *Nanabhivamsadhamma*, p. 18.
31. Cf. John Crawfurd, *Journal of an Embassy to the Court of Ava*, Vol. I (London, 1834), p. 268.
32. Hsaun Sayadaw Buddhanda Wepullabhidhaza, *Thaik sa nyun paun* (Meikhtila 1301/1939), pp. 3-6, 69; Zeyawadi Kyaung Sayadaw (U: Wunna), *Kaba lu' la yei: can: lu-tain: hmyo lin nei: -ca-tho Bodha-Yaza Setkya Min: pyi* (Mandalay, 1314/1952), pp. 52, 54, 55.

33. India Office (unpublished MS), India Secret Consultations, Vol. 17: R. Benson's Journal, Paragraphs 1430, 1432, 1437; Vol. 20, Paragraphs 1677, 1678, cited by Desai, *History of British Residency in Burma*, pp. 399f.; H. Yule, *Narrative of the mission . . . to Ava* (London, 1858), p. 227; Adolf Bastian, *Die Völker des östlichen Asien. Studien und Reisen*, Vol. 1 (Leipzig, 1866), p. 150; Vol. II, p. 72.

34. J. George Scott, *Gazetteer of Upper Burma and the Shan States*, Part I, Vol. i (Rangoon, 1900), pp. 119, 139; Part II, Vol. i, pp. 156f., 170, 172, 175; Tha Aung & Maung Mya Din (R. Alexander, editor), "The Pacification of Upper Burma. A vernacular history," in *JBRS*, XXXI, ii (1941), pp. 93f.; Charles Crosthwaite, *The Pacification of Burma* (London, 1912), pp. 70, 99, 117.

35. *Pinnya Alin* of November 15, 1923, p. 9.

36. Cf. Maurice Collis, *Trials in Burma* (London, 1937), pp. 192ff., 273f.; Ba U, *My Burma: The Autobiography of a President* (New York, 1959), p. 109f.; *Origin and causes of the Burma Rebellion*, 1930-1932, p. 10, cited in Akademia Nauk S.S.S.R., Institut Vostokovedeniia, *Birmansii Soiuz. Sbronik statei* (Moscow, 1958), pp. 84f.; G. E. Harvey, *British Rule in Burma* (London, 1946), pp. 73, 74; Great Britain, Parliament, House of Commons, *Sessional Papers*, Vol. XIX for 1931-32 (Cmd. 3991), pp. 135; Great Britain, Parliament, House of Commons, *Debates*, Vol. 252 (March 9, 1932), pp. 1919, Vol. 254 (June 22, 1932), p. 11.

37. R. Spence Hardy, *The British Government and the idolatry of Ceylon* (London, 1941), p. 6.

38. *JMBS*, IX, No. 1 (May, 1900), p. 3; IX, No. 10 (February, 1901), p. 90f.; cf. Ernst Benz, *Buddhas Wiederkehr und die Zukunft Asiens* (München, 1963), p. 42f.; Anagarika Dharmapala, in *MBUBW*, XIII (1904), No. 5/6, p. 45; *MBUBW*, XIII, No. 11/12 (March/April, 1905), p. 86; XIII, No. 5/6 (September/October, 1904), pp. 46, 47; XVII, No. 9 (September, 1909), p. 236; "Christianity and Buddhism," in *MBUBW*, XVII, No. 10 (October, 1909), pp. 255f.

39. Burma, Imperial Idea Committee, *Report of the Committee appointed to ascertain and advise how the Imperial Idea may be inculcated and fostered in . . . Burma* (Rangoon, 1917), p. 53.

40. P. Lakshmi Narasu, *The Essence of Buddhism* (Madras, 1907), pp. 45-46; Alexander David-Neel, *Le modernisme bouddhiste et le bouddhisme du Bouddha* (Paris, 1911), p. 244f.

41. R. C. Majumdar, *Corporate Life in Ancient India* (Calcutta, 1922), p. 319; H. Nakamura, *Ways of Thinking of Eastern Peoples* (Tokyo, 1960), p. 154.

42. *MBUBW*, XII (1933), p. 348.

43. Zeyawadi U Thilasara's article, in *Pinnya Alin* of Waning-Wagaung 1285 (September 1, 1923), transl. by U Wan Nyunt, Rangoon.

44. Thakin Kudaw Hmain, *Thakin-Tīkā* (Rangoon, 1938), p. 181.

45. Thayawadi U: Nye Ya Sayadaw-thi, *Wunthanu Dhamma neyu Padeytha Can:* (Rangoon, 1319/1957 reprint), Vol. I, p. 10.

46. J. Furnivall, *An introduction to the political economy of Burma* (Rangoon, 1957), p. 77; V. D. Wickizer & M. K. Bennett, *The Rice Economy of Monsoon Asia* (Stanford, 1941), p. 216.

47. Shway Yoe, p. 65.

48. Burma, *Report on the Administration of Burma for the year 1930/1931* (Rangoon, 1932), p. 16; *ibid.*, 1932-1933 (Rangoon, 1934), p. iii.

49. Thakin Kudaw Hmain: "Mi'sata Maung Hmain:," (pseud.) *Bain:kau'Tika-gyi:* (Rangoon, 1927); "Mi'sata Maung Hmain," *Myau' Tika* (Rangoon, n.d.); Thakin Kudaw Hmain, *Hkwei: Ganei'hta* (Rangoon, 1298;1936); V. F. Vasil'iev, "Put' k nezanisimosti": Akademiia Nauk S.S.S.R., Institut Vostokovedeniia, *Birmanskii Soiuz. Sbornik statei* (Moscow, 1958), p. 88.

50. Kudaw Hmain, *Thakin Tīkā* (Rangoon, 1938), pp. 163-165.

51. Than Thun, "Hsou-she-li" wa-da hnin Bama yazawin," in U Thain Pe Myin Ywei: hce ti: hpyat-tho, *Hbun-wada hnin Dobama* (Rangoon, 1954), pp. 106ff.

52. Thakin Soe, *Bama-to hla-mu* (Rangoon, 1934), p. 246.

53. Tet Toe, *English-Burmese Dictionary* (Rangoon, 1957), p. 1288.
54. Ba Swe, "Lokka Nibban-te hsau-ne thu Stalin," in U Thein Pe Myin Ywei: (Editor), *Hbun-wada hnin Dobama* (Rangoon, 1954), p. 122.
55. Kudaw Hmain, *Thakin Tīkā* (Rangoon, 1938), p. 181.
56. Maung Nu [U Nu], "Cun-do buthama," in U Thein Pe Myin Ywei: (Editor), *Hbun-wada hnin Dobama* (Rangoon, 1954), pp. 55, 59, 66, 67, 57, 60-63; U Nu, "Man, the Wolf of Men," in *Guardian* (Rangoon), Vol. I, No. 9 (July, 1954), p. 10; Vol. II, No. 2 (December, 1954), p. 21.
57. Interview with Thakin Thein Maung Gyi (Rangoon, July 8, 1959), who will deal with this topic in detail in a forthcoming book of his.
58. Text of the Naga Ni Song as supplied to the writer by courtesy of the Burmese Broadcasting Corporation in November, 1959.
59. Government of the Union of Burma, Ministry of Agriculture, *The Land Nationalization Act, 1948* (Rangoon, 1950), p. 30 (Paragraph 36); p. 27 (Paragraphs 25-26); p. 28 (Paragraphs 28-30); U Nu's speech of October 11, 1948; Tain: pyei pyu Hlu'to (Pali-man), *Myon-ma naingan-to tain: pyei pyu Hlu'to (Pali-man) satamanyi la hkan kma'tan:* Sa-twei 6 - asi: awe: ahma' 30 (1948 khnuni' −O' to-ba la −11 ye') (Rangoon, 1949), p. 1181, Paragraph xxxx; *ibid.*, pp. 1178-1179 (Paragraph xx-xxiv); *ibid.*, p. 1180 (Paragraph xxvii), p. 1180f. Paragraphs xxx, xxi, xxxiii, xxxiv.
60. Thakin Nu-i mein gun: 1950 hku zulain-la −19 ye' a-za-ni nei twin cin: pa-tho lu-du asi: awei: ji mwe' -ca: tho Nain-gan-to Wungyi: hcou Thakin Nu-i mein gun: *Myan-ma Naingan Thadin: zin*, 1312 hku-ni' dutya wa-zou-la.hsan: 13 ye' (27-7-50), ahma' 26, sa-mye' hna 7. Typescript of the Burmese text supplied to the author by courtesy of the Union of Burma Information Department. On the padeytha Tree, cf. U: Po Sein-tyi, *Hpya' -thyi kan-pe hpon: to-gyi: thyi pyin-hnya kahtein can:* (Rangoon, 1252/1890), pp. 295f.; U Nu's speech of June 13, 1948: Thakin Nu, Mein gun: mya: (Rangoon, 1949), p. 108; A. Judson, *Burmese-English Dictionary* (Rangoon, 1953), p. 1004; Aganna Sutta, *Digha Nikāya*, xxvii, 20-21: transl. by Rhys Davids, p. 38.
61. Po Yarzar [U Ba Yin], "Letters to a Communist Nephew. Letter IV," in *The Burmese Review*, December 6, 1948. For the access to post-war files of the "Burmese Review" and "The Burman" I am indebted to Dr. Virginia Thompson-Adloff who permitted me the use of her collection.
62. U: Ba Swe-i, *Bama to hlan yei: hnin Bama lou'tha: lu-du* (Rangoon, 1955), pp. 44-45.
63. Burma, Ministry of Information, *Towards Peace and Democracy*, by Thakin Nu, pp. 55-64; U Nu's speech of December 11, 1949: U Nu, *From Peace to Stability. Transl. of selected speeches* (Rangoon, 1951), pp. 50f., 64.
64. U Nu, *Towards a socialistic state* (Union of Burma, Department of Information: Rangoon, 1958), pp. 42, 43.
65. U Nu's speech delivered on November 16, 1959 before the Training Classes of the Anti-Fascist People's Freedom League's Clean Faction (Burmese typescript kindly given to the author by U Nu, pp. 14, 15, 23, 25, 32, 24; its text was largely reprinted in the *Bama-khit* of November 17, 1959).

Abbreviations

Cowell, *Jātaka*
    E. B. Cowell (Editor), *The Jātaka or stories of the Buddha's former births* (Cambridge, 1895; London, 1957).

Cūlavamsa
    Cūlavamsa, being the more recent part of the Mahāvamsa, transl. by W. Geiger (Colombo, 1953, Parts I, II, III).

Dīgha Nikāya
    Sacred Books of the Buddhists, edited by T. W. Rhys Davids, Vol. IV (London, 1957); *Dialogues of the Buddha*, transl. from the Pāli of the *Digha Nikāya* by T. W. and C. A. F. Rhys Davids, Part III (London, 1957).

Epigraphia Birmanica
    Archeological Survey of Burma, *Epigraphia Birmanica, being lithic and other inscriptions of Burma*, edited by C. Duroiselle, Vol. I, Part ii; Vol. II, Part i (Rangoon, 1920, 1921).

JBRS
   Journal of the Burma Research Society.
JMBS
   Journal of the Maha-Bodhi Society.
MBUBW
   Maha Bodhi and the United Buddhist World.
Nanabhivamsadhamma
   Nanabhivamsadhammasenapāti, *Rājadhirāja Vilāsini*, Vol. 14, edit. and transl. by
   Maung Tin, "Manifestations of the King of Kings," in *JBRS*, IV, No. 1 (1914).
Sangermano
   (Vicente) Sangermano, *A description of the Burmese Empire, compiled chiefly from
   native documents* (Rome, 1833).
SBE
   F. Max Müller (Editor), *Sacred Books of the East* (Oxford).
Shway Yoe
   Shway Yoe [J. G. Scott], *The Burman, his life and notions* (London, 1896).

Sacral Kingship and National Development: The Case of Thailand

Frank E. Reynolds

The Problem

IN MANY traditional societies, both in Europe and Asia, sacral kingship has held a central position in the religious and political order. And in practically all these societies royal ideologies and royal institutions have played an important role in the process through which modernization has taken place. In some cases the established royal traditions and the forces driving toward modernization became so polarized that choices had to be made which resulted in radically anti-royalist revolutions such as those which took place in France in the eighteenth century, and in Russia and China in the twentieth century.[1] However in other areas such as England, and to a much greater extent Japan, religiously valorized royal traditions assumed a much more positive relationship to the forces which were working toward change and, as a result, continued to exert a direct and significant influence in the life of the emerging nation states.

Though traditions of sacral kingship have both positively and negatively influenced the process of national development in a variety of different ways in several different contexts, this fact has seldom attracted the interest of historians of religion or, for the matter, social scientists. Many historians of religion and anthropologists have devoted learned tomes to the study of sacral kingship, but attention has almost exclusively focused on its "primitive" or "archaic" forms.[2] Many other scholars from these and related disciplines have also been interested in religious and political modernization, but their studies have tended to emphasize either the "specifically religious" or the "folk" aspects of religion, thereby obscuring the role which religion has played at the level of civic order, identity, and transformation.[3] The present essay explores some of the issues which arise when the interaction of sacral kingship and national development are taken seriously. This will be done by focusing specifically on the transformation which has taken place in the Buddhist kingdom of Thailand from the period of the first modern intrusions in the early nineteenth century up to the present time.

The Thai Tradition

Within the traditional Thai order, as this had been developed in the kingdoms of Sukothai (ca. 1230–1350), Ayudhya (1350–1767) and Bangkok (1782–   ), the king held a pre-eminent position.[4] Though always considered to be in some sense under the ultimate spiritual hegemony of the Three Jewels of Buddhism — the Buddha, the Dhamma, and the Samgha — he was looked upon as being a Buddha or Bodhisatta for his subjects, as an embodiment of the Dhamma and the one responsible for its implementation within his realm, and as the protector of the Samgha or Buddhist order.[5] In addition, through the great ceremonies which were supervised by the court Brahmans, he became identified with Hindu gods such as Shiva, Vishnu, and Indra, and was invested with the responsibility for regulating the progression of the seasons and the natural powers of fertility and productivity; and through the complex system of court etiquette associated with the Brahmanic tradition his position at the apex of the national and court hierarchies was vividly expressed and confirmed.[6] In addition, it was recognized that he possessed a special relationship to the great tutelary deities of the territory whose favor was considered to be essential to the maintenance and prosperity of the kingdom.[7]

The main function of the king was, of course, to constitute the central pinnacle — the bond between the divine and the human, around and below which the Thai civil order took form. The king was closely associated with the figure of Indra, the great God who ruled in the heavenly realm which was located at the peak of Mount Meru, the central mountain of the Thai Buddhist cosmology.[8] As Indra ruled and maintained the order of Dhamma in his domain, so the Thai monarch was to rule and maintain the order of Dhamma in his earthly kingdom. However it must also be emphasized, though this aspect has not been highlighted in most of the literature on the subject, that this order which the king was responsible for representing and maintaining was conceived in more than static terms. In fact, it was clearly recognized that if the order was to be preserved continuing adaptation had to take place. And it was the king, particularly in his role as the Bodhisatta (and, in a limited sense, the harbinger of the future Buddha Metteya) who was thought to possess the kind of charisma which would generate and justify change.[9] Thus, for example, it was the king whose prerogative it was to make "interpretations" of the Dhammathat (the Dhamma-based "constitution" of the traditional Thai order), so that its relevance to the changing necessities of practical administration could be preserved.[10] The Thai kings were thus in a position, already in pre-modern times, to take the leadership in introducing new innovations and in domesticating new elements which intruded from beyond the limits of the culture itself.

Kingship as a Modernizing Force

Though the traditional pattern of sacral kingship which had been operative in Thailand during the pre-modern period was basically similar to what had existed in the other Theravada kingdoms of Southeast Asia, only in Thailand did the historical situation provide an opportunity for the established dynasty to play a positive role in the process of modernization. In Burma, the British conquest culminated in the destruction of the indigenous regime, whereas in Cambodia and Laos the French conquest resulted in retaining the monarchy as a formal structure without any real capacity for positive action.[11] In Thailand, however, the inner strength of the newly founded Bangkok kingdom, the political and diplomatic skills of the monarchy and aristocracy, and the need of the British and the French for a buffer zone between their respective spheres of influence combined to maintain Thai independence and the continuation of the power of the Chakri dynasty which had established the Bangkok kingdom at the end of the eighteenth century.

Although the story has sometimes been overly romanticized, it is nevertheless true that the kings of the Chakri dynasty did, in fact, provide the primary leadership through which Thailand became a viable nation-state within the context of the modern world.[12] It is true that these monarchs were forced to sponsor both religious and political reforms in order to assure the continued vitality of Buddhism and the preservation of their own hegemony. Also, they were under some pressure from modernizing groups among those segments of the population which had more extensive contacts with the West. The Thai kings demonstrated, however, a readiness to respond to the necessity of reform which has not been typical of traditional rulers in other areas, and, in most instances, were leading the modernist groups, rather than simply responding to pressures those groups brought to bear.[13]

Within the specifically Buddhist context the Thai leader who had the first extensive exposure to the new Western and modernizing influences and began the work of reformulating the traditional religious doctrine and practice was not a king, but a monk. However, he was a monk who was not only a member of the royal family but also the highest ranking prince in the land. In fact, at the death of his father, King Rama II (reigned 1809–1824), he had been the heir apparent, but because of the experience and prestige of his half-brother and his own youth (he was not yet twenty) the half-brother was chosen in his stead. As a result of this delicate political situation the young prince, whose name was Mongkut, decided to remain in the Buddhist monastic order he had temporarily entered just prior to his father's death.[14] During his long career in the Order, which lasted over twenty-five years, he came to be recognized as a kind of "second king" whose status as heir apparent was made obvious; for example, a royal-style dwelling was built for him within the compound of the monastery with which he was associated.[15] In this situation his close proximity to the throne provided a kind of charisma and prestige which contributed to the attention given to his efforts to reinterpret the Buddhist Dhamma (Teaching) in more modern, "rationalistic" terms, and to his success in organizing a group of supporters who helped to implement and spread his program of reform. This group later became organized into a distinctive sect known as the Thammayutika Nikaya.[16]

At the death of his half-brother in 1851, Prince Mongkut was chosen to succeed to the throne and from that point until recent times the dynasty's concern for Buddhist reform and its favor toward the new and modernist Thammayut community has been well known.[17] King Mongkut (d. 1868) and his successors took their responsibility as head of the entire Thai Samgha very seriously. But their obvious personal preference for the Thammayut group and what it stood for, as well as the participation of many members of the royal family within the new sect, contributed greatly to the steady growth of its prestige and influence. During the reign of Mongkut's son, King Chulalongkorn, who ruled from 1868 until 1910, another one of Mongkut's sons who had become his successor as the Thammayut leader was appointed as the Samgharaja (Samgha-king) or head of the national ecclesiastical hierarchy. He, along with other Thammayut leaders, took the primary initiative in the royally sponsored efforts to reorganize and strengthen the national Samgha organization. In fact, from the time King Chulalongkorn appointed Prince Vajiranana to the position of Samgharaja until halfway through the nineteen-thirties, every monk who served in this post was a member of the Thammayut community. Even as late as 1959 the reformed sect, though representing less than five per cent of the membership of the Thai Buddhist Order, held nearly half of the key legislative and executive positions within the national ecclesiastical structure.[18]

Though it is certainly true that royal interest in Buddhism and in Buddhist reform continued from the time of Mongkut forward, it is also the case that the major contribution of his successor, King Chulalongkorn (Rama V), was made in other areas. Building on the kind of spirit established during his father's reign, Chulalongkorn encouraged many younger members of the Thai court and aristocracy to expose themselves to the new trends of secular thought which were developing in the West. He made it possible for many younger noblemen to study in Europe and he encouraged those who could not actually leave the country to become acquainted with the new ways of thought through reading and study. At the same time, he established a training college in Bangkok whereby the new learning could be disseminated and, with the help of other high-placed officials in both the ecclesiastical and secular spheres, implemented an ambitious program of public education through which the new learning could be spread among the people. Before the end of the nineteenth century he went beyond the level of simply encouraging ideological modernization and implemented a vast program of legal and administrative reforms through which the traditional structures of government which had been operative in Thailand since the fifteenth century were replaced with the kind of bureaucratic order necessary for the unification, maintenance and development of a modern nation state. This new system, though continually modified to meet changing conditions, has persisted even through the various "coups" and "revolutions" which have taken place during the intervening decades.[19] What is more, Chulalongkorn gave great encouragement to the kind of social change (e.g., the elimination of the traditional system of corvée labor) and economic enterprise (e.g., the construction of railway transportation between the major areas of the country) which advanced the cause of national development.[20]

In the main stream of Western interpretation, the towering figures of Mongkut and particularly Chulalongkorn have tended to overshadow a third important royal contributor to the modernization process in Thailand, namely Chulalongkorn's son and immediate successor, King Vajirawut (Rama VI) who ruled from 1910 until 1925. While Vajirawut carried forward many of the Buddhist and governmental reforms initiated by his grandfather and father, his own special contribution, which lay in the evocation and nurturing of a new sense of communal self-consciousness and national identity, has often been overlooked. Even in this area, certain important foundations had been laid by his predecessors. For example, Mongkut had discovered and later established in the royal compound in Bangkok a stele on which the greatest ruler of the ancient and powerful Thai kingdom of Sukhothai had set out a kind of charter for an ideal Thai state.[21] To cite a second and closely related example, both Mongkut and Chulalongkorn had encouraged and personally contributed to the development of a modern style of national Thai historiography. It was only during the reign of Vajirawut, however, that the encouragement of a full blown Thai nationalism became a prime concern of the monarch and his associates.

Through his own writings, many of them in popular, poetic form, Vajirawut sought to re-present the stories of the ancient Thai heroes with a special emphasis on Phra Ruang, the semi-historical, semi-legendary founder of the Suko-

thai dynasty, and Chao-U-Thong, the semi-historical, semi-legendary founder
of the Ayudhya dynasty. He sought to glorify the ancient Thai culture, to establish a sense of Thai identity in relation to the Chinese immigrants, who
were becoming recognized as a threat to the Thai order, and to re-evoke the
martial spirit which had been a predominant characteristic of the ancient Thai
but which had been eroded during more recent periods of Thai history.[22] He
continued and developed the emphasis on the ideal character of the ancient
Sukothai kingdom, with its traditions centering around a benevolent and pa-
ternalistic form of kingship, and at the same time sponsored an experiment in
communal living designed to discover and exemplify a distinctively Thai form
of "democracy." Furthermore, he held up the ideal of Thai cultural achievement and power as exemplified in the period when Ayudhya was the dominant
Thai kingdom and one of the most potent political and military forces on the
mainland of Southeast Asia. In the vision which Vajirawut sought to project
and which did, in fact, become an integral aspect of the modern Thai consciousness, the Thai potential for "democracy" (which was at least suggested
by the sacred history associated with Sukothai) and the Thai potential for
power and greatness (which was recognized through the power achieved for a
short period at Sukothai and for many centuries at Ayudhya) were vigorously
affirmed as the ground for a new kind of national self-consciousness which
could provide the basis upon which a modern Thai nation could be built.[23]

To be sure, the role of the Chakri kings in nurturing the modernization
process was in many respects ambiguous. Especially during the reign of King
Vajirawut and his successor, King Prachathipok (Rama VII), who ruled during
the decade from 1925 to 1935, the pace of change increased and the monarchy
maintained something of a middle position between the traditionalists and
those seeking more radical ideological and institutional reforms. Certainly
after the coup d'etat successfully engineered in 1932, the influence of the
monarchy on the actual practice of government was substantially reduced
and, at certain times, almost eliminated. Nevertheless, without the dynasty's
basic and continuing commitment of both its sacral authority and its considerable intellectual and political skills to the cause of modernization, the kind
of gradual, peaceful transition marking Thailand's entrance into the modern
world could not possibly have been achieved.

Modernization and the Transformation of Kingship

Although the Chakri kings gave leadership and direction to the modernization process and hastened its development by committing to it the authority
and prestige derived from their traditional sacrality, the process inevitably
generated a challenge to the religious basis of kingship and to the king's right
to exercise political authority. On the one hand, the modern, essentially rationalistic world view tended to undercut the cosmological and hierarchical
orientation which had been fundamental to the traditional Buddhist, Hindu
and indigenous conceptions of the royal charisma.[24] On the other hand, the
conceptions of democracy and the values expressed in modern forms of constitutional polity gave the emerging bureaucratic elite a justification for challenging the king's right to rule. However, at least partly because of the way in
which the Chakri kings had used their traditional authority and their flexibility in the face of changing conditions, the challenges to their position resulted

not in the demise of the institution of sacral kingship, but rather in its transformation.

At the outset it is important to recognize that, despite the inroads made by new ways of thinking introduced from the West, the old cosmological conceptions and the forms in which they were expressed were never really abandoned. For example, King Mongkut, who strongly opposed the "Brahmanic" and "superstitious" elements which had, from his perspective, infiltrated and perverted the original, pure Buddhism, at the same time not only participated in the royal rituals but actually reinstituted certain Brahmanic forms which had been neglected by his predecessors.[25] To be sure, during the reigns of his successors these rituals were gradually toned down and declined in importance; the conception of the king's divinity and the taboos associated with his person were modified; and, the extravagance and rigidity of the court etiquette which had expressed and reinforced the hierarchical aspect of the traditional order were steadily ameliorated.[26] However, the older conceptions and the forms through which these conceptions were expressed continued to play a significant role among many segments of the population.

Moreover, there is convincing testimony that in spite of the erosion which obviously occurred, the cosmological, hierarchical perspective continues even today to exert a significant, albeit often hidden, influence. For example, in the specifically royal context, the Thai newspapers recently reported that King Phumipol, the present reigning monarch, was in the process of presenting a specially cast Buddha image to each province within the kingdom and that each image was to be placed in a prominent position in the capital of the province to which it was given.[27] Thus, in twentieth century Thailand the reigning Chakri king was performing an act directly reminiscent of the legendary activity of the great King Asoka of India (reigned third century B..C.) who is believed to have accomplished the simultaneous construction of 84,000 stupas spread throughout his kingdom.[28] His action also calls to mind those actions of Jayavarman VII, the great Buddhist king who ruled during the late twelfth and early thirteenth centuries at the Khmer (Cambodian) capital of Angkor, who had a self-portrait in the form of a Buddha image established in the royal temple he had constructed (the Bayon), with duplicate images distributed to the various provincial centers over which he ruled.[29]

On a rather different level, S. J. Tambiah, in an important anthropological study published in 1970, attests to the fact that the conception of a cosmological order expressed according to the traditional and hierarchical Buddhist mode still remains a living and vital aspect of Thai religion at the village level where, as is well known, the king's sacrality is taken with the greatest seriousness.[30] At the same time another anthropologist, Lucien Hanks, has written a short but classic study entitled "Merit and Power in the Thai Social Order," in which he argues convincingly that the conception of a hierarchical cosmic and social order in which the king stands at the apex and in which merit (in the Buddhist sense of *boon*) ultimately determines the position of the individual, still provides the implicit ideological framework upon which Thai society and Thai politics actually function.[31] In other words, in spite of the impact of modern ideas and ideologies, the deeply ingrained sense of cosmological order, and its role as a context within which royal authority has meaning, remains an important factor both in the villages and in Thai national life.

At the same time, however, the persistence of sacral kingship in Thailand, and the form it has assumed in more recent years, can only be understood by recognizing the crucial importance attached to the king's role as the embodiment and bearer of the distinctively Thai tradition. In fact, many of the king's roles and prerogatives which, in pre-modern times, were primarily associated with his status in the cosmologically grounded order, and which may still be primarily associated with his status in such an order by certain segments of the population, are now accepted and honored by more modernized Thai on the basis of their association with the sacred heritage of the nation. Moreover, the kingship, partly as a result of the achievements of the earlier Chakri monarchs, has come to represent for many citizens all that is sacred and valued in Thai culture and history. Much of the charisma of the later Chakri kings has thus been derived from the fact that they have come to symbolize and focus that sense of national identity and spirit their predecessors had worked, with considerable effectiveness, to evoke and nurture.

Despite the importance of recognizing the persistence of the charisma grounded in the ancient cosmological orientation, and the importance of taking into account the gradually increasing emphasis on a charisma grounded in a basically historical, nationalistic perspective, it is clear that the most dramatic factor in the modern transformation of Thai kingship was the coup d'etat of 1932, with its subsequent establishment of a new form of constitutional monarchy.[32] Actually, the Chakri kings from the time of Mongkut had recognized the necessity for broadening the base of political power and responsibility and had gradually taken steps to foster such a development. As already noted, King Vajirawut had sponsored an intriguing experimental community in the capital in order to explore the possibility of a specifically Thai expression of democracy. His successor, King Prachathipok, was engaged in formulating his own plans for instituting a new modernized constitution when, before taking the actual step, a group of high and middle ranking leaders in the army and civil service staged a coup d'etat and established a new regime according to their own design. Still, in spite of the fact that the way had been prepared by the kings themselves, the establishment of the new order brought about a significant change in the nature of the royal office and the charisma associated with it.

In the new context the king's role was once removed from the exercise of actual political power. He retained his function as the symbolic embodiment of the national tradition and the state, and both his symbolic position as Protector of Buddhism and his authority to appoint the heads of the hierarchy which regulates the affairs of the Buddhist monastic community. However, the actual power to govern and regulate the society was now in the hands of the coup group, the ministers whom it placed in office, and the Parliament which it supported and to a large extent controlled.[33] The king thus served as the legitimizing symbol of a government wherein the coup group and the Parliament, along with the military and civilian bureaucracies, competed for authority and continued the struggle for national development. During the remainder of the 1930s and the years of the second world war the monarchy remained very much in the background; King Prachathipok was not endowed with a strong personality and, following his abdication in 1935, the royal functions were taken over by a regency whose capacity for action was inevitably quite limited.[34]

During the post-war decades the situation remained very much the same.

The monarchy continued to serve an absolutely essential function as a unifying national symbol, but its actual involvement in the governing process was quite minimal. Immediately following the war the possibility that royal activity might once again become a significant factor in the specifically political arena developed when Prachathipok's nephew and successor, King Ananda (Rama VIII) reached his maturity. However, the much discussed possibility that this young, energetic and personally popular king might put the charisma which was still a very obvious aspect of the royal office to use in directly influencing the affairs of the state was summarily cut off when he was killed in a shooting incident or assassination which still today remains deeply shrouded in mystery. The result of this sudden turn of events was the succession of his brother, the present King Phumipol (Rama IX), who was not prepared, either by training or by temperament, to take the kind of initiative many had expected from the much more dynamic and outgoing Ananda. Thus the vitally important but almost exclusively symbolic and formal role which the monarchy had played since the coup of 1932 remained basically unaltered.

The Dynasty Today: Trends and Prospects

Since the early years of King Phumipol's reign important changes have taken place in his own personal maturity and style, in the rapport between himself and his subjects, and in his relationship to the national life of the country. During the more than twenty-five years since the time of his coronation the young monarch has become more accustomed to his role, and appears to have gained a kind of composure and bearing which is fully commensurate with his office. Through his own activities and tours throughout the countryside, and through similar activities and tours undertaken by his extremely attractive and capable wife, Queen Sirikit, he has gradually built a large reservoir of popularity and affection both among a significant number of intellectuals and students, and in the villages as well. At the same time, his role as a center of national self-consciousness and identity has been brought increasingly into the foreground, especially since the coup d'etat led by Field Marshall Sarit Thanarat in 1958 (the present Thai regime is in direct continuity with the one established by Sarit).

This increasing confidence, popularity and public role of King Phumipol has not, however, resulted in any basic deviation from the essentially symbolic and supra-political posture which has characterized the monarchy since 1932. And yet, it has established a situation in which a real possibility exists for the king to exert once again a more active and direct influence upon the affairs of the nation. As a result, the matter has become a focal point for many Thai who are struggling, in the midst of an increasingly critical international and internal situation, to maintain the integrity of the nation and to accelerate its political, economic and social development. On the one hand, many astute observers believe that the monarchy can retain its aura of great sacrality and the obvious popularity it now enjoys only by remaining uninvolved in controversial issues, and that in so doing it will best serve the Thai religion, the Thai state, and the Thai people. On the other side, there are those who believe, with at least equal fervor, that the monarchy must not be content simply to legitimate a rather unsatisfactory status quo, and that it has a unique opportunity to become once again the center for the expression of a self-conscious, Buddhist oriented civic tradition which could serve both as a conscience and stimulus for those engaged in the day to day tasks of government and nation-building. Finally, there are at least some Thai who now look to the monarchy to exert a still more direct kind of influence, believing that the charisma which the king possesses puts him in a unique position to foster a variety of urgently needed governmental and social reforms.

It is, of course, impossible to predict which course the present king will follow, much less to determine the effects which any of these modes of action might actually bring about. There are few other nations in the modern world, however, where a reigning monarch possesses the degree of institutional and personal charisma which is presently associated with King Phumipol, and where the actions of such a monarch have a greater potential for affecting, for good or for ill, the religious and political life of a modernizing nation.[35]

Notes

This article was originally published in March, 1973, seven months before the student uprising of October, 1973, in *Tradition and Change in Theravada Buddhism: Essays on Ceylon and Thailand in the 19th and 20th Centuries* (Leiden: E. J. Brill, 1973), edited by Bardwell L. Smith, in *Contributions to Asian Studies*, Vol. 4, Reprinted with permission.

1. It should be noted that even in these situations symbols and themes drawn from the royal tradition have often reappeared in the new, "revolutionary" contexts.

2. For an example of this emphasis, see *Proceedings of the VIIth International Congress of the History of Religions* which is devoted entirely to the subject of *Sacral Kingship* (Leiden: E. J. Brill, 1959).

3. An exception is to be found in David Apter's essay on "Political Religion and Modernization" in Clifford Geertz, ed., *Old Societies and New Nations* (Glencoe, Ill.: Free Press, 1963). However, the usefulness of this essay is limited by the questionable adequacy of the categories which are employed.

4. A fuller discussion of the role of the king in the Thai order is contained in Frank Reynolds, "Buddhism and Sacral Kingship — A Study in the History of Thai Religion" (Unpublished dissertation, University of Chicago, 1971).

5. The Buddhist heritage which was continued in this Thai tradition is discussed in Frank Reynolds, "The Two Wheels of Dhamma," and Bardwell L. Smith, "The Ideal Social Order as Portrayed in the Chronicles of Ceylon," both of which are included in Bardwell L. Smith, ed., *The Two Wheels of Dhamma: Essay on the Theravada Tradition in India and Ceylon*, American Academy of Religion Studies in Religion, Number Three, 1972.

6. The Brahmanic aspects are discussed in detail in H. G. Quaritch Wales, *Siamese State Ceremonies* (London: Bernard Quaritch, 1931).

7. See the discussions in Frank Reynolds, "The Holy Emerald Jewel" in the present collection.

8. For a description of the Thai Buddhist cosmology, see King Li Thai, *Trai Phum Phra Ruang* (Bangkok: Sueksapan Panit, 1963).

9. The innovative role attributed to the Bodhisatta king in the Theravada tradition is already expressed in the fifth century by the great scholastic systematizer Buddhagosha; see his *Path of Purification*, tr. by Bhikku Nanamoli, Part II, Chap. XIII, p. 54.

10. For an extended discussion of the Dhammathat tradition and the role of the king as interpreter and adaptor, see Robert Lingat, "Evolution of the Conception of Law in Burma and Siam" (*Journal of the Siam Society*, Vol. XXXVIII, Part I, 1950).

11. The very different situation which developed in Burma has been discussed in detail in Emmanuel Sarkisyanz, *Buddhist Backgrounds of the Burmese Revolution*, with a preface by Paul Mus (The Hague: Martinus Nijhoff, 1965), while the Laotian situation has been described by Frank Reynolds in "Ritual and Social Hierarchy: An Aspect of Traditional Religion in Buddhist Laos," in the *History of Religions Journal*, Vol. IX, No. 1 (August, 1969), reprinted in a subsequent chapter in this collection. Further comparative comments

are included in Frank Reynolds and Joseph Kitagawa, "Theravada Buddhism in the Twentieth Century," in Heinrich Dumoulin, ed., *Buddhism and the Modern World* (New York: Macmillan, 1976).

12. One of the more romanticized accounts can be found in Chula Chakrabongse, *Lords of Life* (London: Alvin Redman, 1960).

13. For an account of one aspect of the modernizing process in which the role of the king is portrayed in a vivid and balanced way, see David Kent Wyatt, *The Politics of Reformation in Thailand: Education in the Reign of King Chulalongkorn* (New Haven: Yale University Press, 1969).

14. It was the custom for young men to enter the order for one three-month period in their early adulthood; since the monastic vows were not permanent, men in Thailand could enter and leave the monastery at various times in the course of their life.

15. Robert Lingat, "History of Wat Pavaranaveca," *Journal of the Siam Society*, XXVI, Part I (1933), pp. 73-102.

16. According to Kenneth Wells, *Thai Buddhism: Its Rites and Activities* (2nd ed. Bangkok: The Christian Book Store, 1960), p. 14, the establishment of the sect as such took place in 1892.

17. See Craig J. Reynolds, "The Buddhist Monkhood in Nineteenth Century Thailand," Unpublished Ph.D. dissertation, Cornell University, 1973.

18. Wells, *Thai Buddhism*, p. 15.

19. A number of studies have described the governmental reform carried out under Chulalongkorn's leadership. See, for example, Walter Vella, *The Impact of the West on Government in Thailand* (Berkeley: University of California Press, 1955); Fred Riggs, *Thailand: The Modernization of a Bureaucratic Polity* (Honolulu: East-West Center, 1966); and William Siffen, *The Thai Bureaucracy: Institutional Change and Development* (Honolulu: East-West Center, 1966).

20. For a basic discussion, see James Ingram, *Economic Change in Thailand Since 1850* (Stanford: Stanford University Press, 1955).

21. A translation of the main body of this important inscription is included in P. Schweisguth, *Étude sur la Littérature Siamoise* (Paris: Adrien Maisonneuve, 1951), pp. 30-32.

22. This emphasis on the recovery of the old martial spirit in Vajirawut's court is vividly portrayed in a sermon delivered to him by the Samghaiaja, Piince Vajiianana, which Vajirawut himself translated into English. See Vajiranana, *The Buddhist Attitude Toward Defence and National Administration* (Bangkok: n.p., 1916).

23. For a further discussion of the background and expression of these two themes or ideals as they appear in Thai historiography, see my "Sasana kong Phonlamuang Thai" (Civic Religion in Thai Society) in the felicitation volume for Prince Wan Waithayakorn published in the fall 1971 issue of the *Social Science Review* (Bangkok).

24. See, for example, the statement of a "Modern Buddhist" in Henry Alabaster, *The Wheel of the Law. Buddhism Illustrated from Siamese Sources: The Modern Buddhist, A Life of the Buddha, and an Account of Prabat* (London: Trubner, 1871).

25. In his reformist polemics, King Mongkut went so far as to challenge the scriptural fundamentalism of the Theravada tradition and to seek, within the canon, the pure Buddhism of the founder. See Alexander B. Griswold, *King Mongkut of Siam* (New York: Asia Society, 1961), pp. 13-26. Also compare Guenter Lanczkowski, "Das sogenannte Religionsgesprache des Konigs Mongkut," in *Saeculum: Jahrbuch fur Universalgeschichte*, XVII (1966), pp. 119-130.

26. For references to King Mongkut's actions in regard to the royal court and rituals, see Wales, *Siamese State Ceremonies*, passim.

27. *Prachathipatai*, May 18, 1970, p. 9. I am indebted to Mr. Koson Srisang for referring me to this report.

28. For a full discussion of the beginnings of the Asoka legend, see Jean Przyluski, *La Legende de l'Empereur Açoka (Açoka-Avadana) dans les textes indiens et chinois*, (Paris: Paul Guethner, 1923).

29. For a full discussion of the background and meaning of Jayavarman's action, see George Coedès, *Pour Mieux Comprendre Angkor* (2nd rev. ed., Paris: Bibliotheque de Diffusion of the Musée Guimet, Tome LV, 1947).

30. *Buddhism and Spirit Cults in North-east Thailand* (Cambridge: Cambridge University, 1970).

31. *American Anthropologist*, Vol. LXIV, 1962.

32. Although it deals with the subject from a strictly political science point of view, the best discussion of the coup and subsequent political developments in English is still found in David A. Wilson, *Politics in Thailand* (Ithaca: Cornell University Press, 1962).

33. For a most interesting and insightful discussion of the predominant role of the *khana* or coup group, see Wilson, *Politics in Thailand*, esp. pp. 246-252.

34. It is, however, interesting to note that during the wartime period when the government had allied itself with the Japanese, Pridi Phanomyang, who was acting regent, headed the Free Thai Movement which gave a kind of balance to the Thai posture and thus made the position of the country much more favorable when the Japanese were ultimately defeated.

35. This article was completed in May, 1973, and published just prior to the "October Uprising" in which King Phumipol did, in fact, play a crucial role. For a discussion which takes account of the king's activity in the crisis, see the following essay on "Legitimation and Rebellion."

Sangha and Polity in Modern Thailand: An Overview

S. J. Tambiah

MOST OF MY fieldwork in Thailand, especially in the early sixties, was done in certain villages in the Northeast, North and the Central Plain; and it became clear to me, especially when I was writing *Buddhism and the Spirit Cults in Northeast Thailand*, that my view of Thai religion and society was a projection outwards from the village. I resolved that some day I would attempt a macrocosmic study of religion's connection with Thai society as a whole, particularly in its aspect as a polity.

I already knew that many of the ablest and learning-oriented monks and novices left their village *wat* to go to the metropolis where they lived in the great monasteries of the kingdom, and were invested with ecclesiastical titles and even hob-nobbed with the high and mighty. Thus it was self-evident that if I wanted to study how kingship and Buddhism interrelated, how religion and politics informed each other, I should have to manage a panoramic view of the society from a vantage point high above the dominating metropolis of Bangkok. I began work on this vast topic in 1971, and I shall attempt here to give a thumbnail sketch of some of my findings. These findings are grounded in facts collected from many and diverse sources, but I shall in this overview mention only those sources from which I quote directly.

The Distinctiveness of Thailand

First, let me say a few words on what is distinctive, or perhaps unique, about Thai society — since its distinctiveness certainly has implications for the way religion and politics are interwoven.

Historically, Thailand is the only country in Southeastern Asia that was not subject to Western colonial conquest and domination; this implies a certain continuity of civilization and, therefore, the persistence of certain patterns that other Southeast Asian politics have irrevocably lost.

This historical intactness is linked with another pattern, which is absorbing to the comparativist. It consists of the distinctive mix between Buddhism, *Sangha*, kingship and polity — which terms together traditionally constituted the totality we may call the Buddhist Polity. To resort to a simplification, we can say that the totality of Buddhist Polity had three constituents: (1) Religion (*sāsana*), i.e., Buddhism characterized in terms of the three jewels, Buddha, Dhamma and Sangha; (2) Kingship which was stressed in terms of such idealizations as the righteous ruler (Dharmarāja), the Buddha-to-be (Bodhisattva) and the wheel-rolling emperor (Cakkavatti); and (3) a "people" — the Sinhalese, the Mons, the Burmese, the Thai, and so on — who received their stamp in terms of the above two features, and whose historical destiny was considered to be their preservation. This concept of a people with a historical conservationist destiny had other components as well — ethnic, linguistic, cultural — which were fused with the religio-political ideas. Hence the Theravada Buddhist polities saw themselves on the one hand as being related by virtue of relating themselves to a single Pāli canonical tradition (and by mutual exchanges of the pure texts, and common maintenance of pure ordination lineages), and on the other as different historical totalizations and particularized entities. One sees with clarity this dual theme in the famous chronicles — the *Mahāvamsa* and *Cūlavamsa* of the Sinhalese, the *Jinakālamāli* and the *Cāmadevīvamsa* of the Northern Thai Lanna Kingdom, the *Nidāna Arambhakathā* of the Mons.

My central thesis is that the strain to identify the Buddhist religion with the polity, and the Buddhist polity in turn with the society were deep structure tendencies in the Buddhist kingdoms of Southeast Asia, and that they are more intact in Thailand today than in any other Southeast Asian Buddhist country. It is clear that these tendencies not only show a great continuity through time in Thailand but also inform present-day events.

Before I deal with Thailand, however, I must first indicate how distinctive historically is the mix which I have called the Buddhist polity. To do this I have to go back to early Buddhism in India, and to the time of Emperor Asoka in the third century B.C. The distinctiveness of the mix can be expressed by the proposition that the Buddhist scheme is a transformation of the classical Brahmanical scheme of the relation between *dharma* and *artha,* morality/ righteousness and power, priest and warrior/ruler. I dub this transformation: from *rājadharma* to *dharmarāja.*

From Rājadharma to Dharmarāja

The classical Brahmanical scheme as formulated in the Dharmashāstras requires no detailed recounting. The postulated relation between *dharma* and *artha* is as follows: the Brahmin as expounder and representative of moral law (*dharma*) is eminently situated in the world and legitimates *artha* (instrumental action) as practiced by the *kshatriya.* (*Artha* is the subject matter of Kautalya's *Arthashāstra* and is best translated as covering some features of the domain of "political economy" (as both Adam Smith and Marx would have viewed it). The Kshatriya king implements dharma through the exercise of force (*danda*); his role, described as the practice of *rājadharma* (the whole duty of the king) takes its ranked place in a larger hierarchy of *varna* values. As Dumont has asserted (1970), in the Hindu scheme the world renouncer, *sannyāsin,* is the only true individual who must go outside of Hindu society to pursue his goal.

Now in the Buddhist scheme, the king fills the religio-political space in the world as the representative, embodiment and implementor of dharma — he becomes *dharmarāja* in whom are united both dharma and artha. The Brahmin is either eliminated or is made a subordinate court functionary and a diviniser of the king. The renouncer's religion, as practiced by the institutionalized order of monks (*Sangha*), has a special relation to King and polity. The king as *mahāpurusha* (the great man) ordinates the polity in a morally righteous way. The Sangha as monastic order is situated both inside and outside society in that only a prosperous and virtuous society can set apart, protect and minister to the Sangha, outside society in that the monk's deliverance quest is focused on extra-societal concerns. The king and the polity protect Buddhism and succour it (hence the expression that the king is the protector of the Sangha and the sāsana), but the virtuosi of that religion ideally seek their goals outside it.

This Buddhist formula of the relation between the world renouncer's Sangha and the polity whose corner-stone was the king was already in evidence in the writings of early Buddhism and probably found its realization in the Asokan age. (Incidentally, this observation plus other evidence make Dumont's thesis regarding the renouncer in Indian society only a partially correct one; or rather correct with respect to Hindu society and incorrect in so far as it cannot adequately explain the role of Buddhism in India's most illustrious "empire" as well as certain other principalities.)

Early Buddhism forged a grand conception of the polity as ordered through kingship and imbued with certain Buddhist values. Indeed, early Buddhism had already allied itself with a new conception of kingship and polity, which found its crystallization and elaboration outside India, in Sri Lanka, Mon Burma, and so on. The Buddhist conception is already expressed in the Pāli canon — e.g., in the *Mahāpadāna Suttanta, Lakkahana Sutta, Cakkavattisīhanāda Sutta*. And, what the *Aggañña Suttanta*, the Buddhist myth of genesis, asserts is the twinship and the yoking together of the *bhikkhu* and king, of religion and polity: while the king is the organizing term, the mediator between social disorder and order, the *bhikkhu*, whose origin is in society, mediates between this world of fetters and the state of deliverance. And, if we may allude to a non-canonical, non-Theravada, but early text, Vasubandhu's *Abhidharmakośa* had already constructed the intricacies of the Buddhist social reality and "receptacle world" as the emergent pattern ensuing from the mass of individual *karmic* acts, a pattern that constituted *dharma* as the sovereign moral and cosmic law, and which at a certain level is realized in kingship as the ordinating principle.

The Galactic Polity: the Paradox of Divine Kingship and Perennial Rebellion

Now we must see how the rhetoric of moral and religious conceptions find their implementation and realization in historical circumstances.

The misapprehension is common that the *cakkavatti* concept stands for some absolutist imperial power, when in fact the picture it conjures is that of a king of kings, presiding over lesser kings and their relatively autonomous principalities, who in turn encompass even lesser entities. In other words, the model is that of a center-oriented *mandala*. In actual fact, the historical Buddhist kingdoms are best described in terms of the *mandala* or galactic pattern.

The galactic polity is an apt designation for the Thai kingdoms extending from the fourteenth century Sukhothai era through the Ayutthayan Period (fifteenth to mid-eighteenth centuries) to the early Bangkok era, although in size and scale of the kingdoms and in the degree of centralization and details of administrative organization there were important shifts.

The central features of the traditional galactic polity in Southeast Asia, both Buddhist and otherwise, were as follows as gleaned from many sources:

(a) The political constellations are usually represented as a three concentric circle system: the king at the center in immediate control of the royal domain, provinces ruled by royal princes surrounding it, and at the outer limit tributary or vassal states ruled by traditional rulers or chiefs.

(b) Typically all the political units, though of different sizes, duplicate one another in structure: thus we have the dominant principality, surrounded by smaller principalities which in turn have their satellites. Each political entity is a reproduction of that which encompasses it but on a smaller scale.

(c) The principle of replication on a smaller scale which structures the polity's territorial arrangement finds its counterpart in the principle of bipartition and duplicating of similar units in the administrative system: "departments" are balanced, they replicate each other's functions and organs, and internally, they bipartition into alike units. This administrative involution, like the territorial system of satellites, is rooted in a system of socio-political relations wherein a leader is surrounded by his followers, and circles of leaders and their followers of increasing scale encompass the lesser and build up into a system of competing factions.

(d) The whole galactic polity is held together as a cosmological system: by the king's enactment of cosmic rites and his role as the validator of his satellites' credentials. The system is characterized more by tributary relationships than by a firm exercise of fiscal and judicial control. The imposition of corvée for public tasks was irregular and spasmodic; mobilization for warfare was equally spasmodic and wars were fought for plunder and slaves. The center "holds" its outlying parts more through the king's harem (whose women are presented by the chiefs and nobles), the corps of royal pages (sons of the aristocrats and nobles), the king's own representatives in the provinces, and such like, rather than by direct partimonial control.

(e) Thus the galactic polity was modulated by pulsating alliances, shifting territorial control, frequent rebellions and succession disputes. It is precisely because there were perennial usurpations and unstable reigns that kingship was sought to be buttressed by an elaborate ritual, and kings retroactively tried to prove their "royal" genealogy. The pulsating polity implies expansions and shrinkages of political constellations, with certain strong kings attaining to the strongest modality of the traditional polity and the weak ones opening the floodgates of chaos and disorder. And, in this context, it is better to think of the capital and its palace as having not so much a surrounding circumference of defined and demarcated borders but as being the centers of areas of diminishing control on the analogy of a field of radiation spreading outwards from a light source.

The Sangha and the Polity: The Traditional Relation

Now if the pulsating galactic polity was the actual reality, then in the Buddhist kingdoms — whose distinctive feature was the overarching conception which yoked the Sangha and kingship together in a mutual relation — the fluidity of politics must have had a varying impact on the fortunes of the Sangha. We can speak of this varying relation by employing three concepts — the *normative* formulation, the *normal* relation and the *abnormal* situation.

The ideal or normative relation between the Sangha and the polity is one of complementarity: the king is said to be the patron and protector of sāsana, and the sāsana in turn is the special treasure of the polity and a marker of its legitimacy.

But the formula of complementarity is not unambiguous and holds within itself the germ of a problem. On the one hand, the Sangha and the political authority were separate domains. The king had no specially endowed competence to pronounce on doctrinal matters relating to the salvation quest (though he could and did sponsor the revision of texts, etc.); on the other hand, though monasteries were said to enjoy immunity in their internal matters, yet the king was authorized to intervene in extreme circumstances both to protect and to "purify" the religion. This implies the penetration of the political authority into what is called the "disciplinary" aspect of the Sangha, and even into matters of doctrinal orthodoxy.

Now the king's duty to protect the religion from external invasion and internal civilian disorder is not problematic to grasp. One notes how often in Sri Lanka, Burma, or Siam, invasion by the enemy (who may himself be Buddhist or otherwise) meant the looting of temples and the dispersion of the monks. The following excerpt from an edict promulgated in 1810 by King Rama II in the first year of his reign is forceful, blunt, and informative:

> It has been the custom of kings from old times to preserve the Buddhist religion and to further its prosperity. The way of doing this was by keeping cohorts of good soldiers to form an army, and by the accumulations of weapons, with the royal power at the head. Thereby he vanquished all his enemies in warfare, and he prevented the Buddhist religion from being endangered by the enemy, as kings have always done.

But the king's right to "purify" the religion was usually exercised in circumstances of alleged monastic abuse and degeneracy; "purification" was no doubt sometimes necessitated by abuses generated from within the ranks of the Sangha, but it also was seen as warranted by monks' involvement in the politics of royal succession. Thus, in one way or another, monks were found not to live according to the *vinaya* rules, and the guaranteeing of their disciplinary purity was accepted as part and parcel of the king's competence as *dharmaraja*.

This was the normative formulation of the relation between king and Sangha. What was their relation in both normal and abnormal circumstances?

The normal situation in the traditional galactic polity was that both the polity and the monastic order were not tightly-knit hierarchical structures at all, but were decentralized constellations. In actuality, then, their interpenetration was not close.

But in abnormal circumstances their relation changed in two directions: when a particular king did come to exercise strong power and his kingdom expanded and waxed strong, when he won wars, booty, and prisoners, and when he made attempts at a greater centralization of power, under such a king the Sangha too was built up as an ecclesiastical hierarchy and enjoyed royal liberality. But this resulted in the paradox that the Sangha that was organizationally strengthened was also thereby politically regulated. Conversely, when a king was weak and his rule crumbling, this erosion of political authority meant also the loss of political protection and supervision of the monasteries, resulting in their decline. Witness the revival of *upasampada* ordination at the beginning of many a reign after a period of political collapse.

Hence we must postulate a pulsating relationship between the polity and the Sangha as being representative of traditional times. Political oscillations of short-lived kingdoms, some of which were more vigorous and sturdy than the rest, were paralleled by the prospering and decline of monastic institutions.

Our next thesis is that this pulsation was to change drastically in nineteenth century Thailand into a linear pattern. The Chakkri dynasty established itself in Bangkok, and under them the kingdom became steadily stronger and larger and its political authority more powerful than ever before; correspondingly, the Sangha too attained a centralization and hierarchization hitherto unknown.

The Impact of Colonialism: Linear Change and Political Stabilization

The impact of colonialism on Thailand was double-edged in a special kind of way as compared with the fortunes of those principalities which went under: Burma, Malaysia, Indonesia, Cambodia, Laos, and the others.

On the one hand, although Thailand was not directly colonized, its economy came to have all the familiar features of a colonial economy: exporter of primary products like rice and tea and minerals like tin, low industrialization, and over 80 percent of the population peasants. But, on the other hand, the colonial impact did result in an expansion of the economy. The Bowring Treaty of 1855 by which Thailand's doors were opened for free trade led to an expansion in rice agriculture, colonization of new lands, increased rice exports, growth of commerce (especially in Chinese hands). Progressively, there was also a shift from corvée to wage labor for carrying out state projects (e.g., canal building) — a shift made possible by the influx of cheap immigrant Chinese labor.

Most importantly, the ever-present challenge of the British and French, who were rapidly colonizing adjacent territories, combined with the access to economic resources (through taxation of exports and other fiscal policies) on a scale never before experienced, both compelled and enabled the Thai kings to introduce certain features of provincial and central administrative reorganization and "modernization" in order to stave off the challenge, initiate "progress" and achieve a greater national integration.

The era of Mongkut and Chulalongkorn from 1851 to 1910 was in actual fact one of limited modernization, increased patrimonial bureaucratization combined with enlarged royal absolutism. Never before did the ceremonies of kingship reach such an elaboration as this era; at the same time, never before did the kings exercise effective power as during this era. Thus, as the pool of economic resources expanded, so did the pool of power to be exercised; and correspondingly the ritual elaboration of kingship also took place. Thus we may conclude that the colonial impact on Thailand in the nineteenth and early twentieth centuries produced a linear change from a galactic polity to a polity in which the king and his princely ministers and appointed agents had achieved a greater control over the country, which was dominated by a single primate city and its elite. We may call this polity a radial polity.

Political Stabilization and the Increased Regulation of the Sangha

This process of political stabilization and transformation had two prominent impacts on the Sangha and its organization and practices:

(1) It resulted in periodic purifications of religion and the Sangha on diverse fronts.

(2) On an increasing scale and as an irreversible process, it instituted a hierarchical and politically regulated system of ecclesiastical administration paralleling the civil administration.

I shall dwell only briefly here with the issue of purification and reform of religion in the nineteenth century because we shall return to it as a trend that also informs contemporary events in Thailand. Rama I, the founder of the Chakkri dynasty in 1782, and Mongkut (Rama IV), the princely monk who later became king in 1851, are good examples of royal sponsors of purification of religion. From their acts we learn two lessons: (1) that purification of the Sangha is a recurrent act that is as intimately linked with political necessity as with religious zeal — that is, the cleaning up of the Sangha helps to inaugurate, mark and legitimate a new king, as was the case with Rama I who, whatever his private proclivities, was intensely conscious as the first of a new line of kings of the propriety of being an orthodox Buddhist king; (2) — and this is perhaps a more interesting lesson — that while purification measures seek a sanction in the past ("this is what kings ought to do"), in the Malinowskian sense of charter, they also smuggle in innovations which do not have precedents in the past but which are nevertheless justified in the name of the past. Thus the past as sanction does not exclude innovation, because innovation itself is presented as embodying the spirit and aims of the pristine model.

Let us give supporting evidence. In the case of Rama I some of his first acts were the purification of the Sangha, the sponsorship of a revised canon, and the rewriting of the legal code. He found it necessary to purify and reorganize the Sangha after the ravages of the Burmese wars which destroyed the Ayutthaya kingdom, and, more immediately, after the disputes and dissensions created within the Sangha by the intemperate claims (of being a "stream winner") of King Taksin. It is suggestive that Rama I found it necessary to expel or demote monks who were "unworthy" of the elevation to high positions they received from his predecessor, and to elevate others who he considered had suffered at his hands. Moreover, it appears as if the "purification" of the Sangha was generated by a deep concern deriving from his position as king and protector of Buddhism. On the one hand, it looks as though the king's regulation of the Sangha and ensuring its loyalty were a political necessity, and on the other, the Sangha, if unregulated, threatened to disintegrate in a weak political environment.

During the first two years after his ascension to the throne Rama I issued seven decrees concerning the Buddhist monks in Thailand. Their purpose was to raise the moral level of this class and to restore its prestige and authority. In addition, one more law was passed in each of the following years, 1789, 1794 and 1801. The last law, the tenth, expelled 128 monks from the Buddhist clergy and condemned them to hard labor for "they had been guilty of all kinds of ignoble behaviour, namely drinking, wandering about at night, rubbing shoulders with women, using improper language, buying silly things from Chinese junks" (Wenk, 1968, p. 39).

Another act of Rama I's which is illustrative of our thesis is his causing the existing legal code which he considered to be corrupt to be revised and rewritten (1805) and his charge that this be done to conform with Buddhist canonical prescription. (The immediate provocation was said to be his alleged dim view of a divorce judgement which favored the adulterous wife.) One of the fascinating aspects of this episode is that *the king directed* the committee charged with the revision that the laws "be examined with regard to their agreement with the Pāli Canon, and in cases where they did not agree they were to be altered accordingly in order to restore what was believed to be the original text" (Wenk, *op. cit.*, p. 36). This directive is a patent innovation, for historically the traditional civil laws did not derive, and could not be derived, from the Pāli Canon.* It illustrates how changes can be introduced or legitimated in self-consciously Buddhist polities by using the Pāli Canon as a "charter" for legal innovation.

Mongkut, of course, was by far the greater innovator. He was when a monk the founder of the Thammayut sect to which he believed he was restoring the canonically most orthodox practices as regards *vinaya* discipline, ordination procedure, mode of dressing and chanting, and so on. He was also a champion of scripturalism (a return to the allegedly true version of the canon), the study of the Pāli texts, and an antagonist of impure ritual accretions and superstitious ceremonial. There is no need to repeat here Mongkut's well-known reformist and scripturalist measures. Yet, he again illustrates how an innovator initiates a new orthodoxy which is allegedly grounded in the past. Mongkut introduced certain new Buddhist festivals, he wrote new *paritta* chants and refurbished *wat* ceremonial; when he was a king, he interpolated new Buddhist sequences into the traditional "Brahmanical" royal rites. And, in order to appreciate the complexity of the man and his colonial context, we have to grasp that some of the inspiration for his reformist-conservationist measures derived from his contact with Western Christian missionaries, who simultaneously confronted him with Christian religious thought (which scarcely convinced him) and the new sciences (which impressed him greatly).

The Three Sangha Acts of 1902, 1941, and 1963

The process of political stabilization and augmentation of the Thai polity in the nineteenth and twentieth centuries has resulted in an increased regulation of the Sangha. This political regulation is curiously the product of the creation (or rather the enlargement and tightening) of an ecclesiastical structure which in theory was devised to strengthen the Sangha. Ecclesiastical organization as such implying a head of the Sangha (*mahāsvāmi/sangharāja*), the division into village/town-dwelling monks and forest-dwelling monks with their respective heads, into "northern" and "southern" divisions of the Sangha, etc., is not new. For example, it was operative in Sinhalese Buddhism of the Polonnaruwa period (and earlier) and no doubt influenced the Sukhothai organization of the Sangha. Evidence of ecclesiastical organization and state departments (*krom*) overseeing Sangha affairs is known for Ayutthayan times and for the early Bangkok period. But our point is that the waxing and waning of the overall Sangha organization in traditional times was a common occurrence related to the fortunes of the traditional pulsating polity, and secondly that the normal relation between Sangha and polity was loose because both systems were monolithic. By the end of the nineteenth century, a vertical and national Sangha grid had been erected which represented an immense leap compared to the past and was mainly the product of developments in the political realm. The lesson here is that the setting up of an ecclesiastical ("church-like") organization under the auspices of the state is an index of the political subordination of the Sangha.

Let me run through some of the main provisions and implications of the

---

*The Thai legal code (Thammasat), which is derived from the Mon-Burmese legal codes (Dhammasattham), ultimately seeks its precedent in the Indian Dharmashāstras. The Thai-Burmese codes have a myth of Manu that is transformed to suit the local circumstances. (See Tambiah, in Goody and Tambiah, 1973.)

Sangha Act of 1902 which is a central landmark for our study. It provided for a hierarchical ecclesiastical structure with positions of ecclesiastical governor generals, provincial governors, district governors, all filled by monks. This hierarchy paralleled the civil administrative structure.

The appointment of the major abbotships to the capital's royal temples was in King Chulalongkorn's hands, while, as regards the other positions, the king's civil officials in the provinces and districts had to "counterseal" the letters of appointment issued by the ecclesiastical officers.

The ecclesiastical office-holding titled monks were allowed the privilege (which was by no means new) of appointing retinues of personal assistants and secretaries (e.g., a provincial ecclesiastical governor could appoint six assistants); this again parallels the retinues of the civil departmental officers and administrators.

Monks had to be registered, and had to have fixed residence in monasteries — that is, they were ultimately subject to the supervisory control of the Sangha and the civil administration.

All these measures clearly signal the political regulation of the Sangha, whose "church-organization" is, as I have said before, fashioned in imitation of the civil administrative system.

Why was the Act of 1902 promulgated by King Chulalongkorn? Its drafting coincides with the period of his "modernization" program and the forging of a tighter central and provincial administrative system, particularly with the aid of Prince Damrong (and other able princely half-brothers) the setting up of the Departments of Interior, of Justice, Finance, and so on. When Chulalongkorn turned his attention to the spread of primary education on a country-wide basis, he again enlisted the aid of another prince, but this time a monk, Wachirayan (the abbot of Wat Bowonniwet, and later head of the Thammayut sect), and through him the Sangha and its monks to implement the program. This task was considered appropriate because the monasteries had traditionally run not only monastic schools but imparted the 3 Rs to village children and because there was a dearth of lay teachers. But the Sangha's cooperation with the polity's primary educational program had an unanticipated effect: its participation drove home to Wachirayan and his educator-monks, and through them to the civil authorities, the necessity of forging a national ecclesiastical structure (with agents in communication from the capital to the provinces and districts and finally to the villages) in order to effectively implement the programs.

The Act of 1902 had also another objective. A national Sangha controlled from the capital and encompassing the provinces was seen as conducive to national integration — an objective which at the beginning of this century was interpreted as the ironing out of sub-cultural and dialectical differences existing in the northern, northeastern and southern extremities of the kingdom by a policy of homogenization. The historically autonomous Lanna principalities of Chiangmai and Nan in the north had their own variant tradition of Theravada Buddhism (called the "Yuan Cult" by Dodd) which differed from that obtaining in Central Siam in respect of the sacred script, Sangha organization, and some rites and festivals. (Similarly, the northeast had its Laotian variants.) The Act of 1902 was clearly intended to help effect the incorporation of re-

gional varieties of Buddhism and monastic organization under a national umbrella, though it was a decade before effective measures began to be taken in
the North.

I have dwelt at some length on the provisions and implications of the 1902
Act to drive home a fundamental article of Thai polity. The "modernization"
of the country (by means of administrative reorganization and expansion, economic development, the spread of education) was considered by King Chulalongkorn, Prince Damrong (and his fellow ministers), and the princely-monk
Wachirayan (who in time also became Sangharaja) as being entirely consistent
with the conservation and strengthening of Buddhism. This aim was unam-
biguously stated in the preamble to the Act of 1902. One important method
of strengthening the Sangha was considered to be its administrative "rationalization," which, as we have seen, implied as a corollary the facilitation of its
political regulation.

Changes in ecclesiastical organization have since been introduced by the
Sangha Acts of 1941 and 1963, promulgated in different political contexts,
yet they have not challenged, but rather reinforced, the central implication of
the 1902 Act, namely the creation of a Sangha hierarchy on a national scale
in order to protect, regulate and stimulate religion.

We cannot for reasons of space scrutinize the Acts of 1941 and 1963 in
much detail. I shall confine myself to making those points that reveal how the
character of the polity of the time colored the provisions of the legislation.

The Act of 1941 followed upon the "revolution" of 1932 which was effected by army officers and civilian bureaucrats of non-royal origins, who, though
a product of the new developments initiated by Chulalongkorn and his successors, nevertheless challenged the exclusive exercise of the highest levels of
power by the princes and royalist proteges. In the wake of the "revolution"
and its democratic fervor, certain questions were raised as regards the state of
Buddhism and the role of monks in the modern world, and some criticisms
levelled against alleged disciplinary infractions by monks – criticisms related
to excessive expenditure on and concern with Buddhist rituals and merit-making, to the way in which the Sangha or rather certain monasteries and abbots
were managing *wat* properties and income. By and large, however, the new
politicians were fundamentally orthodox in respect of their attitude to religion. Similarly, the liberal atmosphere stimulated expression by certain monks
of a need for reform in the administration of *wats*, and, quite different, encouraged certain monks of the north (which, as we have mentioned before, had its
own traditions of Buddhism which were felt by the modernizers to be inimical to national unity and security) to challenge the authority of Bangkok. In
actual fact, on the other hand, these movements were short-lived. The high
ecclesiastical authorities and the elders of the Sangha joined the government
in suppressing the ferment. The Sangha easily adapted itself to the new politics, precisely because the new politicians did not question the Sangha and the
Buddhist religion in any fundamental sense. They were traditionalists as far as
religion went, firmly believing that monks should not participate in "politics"
and that the purity of the religion depended (as in the past) on the monks'
obeying the vinaya rules and not indulging in "lax behavior." An example was
set by the supreme patriarch himself, Prince Jinavara, who, until his death in

1937, did not directly engage in politics and is said to have consistently supported the government in power.

Although by 1941 the political system had taken a turn towards authoritarianism and military control under Phibun Songkhram, the Sangha Act that was passed contained democratic features to match the structure of the cabinet system and legislative assembly in the political realm, thus paralleling the legislative, executive and judicial divisions of the government, and the various levels and agencies of civil administration. The Sangha too now had under the headship of the supreme patriarch its own cabinet, assembly, judicial institutions, central administration with departments, etc. Despite these liberalizing measures one should not ignore this important fact: the Sangha continued to be linked to the political authority with hoops of steel, as evidenced by the fact that the appointments made by the Supreme Patriarch had to be countersigned by the Minister of Education, and the Secretariat that implemented Sangha policy and decisions was a department of the Ministry of Education.

The 1963 Sangha Act was a high-handed measure of Field Marshall Sarit's — perhaps the most autocratic of the military rulers in the preceding three decades. This Act constituted a denial of the democratic provisions of the 1941 Act — it concentrated power in the Supreme Patriarch and made the Council of Elders purely an advisory body, and abolished the cabinet system, the ecclesiastical courts and the assembly. The alleged reason for this legislation was the internal rivalry and dissension between the Mahanikai and Thammayut Sects within the Sangha, and the "political" and "subversive" activities of at least one highly-placed Mahanikai monk who was a cabinet minister. It is true that sectarian competition (notably in the form of equality of division of the high posts) intruded into the implementation of the 1941 Act. The Thammayut Sect, though a minority sect, always had aristocratic connections, had a history of close cooperation with the polity, and therefore enjoyed political favor, and was more tightly organized than the flabby polycentric Mahanikai Sect. It, therefore, successfully claimed half share of the high appointments, and also produced more Supreme Patriarchs. It is in this context of competitive factionalism, and rivalry among certain prominent monks, that we should understand the notorious incident of the defrocking of Phra Phimolatham, the abbot of Wat Mahathad, an (Ecclesiastical) Minister of the Interior, and successful propagator of a program of meditation for monks and laymen. We cannot go into the details of this incident here except to say that his religious program gave him a renown and a wide following which was construed as a political threat to a militarily constituted authority.

Let me close this section on the three Sangha Acts of this century with these observations:

(1) All three pieces of legislation, whether they were enacted by a king or lay politicians or generals have as their precedent the historical claim that the king had the right and obligation to purify the sasana in order to protect, preserve and maintain it.

(2) Our access to the circumstances surrounding the promulgation of these recent Acts enable us to reinforce and confirm one aspect of what "purification of religion" may have also been about in the past in certain instances. It is not unlikely that many purifications reported in the chronicles may have

had political implications such that schisms and doctrinal or disciplinary disputes had their refractions in the palace politics of royal patronage and succession to the throne.

(3) The three Acts we have considered show a neat congruence with the character of the political systems of their time. King Chulalongkorn's Act reflected the political system of his day: the "absolute" king was also the head of the Sangha, and he explicitly recognized that he was introducing "rational bureaucracy" into the system of Sangha administration to keep up with changes in the system of civil administration. We have already noted how this Act brought the Sangha into closer relation with the political authority — indeed, one could say that the Act formalized a hierarchical network that was devised in the course of implementing the primary education program and a policy of national politico-cultural integration, and that it gave expression to a fair measure of effective regulation of the Sangha achieved by the political authority.

The second Act of 1941 faithfully reflects the change of the Thai political system from absolute monarchy to an alleged constitutional democracy; it marks the adaptation to each other, and the understanding forged between the revolutionary politicians and the Sangha. And now the third Act of 1963 corresponded to the shift once again back to absolutism under military dictatorship. Just as power in the political system was now concentrated in one person, so was it also concentrated in one person in the religious system, who is made to owe exclusive political allegiance to the former. The political logic of this shift is the dictatorship's attempt to stamp out any possible threat to its supremacy and monopoly of power.

(4) Our final point goes beyond the ambit of the Acts themselves, to point out that Field Marshall Sarit and his regime, whose concern was with "national development" (*kaan phatthana pratheet*) and "national integration" rather than with democracy, appreciated very well that Buddhism and Monarchy were important traditional institutions that would enhance the achievement of his political aims. Thus Sarit's policy of creating a strong and loyal Sangha went hand in hand with his active promotion of the ceremonial role of kingship as a vehicle for promoting national pride, unity and identity. The political climate of the thirties which achieved the erosion of the king's powers was also tepid towards the staging of royal rites that dramatized the divinity of the king and his role in maintaining the prosperity and stability of his country. But, now, with a change in climate again, traditional ceremonies, such as *Raek Na* (First Ploughing), were revived. The king now leads the Oath of Allegiance Ceremony transformed to express loyalty to the country (rather than to himself); he not only conscientiously conducts the presentation of *Kathin* gifts to selected royal *wat* at the end of Lent, but also installs high ecclesiastical monks in office by handing to them the fan and other insignia of office. He also similarly gives ceremonial recognition to Pāli *barian* scholars of the highest grade, and if they are novices, sponsors their higher ordination.

And, projecting forwards into the future from the time of Sarit to the ferment of present times, we can confidently say that any movement seeking changes in the political process will not — at least in the short run — be anti-Buddhist and anti-royalist but rather enthusiastically for them. For, as indicated in the beginning of this essay, there is a deeply entrenched Buddhist conception of political sovereignty and righteousness as the ordinating principle in society, a conception of political ethics and morality which acts as an enduring yardstick by which to measure political performance and as an inspiring but not wrought-in-detail ideal to which political aspirations of different complexion can equally refer themselves. Thus it comes as no surprise that in the 1973 insurrection students marched down Bangkok's Rajadamnern Avenue carrying, right in front, the National Flag, the Buddhist Flag and portraits of the King and Queen. These symbols are as much theirs to display as anyone else's. At the recreation of the ashes of the student martyrs at the Pramane Grounds the King was present, and one of the best known of the student leaders was subsequently ordained monk, presumably to make merit for the dead heroes.

The Monastic Network and Monks' Careers

Let me change tack now and explore a different order of questions: what is the total "grid" or "field" in which contemporary monks are placed; what factors influence their recruitment; what kinds of careers do they have; and what sorts of relationship do the ecclesiastical dignitaries and the educated monks have with the professional politicians — the generals and officers, and civilian bureaucrats.

I raise these questions in order to gauge, by means of the evidence, what the relation is between the Sangha and polity today. I shall try to judge this relation by concentrating on *two segments* within the Sangha: (1) the younger monks who pursue educational objectives of both the traditional Pāli and contemporary secular kinds and are concentrated in Bangkok to a vastly greater degree than elsewhere in the country, and (2) the older ecclesiastical titled dignitaries who are also concentrated in the capital's famous *wat*, especially those of royal status (*wat luang*). I want also to emphasize that my information and analysis relate *up to 1971, and no further*.

The gross, statistical picture is as follows. In 1968, for example, Thailand's population was estimated at 33 to 34 million. During the Lent of that year it was reported (by the Department of Religious Affairs) that there were some 185,000 monks (.5 percent of the total population and 1 percent of the male population) and 109,000 novices (.3 percent of the total population and .6 percent of the male population). Any proportion from 25 to 40 percent of the monks may be considered "temporary" in that the duration of their service would not normally exceed a single Lenten season. The total number of *wat* existing in the same year was about 25,000.

There is a rural-urban difference in the distribution of "temporary" and "permanent" monks (the latter are those who join with the expectation of at least a number of years service). The multitude of rural *wat* are small-sized and have more temporary than permanent inmates, while the urban monasteries are not only larger but the majority of their inmates, say half to two-thirds — the latter proportion is more true of the capital's monasteries — tend to be in the order for many years, progressing from being novices in their teens to being monks, and leaving the Sangha if at all in their thirties. Many, however, remain life-long monks. The educational motive, though by no means the only one, is of great weight for the majority of professional monks who join as novices.

This is another cross-cutting distinction that affects the picture. The royal *wat* (*wat luang*) are usually large, possess a certain amount of property, are conventionally recipients of royal gifts (such as the *kathin* presentation), and are the constituency for the highest ecclesiastical titles. They are predominantly located in Bangkok-Thonburi, the exact number being 78 out of a total of 161. The vast majority of *wat* are of commoner status (*wat raad*) of all sizes and located in rural and urban areas.

The Urban Network

The population of the municipalities of Bangkok-Thonburi in 1970 was 3 million; there exist in the country, apart from the primate city, only two towns with a population of around 100,000, and eleven ranging from 50-100,000. These figures are sufficient to comment on the peculiarity of the hierarchy and network of towns in Thailand. As in many other developing countries, Thailand is overwhelmingly dominated by a single primate city; the other major towns are provincial administrative capitals and commercial centers feeding a rural hinterland. These towns do not so much interrelate with each other as with the metropolis on which they are focused in a radial pattern. This pattern of urban distribution and network has direct implications for the path along which novices and young monks travel from village to district or provincial urban-administrative centers, and from there directly in one long hop to Bangkok. There is a hierarchy of monastic educational institutions (attached to *wat*) which maps on to the urban network. The provincial monastic schools provide the lower rungs of religious education, while the metropolis provides the upper reaches for those who are the most gifted and able and have been able to find accommodation in its *wat*.

The attractions of the metropolis are many to the professional monks who combine education with their Buddhist vocation — indeed, for them the practice of monkhood is closely associated with "learning" *dhamma*. There are first of all the educational institutions imparting higher Pāli learning and also, today, secular knowledge and the English language. The chances of winning or being invested with ecclesiastical titles, or being appointed to important positions within the Sangha, or participating in the higher education of monks by teaching in the monks' universities are either much greater in the capital or only confined to it. In addition to the provision of opportunities for fulfilling these aspirations, there is the additional logistical capacity of the metropolitan *wat* — many of them, besides being architectural achievements, have large and commodious accommodations.

In the entire country it is the northeastern provinces — the poorest and also the alleged breeding ground of insurgents — which contribute the largest number (as judged against population) of monks and novices. The Northeast is fertile ground for the monastic vocation.

Now one of the largest concentrations of monks and novices is to be found in Region 1, which is where Bangkok is located. But the vast majority of this region's religious are not recruited from within its confines, but come from all over the country, and predictably the largest contingent comes from the Northeast. Furthermore, the vast majority of the monks in the capital (as elsewhere) are of rural peasant origins. Thus the paradox that, although the largest monasteries in the country are located in the towns, the most renowned and magnificent of them being in the capital, yet the urban population of the country makes a miniscule contribution to the totality of religious personnel.

I want to submit for consideration one implication of the social origins of the monks and of their monastic path that delivers them from the village to Bangkok. I must first mention, but only to leave aside as difficult to express in words, the spiritual, psychic, intellectual and other satisfactions that the Buddhist monastic regimen in its various facets may provide the religious, not to mention the contemplative life and the quest for liberation itself. Then consider a more immediately perceivable feature, a kind of status reciprocity and symbiosis which is compounded of these elements: the monks are of lowly rural origins but *qua* monks are highly venerated by the laymen. Many of these laymen in Bangkok, the officers of the armed forces, the administrative officers, the professional categories, though usually of socially superior origins solicitously tend the needs of monks and elaborately venerate them who they know to be their moral and ethical superiors and their social inferiors.

Think of a poor rural boy from a farming family in a remote part of Thailand and imagine him in Bangkok with some measure of education, perhaps invested with a title, living in comparative physical comfort in the capital's most imposing architectural monuments (indeed, most urban monks' residential conditions are far superior to the majority of urban dwellers in the capital), but most of all having dealings with and receiving the obeisance and respect of the country's powerful and affluent, the controllers of deference-entitlements in the secular world, with whom no ordinary villager in the normal course of his life could hope to come into contact, let alone receive their prostrations and their respectful addresses. One cannot but sense the social immunity and protection as well as the psychic satisfaction these village-born monks derive when they are being lionized by the middle and upper classes, the powerful and the mighty — at least in terms of outward etiquette, social intercourse and feasting. Add to these gains, the fact that the monastic hierarchy is a path of achievement — there are titles, offices of influence, and privileges and control of real resources at stake — which is there to be exploited by villagers *without competition from the urban population.* In return, a supreme sacrifice is required, i.e., that monks and novices bind themselves to a life of discipline and quietude and observance of the rules laid down in the *vinai* (*vinaya*), particularly those which relate to chastity and restraint in eating.

A second major satisfaction that is to be derived from monkhood — I would claim that either explicitly or implicitly this is a motivation why many youths spend long years as novice and monk — is that it not only allowed for acquisition of education but also enabled the disrobing novice or monk to find an occupation consonant with his educational qualification. Those who receive adequate education and leave the order are able to enter certain lay occupations and become minor government servants or clerks and village school teachers. The majority who secure a degree at the monks' universities are able to become higher civil servants (particularly in the Department of Religious Affairs), army chaplains (which are lay positions), or teachers in secondary schools. (The possibility of rising even higher is open to those who have gone abroad to India or elsewhere and have obtained the M.A. or Ph.D. degrees.)

We should note that this phenomenon of social mobility, when conversion to lay society is made *via* the monastic route, is by no means a recent phenomenon. It is well attested for the Ayutthaya period (seventeenth century), again for the mid-nineteenth century during Mongkut's reign (1851-68) when the trend was seen as so marked that it provoked punitive royal decrees to prevent educated monks from disrobing and finding employment in the more important Ministries (such as Interior, Finance, Foreign Affairs, etc.). Our contemporary evidence, therefore, is information regarding a continuing feature. Traditionally, until the late nineteenth century when monastic schools were the major educational institutions, the connection between donning the robe by intellectually-endowed but deprived youth and the pay-off in the secular world subsequently in terms of a superior social position must have been clearly recognized. Today, when secular education at all levels is spreading, this path becomes relevant only to the under-privileged, but this category is by no means small.

But judged in relation to the members of the Sangha, the recent years in comparison with the preceding decades of this century show a spurt in the proportion of monks who have reverted to lay life at higher levels. These men also marry and found families.

I would therefore conclude this section with the plea to my colleagues that in the interests of the fullest understanding of the picture we take these sociological facts that present themselves to us so conspicuously into account – especially as a balancing counterweight to certain "applications" of psychological theory ventured by Melford Spiro, who, for instance, tells us that what distinguishes monks from non-monks is their greater subjection to dependency, narcissism, emotional timidity, etc., and "from this perspective (i.e., renunciation of sex, etc.) the monastic role may be viewed as an institutionalized and symbolic resolution of the Oedipus complex" (1970, p. 342).

Ecclesiastical Dignitaries and Generals: Symbiosis

What does the Ecclesiastical hierarchy today look like in terms of gradation and numbers? At the very top there is the Supreme Patriarch and the Council of Elders (*Mahatherasamakhon*) made up of about 12 dignitaries.

There are actually two hierarchies of titles (that overlap as regards personnel). The ecclesiastical titles proper – which in 1969 starting from the Supreme Patriarch were the Somdet Phra Rachakhana (4), their deputies (Raung Somdet) (4), the dignitaries of the Phra Rachakhana rank which subdivide into 4 categories (Tham, Thep, Rad, Saman) (444 in all), and finally Phra Khru (2813).

The other hierarchy is composed of official administrative titles pertaining to the territorial framework (paralleling the civil provincial administration). In 1969, there were 22 Regional Ecclesiastical Governors, 110 Provincial Governors, 646 District Governors and 3,614 Commune governors. Now, although most ecclesiastical titles carry insignia of office and entitle their holders to small stipends and to certain number of personal assistants (entourage), we should not be taken in by the formal parallelism between the Sangha and civil administrative hierarchies, for the simple truth is that the ecclesiastics have access to meagre administrative and financial resources to be able to run an effective Sangha administration. As we have pointed out before, it is the civilian Department of Religious Affairs that provides the secretariat, while none of the regional, provincial and lesser ecclesiastical officers have separate offices and staff apart from their own modest quarters in their *wat* and their personal secretaries.

A second noteworthy feature of the ecclesiastical provincial hierarchy is that if there is a close collaboration between the Sangha officials and the civil administrators, it is manifest more in the upper than in the lower reaches. At the base the numerous *wat*, especially of the rural variety, are really pretty autonomous institutions, which are in close relation to their lay constituencies, but on which the hand of Sangha administration rests lightly.

But, for our theme, a matter of capital importance is that the Sangha dignitaries, especially those bearing the highest titles and occupying all administrative positions from regional heads to membership of the Council of Elders, are concentrated in Bangkok. They (as well as the provincial ecclesiastical governors whose seats are in the provincial capitals) usually have had excellent ceremonial and diplomatic relations with the rulers and high bureaucrats.

Thus, for example, the presence of monks is indispensable at all state ceremonies, including the launching of national development programs, for their chanting must commence the proceedings. The monks in turn need the presence and patronage of politicians and generals at the opening of temple fairs and festivals and the launching of drives to collect money for their building schemes. The bigger and more lavish the *bod* and *wihan* and monks' residential quarters that an abbot can build for his monastery, the greater his prestige and veneration.

The king, of course, in true classical style makes royal gifts to the Sangha (e.g., *kathin* presentations to certain royal *wat*). But, most importantly, Government Ministries, and Departments within Ministries, headed by prominent politicians, often act as corporate patrons of Buddhism by making *kathin* presentations or sponsoring the ordinations of indigent youth. Thus, for instance, at the end of the Lent of 1971 several such governmental units made presentations of gifts which were contributed by the member officials or officers, as the case may be. The following are two prominent examples:

The *kathin* presentation on October 18, 1971 to Wat Traimit, a royal *wat* in the capital, was sponsored by the office of the Prime Minister (the Prime Minister Thanom Kittikachorn being an army man). A book written by Dr. Thalerng Thamrongnawasawasdi, the Deputy Under-Secretary of Agriculture, "praising the leadership of Prime Minister Thanom Kittikachorn and saying he had brought much progress to the nation since 1963" was distributed as the procession travelled to the *wat* (*Bangkok Post*, October 19, 1971).

The donor of the *kathin* presentation to the royal *wat* of Rajapatigaram on the King's behalf was the Army, which gave a cash gift of 10,000 baht to the *wat*, and gifts of 50 baht to each of the 60 resident monks and 40 baht to each of the 17 resident novices. In addition, a medicine cupboard and 67 blankets were given the *wat*, plus a typewriter and books and pencils for use by the municipal school situated in the *wat* grounds.

Prominent politicians, especially the ruling field marshalls and generals, in their own right, as individual personages, act in the grand historical manner of Buddhist kings, engaging in conspicuous acts of charity and merit-making. While it is no doubt partly true to say that they act in this manner in the full knowledge of the political advantages to be reaped, it is also true to propose that important politicians are propelled to model certain of their acts and to re-enact parts of the careers of the heroes of traditional chronicles. Examples of philanthropy in the grand style, reported in newspapers in late 1971, were the Minister of Interior, the Minister of Health and Director General of the Police Department, and other prominent ministers.

Let me conclude this section by postulating a certain symbiosis between the leading politicians and generals in 1971 and the country's prominent monks especially the titled dignitaries — a symbiosis from the perspective of the social origins and subsequent achievements of the actors.

From a study of their biographies there is evidence that the military men in power had their origins in the official stratum, the rural landed and urban petit-bourgeoisie. There is overwhelming evidence for the thesis that the vast majority of all categories of monks — the ordinary monks, the famous scholar-monks, the prestige-enjoying ecclesiastical officials and titled monks — basically originate among the poor rural peasantry and have travelled from village to city. Both categories in their own way have moved upwards from their respective but different social strata; both are pre-disposed to be "conservative," "traditionalist" and in favor of a formula that maintains the *status quo* of religion, kingship, and political stability. It is thus not difficult to see why the powerful and mighty, though men of the sword, find it natural to give patronage to the Sangha and to appreciate the political value of the legitimation that monks can give them by officiating at the rituals which they sponsor and by consenting to confer merit upon them by receiving gifts.

This "traditionalism" that characterized the army's ruling elite and the dignitaries and elite-monks of the Sangha should not blind us to the fact that their careers and their achievements represented a real dynamism in Thai society — a dynamism which began with King Chulalongkorn's initiation of modernization but perhaps markedly released by the 1932 Revolution — which has allowed persons from the ranks of commoners (particularly the lower rungs) to utilize certain channels of mobility to make it to the top. Thus Thai society from the 1940s to the 1970s presents us with a face that is both still and mobile. In one sense, the soldiers who captured and exercised power simply replaced the authoritarian and hierarchical system of monarchical times with a structure that manifested the same or similar authoritarianism. There is thus a continuity of political power, although continuity of political legitimacy is problematic. There is one difference which has acted as a constant irritant in the body politic: while the Chakkri kings especially the illustrious Mongkut, and Chulalongkorn (and, more problematically, Wachirawut) enjoyed a legitimacy and were seen as fulfillments of the classical expectations of righteous kings, the ruling generals could not claim to embody the *dharma* of rulers and had to lean on a politically clipped king to invest them with the constitutional right to rule (or, to state in classical idiom, to exercise *danda*, force). Nevertheless, the social origins of the soldiers make clear to us that their political dominance represents an access to power on the part of members of certain strata composed of petty officials and prosperous farmers and petty landowners, who in previous monarchical regimes were excluded from favor and power. The intensification of the process whereby youth of poor rural origins join the monkhood and can achieve along the path of religious vocation fits into the picture as another dynamic feature of modern Thai society.

The Ideological Orientation of Bangkok's Young Educated Monks

While the high ecclesiastical dignitaries sacralize state ceremonials and have symbiotic relations with the rulers, the younger educated monks are concerned with the relevance of Buddhism for contemporary life, the form the education of monks should take to suit present day needs, and, finally, the role of the monks *vis-à-vis* society.

Before we attach labels to the contemporary formulations – labels that are fashionable among modernization theorists, e.g., neo-traditionalism, reformism, scripturalism, secularism and the like – I should like to make two observations on the interpretation of Buddhist doctrine.

The first observation is that many of us, perhaps because of our dependence on a few secondary sources for our understanding of Buddhist concepts, appear to accept the notion that Buddhist doctrine asserts a categorical negation of the world, that nirvāna (the goal of the Buddhist quest) is annihilation or void.[1] An antidote to this narrow dogmatism is, for example, Guy Richard Welbon's *The Buddhist Nirvāna and its Western Interpreters* (1968), where he shows that a gallery of scholars from the 1830s onwards consisting, among others, of Max Müller, James D'Alwis, R. C. Childers, Oldenberg, the Rhys Davids, La Vallee Poussin, and Stcherbatsky, took a number of sharply differing positions in regard to their interpretation of nirvāna. We cannot here wade into the deep waters of this philosophical and philological problem; we merely take notice of the fact that the views of these scholars form a spectrum ranging from nirvāna as annihilation to nirvāna as bliss, between a pre-mortem achievement of a psychic state and a post-mortem release into annihilation, between a this-worldly experience and an eternal other-worldly rest. There is a noteworthy concordance between a certain interpretive strand of Western scholarship and the views of modern Thai interpreters. This strand stresses the this-worldly dimension of Buddhism. For example, Oldenberg expounded the view that nirvāna is the state of sinlessness and painlessness, the state of deliverance from the law of causality through sanctification in this life; nirvāna, as annihilation, he said, is a secondary derivation, a dialectical development of the philosophy and not the pristine kernel of the Buddha's teaching. For Rhys Davids too, nirvāna is an ineffable state of human achievement in this world, an achievement while alive of perfect peace and wisdom.

My second observation is that the canonical texts of Buddhism, just as the Bible of Christianity and the core texts of other religions, are complex, paradoxical, ambiguous and capable of different levels of interpretation at critical points. Christian sectarianism itself exemplifies how the canon can serve as a language of religious and social controversy. The same in principle applies to Buddhist interpretations in modern times. Instead of naively assuming that there are unambiguous prescriptions and value orientations in Buddhism from which can be deduced behavioral correlates which bear an intrinsic relation to the doctrine, let us creatively apply the Weberian concept of "elective affinity" to the Asian materials in a manner more sophisticated than Weber's own diagnosis of Asian religions.

The Ethic of the Contemporary Monk-Interpreters

Briefly stated, the preoccupation of modern Thailand's elite monks is the relevance of Buddhism as a positive ethic of action for both monks and laymen. Since I have already discussed the main features of the present day ideological thrust in another essay,[2] I shall limit myself to a few examples.

Thailand's foremost expounder of Buddhism is Bhikkhu Buddhadasa, who presides over the forest hermitage of *Suan Mokh* in Southern Thailand. His thought is influenced in part by Zen Buddhism. While he is doctrinally "orthodox" about the nature of the Buddhist quest, his interpretations are firmly grounded in the view that for the Buddhist the world here and now is relevant and hence action here and now is productive of results. He expounds that the cosmological levels such as heaven and hell, and processes and states such as *saṃsāra* and *nirvāna*, are not out there but really interiorized states of the mind. His exhortation to his fellow bhikkhus is that religious practice involves the propagation of Buddhism to all the nations of the world, and cites in support the slogan from the *Mahāvagga*: "Proclaim O Bhikkhus, the Doctrine glorious, preach ye a life of holiness perfect and pure." He sees Christianity and Buddhism as having this orientation in common. In sum, what Buddhadasa tries forcefully to refute and deny is the fatalism, the suspension of action because of the unreality of the world, and therefore the apathy attributed to Buddhism by certain stereotype commentators.

A transformation from this position to an even more activistic orientation is portrayed by various young scholar monks who man and run the Sangha's higher educational institutions — the two universities (Mahachulalongkorn and Mahamakut), the adult schools, and so on. The main planks in their platform are that the education of monks should be broadened to include knowledge of secular subjects, that monks have a duty to make a return to society, and that monks should recover their lost roles as educators and moral leaders of laymen. In support of this last thesis, they cite the Asokan precedent, but more forcefully the last decade of the last century when King Chulalongkorn relied on the princely monk Wachirayan (then abbot of Wat Bowonniwet and Head of the Thammayut Sect) and teacher-monks recruited by him to implement a primary education program in the provinces.

I could cite the opinions of numerous individual monks which reflect this perspective. They are all uneasy about being confined to their monasteries and being restricted to the enactment essentially of ceremonial roles and itch to contribute more positively to society. For lack of space let me cite only one telling example which is taken from a survey of the opinions of a sample of 324 monk-students attending Mahachulalongkorn University. To an open-ended question "In your view what should be the role of monks in society today?," the vast majority (75.9 percent) said they favored active engagement with society in the traditionally acceptable role as teachers and preachers. And, perhaps more interestingly, 45.6 percent of the respondents said they were in favor of participating in the government's current programs of national and community development as "missionary monks" (*thammathud*). In striking contrast, the contemplative life of a recluse, though admired, was personally favored by a miniscule minority. Another query produced the response that 93.2 percent of the sample approved of the *thammathud* program, 66 percent said they wished to participate in it, and 26 percent (mainly the seniors to whom only participation is mainly open) had already taken part.

In the *thammathud* movement I studied in 1971 (for details see the essay mentioned earlier: Tambiah, 1973), the orientations of the government, which wanted to stem and contain communism, intensify the loyalty of the people to Religion, King, and Nation, happily converged with the propensities of both the "conservative" ecclesiastical dignitaries who approved of these larger aims and the young educated monks who wanted to commit themselves to a more activistic role in society. The program is directed primarily at the far-away underdeveloped provinces, the frontier provinces, and the Hill Tribes.

Some Tentative Reflections

Let me close this overview by making a few observations on how we may read in a comparative sense the relation between religion and politics in Thailand.

The current interpretive dogma that I have described tends to generate the scripturalist (and, perhaps, "puritanical") attitude of deprecation, if not denunciation, of popular rituals and ceremonials — to ensure prosperity and good health and to dispel misfortune — as obstacles to salvation. This orientation is not new: we saw it manifest itself in the Mongkut era, again in the 1930s, and it is once more a feature of the present-day monk-ideologists, who express a devaluation, if not slight contempt, for the ordinary layman's requesting and the majority of monks' performing prosperity-inducing ritual acts. As one monk put it, no doubt harking back with fidelity to canonical prescription: "the way of deliverance lies within man's reach. No priest nor any external power can deliver a man."

We see here the familiar reformist attitude that the "word" takes precedence over "ritual act" (only later in turn to generate its own cult); and the accompanying assertion that a gap separates the true "interiorized" view held by the prophet or philosopher-monk from the fallacious "exteriorized" beliefs of the ordinary peasant.

From a comparative point of view, it seems relevant to comment on the applicability of some of Clifford Geertz's assertions, relating to the implications of "scripturalism," as it has manifested itself in the Islam he observed in Indonesia and Morocco:[3]

Scripturalism, according to Geertz, leads to an "ideologization of religion," which represents a shift from "religiousness" to "religious-mindedness" accompanied by scepticism and a loss of spiritual self-confidence.

The relationship between scripturalism and nationalism is stated as one in which nationalism grows out of scripturalism and advances further by superseding it. "In both Indonesia and Morocco the prologue to nationalism coincides with the epilogue to scripturalism" (*ibid.*, p. 73). At the early stages, a religious self-purification is combined with political nationalist self-assertion; in the end, the scripturalists are left behind and become isolated.

As regards modern Thailand, these propositions do not fit conclusively. Thailand's contemporary Buddhist revitalization, of which scripturalism is a part, is in some ways not a *unique* modern phenomenon, but an expression of other similar vitalization movements that have occurred in the past in Buddhist polities. Extending from as far back as the Asokan era "purifications" of religion have occurred in the reigns of famous kings in Ceylon, Burma, and Thailand. These purifications have been "scripturalist"; they also carried an ideology of political action (e.g., unification of the country, war against the enemy, and building a prosperous society).

Thus, as far as most Thai are concerned, it would be difficult to detect in present-day events a shift from religiousness, from Buddhism as a way of life in all its ramifications, to a more sceptical narrower on-the-defensive religious-mindedness. Virtually at all levels of society, the integral relevance of their religion for conduct is not in doubt. Buddhism is as much the religion of the bourgeoisie as of the peasant, of the soldier as much as the recluse.

This attitude is partly the result of the greater sense of intactness and continuity experienced by the Thai as compared with other Asian societies actually colonized by Western imperial powers. But, it also derives from the intrinsic character of Buddhism itself – how its tenets relate to the concerns of the politico-social order.

It is perhaps in this area that I see a real departure from Geertz's Islamic cases. While in the Islamic societies treated by him scripturalism may initiate nationalism but is later superseded by it, it is difficult to imagine this divorce taking place in Thailand in our time. A secularist politics that does not seek its legitimacy in Buddhism is implausible as things stand now. This is partly because – as indeed the Sinhalese *Mahāvamsa* states as a root paradigm – the traditional politics of Sri Lanka, Burma, Thailand, and so on, have always been Buddhist kingdoms in the sense that the consciousness of being a political collectivity is tied up with the possession and guardianship of the religion under the aegis of a dharma-practicing Buddhist king.

In other words, one of the central theses of this presentation is that from early times Buddhism has been positively related to a conception of an ideal politico-social order, whose cornerstone was a "righteous" monarch who would promote a prosperous society and religion. This Buddhist conception of a moral polity readily fits with a formulation that only a materially prosperous society can be ready for the pursuit of spiritual concerns; it also fits equally with a political ideology of benevolent absolutism combined with welfare socialism, of non-violence and peace existing side by side with aggressive militant protection of the treasure of religion. Given this interlaced totality of religion and politics, of national consciousness and religious identity, of righteous morality and politics, it is difficult to see in Thailand in the near future a secular nationalism dispensing with Buddhist referents.

Let me finally conclude with a paradox. The encompassing dharma doctrine of the Buddhist polity to be realized *via* righteous kingship did not specify with any firmness or finality of detail specific norms and codes relating to the status and freedom of women, marriage customs and rituals of family life, and the form and shape of intermediate corporate groupings standing between the individual householder and the state. There are no castes or religious congregations or sectarian associations among the Thai Buddhists separating themselves from non-members, outsiders, aliens, or non-believers. Therefore, unlike Islamic societies, where a revivalist position is inescapably tied to traditional social codes that might be viewed by modernizing nationalists as obstacles deserving to be blasted away, a view that inevitably generates an anti-religious or secularist opposition group, in the Buddhist polities new content can be poured into the socio-political mould because they are like hollow vessels which have in the past and will in the future hold varying contents. The ethic of the householder recommended by Buddhism, though perhaps not

the "colorless bourgeois ethic" of Max Weber's description, escaped being a
jurisprudential code grounded in the religious canon.[4] Hence Thai nationalism
can wrap around itself a cloak of Buddhist aura without fear of finding religious obstacles to the social objectives it may wish to promote.

References

Dumont, Louis.
    Homo Hierarchicus. The Caste System and its Implications. London, 1970.
Geertz, Clifford.
    Islam Observed. Religious Development in Morocco and Indonesia. University of
    Chicago Press, 1971.
Goody, Jack and S. J. Tambiah.
    Bridewealth and Dowry. Cambridge Papers in Social Anthropology, 7. Cambridge
    University Press, 1973.
Tambiah, S. J.
    Buddhism and the Spirit Cults in Northeast Thailand. Cambridge University Press,
    1970
    "The Persistence and Transformation of Tradition in Southeast Asia, with special
    reference to Thailand," in *Daedalus: Post Traditional Societies,* 1973.
Wenk, Klaus.
    The Restoration of Thailand under Rama I, 1782-1809. University of Arizona
    Press, 1968.

Notes

1. Max Weber, partly because he was a victim of the nature of Buddhist scholarship of his
time, and partly because of his dependence on available secondary sources, has been responsible for transmitting to the social scientists such an uncomplicated view.
2. See "The Persistence and Transformation of Tradition in Southeast Asia, with special
reference to Thailand," in *Daedalus,* Winter 1973: *Post Traditional Societies*
3. Clifford Geertz, *Islam Observed* (Chicago, 1971).
4. Buddhism wherever it went tended to accept the local social codes and customs. Its religious provenance, outside of a few basic norms (*sīla*), did not directly impinge on the
moral acceptability of social customs. Buddhism could also incorporate and hierarchise
in a total scheme the particularities of the context in which it found itself. Unlike in
Medieval Christian or Islamic Universities and Rabbinical and Brahmanical schools, Law
and Jurisprudence formed no part of Buddhist monastic education.

Legitimation and Rebellion: Thailand's Civic Religion and the Student Uprising of October, 1973

Frank E. Reynolds

THROUGHOUT HUMAN history the life of men has always involved a religious and a political dimension. Men have always expressed themselves as religious beings — that is to say, as beings who order their world and live their lives in terms of realities which they consider to be sacred. And they have always expressed themselves as political beings — that is to say, as beings who are consciously and persistently concerned with the organization and distribution of communal power. Moreover, in every society with which we have become acquainted, these two dimensions have been to some degree distinct, but at the same time they have been inextricably interwoven and interdependent.

Most historians of religion and political development are agreed that in the primitive and archaic world the differentiation between religious and political expression is relatively limited. Religious forms such as myths (which, among other things, often constitute a kind of sacred history through which people come to understand and express the order and meaning of their existence), symbols (which are those basic forms through which men apprehend and express the complex structure of the world and of their own being), and rituals (which are the forms of action through which men seek to maintain, to renew, and to participate in those realities which they consider to be basic to their life and meaning) provide the context within which the political order is conceptualized and maintained. To be sure, there is a division of responsibility and sometimes even a tension between those individuals who are primarily concerned with preserving and adapting the religious tradition on the one hand, and those who exercise political authority on the other. Nevertheless, the community which these leaders serve is fundamentally one community.

However, with the emergence of the great classical civilizations a profound change takes place, a change which most previous interpreters have perceived as one which should be characterized as a more or less radical separation of the religious and political spheres. For example, Joachim Wach, the great German historian of religions, has placed a strong emphasis on the emergence of what he calls "specifically religious communities," a development which came to full fruition first in India (the Buddhist Sangha being the prime example) and somewhat later in the West, where the classic example is, of course, the Christian Church (Wach, 1944:109-204). And, more recently, historians like Arnold Toynbee and philosophers such as Karl Jaspers have reiterated the same theme concerning this presumed bifurcation between religion and politics.

Certainly this interpretation of the changes which took place with the emergence of at least some of the so-called high religions brings into focus certain very important developments which have occurred both in Asia and in the West.

Nevertheless, this way of conceptualizing the development has tended to obscure other very important elements in the total religio-political situation not only in classical times, but in the modern period as well. For one thing, it has encouraged scholars interested in understanding the development of traditions such as Buddhism and Christianity to concentrate on the religious aspects of myth, doctrine, ritual, devotion, and ethics, and to pass too lightly over the very obvious fact that these communities are also political communities which are deeply concerned with the distribution of authority and power within their own group and within society as a whole. And — what is more important for our specific purpose here — this too-simple kind of dichotomy has tended to encourage scholars interested in understanding national communities to concentrate on political, economic and social factors, and to pass too lightly over the very obvious fact that specifically civic myths, symbols, rituals, and sacralized norms of behavior have provided a basis for the legitimation and maintenance of civic order and, in many cases have also provided a basis for the legitimation of civic rebellion and even revolution.

In the present paper my purpose is to demonstrate that important insights into certain "political" events in recent Thai history can be gained by holding in abeyance the traditional way of making the dichotomy between the religious order and the political order (in this case between Buddhism and the state), and by taking serious account of the existence and role of a distinctively civic religion. I will begin by sketching, in very broad strokes, the emergence and development of the most influential formulations of civic religion in modern Thailand. I will then move directly into an account of the student uprising of October, 1973 in which special attention will be given to the presence and power of the traditions of Thai civic religion, and the ways in which these traditions contributed to the students' success in bringing about the overthrow of the ruling military clique.

The Tradition of Civic Religion in Modern Thailand

The form of civic religion which developed in modern Thailand has deep roots in the traditions of the earlier period of the Thonburi-Bangkok kingdom (late eighteenth century) and beyond that, in the traditions of the more ancient Thai kingdoms of Ayutthaya, Chiangmai, and Sukothai.[1] However, the specifically modern form of Thai civic religion did not really emerge in any clear or identifiable way until the second, third, and fourth decades of the twentieth century. The prime mover in the formulation and stabilization of this tradition was King Vajirawut (reigned 1910-25) who, in addition to maintaining many of the progressive policies of his grandfather (King Mongkut) and his father (King Chulalongkorn), chose to invest a great deal of effort in the propagation of a kind of civic religion which would incorporate both the appeal of new "modern" ideologies and also the vitalities of the older Thai tradition. Following the coup d'état of 1932, Vajirawut's classic expression of the tradition was revised and supplemented in accord with the more democratic ideals of the new order.

In his efforts to rally a renewed sense of Thai civic identity and meaning King Vajirawut spent a significant portion of his considerable talent as a writer and poet highlighting and nurturing three distinct foci of Thai civic religious consciousness. First of all, he put into the foreground the nationalistic fervor which was just beginning to gain strength at the time by emphasizing the primacy of the *chat* or nation which, in his usage, refers both to the land on which the Thai dwell, and also to the bond of peoplehood through which they have maintained their freedom and expressed their greatness. But he gave this nationalistic focus a distinctive and traditionalist thrust by also placing in the foreground the co-equal sacrality of the established *sāsana* or religion (i.e., Buddhism) which, as he interpreted it, provides the spiritual and moral fabric undergirding and giving meaning to the life of the community as well as to the lives of its individual members. And, in a similarly traditionalist vein, he centered attention on the coequality and sacrality of the monarchy or *mahakesat* which he considered to be a personification of the Thai heritage and the integrating axis providing both stability and the dynamism in the Thai civic order. Thus, when Vajirawut took the responsibility for introducing a new national symbol, namely a Thai flag, it was constituted by three stripes representing this triad of inter-related and inter-dependent elements – a red stripe representing the *chat*, a white stripe representing the *sāsana*, and a blue stripe representing the *mahakesat.*

Following the coup d'état of 1932, Vajirawut's formulation, which had gained widespread acceptance, obviously needed modification. To be sure, the leaders of the new order were fully committed to the sacrality of the *chat* and the *sāsana*. For example, the date of the coup came to be celebrated as a *wan chat* or national day, and both the symbolic and practical support of Buddhism were continued. Moreover, though the primary purpose of the coup leaders had been to wrest actual political power from the hands of the king, they came to recognize the propriety and even the necessity of retaining the sacral functions of the monarchy as an embodiment of the distinctively Thai heritage and as an integrating axis of civic order and life. But, in addition, they made every effort to formalize the role of the *ratatamanun* (or constitution) as a fourth, democratizing element in the established pattern of civic religion. Thus, on the one hand, Vajirawut's triad of civic religious elements were reinterpreted so that they could be correlated with the more democratic ideal which was most explicitly expressed in the *ratatamanun*; and, on the other, a number of related symbolic actions were taken including the construction of an appropriate commemorative monument in the heart of the governmental center in Bangkok, and the incorporation of a *wan ratatamanun* or constitution day into the calendar of civic religious celebrations which were observed in every section of the country, and particularly in all of the nation's schools.

During the decades since the 1932 coup the various elements in the civic religious tradition in Thailand have been understood and utilized in differing ways. In the case of the *chat*, there have been chauvinistic understandings which emphasize a complete or exclusive correlation between the *chat* and Thai ethnicity (though the complete correlation was particularly evident in the propaganda of the expansionist pan-Thai movement of the late 1930s and early 1940s, the continuing influence of this tendency toward exclusiveness is reflected in the fact that certain non-Thai ethnic groups are still not legally recognized as full citizens of the Thai nation); and, at the same time, there have been more truly national understandings which have emphasized the correlation between the *chat* and all of the peoples who live within the borders of Thailand and identify their destiny with that of the country as a whole.

Similarly in the case of the *sāsana*, there have been reactionary forces which have emphasized an exclusive correlation between the *sāsana* and Buddhism (such interpretations were particularly evident during the Second World War) and there have also been more liberal interpretations which have maintained that the *sāsana* includes not only Buddhism but also other religions such as Islam and Christianity which are practiced by significant numbers of Thai people. In the case of the monarchy, there have been serious debates concerning the specific role of the king in the new order.[2] And, also, the relative significance and form of the constitution have tended to generate continuing controversy.

Nevertheless, in spite of the divergences of interpretation and the changes which have taken place since the coup d'état of 1932, the *chat* , the *sāsana*, the *mahakasat*, and the *ratatamanun* have retained their sacrality and have served to express and mold the civic religious consciousness of the Thai people at all levels of society. As a result, they have exerted an important influence on both the rhetoric and the substance of Thai political life. Though there have been differences in emphasis between various leaders and governments, particularly with regard to the degree of ideological and practical importance accorded to the king and the constitution, every Thai regime since 1932 has grounded its claim to legitimacy in an appeal to these basic symbols.[3] And, what is equally important, every significant change in government leadership or structure has involved some kind of appeal to one or more aspects of this civic religious tradition. In no instance, however, has the role of the civic religious tradition in the process of change been as obvious or dramatic as in the case of the student uprising of October, 1973, through which the regime headed by Field Marshalls Thanom Kittikachorn and Prapat Charusathiara was toppled from power, and through which a new royally appointed interim government headed by the Sanya Thammasakdi was established in its place.

Sarit, Thanom, and the Immediate Background of October, 1973.

In the decades following the coup d'état of 1932 the continuity in the established tradition of civic religion in Thailand was closely associated with the fact that the political and social order remained fundamentally stable. The control of the bureaucracy which was institutionalized by the coup was continuously preserved. Despite the never-ceasing power struggles between the military and civilian components of this bureaucracy and between the more conservative and more liberal elements in the top leadership, the military elite (particularly the army) has predominated. Structural innovations have been effected only gradually, and, until the 1970s at least, broadly based popular dissatisfaction has been limited primarily to the border provinces.

The basic preeminence of the military, though threatened for a short time during the period immediately following the Second World War, was firmly reasserted in December, 1958 when a successful coup d'état led to the suspension of the constitution then in force and to the establishment of a new regime under the strong direct leadership of Field Marshall Sarit Thanarat. Despite some internal problems and various scandals involving official corruption, Sarit's regime enjoyed considerable success in achieving its goals of political stability and national development. As a result of this success, along with a reliance on the role of the monarchy, his regime was able to delay the promulgation of a new constitution. After Sarit's death the same pattern was continued, with considerable success, by his personally chosen successor, Field Marshall Thanom Kittikachorn. However, in the late 1960s, the problems of the government increased, and in 1968 civilian and popular pressures finally led to the promulgation of a new constitution. But, as soon as serious tensions developed between the new legislature and the military leaders who still controlled the executive, F. M. Thanom, with the support of the widely disliked though very powerful General Prapat Charusathiara, effected a bloodless coup through which the constitution was abrogated and undisguised military rule was reestablished.

Under the new Thanom-Prapat regime the problems which had developed in the late 1960s not only continued, but actually accelerated. Dissatisfaction with Thanom (and with his wife who also played an important role) and especially with Prapat increased, and was exacerbated by the rapid rise to power of Narong Kittikachorn, an arrogant young Colonel who was Thanom's son and had married Prapat's daughter. Even among the military itself there were growing fears that the ruling clique was becoming irresponsible, and that something like a new dynasty was being established. At the same time, the international situation was changing rapidly, and the regime's long-established association with American policy and support became a source of serious discontent among the more educated groups, as did the fact that the government seemed to be either unwilling or unable to stem the tide of growing Japanese influence in the Thai economy. And, what is more, the escalating price of rice and other basic commodities, for which government policies and corruption were blamed, nurtured a growing unrest and bitterness among the populace.

As this dissatisfaction with the Thanom-Prapat-Narong regime developed, the gap between the various legitimizing facets of Thai civic religion, on the one hand, and the realities of the established regime, on the other, became accentuated. The accusation that the ruling clique had become utterly corrupt and was governing for its own benefit to the exclusion of the benefit of the *chat* became a pervasive theme of anti-government criticism, and became more widely accepted as time passed. Though most Buddhist leaders did not criticize the regime directly, and many seemed to give it their tacit support, there was an increasingly articulated concern with the breakdown of dhammic values in government and society, and an increasing emphasis on the need for reform. Though the king remained above the political arena as such, his lack of enthusiasm for the ruling clique did not go unnoticed, and the fact that the people felt that a tension existed was evident in a variety of ways. For example, in early 1973 many people were recounting – with no small degree of disgust – a story to the effect that at a drunken party with some of his fellow officers Col. Narong had explicitly announced his intention to become the first president of a new republican government in Thailand. Or, to cite another similar example, during the summer of 1973 rumors became widespread that an attempt had been made on the life of the crown prince who was then in Australia, and it was implied by many that this attempt had been instigated by Prapat and/or Narong. Finally, as time went on and no action was taken to begin the task of formulating a new constitution, the accusation that the regime had no intention of proceeding in this matter became more widespread and more believable. In fact, just a few days prior to the beginning of the uprising, the Bangkok papers reported that the government was developing plans to "update" the references to democracy and the importance of the constitution which, despite the absence of an actual constitution, had retained their place in the civics curriculum of the Thai schools.

Thus, during the period following the coup d'état of 1971 many diverse segments of Thai society became increasingly dissatisfied and bitter toward the ruling clique of Thanom, Prapat and Narong; and this prepared the political ground for the student uprising of 1973. What is more, these same segments of Thai society came to perceive a widening gap between the major elements of Thai civic religion and the ruling clique. This established a context in which the traditional symbols of this Thai civic religion could emerge as crucial factors in the sudden and quite unexpected success which the students were able to achieve.

The Student Movement and the Uprising of October, 1973.

During the late 1960s and early 1970s rising dissatisfaction with the established government was closely correlated with the emergence, for the first time in Thai history, of an active student movement. To be sure, there had been some student participation in the coup which F. M. Sarit had carried out in 1958, but in this instance the involvement had been largely instigated by the Sarit forces outside the university. So too, in the early 1960s a number of conferences and work camps were held which stimulated student interest in national issues. However, in the late 1960s, and especially after the Thanom-Prapat coup of 1971, younger university teachers began to become more articulate in questioning the leadership and direction of the government, the pace of student interest accelerated, student organizations began to take form, and student activism emerged as a significant political factor. In 1969 the National Student Council of Thailand was established, and, following the rise of Tirayudh Boonmee to a prime leadership role in August, 1972, the NSCT grew rapidly in size and organizational strength. In November, 1972 a major demonstration was mounted against Japanese influence in the Thai economy, and in the spring of 1973 the students at Chulalongkorn University in Bangkok engaged in a major protest against government policies concerning the export of rice. Though neither endeavor achieved its goals, the students made their presence felt and, at the same time, gained invaluable organizational experience. Also in 1973, a very important student protest at Ramkemheng University succeeded in disrupting the University and in bringing about the ouster of its rector. Thus, in the context of this long-term development of student activism, it came as no great surprise when, in early October, a group of dissident leaders including Tirayudh (who in the meantime had been graduated from the university and had therefore left his position as the head of the NSCT) and a number of others involved in the student movement began to distribute leaflets in support of a petition by a group of 100 prominent national leaders demanding the rapid promulgation of a new constitution. However, at the time, no one, including the dissidents themselves, had any idea that this small action would quickly escalate into a student-led uprising of major proportions, and that such an uprising could bring about the demise of the seemingly well-entrenched regime of Field Marshalls Thanom and Prapat. But all of this did, in fact, occur. In the period from October 6 to noon on October 12 there was a rapid escalation of tension; from that point until the early morning of October 14 there was a restrained confrontation which culminated in a partial realization of student goals; and finally, beginning a few hours later and lasting until the evening of October 15, there was a violent confrontation which resulted in the exile of the three preeminent leaders of the old regime and the establishment of a new government under the leadership of Nai Sanya Thammasakdi.

The crisis began on Saturday, October 6, when the government arrested 12 leaders of the constitution movement; it was extended the next day when still another dissident was taken into custody; and it took on ominous proportions on Monday, October 8, when F. M. Prapat announced that since the police had discovered evidence that the movement was part of a plan to overthrow the government, and since communist literature had been found in the possession of members of the arrested group, the possibility of bail could not be considered. In the face of these actions the NSCT responded immediately, calling for the release of the activists; and then on Tuesday, following F. M. Prapat's announcement, students at Thammasat University began serious efforts to organize a protest rally in the university compound. On that same day the student legislative body at Thammasat voted to suggest a postponement of the semester examinations which were imminent, affirmed their intention to carry out nonviolent protests, and warned that if these protests failed to secure the release of the arrested leaders, violence could result. By Wednesday the demonstrations at Thammasat had attracted several thousand students, including an increasing number from other universities and colleges, many of which had by this time been closed down either by administrative decision or by independent student action. On Thursday the number of demonstrators swelled into the tens of thousands and by Friday, after practically all of the universities, colleges and vocational schools in Bangkok had been closed, over 50,000 students were actually participating in the protest.

During the course of the week the students, putting to good use both the experience which they had gained in previous demonstrations and the widespread public support which they enjoyed, developed a network of facilities and a flow of supplies which was able to sustain the rapidly expanding number of demonstrators. They were also involved in laying concrete plans for possible encounters — either peaceful or violent — with police or government troops. And, what is at least equally important, they were making a very serious and self-conscious effort to identify their cause with the basic symbols of Thai civic religion. The rhetoric which the students used throughout the duration of the protest combined increasingly vitriolic and bitter attacks on the arrogance and corruption of Thanom, Prapat and Narong with fervent expressions of the identity between their own cause and the long-established ideals of the nation. In this connection it is not insignificant that the songs which were sung to pass many of the long hours of waiting were for the most part well-known expressions of traditional patriotic sentiment and loyalty to the nation. Moreover, in the course of the week, as the scenario developed, the leaders, following the advice of some of the younger Thammasat professors who were working with them, pressed this association of their cause with basic civic religious symbols still further by quite self-consciously setting out to establish clear and visible associations between themselves and their movement on the one hand, and the monarchy and Buddhism on the other. For example, pictures of the king and queen were displayed with increasing regularity, a huge figure of the Buddha was established in a prominent and highly photogenic position in the compound where the demonstration was centered, and the traditional morning ritual of feeding the monks was publicly performed by a number of the protestors. Moreover, it was of course self-evident that the cause of the students was integrally bound up with the struggle for a constitution and for the more democratic form of political and social order which a constitution had come to signify.

Partly due to the students' own efforts, partly due to the king's public statement emphasizing his desire that the students not be harmed, and partly due to the cooperation which was given by the media in both verbally and visually highlighting these highly charged symbolic associations, the students succeeded in creating a firmly entrenched public image of themselves as the true defenders of the most sacred values of the Thai civic order, and in thoroughly discrediting the continuing efforts of the government to tar their protest with the brush of either youthful irresponsibility or communist subversion[4]. Thus the protesting students were able to capitalize fully on the deep-seated resentment against the military government which existed even among basically conservative groups, and thereby to attract an increasingly broad base of support not only among their fellow students, but in practically every segment of Thai society as well. By Thursday the extent of this support which was gathering in Bangkok and in other areas of the country was becoming more and more evident; and at this point the first hints of possible compromise began to be dropped by government officials. However, no concrete proposals were made, and by mid-day on Friday the students felt sufficiently strong to issue an ultimatum: if the arrested activists were not released within 24 hours, they announced, the protestors would move out from the Thammasat campus and carry their demonstration into the very heart of the governmental center in Bangkok.

With the announcement of this ultimatum a new stage in the struggle – what I have called the stage of restrained confrontation – began. On Friday evening the government announced that the imprisoned dissidents would be released on bail; but after some deliberation the NSCT leaders determined that this did not meet their demand for an "unconditional" release. Thus, despite a last minute effort in which the government tried to rid itself of the physical presence of their prisoners, the plans for the demonstration continued. And at noon on Saturday the protestors and their supporters, whose numbers had now swelled to an almost incredible extent (press estimates placed the figure at ca. 200,000), began their historic march. The plans had been carefully laid. The marchers were organized into discrete groups including, for example, scouts who went out ahead of the main column, a very prominent forward contingent from a girl's academy attended largely by daughters of ranking military personnel, male students who carried sacks to be placed over any barbed wire which might have been laid to obstruct the way, first aid units, groups of engineering students with sticks, clubs, and, in some cases, tear gas masks, supply units with food and water, and other necessities. And what is more, more specifically religio-national symbolism was very much in evidence – many of the various groups, including especially those in the most exposed positions in the column carried before them Thai national flags and Buddhist flags as well as large posters bearing the likenesses of the king and the queen; and the goal of the march was appropriately enough the Democracy Monument which had been erected after the coup d'état of 1932 to commemorate the promulgation of the first Thai constitution.

The march proceeded in a highly orderly manner, and the police made no attempt to interfere. By early afternoon the demonstrators filled to overflowing the entire area around the Democracy Monument; and there they remained quite peacefully as a delegation of students, including some of the activists who had in the meantime been released from custody, went to the royal palace where an audience had been arranged with the king. In this audience the student leaders were assured that the government had agreed to their demands, and that a new constitution would be promulgated within a year. The delegation then returned to the monument, and the news was conveyed to the waiting demonstrators via loud speaker. The demonstration was then brought to an "official" close, and many of the students returned to the Thammasat campus to celebrate the victory which they had achieved.

However, a very significant number of the more militant students (perhaps somewhat less than half of the original 200,000), either because they were eager to press further the advantage which they felt they had gained, or because they had not clearly understood the nature of the solution which had been achieved, failed to disperse and, as the evening proceeded, became increasingly restive. Around midnight, in order to retain their leadership and to clarify the situation, the NSCT leadership directed the students to march to the king's palace. After they had been congregated for some time at the palace (by this time it was just before dawn on Sunday morning), an official aide of the king again informed them of the government's agreement regarding the promulgation of a new constitution, and apprised them of the king's ardent desire that the demonstration be brought to an end. At this point (shortly after 6 A.M. on Sunday morning) many of the remaining students began to disperse; however, a militant core group still was not satisfied and refused to clear the area. Exactly what happened next cannot be determined with any degree of certainty, but what *is* definitely known is that at about 6:30 A.M. on the southern side of the palace tear gas bombs began to explode and the police unit which had been on duty began to fire on a crowd of fleeing students. The period of restrained confrontation had come to an end, and a period of violent confrontation had begun.

The first shots having been fired, the pent up hostilities on both sides exploded into violence which spread rapidly throughout the city. The students, and particularly the vocational students who had for years been involved in violent inter-school brawling and related encounters with the police, mounted attacks on various government centers and succeeded in burning several key buildings which housed agencies which had long been particular objects of popular hostility.[5] For their part, the police and other government forces responded with tear gas and gunfire, killing and wounding not only some of the attackers but many of the less militant students and other bystanders as well. As it turned out, something less than one hundred persons (including a number of policemen and soldiers) were actually killed during the entire two days of fighting, but at the time reports were circulating which put the number in the thousands. Moreover, the impression of government brutality was enhanced by very obvious and rapidly reported incidents which involved indiscriminant shooting from government helicopters, one of which was widely believed to have been piloted by Colonel Narong himself. It is clear that in the minds of the great mass of students and people, the government, through its direct involvement in the killing of students and others, had broken its last tie with the nation and had thereby destroyed the last vestiges of its own legitimacy.

Clearly, at this point, the issue had been drawn. To be sure, the government had lost its legitimacy in the eyes of its subjects, but there was still a very real possibility that it could maintain its control through the exercise of brute military force. However, this did not occur, and the reason is made clear by an account of a meeting which involved the king, F. M. Thanom, and the commanders of the three major military services. In that meeting, according to a later newspaper report, F. M. Thanom asked his commanders if they were willing to stand by him in an effort to crush the uprising. The response from the commander of the army was that he would remain loyal, but that he could not guarantee that his men would follow. The response from the commander of the navy was that the navy had always sided with the people. And the response from the commander of the air force was that the air force awaited the orders of his Majesty the King. What this report signifies, quite apart from whether or not it is a precise word-by-word rendering of what actually transpired in the meeting, is that the government's loss of any claim to exercise legitimate authority had been recognized by very significant individuals and groups within the military establishment itself. It was this recognition which sealed the fate of the old regime and made possible the victory of the students. At approximately 8:45 on Sunday evening King Phumipol appeared on national television and in a short, highly formal, but intensely emotional speech expressed the sorrow and shame of the nation concerning the violence and killing that had occurred during the day; and he then went on to announce that the Thanom government had resigned, and that he had appointed Nai Sanya Thammasakdi to serve as interim prime minister until a new constitution could be drafted.[6]

However, despite the king's announcement and his personal plea for a cessation of the violence and a return to normalcy, and despite a subsequent, strongly Buddhist-oriented plea from the Princess Mother which was also broadcast over national television, the fighting in the streets did not abate. Clearly, the militant vocational students had tasted the first fruits of success and were now determined to bring about the complete demise of Thanom, Prapat, and Narong. And shortly after midnight it became clear that Thanom himself had not given up the battle; now acting in his role as commander-in-chief of the armed forces he issued a strongly worded statement indicating that since communist terrorists had infiltrated the student ranks and posed an immediate threat to the security of the nation and its heritage, the military would act decisively to restore order. During the day on Monday the fighting continued, but, as the day proceeded, it became increasingly clear that Thanom's accusation concerning the communist subversion of the movement was not being accepted, and that he and his supporters simply could not marshall the military support which they needed in order to carry out their announced purpose of crushing the uprising.[7] During the afternoon an agreement was reached among the king, Nai Sanya, the NSCT leaders (who, ironically, had not shown any great enthusiasm for the more militant student actions which had occurred since the original compromise "solution" had been announced during the demonstrations at the Democracy Monument on Saturday afternoon) on the one hand, and Thanom, Prapat and Narong on the other. Shortly thereafter, at the official request of the king himself, the three former leaders, their families and a few followers were escorted to the airport where they boarded a plane for Taipei. Later in the afternoon their departure was publicly announced, and within a remarkably short time the fighting had ceased.

In retrospect, it is obvious that a great variety of different kinds of factors contributed to the process through which the tiny movement for the promulgation of a constitution burgeoned within one short week into a full-fledged student uprising, and the process through which this student uprising within a few additional days toppled the military government which had ruled in Bangkok for the better part of fifteen years. The overall political and economic situation, international as well as national, provided a potentially explosive context for a reaction against the established authority. Disillusionment with the ruling clique, especially within the military group itself, had cut much deeper than most observers (including, most importantly, the ruling clique itself) had imagined. The long-standing tension between the monarchy and the government played a crucial role, as did the very adept and effective ways in which the king acted in the midst of the crisis to maintain the integrity of the nation while at the same time advancing, as far as was practicable at each given stage, the cause of the students. Moreover, many other kinds of factors were involved. For example, in the early stages of the crisis the government followed a kind of middle course between decisive repression and discreet compromise which, as it turned out, actually fed the flames of discontent and therefore played directly into the hands of the more ambitious protestors. Indeed, the psychological factor of the numerous predictions of local astrologers, who had for some time been pointing to a governmental crisis, as well as the astrological calculations which were associated with the timing of various aspects of the demonstration itself, should not be underestimated. And certainly the importance of the quite arbitrary fact that the weather held good played a crucial role. Had a heavy seasonal rain occurred on Friday or Saturday, it is possible or even probable that the demonstration would have fizzled, and that Thanom, Prapat, and Narong would still be in power in Bangkok today.[8]

However, the primary point we have sought to highlight is that among these many various factors which contributed to the outbreak of the demonstrations and the success of the uprising, the legitimating role of Thai civic religion must be taken seriously into account. The issue which became the catalyst for the uprising and which enabled the students to capture very broad-based support from practically all segments of the population was the demand for the promulgation of a constitution, the absence of which had, since the Thanom-Prapat coup of 1971, been fostering increasingly serious doubts concerning the legitimacy of the military'regime. Throughout the period of escalating tension the students quite self-consciously challenged the legitimacy of the government on the basis that it was no longer serving the interests of the people, and had great success in identifying their own cause with that of the nation. And, as time went on, they mounted a serious effort to establish in the public mind a close association between their movement and the two other major foci of Thai civic religious consciousness — the monarchy and religion (most specifically, Buddhism). By the time of the massive march on Saturday, and through the skillful use of civic religious symbolism in the context of the march itself, the patriotism of the students and the legitimacy of their protest movement in traditional Thai terms came to be almost universally accepted. It was this fact, along with the impressiveness of their numbers and the not-so-subtle threats of physical force, which provided the leverage the students needed in order to force the government to accede to their demands.

Though, as I have suggested, it is by no means certain exactly how the first outbreak of real violence which took place early Sunday morning at the royal palace actually occurred, it *is* clear that the students and the public were practically unanimous in their assumption that the police were the aggressors. It is also clear that this assumption resulted in the government's loss of the last vestiges of its claim to exercise legitimate authority. And, at the same time, a corresponding boost was given to the legitimacy of the students' cause by the obvious and quite public sympathy and aid which the king and the royal household gave to the students who were on the scene, especially to those who had been injured in the encounter. (Again, the publicity given to these expressions by the media was equally as important a factor as the actions themselves.) Thus, those public images which had been carefully developed during the course of the preceding week were now dramatically confirmed. And these images, now decisively reinforced by the blood of martyrs, provided a highly effective source of legitimation for the ensuing violence of the more militant students, and made a crucial contribution to the ethos in which Thanom's final, desperate effort to identify these students as communist terrorists fell on totally deaf ears.

Conclusion

In this paper my purpose has been two-fold. On the one hand, I have highlighted the existence of a specifically civic religion in Thai history, particularly in recent Thai history. And, in addition, I have described the fascinating and crucial role which this civic religious tradition played in setting the stage for the student uprising of October 1973, and in the success which the students achieved in securing the ouster of Thanom, Prapat and Narong. This account could, of course, be continued through a discussion of the very important role which the sacrality of the *chat*, the *sāsana*, the *mahakesat* and the *ratatamanun* played in the efforts to restore national unity, in the subsequent reinstatement of constitutional government, and in the various controversies which have developed in the more recent phases of Thai national life. And, it could also be continued through a discussion of the very significant changes which the traditions of Thai civic religion have themselves undergone in the context of the student uprising and of subsequent events. Both of these avenues of research should yield interesting results, and we hope to pursue them in future studies.

Notes

The interviews and materials on which this paper is based were gathered between September, 1973 and February, 1974 when my wife and I were in Thailand under the sponsorship of a Fulbright/Hayes faculty research fellowship and were receiving supplementary support from the American Philosophical Society and the Committee on Southern Asian Studies at the University of Chicago. Our thanks go to these organizations, and also to the National Research Council which granted us permission to carry out our work in Thailand.

1. For a discussion of this background, see my articles on "Sasana Kong phonlamuang nai pra-prawatsat Thai" in the festschrift for Prince Wan Wathayakorn published as a special issue of the *Social Science Review* (1971) and on "Civic Religion and National Community in Thailand," *Journal of Asian Studies* (February, 1977), 267-282.

2. I have discussed some of the relevant material in an article which, though it was written several months before the October uprising contains material concerning the role of the monarchy which is extremely relevant to the present paper. See "Sacral Kingship and National Development" (1973), which is reprinted in the present collection of essays.

3. For an excellent discussion of the king and constitution as well as other highly relevant aspects of Thai civic religion, see Koson Srisang, "Dhammocracy in Thailand: A Study of Social Ethics as a Hermeneutic of Dhamma" (Unpublished doctoral dissertation, University of Chicago, 1973).

4. The role of the press, particularly the Prachatipatai and Sayamrat dailies, in conveying these legitimizing images (the former focusing especially on the connection with the constitution and democracy, and the latter on the connection with the monarchy) was crucial, and is in itself worthy of an independent study. In this connection it is perhaps worth noting the fact that many citizens believed that the Sayamrat editorials (written by Kukrit Pramoj, who later became the prime minister under the new constitution), which were strongly positive toward the protest movement and which culminated on Thursday in a call for the government's resignation, represented a true reflection of the views of the king himself.

5. Earlier in the week the various groups of vocational students had agreed with one another that they would temporarily put aside their differences and join together in the protest movement.

6. It is perhaps not purely fortuitous that the man whom the king chose to lead Thailand through the profound crisis which it was undergoing was not only one who was acquainted with students and respected by them (he had for several years been the Rector of Thammasat University), but was also a leader who was closely associated with the prime symbols of Thai civic life. In this connection, it is significant that Nai Sanya had long been a staunch nationalist, that he was at the time serving as a member of the king's privy council, that he had for many years been one of the country's most prominent lay Buddhists, and that in his earlier years he had built a long record of distinguished service as the Chief Justice of the Supreme Court of Thailand.

7. Actually, the military leader's propaganda concerning the communist subversion of the movement, which was conveyed during the morning hours by the government radio, which seems to have been accepted by some of the peasants in outlying areas who had no other sources of information (at least after the uprising was successful many were surprised by the fact that no communists were included in the new government). However, in Bangkok and other major centers where the action was taking place and where the crucial decisions were being made, Thanom and his supporters had, by this time, lost all effective credibility.

8. The danger which a change in the weather posed was clearly recognized by the students. In fact, during the demonstrations special ceremonies were organized in order to offer prayers to the guardian deity of the city in order that rain might be averted.

Political Crisis and Militant Buddhism in Contemporary Thailand

Charles F. Keyes

Militant Buddhism in Theravada Buddhist History

IN THE *Mahāvaṃsa*, the great mythical history of Buddhism in Sri Lanka, it is related that in the second century B.C. a Tamil king from South India had taken control of Anurādhapura, the ancient capital of Sri Lanka. During the more than forty years of his reign, Buddhism was not given royal support and the faith which had only been established in the country a short time previously was in danger of being destroyed. However, a young Sri Lankan prince from the southeastern part of the island, known as Duṭṭhagāmaṇi (or Dutugemunu), finally succeeded in mobilizing sufficient force to defeat the Tamils, kill the Tamil ruler, and become the king of the whole country. The war which Duṭṭhagāmaṇi waged against the Tamils portrayed in the *Mahāvaṃsa* is depicted in terms which make it the nearest approximation to a holy war which can be found almost anywhere in the literature of Theravada Buddhism.

Duṭṭhagāmaṇi is said to have carried into battle a spear in which was embedded a Buddhist relic and he is said to have marched with five hundred ascetic monks. His object in attacking the Tamils was "to bring glory to the doctrine."[2] Yet, in the process of attaining this worthy objective, Duṭṭhagāmaṇi was greatly distraught by the thought of the demerit which was created by the slaughter in battle and he told eight *arhats* (Buddhist saints) who came to him that he could not be comforted because he had been responsible for the death of so many. However, the *arhats* told him:

> From this deed arises no hindrance in thy way to heaven. Only one and a half human beings were slain here by thee, O lord of men. The one had come unto the refuges, the other had taken on himself the five precepts. Unbelievers and men of evil life were the rest, not more to be esteemed than beasts. But as for thee, thou wilt bring glory to the doctrine of the Buddha in manifold ways; therefore cast away care from thy heart, O ruler of men.[3]

And, true to their words, after his own death, Duṭṭhagāmaṇi was said to have been reborn in the Tusita heaven where he became the first disciple of the Maitreya (Mettayya) Buddha, the future Buddha.

Obeyesekere, commenting on this myth, says that:

> This is the only instance in the Ceylon chronicles where there is an explicit justification for war and killing in terms which perhaps better fit the *Bhagavata Gita* than the Buddhist *suttas*. I have heard historians of Ceylon argue that this was simply a lone exception in the history of Ceylon.[4]

In all of the societies where Theravada Buddhism has become dominant — that is, in Burma, Thailand, Laos, and Cambodia as well as Sri Lanka — Buddhism has been construed as fundamental to the legitimacy of power.[5] Moreover, in

147

periods where there have been crises of power, men have arisen in these societies who have claimed to have extraordinary Buddhist merit and therefore able
to restore the world to a state of less suffering.[6] Yet, Obeyesekere's conclusion is probably as valid for most of the history of Theravada Buddhist societies.
Buddhism has traditionally in these societies been seen as a refuge of peace
from a world of incessant conflict or as a source of strength for those who
would restore peace in a disturbed mundane world. It has rarely been seen as
a cause for taking up arms and destroying one's enemies.

Given that Buddhism has long been seen as representing peace, not war, it
was extremely shocking to many when in 1976 in Thailand a widely-respected
monk publically advocated a holy war on "Communists" in terms which
echoes strongly the justifications for killing given to Duṭṭhagāmaṇi. In this
paper I shall attempt an interpretation of the radical call to a militant Buddhism by this monk, attending to the political events which led up to his public espousal of the position, to the claims to authority which he made in advocating the message, and to the "social drama," to use Victor Turner's concept,[7]
which was set in motion by this highly unusual action.

It is my thesis that the rise of militant Buddhism in Thailand is a direct consequence of a political crisis in which the moral basis for political authority
became problematic. In turn, once militant Buddhism had emerged as a significant ideology, that is, an ideology which had wide support, it became a
critical element in the efforts to order events in order to achieve a resolution
to this crisis. Implicit in this argument is a theoretical assumption that neither
political action nor political ideology can be seen as mere reflections of the
other but that they are related dialectically.

Kittivuḍḍho Bhikkhu and Right-Wing Politics in Thailand

Biography of Kittivuḍḍho Bhikkhu[8]

For a monk as famous as Kittivuḍḍho Bhikkhu it is noteworthy that there
are few public facts known about him prior to his ordination as a monk in
1957, the year in which Thailand and the rest of the Buddhist world celebrated the 2500 year anniversary of the Buddhist era.[9] It is quite possible that the
facts about Kittivuḍḍho's early, pre-clerical life have been purposely restricted to permit possible hagiographic treatment at a later stage. What is known is
that he was born in 1936 in Bāng Len District of Nakhōn Pathom province,
some 55 kilometers northwest of Bangkok-Thonburi. In 1957, when he was
21, he was one of a very large number of young men who was ordained into
the monkhood on the auspicious occasion of the 2500 year anniversary of
the Buddhist era. He was ordained into the Mahānikāya order and took up
residence at Wat Paknām Phāsīcarōēn in Thonburi. He later moved to the
famous temple, Wat Mahādhātu in Bangkok, a temple to which he is still formally affiliated.

Within a few years of his ordination, he began to develop a reputation as a
public speaker and, although he apparently never undertook the study of the
Dhamma and of Pāli language as structured in the curriculum taught in all
major monasteries in Thailand, he staked a claim to being a significant interpreter of the Buddhist scriptures by establishing in 1967 the Abhidhamma

Foundation College of Wat Mahādhātu. As the name suggests, the ostensible purpose of the Abhidhamma Foundation was to foster the study of the *Abhidhamma-pitaka*, the metaphysical basket of the Buddhist scriptures, the part of the scriptures which is most difficult to interpret.

While the Abhidhamma Foundation has remained as an important institutional outlet for the spread of Kittivuḍḍho's ideas, it has not achieved the reputation of Cittabhāvana (Thai, *Cittaphāwan*) College which he founded in the same year. Cittabhāvana College is located some 100 kilometers away from Bangkok-Thonburi in a beach-resort area in Chonburi Province. According to a booklet written by Kittivuḍḍho himself, Cittabhāvana means "elevating the mind or developing the mind, improving it through moral practice . . . . The promulgation of Buddhism is the elevation of the minds of the people of the world to a higher level through moral practice."[10]

Cittabhāvana College is a unique religious institution. Although it has no formal place in the organizational structure of the Thai Sangha, it has become a center at which thousands of boys have been ordained as novices, and at which hundreds of monks each year have been instructed in Kittivuḍḍho's own particular version of Buddhist social action. For Kittivuḍḍho, members of the Sangha must not remain in their temples waiting for the laity to seek them out for purposes of merit-making. Rather, Kittivuḍḍho has strongly advocated that since "monks are people in the world, they should help the world, too."[11] Monks should go out to propagate the Dhamma of the Buddha, to guide those who are Buddhists in finding moral bases for their actions, and to convert those who are not Buddhists.

The activist Buddhism promoted by Kittivuḍḍho at Cittabhāvana College has strong similarities to a number of other programs, mainly government-promoted, which were created in the 1960s. Such programs as the government financed *thammathūt* (Pāli, *Dhammadhūta*, or "Dhammic-ambassador" project) and the *thammacārik* (*Dhammacārika*, "wandering Dhamma" project), the privately supported *thammaphatthanā* (*Dhammabadhanā*, "Dhammic-development" project) financed mainly by the Asia Foundation, and community development programs of the Buddhist universities, all have been predicated upon the idea that monks should be much more active in working to bring about a reduction of suffering in the world. While many of the monks who have participated in these programs have done so with true concern about the conditions under which many in Thailand live, the basic purpose of all of these programs has been ideological. All seek to instill in the populace a sense of Buddhist morality which can be utilized in the quest of mundane goals. Many government officials who have accompanied the activist monks in their travels in the countryside and a few of the activist monks themselves have also made explicit the contention that Buddhism must serve as the bulwark against Communism.[12]

At the outset, the activist Buddhism promoted by Kittivuḍḍho did not appear to have an explicitly anti-Communist flavor. However, events of the period between October 1973 and about the middle of 1975 led him to become stridently anti-Communist and to attempt to create a movement which sought to destroy, by force if necessary, the "enemies" of the religion, the nation, and the monarchy.

Kittivuḍḍho and the Nawaphon Movement

In early October 1973, university students in Thailand began a protest movement against the military government led by Field Marshal Thanom Kittikachorn and Field Marshal Praphat Charusathien which had arrested a number of leaders of an organization demanding the promulgation of a Constitution. By the 14th of October, the protest had attracted upwards of a quarter million people. While the protest had been non-violent, it now began to take on a new cast as some of the demonstrators set fire to a police station and the National Lottery building, both located in the vicinity of Thammasat University where the demonstration was centered. On the 14th of October, the demonstrators were attacked at Thammasat University by police and military units. The resultant bloodshed, leaving perhaps as many as 74 dead, was greatly shocking to most Thai and, apparently, particularly so to the king. Although the events of the 14th and 15th of October, 1973 are still not entirely clear, it is apparent that both the king and General Kris Sivara, the head of the army, intervened to end the violence and to arrange for Thanom, Praphat, and Narong, Thanom's son and Praphat's son-in-law, to leave the country.

While the October Revolution of 1973 succeeded in toppling the existing military dictatorship, it also created a serious crisis of political legitimacy in Thailand. The military had refrained or had been prevented from exercising its control of force in making a claim for power and the revolutionary leaders, mainly students, lacked control of any force which they might have used in establishing themselves in power. Without a constitution — the goal which the protestors had sought — there was also no legal basis for determining who should exercise power. The only source of legitimation in the aftermath of the October Revolution was the king and the recognition of his legitimating quality was not predicated upon any legally defined rights but on a traditional Buddhist idea that the king embodied greater merit than anyone else in the kingdom. That King Phumiphon Adunlayadet was a "man of merit" had been demonstrated time and again in the previous two decades through the linking of symbols of monarchy and Buddhism in school texts, in the press, in almost every public ceremony, and in special rituals initiated by the king himself.[13]

The king chose neither a military man nor one of the revolutionary leaders to head a new government; rather, he chose one of his own counsellors, Sanya Dhammasakdi, a man who as Rector of Thammasat University was also acceptable to the students. Sanya was charged with establishing an interim government whose term would last only until a new constitution could be written and promulgated and a constitutionally-based government established. The constitution which was finally promulgated by the king in October 1974, was very different from other constitutions which had existed previously in Thailand. Not only was it drafted by a civilian group, appointed by the king, but it was passed by an Assembly which had been chosen from representatives of all segments of the Thai population. Symbolically, at least, the constitution was the people's constitution. This constitution also provided for a government, responsible to a Parliament, whose members were to be elected by the people.

Political parties, except for the Communist Party, were legalized shortly after the promulgation of the constitution. Then many groups — from elements of the old military and commercial elites, to the now expanded middle classes, to liberal and socialist intellectuals — began to work to mobilize support from among the populace for their varying approaches to governing. Elections were held in January 1975, contested by what seemed to be a bewildering number of parties. The results of the elections were not conclusive for any party and it was only after some maneuvering that a centrist-right-wing coalition government led by M. R. Kukrit Pramote took office.

During this period of transition from the royally-appointed Sanya government to the Parliamentary government, another movement was created which almost went unnoticed at the time because it did not claim to be a political party seeking parliamentary representation. This movement, known as *Nawaphon* (Skt., *navabala*, "the nine strengths"), received its name because of the nine points of its program designed to preserve Thai nationalism.[14] While Nawaphon is known to have drawn its financial support from a number of strongly anti-Communist military officers, the most significant fact about it is that it developed into a popular movement which acquired adherents mainly because of its ultra-nationalistic ideology. From what little is known about the movement to date, it appears that those who were attracted to the movement were mainly low-level government functionaries and clerks, urban petit-bourgeoisie, and rural village and commune headmen. It also attracted the support of a number of monks, most notably Kittivuddho Bhikkhu.

When Kittivuddho began to play an active role in the Nawaphon movement is not clear, but it most probably occurred after Communist governments were established in Cambodia and South Vietnam in April 1975. These events made, according to Kittivuddho's own words, a very strong impression on him. He tells of visiting Cambodia just before the fall of that country and describes the terrible state of mind in which he found Khmer monks who anticipated the coming of Communist rule. And he tells of hearing accounts after the fall about the destruction and desecration of temple-monasteries and the killing of monks, as well as ordinary people.[15] What happened in Cambodia clearly demonstrated to him that Communism represented a dire threat to the religion. Moreover, when the new Communist government of Laos abolished the Lao monarchy in December 1975, he was convinced that Communism also represented a threat to the institution of the monarchy. In addition to these events which obviously influenced Kittivuddho's thinking, it is also important to note that his support was drawn from much the same class of people as was the support for the Nawaphon movement.

By the end of 1975 Kittivuddho was clearly a leader of the Nawaphon movement and his stature as a distinguished monk most certainly made the movement attractive to many who might otherwise have been more wary of the lay leaders with their close military connections. Kittivuddho's role in the Nawaphon became a public issue in early January 1976 when he was conspicuously present at a demonstration of some 2000 commune and village headmen who came directly from a meeting at Cittabhāvana College to Government House in Bangkok. The demonstrators called for the government to resign and to turn over power to a "National Reform Council" led by the military. They also railed against those members of Parliament who were Communists disguised as Socialists.[16]

Kittivuddho's apparent participation in what was unquestionably a political demonstration became an immediate public issue. Two years previously, in

May 1974, about 20 monks had participated in a demonstration involving perhaps 20,000 people who had gathered to protest government policy towards the peasantry. Subsequently, a number of the monks who had participated in the demonstration had been subjected to investigations by the abbots of their temple-monasteries and at least one had been expelled by his abbot. In December 1974, supporters of this monk had demanded that the expulsion order against him be lifted and that the Sangha be reformed so that it would be more responsive to the problems of the people.[17] Because of this outcry, the Mahā Thera Samāgama known in English as the Ecclesiastical Council, the highest Sangha body in the country headed by the Supreme Patriarch, considered the question of monks participation in political activities. The Council issued a statement on December 2, 1974, which said that "It was not appropriate for monks to join in the demonstration by the peasants and that the abbots [of temple-monasteries] have the duty to determine punishment."[18] While the monk in question was eventually allowed to resume his clerical life, the Council reaffirmed its position several times in the ensuing months that monks should not participate in political demonstrations. Thus, when Kittivuḍḍho was seen to be among the Nawaphon demonstrators in January 1976, questions were raised, most notably by liberal newspapers, about whether he would be punished for the action.

The Supreme Patriarch, who was interviewed a day or two after the demonstration, was said by the Thai newspaper, *Daily Times*, that while he did not know all the facts, he thought that Kittivuḍḍho had committed a minor infraction of the monk's discipline. The Patriarch said that an investigation would be made to determine if all the facts are correct, and, if necessary, the question would be taken up by the Ecclesiastical Council. If he were judged to have committed an infraction, he would, according to the Supreme Patriarch, probably be reproached (*tamni*) and not punished in any other way since this was the first time that he had done anything like this.[19] Kittivuḍḍho, himself, had told reporters after the demonstration that he had "acted like this in order to protect the country because if the nation does not exist, the religion cannot exist."[20] The Supreme Patriarch was asked to comment on this statement and had said that "if the facts be that Kittivuḍḍho acted to protect the country, that is a good purpose; but I do not see that what he did was of any utility and also as monks it is not necessary to act like this."[21]

Rather curiously, among those who complained about Kittivuḍḍho's participation in the Nawaphon demonstration in the following weeks was a leader of the "Red Gaur" (*krathing dāeng*), another radical right-wing movement. A Mr. Praphan Wongkham, advisor to the Krathing Dāeng, attacked those on the right who acted in such a way to hurt the cause and pointed specifically to Kittivuḍḍho "who is in such a position that he ought not to become involved in politics."[22] This attack may have been based on ideological grounds, but it may also have reflected some sort of competition between the Red Gaur and Nawaphon.

An investigation into Kittivuḍḍho's action was apparently launched by the Ecclesiastical Council at the instigation of Ministry of Education which has responsibility for religious affairs.[23] However, after an announcement made in early February that the Ecclesiastical Council was considering the issue, no further action seems to have been taken.[24]

Kittivuḍḍho, for his part, however, strongly defended his action. In an interview in the newspaper, *Prachāchāt* ("The Nation"), he said that he had not led the demonstration. Rather the commune and village headmen who had been at a training session at Cittabhāvana College had wished to go to Bangkok. He had gone along to see that the affair remained orderly.[25] In a speech given on July 2, 1976, Kittivuḍḍho reiterated this same point. He added that he was only a "binding agent" (*tua chṳam*) for the headmen and that although nothing had happened at the demonstration, the newspapers had made it "headline news."[26] Yet, while attempting to excuse his action, Kittivuḍḍho reaffirmed strongly his support of the purpose of the Nawaphon movement. He said:

> I would like to point out that it is understood that this Nawaphon is not a political party. Nawaphon is a principle of nationalism. It is only a name of a philosophy whereby we take the middle way of Buddhism as the way to act in order to solve all problems of government, economics, and society.[27]

For Kittivuḍḍho, Nawaphon is the only ideology which a true Thai nationalist (who must also be a Buddhist) can take. Anyone who opposes Nawaphon must, therefore, be an enemy of the nation, the religion, and the monarchy. And, those enemies are to be destroyed.

Kittivuḍḍho's Call to Preserve the Nation, the Religion and the Monarchy: "Killing Communists Is Not Demeritorious"

In about mid-June Kittivuḍḍho gave an interview with the liberal magazine, *Caturat*. This interview allowed him to make public an extended statement of his ideas about the role of the monk in the context of a political crisis brought about by the student-led revolution of 1973, the creation of Parliamentary system of government in Thailand, and the Communist victories in neighboring Laos, Cambodia, and Vietnam.[28] In the context of this interview, Kittivuḍḍho was asked whether killing of leftists or Communists produced demerit (*pāppa*), i.e., the negative karma which would have the consequence of more suffering in some future time in this life or the next. Kittivuḍḍho replied that Buddhists must do this (i.e., kill Communists). However, he said, such killing is not killing persons "because whoever destroys the nation, the religion, or the monarchy, such bestial types (*man*) are not complete persons. Thus, we must intend not to kill people but to kill the Devil (Māra); this is the duty of all Thai." He continued, under questioning, to say that while any killing is demeritorious, the demerit is very little and the merit very great for such an act which serves to preserve the nation, the religion, and the monarchy. "It is just like," he said, "when we kill a fish to make a stew to place in the alms bowl for a monk. There is certainly demerit in killing the fish, but we place it in the alms bowl of a monk and gain much greater merit."[29]

This interview caused quite a furor and was discussed at length in the press. In the subsequent weeks, Kittivuḍḍho himself attempted to clarify his position through interviews with various newspapers and magazines and in public lectures. The most extended (and bitter) such self-justification was made in a speech at Cittabhāvana College to an audience described as monks belonging to the first twelve "spiritual development units" (*phra nuai phatthanākān thāng cit*) – that is, monks trained in activist programs at Cittabhāvana. The audience was also said to contain provincial abbots or their representatives. Obviously not backing down one whit under attack, Kittivuḍḍho entitled his speech, "Killing Communists is Not Demeritorious." The speech was subsequently published as a pamphlet under the imprint of Kittivuḍḍho's Abhid-hamma Foundation.[30]

In this speech, Kittivuḍḍho attempted to mobilize a number of religious arguments to justify his position. One of his arguments turned on the question of intention (*cetanā*). He says that for a death to be considered to have been caused by an act of killing, and thus to have demerit as a result, doctrine (the *vinaya*) requires that five conditions be met:

(1) "*pāṇo*, the animal must have life;"

(2) "*paṇasaññitā*, one must know that the animal has life;"

(3) "*vadhakacittaṅ*, one must intend to kill;"

(4) "*upakkamo*, one must act only in order to kill;"

(5) "*tenamaraṇaṅ*, the animal must die by that act."[31]

Although he does not make the connection explicit at this point, he does say that soldiers are justified in killing if they do not intend to kill people, but act on their intention to protect the country.[32]

Kittivuḍḍho invokes the teachings of the Buddha as a source of support for his position in several different ways. He says that as the Buddha taught that one must sacrifice the lesser good for the greater good, so too must "our heroes sacrifice their lives in order to preserve the nation, religion and monarchy for all of us." Then, in a superb *non sequitur*, he continues as follows:

> Our heroes must kill people; however, those people are enemies of the country. This [act of killing] is certainly demeritorious, but the merit is greater. I believe that all those [heroes] make greater merit. Today, when I make merit, the first thing I think about are our heroes who do their duty to protect the country, the religion, and the institution of the monarchy. I always dedicate a portion of the merit I make to all these.[33]

In another place in his speech, Kittivuḍḍho asks, "Did the Lord Buddha teach us to kill or not? He taught [us to do so]. He taught us to kill. Venerable sirs, you are likely to be suspicious about this teaching. I will tell you the sutta and you can investigate: [It is] the *Kesi-sutta* in the *Kesiya-vagga*, the *sutta-nipiṭaka, aṅguttara-nikāya, catukaka-nipāta*. If you open [this text] venerable sirs, you will find in the sutta that the Lord Buddha ordered killing."[34] Having made this startling claim, Kittivuḍḍho then tells the story contained in this sutta. There was a famous horse trainer who visited the Buddha. The Buddha asked him what methods he used to train horses such that he had obtained the reputation which he had. The trainer replies that for some horses he uses a gentle technique, for others a severe technique, and for others a combination of these. What if none of these methods work, the Buddha asks. Then I kill the horse, the trainer replied. Why? asked the Buddha. "In order not to destroy the reputation of the teacher." The Buddha makes an analogy between himself and the trainer regarding his teaching of the Dhamma. However, what the Buddha means, he explains, is that one kills by ceasing to teach the person who cannot be taught.[35] Kittivuḍḍho then interprets the sutta:

> The Buddha kills and discards, but the word "kill" according to the principles of the Buddha is killing according to the Dhamma and Vinaya of Buddhism. To kill and discard by not teaching is the method of killing. I don't mean that the Lord Buddha ordered the killing of persons. But [he ordered] the killing of the impurities of people.[36]

He then says that to kill Communists is to kill ideology, "to kill the impurities (*kilesa*) in the hearts of people."[37] Again in another *non sequitur*, in the next sentence he says that soldiers who kill people, use the methods of the world. However, "They kill to protect themselves, to protect the nation, the religion, the monarchy. They kill like that, and that is demeritorious, but it is little demerit and the merit is greater."[38] Having said this, he then tells his audience that if they are ever asked to justify people killing Communists they should refer to the scriptural source cited.

In this speech, as in his other speeches and interviews, Kittivuḍḍho shows himself to be a masterful rhetorician. He is able to link the powerful emotional meanings associated in Thailand with the term "to kill" with a clear political philosophy. Here is a representative of a religion noted for its categorical rejection of killing, a monk who in his own actions should be suppressing all feelings of anger since anger (dōsa) is one of the cardinal sins recognized by Buddhism. When a monk, a man in the yellow robes, says "Killing Communists is not demeritorious," he immediately gains an audience. Then he tells us that because he is a monk, only enemies of the religion would attack him. If these enemies succeed the religion will be destroyed, and the Communists will kill all good people. Look, he tells us, at the slaughter in Cambodia. He conjures up images of desecrated temples, of monks being killed by bestial types, the Communists. Then he says, I did not order people to kill each other. It is the Communists who order people to kill. But if we are to protect our religion, our nation, our monarchy, it is necessary to kill Communists. Communists are not people, however; they are the devil, impurities and ideology personified, abstractions. It is all right to kill an ideology; the Buddha taught us to do so, and he gave us the Dhamma with which to do it. Yet, if defenders of the nation, religion, and monarchy use the methods of the world (i.e., weapons) to kill Communists, that is all right because their intention was morally correct. Thus, the merit they gain will be far more than the demerit acquired.

But Kittivuḍḍho is not only a rhetorician, seeking to persuade people to his views through the skillful manipulation of symbols. He also makes another claim to authority which gives his message particular impact for those who are able to believe.

Kittivuḍḍho as a Saint

It is well known to all monks that to claim to have extraordinary powers, to claim that some "superior human state worthy of the 'Noble Ones' [Arhats] knowledge and vision is present in himself," and not, in fact, to possess such extraordinary powers results in a pārājika-āpatti, a defeat of the monk's efforts to follow the religious life.[39] A monk who incurs pārājika-āpatti must leave the monkhood. For this reason alone, a monk must be very wary of claiming to have extraordinary powers or of being an Arhat, a Saint, whose characteristics include such powers.

Kittivuḍḍho has raised the question of his being a saint and while he has refrained from making any claims which might be misinterpreted, he certainly has succeeded in planting in the minds of some of his followers the thought that he might well be an Arhat. In an interview which he gave to the Prachāchāt newspaper in late June, 1976, he said that while he could easily achieve nibbāna if he wished, he had not done so because the conditions were not suitable:

> How can one seek after Nibbāna when a gun is pointed at one's throat? I have gone and seen in Laos and Cambodia monks without number that have died. In Thailand at this time, the conditions are not right for seeking after Nibbāna. I could seek after

Nibbāna easily. I only have to shut my eyes for a moment and it would be Nibbāna (*ātamā ca mung niphān nan ngāi; lap tā pradiao pradāo ko niphān lāēo*).[40]

The implicit meaning in this statement is that Kittivuḍḍho is a Arhat who has foregone attainment of nibbāna in order to help a troubled world.

In his speech to monks on July 2, 1976, he even appears to substitute a heavenly state for Nibbāna while still implying that he might be a Arhat:

Ever since I was ordained, I have not hoped for Nibbāna. I speak straight. I do not desire Nibbāna in this life. I desire the Buddha-land (Buddha-bhūmi; Thai, *phuttha phūmi*). Perhaps I will go to Hell (*naraka*) instead; it is not certain. But I believe this; my virtues (*pārami*) are such that I must do [what I do]. Thus, I am not afraid [except] if anyone misrepresents me as a Arhat. Then I am very afraid. . . . Do not extol me as an Arhat; I do not like it.[41]

Earlier in the same speech he had also protested being called an Arhat:

When they accuse me of being shameless, I remain content. If they accuse me of being a stupid person, I am still content. But if they come and praise me as an Arhat, I am extremely frightened. I have fled from the Arhat [role] ever since [my] first lent [as a monk] and that is the veritable truth, venerable sirs. At the time I lived in a cave, when anyone came with the understanding that I was an Arhat, I hurriedly leapt away. I have opposed anyone [making this claim] since my first lent [in the monk-hood]. Thus, I am not afraid at all of being accused of being anything . . . [except] I am most frightened when I am extolled as being an Arhat. I would go to Hell if [I claimed] to be an Arhat. If I am accused of being an Arhat, I will not go to Hell. At least, I am free of the [infraction of the monk's discipline which would incur *pārājika-āpatti*].[41]

Kittivuḍḍho has thus articulated the possibility that he is an Arhat, but has kept himself free of canonical punishment by emphasizing that he makes no claim himself. He alludes, in the reference to having dwelt in a cave, to behavior often thought typical of Arhat even though such behavior has not typified his clerical career. And he also suggests, indirectly but quite clearly, that if he is an Arhat, he has foregone attaining Nibbāna in order to help alleviate the suffering in the world.

There is no evidence available which would make possible any assessment of how many and what kinds of people might think of Kittivuḍḍho as an Arhat. It is likely, however, that this idea certainly has some currency among his followers at Cittabhāvana College and among the members of Nawaphon. Moreover, this identity gains credulity insofar as his plan for the reduction of suffering in the world actually succeeds. For Kittivuḍḍho, his plan involves the complete triumph of a militant Buddhist nationalism over all enemies.

The Enemies of the Nation, Religion, and Monarchy

Kittivuḍḍho calls for unrelenting and uncompromising attack on Communists and those who would bring about a Communist victory. This attack, he sees, as being mounted by monks and by soldiers, each using different weapons.

In speaking to an audience of monks, Kittivuḍḍho said:

All of you venerable sirs please consider. We are owners (*cao khǭng*) of the country. True, we are monks, but monks have always been among the owners of the country as a pillar of the nation since ancient times. Are we going to allow our country [to become Communist like Laos and Cambodia] by not helping? . . . [If Communism or Socialism triumphs] the religion will be attacked constantly and the nation will be shattered in many parts.[43]

Thus, monks must not sit on their mats in their temple-monasteries, waiting for lay people to seek them out. They must go out among the people and teach them who the enemies of the religion are.[44] Monks should attack the enemy with their special tools, their moral wisdom (*paññā*) and the Dhamma of the Buddha.[45]

Not all monks, unfortunately in Kittivuḍḍho's eyes, recognize the danger in which the country is. In addition to those monks who remain in their temple-monasteries, there are even leftist monks.

> Today even monks themselves are divided into left-wing monks and right-wing monks. They [presumably the Communist] divide the monks. This was the plan used in Laos and one can see the results in Cambodia. . . . I warn you strongly that when [aspirants] come to be ordained, be cautious.[46]

He specifically points to the "illegal" (*thŷan*) organization of the Young Sangha (*yuwa song*) and the National Center of Monks and Novices of Thailand (*Sūn klāng phra phiksu sammanēn hāeng prathēt thai*) as being organizations of leftist monks. Both these organizations emerged in Thailand after the Revolution of 1973.

For Kittivuḍḍho, *soldiers* includes both those who are actually in the armed services and also any other lay people who are willing to dedicate themselves to fight to preserve the religion, the nation, and the monarchy. Through the Nawaphon movement, Kittivuḍḍho would appear to have ties with right-wing elements of the military, many of whom being involved in Internal Security Operations Command. As to the other dedicated lay antagonists to Communists, for Kittivuḍḍho these were most likely to be affiliated with Nawaphon and/or the Village Scout (*lūk sŷa chāo bān*) movements. Members of these movements are described by Kittivuḍḍho as being "very angry. They are angry with those who attack me."[47]

Kittivuḍḍho is very explicit as to who the enemies of the religion, the nation, and the monarchy are. Foremost among the enemies are the students in the National Student Center of Thailand, the coordinating body which had led the Revolution of 1973. For Kittivuḍḍho, the October Revolution was caused by a major blunder and led to general unrest. It was most certainly part of Communist plan.[48] Since then, the students have been involved in a well-organized plan which will, if it succeeds, lead ultimately to a Communist society and to the destruction of the religion, the nation, and the monarchy.[49] In fact, the student leftists (whose organization began, he claims, in England in 1956[50]) are "even more evil than the Communists because they would destroy all the foundations of society . . . and build a completely new society."[51] Moreover, they are being manipulated and supported by "foreign Communists."[52]

In addition to the students, the other enemies are known because they have attacked him. These other enemies include most of the newspapers in the country,[53] but especially *Prachāchāt*, which is "the mouthpiece of the left,[54] and *Caturat* magazine which is clearly left-leaning.[55] Socialist MP's, and particularly those like Khlāeo Norapati, MP for Khŏnkaen, who have attacked Kittivuḍḍho, are clearly enemies.[56] And then there are the "illegal" Sangha organizations already mentioned above.

By mid-1976, Kittivuḍḍho had undertaken a major effort, in concert with the Nawaphon movement and probably with others on the far right to assert a very narrow definition of Thai nationalism. While others in the right-wing movements were pointing to (and in some cases helping to create) a floundering parliamentary system, growing labor and farmer unrest, increasing numbers of political assassinations, rampant corruption, persistent insurrection in some rural areas, and so on, Kittivuḍḍho offered people a plan of action which would lead to a marked alleviation of their troubles. His plan pitted him in direct opposition not only to "real" Communists (whoever they might be), but also to the liberals and socialists who had committed themselves to creating a constitutionally-based democratic government. In this confrontation were all the elements of a social drama whose outcome would have marked implications not only for Thailand's political future but also for the future of the relationship between Buddhism, nationalism, and the legitimation of power in Thailand.

Militant Buddhism and the Resolution of Political Crisis in Thailand: Kittivuḍḍho Is Accused of Behavior Unsuitable for a Monk

Demands were made for an investigation to determine whether or not he had committed an infraction of the code binding on monks. Whatever the outcome of this investigation, there could be hardly any doubt that he had clearly breached a norm which most people thought guided the behavior of monks. This breach was underscored by the fact that only a couple of months previous the Supreme Patriarch himself had issued a statement which denounced killing as being behavior beyond the pale for people who were Buddhists.

On March 3, 1976, the Supreme Patriarch had addressed the nation on the occasion of his birthday. His remarks had been formulated with regard to the growing number of political assassinations, including that of the Secretary-General of the Socialist Party of Thailand only a few weeks before. The Supreme Patriarch is quoted by the *Bangkok Post* as saying:

> Murders and killings should never take place in Thailand because the majority of the people are Buddhists. Lord Buddha's teachings specifically state that killing is forbidden. It is therefore tantamount to a sinful, shameful act for Buddhists especially in a Buddhist country like Thailand — we are behaving unreasonably, killing each other as if we are worse than animals.[57]

However Kittivuḍḍho might justify his statements, he had turned the Supreme Patriarch's position on its head and made killing a morally acceptable act for Buddhists.

The National Student Center of Thailand requested that the Ecclesiastical Council investigate whether or not Kittivuḍḍho had been in violation of the monk's discipline. The same demand was also made by the Young Sangha movement, by Khlāēo Norapati, Socialist MP from Khonkaen, and others. For obvious reasons, the Prime Minister, Seni Pramote, said that the government could do nothing in the matter as it was an affair of the Sangha.[59] On the 30th of June, the Ecclesiastical Council was said to be considering the matter.[60]

During the next several weeks, there were heated attacks in the press on Kittivuḍḍho's position. Among those who attacked him were editorialists in the *Prachāchāt* newspaper who accused Kittivuḍḍho of founding a "new religion," one predicated upon killing.[61] He was also attacked by the head of the Sangha in Laos,[62] and his arguments were rebutted *in extenso* by the well-known lay Buddhist intellectual, Sulak Sivaraksa.[63] Kittivuḍḍho, for his part, lashed back at his critics in speeches before groups of monks and lower-echelon government officials and even in interviews with the newspapers he most strongly distrusted.[64]

Finally on August 11, 1976, it was announced that the Ecclesiastical Council would not conduct an investigation regarding Kittivuḍḍho because the evidence was insufficient.

> Phra Wisutthāthibodī . . . [acting on behalf of the Ecclesiastical Council] reported to the Department of Religious Affairs [regarding] the case in which the National Center of Students and Teachers in Thailand had requested an investigation of Kittivuḍḍho Bhikkhu, the director of Cittabhāvana College. [The report] pointed out that
>
> (1) The purpose of the Nawaphon Group about which the Department of Religion affairs had collected facts and announced them is not known;
>
> (2) The assertion that Kittivuḍḍho's interview caused dissension is ambiguous and not clearly specified and cannot, thus, be considered;
>
> (3) The Department of Religious Affairs had sent [to the Ecclesiastical Council] articles [appearing in various newspapers], but it is not possible to determine whether these articles are true or not.[65]

This decision would appear to suggest that the high Sangha authorities were unwilling to issue even a mild public reprimand of Kittivuḍḍho.

It is possible that the drama would not have ended here for certainly the decision by the Ecclesiastical Council was hardly satisfactory to many of Kittivuddho's opponents. However, this drama was eclipsed shortly thereafter by another drama which had a more conclusive resolution.

Militant Buddhism and the Dialectics of Political Change in Thailand

By the end of August 1976, rumors were rife in Bangkok that former Prime Minister Thanom Kittikachorn was about to return to the country and that he would be returning in order to be ordained into the Buddhist monkhood. In mid-September Thanom was ordained as a novice in a temple-monastery in Singapore and on the 19th of September returned to Bangkok where he was immediately taken to Wat Bowǫnniwēt, one of the most famous monasteries in Thailand. Here he was ordained as a monk.

In the following two weeks, there were numerous protests against Thanom's presence in the country, these finally culminating in large-scale demonstrations held, as in October 1973, at Thammasat University and again as three years previous organized by the students. This time, however, the outcome was very different. On October 5 and 6, police units, supported by right-wing mobs, carried out a sustained attack on the protestors, during which hundreds of students were killed or badly wounded and thousands were arrested. On October 6, a military coup was staged and a military National Reform Council abrogated the constitution, abolished parliament, and brought to an end the three year old experiment with democracy in Thailand.

It would require another lengthy paper to discuss the implications of Thanom's return to Thailand in order to become ordained as a monk for the relationship between Buddhism and power in Thailand. For the purposes of this paper, it is important to note that the *coup* of October 6, 1976, was conditioned, in part, by the definition of the situation imposed by Kittivuḍḍho and the radical right. The new National Reform Council had to make quite explicit at the outset its goal to combat Communism and those arrested in the aftermath of the coup or forced to go into exile included all those whom Kittivuḍḍho had identified as enemies of the religion, the nation and the monarchy. The newspapers and magazines which Kittivuḍḍho and other rightists had found most offensive – e.g., *Prachāchāt* and *Caturat* – were closed. The National Student Center of Thailand was destroyed, and many of those student leaders who had not been killed or arrested fled into the hills to join the Communist insurrectionaries. Seemingly, at least, the goals sought by Kittivuḍḍho were realized in the October 6, 1976 coup.

And yet, the new government was not made up of members of Nawaphon or, with perhaps a few exceptions, of the military men who had backed Nawaphon. In the post-coup period, the movement which has been most successful has been the Village Scouts, whose leader, at least nominally, is the king, rather than Nawaphon whose moral leader is Kittivuḍḍho. While it is still too early to say, it would appear that militant Buddhism makes even ardent Thai nationalists a little uneasy.

Certainly, militant Buddhism as it has been formulated by Kittivuḍḍho and institutionalized in the Nawaphon movement, is markedly discordant with what Reynolds has portrayed as the "civic religion" of Thailand, both traditional and modern.[66] Or, more correctly, perhaps it can be seen as the "darker side" of the civic religion, a dimension which Bennett has suggested has been a counterpoint to the more usually dominant lighter side of civic religion. Bennett says that this darker side involves "a sanctification of death and aggression."

The primordial fears, the violence, the brutality, and the mortification that often accompany threats and responses to threat can be transformed for the preservation of members' sensibilities via the suggestion of religious interpretations.

The most powerful of these interpretations are expressed as moral imperatives. The symbolic construction of moral imperatives around even the most violent of acts can transform both the meaning of the action and its visceral impact.[67]

The idea of Buddhist holy war probably has been as rarely formulated as Obeyesekere suggests in his comment on the early Singhalese version under Duṭṭhagāmaṇī. However, in times of political crisis in all Buddhist societies, there have often emerged millenial movements which seek to establish often by very violent means a utopian order in the place of the prevailing political chaos.[68] And, we can even see in Kittivuḍḍho's words and actions at least an echo of Buddhist messianic ideas. Nonetheless, as Bechert has suggested, "The Buddhist public [accepts] political activity of the Sangha as legitimate only in periods of crisis when the survival of Buddhism itself [is] considered to be at stake."[69] Given the obvious discomfiture by many in Thailand, both in and outside of the Sangha, at the spectacle of the politicization of the Thai Sangha during the period between 1973 and 1976, and given that the political crisis was resolved, at least for the moment, by the coup of October 6, 1976, it is likely that there will be a dissociation of the populace from the effort to launch a Buddhist holy war.

Even if this should prove to be the case, the militant Buddhism which emerged in Thailand in the mid-1970s cannot be dismissed as a transitory phenomenon, without any lasting impact on Thai political life. As Turner and Cohen have shown, every social drama has its own dialectical process. Following some *breach* or "deliberate nonfulfillment of some crucial norm regulating the intercourse of the parties, . . . a phase of mounting *crisis* supervenes."[70] Once a crisis has occurred, those who have been drawn into its vortex are in what Turner has called a "liminal" state, a state in which the ordinary conventions of social structure no longer obtain and in which the character of that social structure is fundamentally questioned. At this stage, there will be a polarization of the parties, each taking its guidance from a particular set of symbols, an ideology. The symbols which will define the situation for the participants are those which have strong "orectic," to use another of Turner's terms, or emotional meanings as well as conceptual meanings. Cohen, drawing on Turner's ideas, has pointed to the significance of this emotional meaning of symbols during a political drama:

The essence of the drama is the struggle to achieve communion between disparate individuals or potential enemies and to give a tangible expression to this communion. In the course of the drama the struggle is internalized within the psyches of the participants.[71]

In other words, the political struggle becomes for the participants not merely something that is happening externally to themselves; it also becomes a crisis of self-identity.[72] Kittivuddho calls people to fight for Buddhism because to be Thai is to be Buddhist. Threats to the nation and religion are perceived, thus, as threats to personal identity.

Those who opposed Kittivuddho were constrained by the symbolic appeal which he had made. They could not, with any hope of success, define Thai nationalism in other than Buddhist terms. They were, thus, led to confront Kittivuddho by appeal to interpretations of Buddhist symbols which would persuade people that Kittivuddho was going against Buddhist morality in advocating that to kill enemies of the nation would bring more merit than demerit.

In the next phase of the social drama, a phase which involves what Turner calls redressive action,[73] Kittivuddho appealed for popular support for his position. His message had considerable impact for many people definitely felt that the nation, and their identity as Thai nationals, was under attack by radical elements in Thailand and the new Communist governments in neighboring Vietnam, Cambodia, and Laos. Kittivuddho's opponents, in their turn, looked for support not only to the public but also to the authorities in the Sangha. If Kittivuddho could be shown to have violated the disciplinary code regulating the behavior of monks, then his message would be sharply undermined. Instead, the Sangha authorities refused to consider the case.

At this point, a new social drama overtook the one we have been considering here. This new drama, involving the return of former Prime Minister Thanom as a monk, was, I suspect, not entirely unrelated to the events surrounding Kittivuddho, since high Sangha authorities had also to determine whether Thanom would be allowed to be ordained. It could well be that given their perception of the popularity of Kittivuddho's position they felt that the situation was suitable for permitting Thanom to return. However this may be, Kittivuddho's militant Buddhism was certainly a major factor in the new crisis which was resolved by the October 6, 1976 coup. While militant Buddhism may now recede in importance in Thailand, it has already altered significantly the direction which political action will take in the future. In the final stage of this social drama, the stage which Turner calls reintegration,[74] the ordering of political relations was radically different from what it was at the outset of the drama.

Notes

1. I am indebted to Roger Harmon for making available to me a number of documents on which this paper is based and for the many conversations which we have had about the topic of the paper. I would also like to thank those who first heard this paper when it was delivered at the University of Chicago and Northern Illinois University in April 1977

for their comments and ideas. Finally, I would like to acknowledge with special gratitude the comments made on the paper by Frank Reynolds, Sulak Sivaraksa, and Jane Keyes.

2. *Mahāvaṃsa.* Tr. by W. Geiger. (London: Pali Text Society, 1912), p. 171.

3. *Op. cit.*, p. 178.

4. Gananath Obeyesekere, "Sinhalese-Buddhist Identity in Ceylon," in *Ethnic Identity: Cultural Continuities and Change*, ed. by George de Vos and Lola Ramanucci-Ross (Palo Alto, California: Mayfield Publishing Co., 1975), p. 236.

5. See E. Sarkisyanz, *Buddhist Backgrounds of the Burmese Revolution* (The Hague: Martinus Nijhoff, 1965); S. J. Tambiah, *World Renouncer and World Conqueror* (Cambridge: Cambridge University Press, 1976); Frank E. Reynolds, "Sacred Kingship and National Development: The Case of Thailand," *Contribution to Asian Studies*, 4:40-50; and Reynolds, "Civic Religion and National Community in Thailand," *Journal of Asian Studies,* 36.2:267-282, 1977.

6. Cf. Kitsiri Malalgoda, "Millenialism in Relation to Buddhism," *Comparative Studies in Society and History*, 12:424-441, 1970; Charles F. Keyes, "Millenialism, Theravāda Buddhism and Thai Society," *Journal of Asian Studies*, 36.2:283-302, 1977.

7. Victor Turner, *Dramas, Fields, and Metaphors* (Ithaca, New York: Cornell University Press, 1974).

8. In this paper, I transliterate names and terms which are derived from Pāli according to the system used by the Pali Text Society. In transliterating words from the Thai, I have indicated vowel length, but not tone. The consonants used for transcription are: -p-, -t-, -c-, -k-, ph-, th-, ch-, kh-, b-, d-, f-, s-, h-, -m-, -n-, -ng-, l-, r-, w-, y-. Vowels are: i, e, ae, u, o, ǫ, ṳ, oe, and a. Sometimes both Pāli and Thai transliterations are given. Some well-known names have been written in the form in which they generally appear.

9. The following discussion of the biography of Kittivuḍḍho Bhikkhu is based on information collated by Roger Harmon in his as yet unpublished paper, "Drawing on the Ancient and the New: The Symbolism of Two Monks in Contemporary Thailand," 1977.

10. Quoted in translation in Harmon, *op. cit.*, p. 11.

11. Quoted in translation in Harmon, *op. cit.*, p. 13.

12. For further discussion of these various programs, see Donald K. Swearer, "Community Development and Thai Buddhism: The Dynamics of Tradition and Change," *Visakha Puja B. E. 2516* (Bangkok: The Buddhist Association of Thailand, 1973), pp. 59-68; Charles F. Keyes, "Buddhism and National Integration in Thailand," *Journal of Asian Studies*, 30:551-68, 1971; S. J. Tambiah, "The Persistence and Transformation of Tradition in Southeast Asia, with Special Reference to Thailand," *Daelalus*, 102.1:55-84, 1973. The *thammathūt* program is the focus of a forthcoming Ph.D. dissertation by Roger Harmon at the University of Washington.

13. In another paper, I will discuss rituals of legitimation engaged in by King Phumiphon.

14. *Nawaphon* has been translated by some Western sources as "the new force," a translation which is not only incorrect but which also makes for confusion since a left-liberal party of the time, *phlang mai*, is also known in English as the "New Force." For a discussion of the development of Nawaphon based on Thai newspaper accounts, see E. Thadeus Flood, *The United States and the Military Coup in Thailand: A Background Study* (Washington, D. C.: Indochina Resource Center, 1976, pp. 6-7).

15. Kittivuḍḍho Bhikkhu, *Khā Khǫmmūnit mai bāp* ("Killing Communists is Not Demeritorious") (Bangkok: Abhidhamma Foundation of Wat Mahādhātu, 1976), pp. 5, 9-11. Hereafter, this work will be abbreviated as KKMB.

16. *Bangkok Post*, January 5, 1976; Flood, *op. cit.*, pp. 6, 7.

17. *Prachātipatai*, December 2, 1974.

18. *Ibid.*, December 3, 1974.

19. *Deli Thaim* (Daily Times), January 6, 1976.

20. *Ibid.*; also see *Bangkok Post*, January 5, 1976.

21. *Deli Thaim, loc. cit.*

22. *Prachāchāt*, January 13, 1976.

23. *Bangkok Post*, January 16, 1976.

24. *Deli Thaim*, February 5, 1976.
25. *Prachāchāt*, June 28, 1976.
26. KKMB, pp. 2-6.
27. *Ibid.*, p. 7.
28. The interview was published in the issue of *Caturat* dated June 29, 1976, but the issue was released a week earlier and the interview was reported upon in *Prachāchāt* on June 22, 1976.
29. *Caturat, op. cit.*, pp. 31-32.
30. KKMB, *op. cit.*
31. KKMB, p. 43.
32. KKMB, pp. 17-18.
33. KKMB, pp. 25-26.
34. KKMB, p. 49.
35. KKMB, pp. 49-51.
36. KKMB, pp. 51-52.
37. KKMB, p. 52.
38. *Ibid.*
39. See Prince Vajirañānavarorasa, *The Entrance to the Vinaya: Vinayamukha*, Vol. I (Bangkok: Mahāmakuṭarājavidyālaya, 1969), pp. 48ff.
40. *Prachāchāt*, June 28, 1976.
41. KKMB, p. 58.
42. KKMB, p. 31.
43. KKMB, p. 11.
44. KKMB, pp. 36-38; also see p. 27 and p. 33.
45. KKMB, p. 54.
46. KKMB, p. 39.
47. KKMB, pp. 32-33.
48. *Caturat*, June 29, 1976, p. 30.
49. KKMB, pp. 33-36; also see p. 32.
50. KKMB, p. 46.
51. KKMB, p. 47.
52. *Ibid.*
53. KKMB, p. 40.
54. KKMB, p. 19.
55. KKMB, p. 17.
56. KKMB, pp. 20-21, 23.
57. *Bangkok Post*, March 4, 1976.
58. See *Prachāchāt*, June 27, 1976; *Deli Thaim*, June 29, 1976.
59. *Prachāchāt*, June 29, 1976
60. *Ibid.*, June 30, 1976.
61. *Ibid.*, June 24, 1976; also June 30, 1976.
62. *Ibid.*, July 5, 1976.
63. *Pācārayasān*, Vol. 5, No. 20, September-October 1976.
64. See KKMB, *op. cit.*; *Chōfā*, July 8, 1976; *Prachāchāt*, June 28, 1976 and *Prachāchāt*, June 30, 1976.
65. *Prachāchāt*, August 11, 1976.
66. Frank E. Reynolds, "Civic Religion and National Community in Thailand," *op. cit.*
67. W. Lance Bennett, "Imitation, Ambiguity and Drama in the Political Order: An Essay on the Civil Religion," mimeo., Seattle, 1976. Also compare Bennett, "Political Sanctification: The Civil Religion and American Politics," *Social Science Information*, 14.6:79-102, 1975.

68. See Malalgoda, *op. cit.*; Sarkisyanz, *op. cit.*; Keyes, "Millenialism . . .," *op. cit.*

69. Heinz Bechert, "Sangha, State, Society, 'Nation': Persistence of Tradition in 'Post-Traditional' Buddhist Societies," *Daedalus*, 102.1:90, 1973.

70. Turner, *op. cit.*, p. 38. Abner Cohen, in *Two-Dimensional Man* (Berkeley and Los Angeles: University of California Press, 1974) elaborates on the dialectical character of social dramas.

71. Cohen, *op. cit.*, p. 134.

72. In this connection, also see Obeyesekere, *op. cit.*

73. Turner, *op. cit.*, pp. 39-41.

74. *Op. cit.*, pp. 41-43.

Part Two

Ritual, Symbolism, and Patterns of Legitimation

Ritual and Social Hierarchy:
An Aspect of Traditional Religion in
Buddhist Laos

Frank E. Reynolds

IN ANY HIGHLY developed religious tradition it is possible to discern a variety of social ideals. In the corpus of myths, scriptures, legends, and doctrinal formulations, different and often contradictory conceptions are expressed. However, in the central cultic festivals in traditional societies, a particular ideal of social order is often articulated, an ideal in terms of which the empirical order is actually structured. Students of primitive religions have often discussed the character and importance of such cultically expressed ideals in the groups which they have studied.[1] In the present paper, I propose to focus attention on the same kind of phenomenon as it is found in the quite different context of a Theravada Buddhist kingdom in Southeast Asia.

The problem of social ideals in the pre-modern Theravada world has already been treated by a number of scholars, working in different areas, who have approached the subject from a variety of disciplinary perspectives. The three major ideals of social order depicted in the Pali canon (the republican ideal recommended in the Mahāparinibbāna Sutta, the Mahāsammanta ideal depicted in the Aggañña Sutta, and the Chakravartin ideal which is touched upon in a variety of texts) have been described by a number of Buddhologists and historians.[2] The ideals expressed in the Asokan edicts and the Sinhalese Chronicles have also been explored from the perspective of both of these disciplines.[3] In their classic discussions, Robert Heine-Geldern and Paul Mus have provided brilliant interpretations of the relationship between Theravada cosmology, architecture, and social order.[4] And more recently the social ideals expressed in the Burmese tradition have been depicted with great skill by Emmanual Sarkisyanz, notably in the first chapters of his study, *Buddhist Backgrounds of the Burmese Revolution*, and analyzed from the point of view of a political scientist by John Badgley in his article, "Theravada Polity in Burma."[5] Nevertheless, in spite of the very substantial contributions which these and other authors have made, none of them have grounded their work in a study of specific cultic scenarios.[6]

I have selected the north Laotian tradition which developed at Luang Prabang as the locus for pursuing this issue for two reasons, both of which are closely bound up with the fact that during recent centuries the city has been comparatively isolated from the mainstream of affairs in southeast Asia. In the first place, though Luang Prabang was for more than two hundred years (*ca.* 1315-1550) the capital of one of the most important Buddhist kingdoms in the area, it has attracted little attention from either Buddhologists or historians of religions.[7] And second, the persistence of the ancient tradition into the contemporary period makes it possible to investigate aspects of it which are not accessible in other comparable traditions. For our purposes this is crucial, since the reports provided by contemporary observers, including anthropologists and others, give us the kind of access to the traditional cultic life of the community which in most other situations simply cannot be obtained.[8]

Both the more usual types of historical data and the contemporary descriptions show that the official ceremonies at Luang Prabang have been organized on the basis of an annual cycle and include at least one major celebration for each month of the year.[9] A somewhat closer look at the situation makes it clear that there are three festivals which have assumed special importance and involve the whole community over a considerable period of time. The first of these is the festival which marks the beginning of the calendric year (November). The second is actually called the New Year's celebration; it takes place during the fifth to sixth months of the calendric year (March-April), roughly at the time when the first rains presage the coming of the monsoons. The third festival, which also has the structure of a new year celebration, is known as the festival of the *stupa* and takes place during the twelfth month (October), at the point when the monsoons have ended and the flood waters are beginning to recede. Since these three ceremonies dominate the religious calendar and provide the major cultic contexts in which the social ideal is expressed, our discussion will deal primarily with them.[10]

These festivals are highly complex and incorporate many types and levels of religious meaning. As their positions in the annual cycle would indicate, they are seasonal festivals through which the community seeks to assure the great transformations in the realm of nature which are essential for the proper growth of the crops. Over and above this they provide, as do similar festivals the world over, the occasion at which the community acts to renew and to reaffirm the basic structures which undergird its own existence.[11] At Luang Prabang this is done through the use of many forms which are very widespread in their distribution; but interwoven with these more or less universal patterns there is a series of very distinctive ritual performances which play an important role. In these performances what might be called the sacred history of the city (including mythic episodes, legendary occurrences, and events which can actually be documented) is dramatically recalled and its religio-social ideal is vividly reaffirmed.

Certainly the most striking figures to be found in the sacred history of Luang Prabang and in the cultic life which represents it are the two primal ancestors Pu No and Na No (Grandfather and Grandmother No). According to the tradition, this pair originally lived in the celestial regions but because of their grotesque features were banished from their homeland. They were sent here below where the waters still covered everything, but they were told that where they stepped the dry land would emerge.[12] In the ritual performances the two ancestors, depicted by men wearing masks which vividly attest to the grotesqueness mentioned in the myth, perform the dances through which the world is made to appear.[13] The dances depict not just the emergence of the earth as such but also the establishment of the geographic units which make up the city and the kingdom. Moreover, through the dances not only the watery demons but also all other forms of evil are dispersed or tamed.[14]

As the creators of the Laotian world, these primal ancestors assume an important position in the socio-religious organization. At the end of the ceremonies in which they are used, the masks which represent them are returned to their place at the most important altar of the city. A depiction of their dances is utilized as the emblem of the royal dynasty. By virtue of the power which they demostrate each year by again creating, purifying, and organizing the land, they are accepted as the *devata luang*, the guardian divinities of the city.

The same mythic complex which recounts the original creative acts of Pu No and Na No mentions that before their death and transformation into guardian deities they established the institution of kingship. They chose one of the members of the royal clan — Khun Borom (the Supreme Chief) — to be their adopted son, thus making him and his descendants the prime beneficiaries of their work and the legitimate rulers of the city.[15] Though this episode is not directly reenacted in the ritual, there is an important cult devoted to King Borom, his immediate successors, and the more charismatic of the later kings; and the structure of this cult confirms the hierarchic position of the dynasty suggested by the imagery of adoption. Those in the royal line clearly possess the potential for divinity; they are capable of attaining the post-mortem status of guardian deities. However, it is also apparent that only those who demonstrated their divine charisma actually realized this potential. And it is clear that those who did achieve apotheosis hold a position beneath that of the *devata luang*, that they exercise less continuing power. This is reflected in the lesser importance of the cult which is devoted to them and by the fact that its maintenance is the responsibility of the royal family rather than the community as a whole. It is also reflected in a number of legends: In contrast to the *devata luang* who remain clearly superior to the local spirits and demons whom they have subdued, the divinized kings are often associated with these spirits and demons in various kinds of alliances.

The creation myth associated with the cult also recounts how Pu No and Na No brought about the peopling of the world, and it does so in a way which shows the basic hierarchical divisions of society which were inherent "from the beginning." According to the myth the ancestral pair, after bringing forth the earth, were lonely and asked the celestial beings for companions. They subsequently found three gourds which they proceeded to break open. Out of the first came the royal clan (from which Khun Borom was chosen), out of the second came the Lao commoners, and from the third the Kha (the pre-Thai peoples of the area who presently live on the fringes of Lao society).[16] Though this episode itself is not explicitly dramatized in the rites, the division is adhered to and thus reaffirmed through the entire course of the festival. Moreover, in a number of ceremonies the relationships within these three groups and some of the more complex relationships between them are portrayed and renewed.

An intricate pattern of social differentiation among the nobles is established in the procession of the boats which takes place following the ritual dances of creation in the festival of the *stupa*. This ceremony has, as one primary purpose, the regulation of the flow of the *nagas* (serpentine water spirits) back to the places which they occupy during the dry season — that is, to the more remote river sources — and through an obvious homology it serves to reinforce the purifying action of the ritual dances. At the same time, however, the procession includes boats belonging to the various nobles and involves a carefully regulated series of nautical maneuvers which serve to reestablish a minutely articulated hierarchy of prestige. The ritual is thus an act of installation through which this hierarchy is annually renewed.[17]

Many of the basic relationships between different groups of commoners are similarly renewed, especially during the New Year's ceremonies of the first and fifth to sixth months. Again a series of carefully regulated jousts is involved, this time between the different socio-geographic units into which the city and the kingdom are divided.[18] Unfortunately, the reports which are available do not permit a detailed analysis of these jousts and their more specific relationships to kinship patterns, division of labor, and the like. However, it is very probable that such relationships do exist and that they have their roots in the kind of dual organization which characterized the city during the pre-Buddhist period.[19]

Finally, the position of the Kha is delineated with considerable precision, particularly in the festival of the *stupa*. On this occasion the Laotian conquest of the aborigines – a historical occurrence or series of occurrences which actually took place during the ninth and tenth centuries – is ritually reenacted in the form of a game of hockey called the Ti Ki.[20] At another point in the ceremonies the Kha confirm their acceptance of the Laotian king's authority through a ceremony reportedly instituted by the great fourteenth-century monarch Fa Ngum. A similar rite is performed on a triennial basis at the March-April New Year's ceremony where once again the Kha symbolize their submission and participation in the Laotian order through a gift of goods produced from the land. Thus through the whole procedure the original territorial rights of the Kha are recognized, the prosperity of the realm is assured, and the hierarchy which culminates in the king is reasserted and renewed.[21]

The festivals thus involve the re-establishment of a Laotian world and a Laotian ideal of social order which appear to be quite independent of any Indian or Buddhist tradition. Nevertheless, in the ritual context it is quite evident that the whole process of re-creation and the re-establishment of proper order in the world takes place within a Buddhist setting. Buddhist temples and monuments provide the environment for the ritual; Buddhist symbols impinge on every ceremony. Buddhist monks are omnipresent and the reciting of Buddhist texts provides a continuing accompaniment to all that occurs. Moreover, each of the three festivals which we are considering has as its high point a ceremony in which the ultimate hegemony of Buddhism is made explicit.

The rites which climax the March/April New Year's festival focus around a symbol which recalls still another crucial event in the sacred history of the city – in this case the establishment of the present form of Buddhism.[22] This central symbol is the Prabang, the Buddha image of miraculous origin and power which has given its name to the city.[23] According to the well-known tradition, which most scholars accept as historically accurate, the image was brought from Angkor by Fa Ngum in the early fourteenth century when he returned from exile to begin his long career of Buddhist reform and military conquest.[24] The rites themselves, which almost certainly go back to the fourteenth century, center around the lustration of the image, an act which seeks to assure the coming of the rains, the renewal of the magical power of the image, and its continued beneficence toward the community.[25]

For our purposes it is crucial that these lustrations are performed both by the masked dancers representing the primal ancestors (the *devata luang*) and by the king. Since, in addition to its other functions, the lustration is an act of veneration and commitment, the participation by the ancestors signals the acceptance by the whole community of Laotians, past, present, and future, of the supremacy and authority of the image (and hence of the Buddha whom the image represents). In the same vein the lustration by the king confirms his

own acceptance of the Buddha's authority and prepares the way for the ceremony which immediately follows — the oath of loyalty to him (the king)
taken by the nobles.

The ceremony which provides the culminating point in the festivities of the
twelfth month focuses around the Sridhammasoka Stupa. As the name itself
implies, this *stupa* is closely associated with Asoka, the great Indian monarch
who ruled during the third century B.C. and subsequently came to be ideal-
ized as the perfect model of Buddhist kingship. Asoka, according to the Laotian
tradition, brought to Luang Prabang a relic of the Buddha, which was installed
in a *stupa* (a predecessor of the present one) erected on a spot previously made
sacred by the presence of a local deity.[26] In the ceremonies the king, having
left his palace in the charge of his subordinates, enters a specially constructed
pavilion located next to the *stupa* and above the area where the ancestral
dances and the related rituals are performed. Acting in imitation of Asoka (i.e.,
the Asoka of the tradition) — even identifying himself with him — the king
enters a period of meditation which was formerly seven days in length but was
subsequently reduced to three days and finally to one. Through this meditation,
which functions in the manner of a sacrifice, the king is believed to assimilate
the essence of the sacred monument which has the structure of a symbolic universe, a world ordered according to the Buddhist vision of reality.[27] He thus
recognizes the ultimacy of the Dhamma and prepares himself to become the
channel through which the rule of Dhamma can become established in the
world created by the strictly Laotian rites being carried on below him. It is
after this meditation has been completed that the king is invited to "return to
rule as before" and the festival of the twelfth month comes to its conclusion.[28]

Whereas the veneration of the Prabang Buddha image culminates the March/
April New Year's festivities and the king's meditation on the *stupa* conceived
as a "reservoir of Dhamma" culminates the festival of the twelfth month, the
calendrical New Year's ceremonies reach their climax with the lustration of
the monks who preside over the temples of the four quarters. At one level this
ceremony, which takes place in the central courtyard of the royal palace, cli-
maxes a series of rites which seek to renew the sacred power that is inherent in
the territories that make up the kingdom and to reinforce the unity which binds
it into a single unit. At another level, however, this rite culminates the entire
festival in an act symbolizing the sovereign's recognition that beyond his own
temporal authority and power stands the ultimate spiritual authority and power
of the third jewel of the Buddhist Triratna, the Samgha.

When one telescopes these various ceremonial episodes which we have discussed — and in fact they are telescoped in a variety of different ways in the
ritual context itself — the lineaments of a strongly hierarchical religio-social
ideal can be discerned. The three jewels of Buddhism (the Buddha, Dhamma,
and Samgha) appear at the peak of the hierarchy, providing the ultimate norms
which regulate the structure and circumscribe the cosmos in which it operates.
Below the three jewels and within the world which they define stand the *devata
luang*, the ancient divinized kings, and the living monarch who is himself at
least potentially divine. Under them are ranged, on one side, the lesser spirits
and demons which they have "tamed" and drawn into the service of Buddhism
and, on the other, the hierarchy of court nobles committed to the ruling king
and responsible for the implementation of his rule of Dhamma. Next in the

order come the commoners who are organized in socio-territorial units established by the ancestors and given particular segments of the Dhamma which it is their special responsibility to maintain.[29] Finally, at the bottom of this ideal order, but through their original association with the territory still necessary participants in it, are the aborigines of the area, the Kha.

As we mentioned at the beginning of our discussion, these festivities at Luang Prabang and the religio-social ideal which they depict, attained their classical form during the period from 1315 to 1550 when the city was the capital of a powerful Buddhist kingdom. The amazing persistence of this tradition, though made possible by the subsequent isolation of the city, nevertheless suggests the capacity of this ideal to structure a livable human environment. During the entire period, so far as we are able to determine, no significant movement of religious or social protest ever developed. Though the ideal was hierarchical — or perhaps because it was hierarchical — it has provided the undergirding for a society in which there has been a significant and meaningful participation at all levels, even down to that of the Kha.[30]

However, by way of conclusion, it should be noted that the isolation which allowed this type of ideal and this type of environment to persist is very rapidly coming to an end. Unfortunately, the suddenness with which this is happening has left the city, and for that matter all of Laos, totally unprepared and ill-equipped to respond. The old ideals and the type of society which correspond to them are no longer viable in contemporary Southeast Asia; however, there is no indication that any new ideals have even begun to make an appearance.[31] Thus, the same situation which has opened up such unique opportunities for a historian of traditional religions to view the past has, at the same time, set the stage for the tragic religious and human crisis which is engulfing contemporary Laos.

Originally published in *History of Religions*, Vol. 9, No. 1, August, 1969, pp. 78-89. Reprinted with permission.

Notes

1. For example, see A. Jensen, *Myth and Cult among Primitive Peoples*, translated by Choldin and Weissleder (Chicago, 1963), esp. pp. 34-45 and the chapter on "The Religious Ethos."
2. For example, see Richard Gard's article, "Buddhist and Political Authority," in Laswell and Cleveland (eds.), *The Ethics of Power* (Harper, 1962).
3. For example, see B. G. Gokhale, "Early Buddhist Kingship," *Journal of Asian Studies*, XXVI, No. 1 (1966), as well as the paper by Bardwell Smith, "The Ideal Social Order as Portrayed in the Chronicles of Ceylon," in *The Two Wheels of Dhamma: Essays on the Theravada Tradition in India and Ceylon*, edited by Bardwell Smith, American Academy of Religion, Studies in Religion, No. 3 (Missoula, Mont.: Scholars Press, 1972).
4. Heine-Geldern's discussion is found in his article, "Weltbild und Bauform in Sudostasiens," in the *Wiener Beitrage zur Kunst und Kultur Asiens* (1930). A condensed version in English was published under the title "Conceptions of State and Kingship in Southeast Asia," *Far Eastern Quarterly* (presently the *Journal of Asian Studies*), II, No. 2 (1942), 1-15, and republished by the Southeast Asia Program at Cornell (Data Paper No. 18, 1956). Mus's position is most exhaustively developed in his *Barabadur: Esquisse d'une histoire du Bouddhisme fondée sur la critique archéologique des textes* (Hanoi, 1935).
5. Sarkisyanz, E., *Buddhist Backgrounds of the Burmese Revolution* (The Hague: Mouton & Co., 1965), chaps. i-v. See also his essay, "On U Nu's Buddhist Socialism in Burma's History of Ideas," in R. Sakai (ed.) *Studies in Asia—1961* (Lincoln, Nebraska, 1961). Badgley's article appeared in *Ionam Asia Kenkyu*, II, No. 4 (March, 1965). He provides a

more extensive treatment in his unpublished doctoral dissertation on politics and progress in modern Burma (University of California, 1959).

6. Mus goes further than any of the others in this direction, especialiy in his introduction to René Berval (ed.), *Présence du Bouddhisme* (Saigon, 1956).

7. During the early decades of the fourteenth century, the Thai-Laotian rulers who had established themselves in the area accepted the Sinhalese version of Theravada Buddhism and simultaneously embarked on a campaign of conquest which extended their control over an area roughly equivalent to that of contemporary Laos. For more than two centuries thereafter Luang Prabang competed on equal footing with other Thai Buddhist centers such as Sukothai, Chiengmai, and Ayuddhia. However, in 1550 the situation was radically altered when the reigning dynasty moved its capital to the more strategically located city of Vientienne. Unfortunately, it is impossible to refer the reader to any adequate comprehensive history of Laos. The two major efforts in this direction are the treatments by Le Boulanger in *Histoire du Laos Français* (Paris, 1931) and by Mahasila Viravong in *History of Laos* (New York: Paragon Books, 1964). Similarly, no adequate comprehensive discussion of Laotian religion or Laotian Buddhism has yet appeared. Perhaps the best available survey of the latter is to be found in Thao Rhou Abhav's essay in René de Berval (ed.), *Kingdom of Laos* (Saigon: France–Asie, 1959).

8. The degree of access varies from one area to another. In several other Laotian centers the cultic patterns have persisted and certain aspects have been carefully described. For example, Charles Archaimbault has provided a detailed report, "L'histoire et l'organization rituelle de Basak-Campasak," in his unpublished dissertation for the Sorbonne (1959) and a short but intriguing study, "La Fête du T'at à S'ieng Khwang," *Artibus Asiae*, XXIV, No. 3/4 (1961), 187-199. The same can be said for Cambodia where excellent work has been done by Evelyn Poree-Maspero. (See *Ceremonies des douze mois* [Commission des Moeurs et Coutumes des Cambodge, Pnon Pehn, Portail, 1950] and the first two volumes of her projected three-volume *Étude sur les rites agraires des Cambodgiens* [The Hague: Mouton & Co., 1962 and 1964]). In Thailand a few remnants of the royal ceremonies which were important in the Ayuddhia-early-Bangkok tradition have been preserved, but here the major source must be the accounts provided by King Chulalongkorn in the nineteenth century. See H. G. Quaritch Wales, *Siamese State Ceremonies* (London, 1931) and King Chulalongkorn, *Prarajapithi Sipsong Duan* (republished in three volumes, Bangkok, 1963). In Ceylon and Burma, where the British colonial rule radically disrupted the traditional religious and social patterns, detailed research along these lines is practically impossible.

9. A Siamese abstract of a Laotian account has been published under the title, "The Royal Traditions of Lan Sang," by Kricak (Bangkok, 1936). The accounts on which the following discussion depends most heavily are those given by Henri Deydier in his *Lokapala: Genies, Totems, et Corciers dur Nord Laos*, Part IV (Paris, 1954); and by Charles Archaimbault in his article, "La Fête du T'at à Luang Prabang," in *Essays offered to G. H. Luce*, by Ba Shin, Jean Boisselier, and A. B. Griswold (*Artibus Asie*, Suppl. XXIII, Vol. I [Ascona, 1966)], 5-47. For the oral tradition accompanying the cult our major source is Archaimbault's report in his "La naissance du monde selon les traditions lao," in *Sources Orientale*, Vol. I (Editions du Seuil, 1959), 385-414. Where other sources are used, reference will be made in the footnotes.

10. For a description of two closely parallel ceremonies which dominate the religious calendar of a nearby Thai (Tai) group which has not been converted to Buddhism, see Henri Maspero, "La Société et les Religions des Chinois Anciens et celles des Tai Modernes," in his *Mélanges Posthumes* (Paris, 1950), Vol. I.

11. For a discussion of the basic structure of this type of festival as it appears in the history of religions, see Robert Challois, *Man and the Sacred*, translated by Barash (Free Press, Glencoe, 1959) chap. v; and Theodore Gaster, *New Year: Its History, Customs, and Superstitions* (New York, 1955).

12. The imagery indicates the close connection between the episode and the recession of the waters which occurs after the end of the monsoons.

13. Though the pair of primal ancestors is included in the mythology of the most remote Thai (Tai) peoples among these groups, they are not depicted as creators and they are not associated with any ritual dances. The dances do, however, have very deep roots in the religious history of the area. See Marcel Granet, *Danses et legendes de la Chine ancienne* (new edition, Paris, 1959), esp. Vol. I.

14. The power of Pu No and Pu Na to control all libidinal forces is symbolically portrayed in the story of their visit to the Himalaya forest where they domesticated a great lion (Sing Keu Sing Kam, the Golden Crystal Lion) which thereafter became their ward. The mask representing this lion is kept at Luang Prabang and the dances performed by its wearer play an important role in the ceremonies.

15. The relationship between the primal ancestors and the royal founder is directly reversed in the dynastic chronicles. In this context Khun Borom is a divine figure who comes from the celestial regions to organize the earth, while Pu No and Pu Na are two servants sent to aid him by dispersing the demons. In the cosmogony of the more remote Black Thai (Tai), the founding chief is even more exalted, being considered as the incarnation of the chief celestial deity. The relevant parts of the chronicles are translated in Archaimbault's article in Sources Orientale Vol. I (see n. 9 above), and the reference to the Black Thai is from his article "Religious Structures in Laos," Journal of the Siam Society, LII, Part I (April, 1964), 57.

16. The emergence of humanity from gourds is a theme common to most of the more remote Thai (Tai) peoples and to most Thai-Laotian communities. However, the number of gourds and the specific divisions which are thereby established vary from one context to another.

17. This ritual pattern which appears in the ceremonies held at various Laotian centers is discussed in Charles Archaimbault, "Un Complexe Culturel: La Course de Pirogues au Laos," in Anthony Wallace (ed.), Men and Cultures (Philadelphia, 1966), pp. 384-389.

18. It should be noted that each of the major units is entrusted with a specific segment of the Buddhist literature and that the jousts are interpreted at the Buddhist level as a test and renewal of the potency of these texts (in this context called mantras).

19. The evidence for an early dual structure and a discussion of it can be found in Paul Levy, "Doublets onomastiques au Laos et ailleurs dans l'Asie du Sud-Est. A propos de S'ien Dong-S'ien T'ong, un ancien nom de Luang Prabang," in Bulletin de l'Institut Indochinois pour l'étude de l'Homme, Vol. V (1942).

20. By 1952 the Ti Ki ritual, which had replaced an earlier, more realistic method of representing the struggle, had itself disappeared from the actual performance. Two interesting studies of the Ti Ki have been done, one by Archaimbault ("La Fête du T'at à S'ieng Kwang. Contribution à l'étude du Ti K'i," see n. 8, above); the other by Paul Leyy ("Ti-Khi: un jeu de mail rituel au Laos" in Annuaire de l'École Pratiques des Hautes Études (1952-53), pp. 1-15). As these studies show, this ritual hockey game forms an important part of the ceremonial in many Laotian centers (as well as elsewhere in Southeast Asia), though it is associated with different specific historical referents in each case.

21. The great importance of the expression of land rights in Southeast Asian religion has been discussed in Paul Mus, "Cultes indiens et indigènes au Champa," Bulletin de l'École Française Extrême-Orient, XXXIII (1933), 367-410. He has gone so far as to use the term "cadastral religion" to emphasize the basic importance of this element in the pre-Indian tradition in Southeast Asia.

22. In a very helpful article Paul Levy has shown that, contrary to some earlier opinions, a type of Buddhism was being practiced at Luang Prabang prior to the fourteenth century. See "Les traces de l'introduction du bouddhisme à Luang Prabang," Bulletin de l'École Française Extrême-Orient, XL (1940), 411-424.

23. Miraculous images have been very common and important throughout the Theravada areas of Southeast Asia. See, for example, my article on "The Holy Emerald Jewel" in the present volume.

24. By the end of the thirteenth century and the beginning of the fourteenth, Angkor had become a center of the reformed Sinhalese sect of Buddhism and was playing a significant role in its further spread. The case for this early dating of the rise of Theravada Buddhism at Angkor and for the role of the city in its spread is made by Lawrence Briggs, in The Ancient Khmer Empire (Transactions of the American Philosophical Society, Philadelphia, 1951), esp. pp. 237-261.

25. The emphasis on assuring the coming of the rains through the lustration accounts for the fact that whereas this ritual complex appears in all three festivals it takes over the foreground in the festivities which are held in March/April.

26. The belief that Asoka was responsible for the introduction of Buddhism into Southeast Asia is very widespread. Also, the Thai (Tai) groups in the Yunan area of southern China have a little known but important tradition that Asoka himself came to rule over them

and that he left a line of descendants which continued to rule for more than a millennium (these traditions and their connection with the stupa cult are mentioned in M. Carthew, "The History of the Tais in Yunan 250 B.C.-1253 A.D.," *Journal of the Siam Society, Selected Articles*, Vol. III (Bangkok 1959). However, in the absence of any kind of corroborative evidence most scholars have concluded that these are later legends rather than an account of actual historical occurrences.

27. The interpretation of the symbolism of the stupa which is suggested here has been worked through with great detail and brilliance by Paul Mus in his monumental study of Barabudur (see n. 4, above).

28. The pre-Buddhist symbolic and ritual complex which is here expressed in its Buddhist transformation has been discussed by many students of southeast Asian history and religions. For two studies which refer to many other important works, see H. G. Quaritich Wales, *Mountain of God* (London, 1953), and *Prehistory and Religion in Southeast Asia* (London, 1957).

29. See n. 18.

30. However, in order to balance the picture, it is well to keep in mind the fact that in the Laotian idiom *Kha* means both "aborigines" and "slaves."

31. For a discussion of contemporary Buddhism in Laos, including comparisons with other Theravada countries, see Heinz Bechert's two-volume work, *Buddhismus, Staat, und Gesellschaft* (published as Band XVII/1 and XVII/2 der Schriften des Instituts für Asienkunde in Hamburg by A. Metzner: Frankfort and Berlin, 1966 and 1967). The section dealing specifically with Laos appears in Vol. II, pp. 261-403.

The Holy Emerald Jewel: Some Aspects of Buddhist Symbolism and Political Legitimation in Thailand and Laos

Frank E. Reynolds

THE FACT THAT Theravada Buddhism has traditionally provided various modes of religious legitimation for political authority in South and Southeast Asia is no longer a matter of serious dispute either among Buddhologists or area specialists. After many decades of modern scholarship in which the re-ligio-political aspects of Theravada concern were either ignored or summarily dismissed, their importance has now become widely recognized among historians of religion, area historians, political scientists and anthropologists. More directly related to the focus of the present paper, investigators representing these various disciplines have already explored several different Theravada scenarios in which conceptions of legitimation have been given both mythic and cultic expression, and in which various elements of the indigenous tradition have been incorporated.[1]

However, in spite of the recent proliferation of this kind of study, the insights first generated by Paul Mus more than forty years ago still remain basic. For example, Mus, in his classic and far-ranging study of the great stupa at Barabadour, highlighted the "political" importance of cultic representations of the Buddha and — more importantly — focussed attention on the richness and complexity of the symbolism which they often embody.[2] In the same work Mus went to great pains to highlight the central significance of the ortho-dox Theravada distinction between the *dhammakāya* (dhamma body) of the Buddha which was traditionally associated with the scriptures and with the monks who recited and preserved them, and his *rūpakāya* (rūpa body) which was traditionally associated not only with his relics but also with architectural and iconographic representations of his person and with the kings who con-structed and venerated them.[3] In another seminal study, also published in the early 1930s, the great French Buddhologist emphasized the crucial role of the indigenous "cadastral" religion of Southeast Asia, especially the way in which the aniconic representations of the ancestrally mediated deities of the soil gradually evolved into the stupas and images Theravadins have traditionally used to represent the figure of the Buddha.[4]

In the following study of the Holy Emerald Jewel (this Jewel, presently the palladium of the Chakri dynasty in Bangkok, is better known in Western circles as the image of the Emerald Buddha) we intend to carry forward this line of research concerning the mythic and cultic modes of Theravada legitimation in a way which will both utilize and extend the insights which Mus generated. Our discussion will be divided into the following four segments: (1) a brief review of the mythical and historical adventures of the Jewel and its cult; (2) an investigation of the dimensions of sacred power manifested by the Jewel

175

qua jewel; (3) a study of the mythic associations which enhanced the sacrality of the Jewel and gave it a specifically Buddhist and royal focus; (4) an exploration of the relationships which developed between the Jewel and other Buddhist symbols of legitimation, as well as between the Buddhist pattern of legitimation and the basic pattern of cadastral religion in the "Asia of the monsoons."

From Myth to History

Despite the diversity of northern Thai texts which recount the origins of the Holy Emerald Jewel, those texts do not differ in their basic account.[5] The story goes as follows: Some 500 years after the death (or *Parinibbāna*) of the Buddha the Thera Nāgasena, who was at the time a spiritual counselor to King Milinda, wanted to make an image of the Buddha in order to encourage the expansion of the faith. Fearing that an image of silver or gold would be destroyed by a degenerate humanity, he wanted to make the image from a precious stone endowed with special spiritual power. Sakka (i.e., Indra) became aware of his desire, decided that he would provide the Jewel, and went to the fabulous Vibulapabbata (Mt. Vibul) hoping to obtain the gem Jewel of the great Chakkavatti king (according to Buddhist mythology when a great Chakkavatti king or Universal Monarch appears in the world, this gem Jewel, which normally resides on Mt. Vibul, comes to him along with six other great gem possessions and remains in his care until the very end of his reign). Since no one but a Chakkavatti king could possess the gem Jewel, its guardians refused to relinquish it to Sakka; but in its place they offered an Emerald Jewel which was of the same essence and came from the same place. Sakka brought the Emerald Jewel to Nāgasena and then Vissukamma, the divine architect and craftsman, appeared in the guise of an artisan and fashioned the Jewel into an image of the Buddha — a task which took seven days and nights during which all sorts of miracles transpired. When the image was completed, the Thera invited the seven relics of the Buddha to enter into it, and they did so. Thereupon, the Thera prophesied that the image would be worshiped in Cambodia, Burma, and Thailand.

As we shall subsequently see, this story of the acquisition and fashioning of the Jewel is pregnant with religious significance, but all of the modern scholars who have commented upon it from the time of King Mongkut (mid-nineteenth century) have agreed that it falls into the realm of mythology.[6] The account may reflect certain historical facts such as the existence of the Thera Nāgasena and possibly his relationship to the widely famed King Milinda, the emergence in early Buddhist history of the previously avoided practice of fashioning images, and even the ancient use of jewels of the emerald type as a material from which images were made.[7] However, there is no external evidence to suggest an Indian origin for the image; what is more, the fabrication of Indian origins for images and other sacred objects was a common practice in Southeast Asia.

The various chronicles continue by providing a brief sketch of the Jewel's early career. According to the account, the image remained in India until a series of calamities caused the people who possessed it to move to Sri Lanka where it was then established. Much later, the chronicles continue, King Anawartha of the Burmese kingdom of Pagan felt the need to obtain a full and correct version of the sacred scriptures, and in order to acquire such a copy he used his magical power to go to Sri Lanka. There the king made copies of the three major segments of the Pāli canon, and also of an additional collection of grammatical works. In order to send them back to Pagan he placed two of the texts in one boat and he placed the other two texts, along with the Holy Emerald Jewel, in a second boat. However, in the course of the journey back to Burma a great storm arose and the second boat was diverted to the Khmer country (Cambodia). When King Anawartha discovered what had happened, he used his magic power to travel to the Khmer capital of Angkor where he obtained the writings but forgot his intention to take the Jewel. Later, as a result of a flood occasioned by the anger of a royal chaplain whom the Khmer king had mistreated, the people fled from Angkor and took the Jewel to a neighboring village.

As in the case of the preliminary account of the origins of the image, this recital of its travels from India to a village near Angkor owes more to the chronicler's efforts to establish its religio-political meaning than to actual historical events. Even though King Anawartha was a powerful ruler of Pagan who instituted a Theravada Buddhist reform, the story of his travels to Sri Lanka and Angkor and the related account of the Jewel's misadventures at sea and arrival at Angkor cannot be accepted as historical facts. Nevertheless, Robert Lingat, who has carefully surveyed all of the sources, has strongly argued that the Holy Emerald Jewel is identical with the Holy Jewel mentioned in an ancient Khmer inscription from the reign of King Sūryavarman I (early eleventh century A.D.).[8] He has noted a commonality of both name and function and has ingeniously dealt with the problem posed by the Brahmanic rather than the Buddhist associations of Sūryavarman's Jewel and the obviously later northern Thai style of the iconography of the Holy Emerald Jewel. At the time when it was being venerated in Sūryavarman's court, Lingat argues, the Jewel had not yet received its image form; its transformation into an image occurred, he contends, in the context of the Theravada reform movement which took place in Thailand during the late fourteenth and early fifteenth centuries and should be attributed to the period during which, according to the unanimous testimony of the chronicles, the whereabouts of the image was unknown.

Lingat's hypothesis has much to commend it, but the actual physical identity of the two Jewels remains problematic. There is no really valid evidence for the occurrence of any flood of the kind reported in the chronicles, and Thai incursions into the Khmer heartland before the middle of the fourteenth century were rare.[9] What is more, there are stories of Thai acquisitions of sacred objects of indigenous peoples which suggest that the Jewel may well have been acquired in this context and only later associated with *the* Holy Jewel of the Angkor court. In this connection it is perhaps significant to note that in the chronicles of southern Laos it is reported that a precious stone considered to be an image of the Buddha was found by the aborigines in the region of Sarvanne.[10] The chronicles recount that it was originally treated as a genie of the hunt, that after many adventures it was brought to Champassac and established in that vicinity, and that during a dynastic crisis the Jewel, by then considered to be the palladium of the kingdom, was seized and carried away by the Siamese.[11]

But whatever we may conclude concerning the actual physical identity between the Angkor Jewel and the Holy Emerald Jewel, the chroniclers' accounts of the subsequent adventures of the Holy Emerald Jewel in central and northern Thailand almost certainly contain at least a germ of historical fact. Though the various versions involve inconsistencies which cannot be definitively resolved, the Jewel seems at different times to have fallen into the hands of the princes of Ayudhiā, Kampeng Phet, and Chiangrai. And, what is most important, the accounts all agree on the fully confirmed historical fact that in the late fifteenth century the Holy Emerald Jewel came into the possession of King Tilok of Lannathai, who brought it to his capital of Chiangmai and established it in the compound of the new central stupa which he had constructed.

From this point forward the history of the Jewel's adventures can be traced quite precisely. In 1545 the son of the king of Luang Prabang acceded to a request to take the throne at Chiangmai where he ruled for several years. At the death of his father he returned to his homeland and when he did so he took the Holy Emerald Jewel with him. Much to the distress of the populace of Chiangmai he refused to return the image, but rather established it in a temple near his own palace. A few years later he moved his capital to Vientienne, and again the Jewel was established in a similar location where the traditional cult was maintained. The Jewel remained in Vientienne for two hundred years until 1778 when a Thai general who conquered the country sent it back to the Thai capital of Thonburi where it was received by the monks with all appropriate honors. A number of years later, when the same general led a coup d'état and established himself as King Rāma I, he placed the Holy Emerald Jewel in its own Chapel in the compound of the Grand Palace in Bangkok where it still remains, and where it still continues to be venerated as the protector of the Chakri dynasty and of the kingdom over which it rules.[12]

The Jewel as Hierophany

The various chroniclers' versions of the myth of the origins of the Holy Emerald Jewel are quite explicit in recounting that the Thera Nāgasena, when he became interested in the project of fashioning an image, wanted to have it carved from a sacred stone; and the versions are equally explicit in affirming that the Jewel which was actually obtained was one which manifested great supernatural power. From an historian's point of view Robert Lingat has noted that the Holy Emerald Jewel was one of an important group of Thai and Laotian images which were associated with a *phi* (an indigenous guardian spirit similar to the *nats* of Burma) whose sacred power was a direct function of the material from which the image was made.[13] By taking this emphasis on the material from which the image was fashioned more seriously into account, it is possible to specify more precisely the mode of sacrality which it manifests.

At the outset it should be noted that despite the fact that it is called by the name of Holy Emerald Jewel, the image is not made from an emerald as that stone is usually defined by minerologists. Though the Holy Emerald Jewel is fashioned from a kind of jewel which is relatively common around the northern Thai city of Nan, and though the material has sometimes been vaguely designated by scholars as a kind of jasper, its exact minerological character remains to be established. More important, however, is the immediate impression which the Jewel makes upon an observer, specifically the deep bluish-green luminosity which conveys different aspects depending upon the lighting and the angle from which it is viewed. It is this curious and mysterious character of the appearance of the Jewel which has led to its identification as an emerald, and which helps to explain the specific modes of sacred power which it has conveyed to those who have venerated it.[14]

Emerald Jewels of the emerald type have appeared at many points in the history of religions, and have demonstrated their ability to manifest various dimensions of sacrality. Through their greenish color they have become associated with the positive aspects of vegetation and fertility, and with the power of the sacred to regenerate and renew.[15] In other instances their bluish-green cast has provided the basis for affirming their association with the waters in general, and with the rains in particular.[16] Especially in those cases where the luminosity of the emerald has been most apparent associations with the sky and lightning have been evoked, and thus the connections between the emerald and the rains have been reinforced. On occasions emeralds have been credited with origins in the heavenly regions,[17] while on other occasions their celestial character has been attested through their close association with birds.[18] Variously expressed in the accompanying mythologies, the transcendent and sacred dimensions of the sacred revealed by celestial hierophanies have made themselves manifest in forms which attest to the continuing immediacy and efficacy of the sacred in the affairs of the world.

These various dimensions of sacred power which men have perceived in this type of jewel focus around its positive aspects, around regeneration and renewal, around active beneficence provided from above and beyond the profane. It is in this context that the power of such jewels to bring relief from disease, to hasten childbirth, to restore sight, to increase wealth and the like make sense.[19] Also it is from these associations that George Kunz, in his *Magic of Jewels and Charms*, has derived what he calls the usual meanings of the emerald — namely, faith, hope and resurrection.[20]

These possibilities of the emerald for manifesting sacred power have been widely recognized and adapted in Southeast Asia. This fact is demonstrated by a very popular myth concerning the goddess Mani Mekhala which has been incorporated into the *Ramakien* (the Thai version of the *Rāmāyana*) and provides the story line for one of the most renowned classical Thai dances.[21] The light which this myth throws on the way in which the symbolic possibilities of the emerald have been exploited in this particular environment justifies quoting a part of a summary of the myth given by René Nicholas: "Mani Mekhala, the nymph of the waters, possesses a marvelous emerald which produces the lightning. When she joins in with the joyous troups of gods and goddesses who, by their dances, celebrate the coming of the rains, Rama-sua, the grandson of Brahmā, covets the emerald and desires to rip it away from the nymph. The nymph flees from him and the rays from the jewel shine in his face so that they blind him. The demon pursues her across the heavens, throwing his hatchet in her direction; but she evades the weapon and, striking the clouds, it causes the thunder."[22] In this episode the general association of emerald jewels with the rains and with regeneration and renewal are made more specific. The myth of the goddess and her jewel are connected directly with the coming of the monsoons, the most dramatic and positive event in the life of the agricultural communities of Southeast Asia. Furthermore, in the myth the jewel is intimately related to the lightning; in fact it is recognized as the very source of the light which comes from the sky.

Turning to the case of the Holy Emerald Jewel itself, the chronicles of Chiangmai clearly testify to the fact that while the image was in Chiangmai it came to serve as the preeminent guardian of the city. And, just as in the case of the indigenous guardian *phi* which it superseded, it was venerated in special ceremonies held in April/May in order to assure the onset of the rains and to guarantee the prosperity and security of the realm for the coming year.[23] The Jewel also assumed a role as the preeminent guardian of the city in Vientienne and Bangkok where special veneration at the time of the onset of the monsoons remained a regular focus of the cult. In addition, other special observances were held, particularly in times of crisis. For example, a great ceremony was performed in Bangkok at the time of the terrible cholera epidemic of 1820; on this occasion, an attempt was made to purify the city through an elaborate procession in which the Holy Emerald Jewel was taken around the city while the monks engaged in the recitation of sacred texts (*paritta*) which were believed to possess a special magical potency.[24]

The specific manifestations of sacred power which were associated with the particular character of the Jewel from which the image was carved were also closely related to various affinities and antagonisms which the image reportedly displayed during the course of its history. For example, consider the well-known affinity between the Holy Emerald Jewel and the almost equally famous image known as the Phra Sihing. In this case the Holy Emerald Jewel, both because of the symbolism inherent in the material from which it was made and because of the associations made in its mythology, was correlated with celestial powers; in contrast, the Phra Sihing had explicit mythological connections with the underworld (according to the chronicles which recount the origins of the Phra Sihing, it was cast in the likeness of a nāga king who had assumed the form of the Buddha, and in a local Chiengmai chronicle it is reported that immediately after its casting the nāga king took it with him and descended into his underworld realm).[25] Thus, according to the tradition which also affirms that the two images were made on the same day, they complement one another, and their "reuniting" in one place is most beneficial.[26] On the other hand, consider the equally well-known antipathy between the Holy Emerald Jewel and the Phra Bang image of Laotian fame, an antipathy which was believed to have wrought great havoc when the two images were brought together in Bangkok, thus leading to the return of the Prabang image to its earlier "home" in Luang Prabang. In this case both images were associated with the celestial dimensions of power (like the Holy Emerald Jewel, the Prabang image had close mythological connections with the celestial realm) and thus they were considered to be competitive, antagonistic and prone to cause problems when they were kept together within the confines of a single kingdom.[27]

The significance of the emerald hierophany is also evident in the close and very important connection which is made in the cult between the image, the lightning and the use of sacred fire. In the chronicles a number of instances are reported in which the image effects its will through the power of lightning. For example, when the image does not desire to be placed in a shelter built for it by a local sovereign, the shelter is destroyed by a bolt of lightning. The chronicles also report that, at a certain crucial juncture in the Jewel's career the plaster in which it had been encased and hidden was broken off by a similar bolt. The lightning was identified as the source of the sacred fire which was kept beside it through which its power became especially manifest. This connection between the lightning and the sacred fire was clearly stated in the local chronicles; and in the nineteenth century it was noted by Anna Leonowens who reported that on one occasion after the fire had been allowed to go out by

a careless attendant it was not rekindled until lightning struck the Royal Audience Hall, thus providing a flame which was appropriate for the purpose.[28]

Though our data concerning the character of the cultic practices which were
traditionally associated with the sacred fire is very sketchy, some indications
may be gleaned from the chronicles. For example, the *Ratanabimbavamsa* refers to a fascinating ritual which was supposedly performed shortly after the
Jewel had been "rediscovered" and established in the city of Chiangrai. According to this report, "all of the inhabitants of the village lustrated (the Jewel)
with perfumed liquid. When those who performed the lustration were endowed
with good qualities such as a pure faith, when they had acquired merit by the
practice of alms-giving and other virtues, when they had always fulfilled their
duties toward their parents, and when they had always shown respect for the
elder members of their family, the liquid which they used to lustrate the image
spread over all of it, and the oil which they poured fell into the bowl of their
lamp, and their lamp, being lit, burned brightly and perfectly. When those who
lustrated the image were evil-doers who had committed evil actions such as
striking or killing their parents, not even a single drop of the liquid which they
used to lustrate the image spread over it, the oil which they poured did not
flow into the bowl of their lamp, and whatever they did, their lamp would not
burn."[29]

Jewel, Buddha and King

Without an appreciation for the basic religious character of the Holy Emerald Jewel *qua* jewel no integral understanding of its legitimating power can
be generated. But at the same time a full understanding of the Jewel's potency
must also take seriously into account the specifically Buddhist and royal associations which it has acquired. Among these associations those with Indra, the
Buddha-Chakkavatti, Mahāvessantara, and Rāma have been of central importance.

Whatever its previous career may have been, when the Holy Emerald Jewel
appeared clearly on the stage of history it was fully integrated into the Buddhist framework. And within this framework its association with Indra — the
divine king who rules over the gods in the Tāvatimsa heaven — has been consistently recognized. This is not surprising since there is an intrinsic connection between the dimensions of sacred power traditionally manifested by emeralds
and those associated by Buddhists with the figure of Indra (for example, the
connections with the rains and fertility, with the sky and the lightning, and so
on). This association between the Jewel and Indra is visually communicated
through the fact that a deep green emerald-like color is used within the Thai
tradition to identify the figure of Indra. Moreover, the association is quite
clearly expressed in the accounts recorded in the chronicles. We have already
referred to the myth of the origins of the image in which it is reported that it
was Indra who obtained the Jewel which Vissukamma, his assistant, fashioned
into an image. To this can be added the fact that the chronicles explicitly state
that the oil for the lamps which stood before the image had been given by
Indra, and that the flame had come from the celestial fire (i.e., the lightning)
which he had provided.[30] What is perhaps most significant of all, there are a
series of tantalizing connections which seem to link the Holy Emerald Jewel

with a very important cult object in northern Thailand known as an Indrakhila (column of Indra).[31]

The cult of the Indrakhila seems to have been introduced into northern Thailand by early Buddhist ascetics as a part of their activities which included the founding of settlements, bringing in Indianized chieftains from the south, and the establishment of their (probably Sanskritic) form of the Buddhist tradition.[32] In many respects the cult was similar to that which had previously been rendered to the indigenous guardian deities. However, the center of worship was an Indrakhila which was thought to perform the function of guaranteeing fertility, security and prosperity so long as the sovereign and the people followed the five and eight precepts and offered the proper veneration to it and to the Kumphan (lesser deities) who guarded it.[33] But what particularly interests us here is the fact that the mythology associated with the Indrakhila correlates closely with the mythology associated with the Holy Emerald Jewel, that some of the descriptions of its form reveal striking parallels between the two sacred objects, and that the accounts of the cult suggest a strong similarity of function.

At the level of mythology the Indrakhila had its original home in the Tāvatimsa heaven, and was given by Indra to an ascetic or sovereign who desired to have it established in the earthly realm in order to assure the well-being of a village or kingdom. To be sure, there are differences between this kind of account of the origins of the Indrakhila and the accounts of the origin of the Holy Emerald Jewel, but the fact that they belong to the same family of stories can hardly be denied. In contrast to the accounts of the Indrakhila's origins, which remain basically constant in the different sources, the descriptions of the object itself vary a great deal. In some cases the Indrakhila is described simply as a column of bricks. But in other cases it is identified as a precious stone or is associated with an object which had an appearance very similar to that of the Holy Emerald Jewel. This latter kind of description is provided in a fascinating account in the Chronicle of Mahāthera Fa Bot in which it is reported that Indra ordered an ascetic to make a vase of alloy in the shape of an egg of the rain bird. He was instructed to polish this vase until it took on a deep green coloring, and then to fill it with statues of the 101 species of animals. When this was completed, two Kumphan came and placed the Indrakhila in the vase (an event which was accompanied by a frightening clap of thunder) and thereafter the vase-Indrakhila and its Kumphan guardians became the object of the cult.[34] In a parallel version the green, egg-shaped vase is identified directly with the Indrakhila itself.[35] In addition to these remarkable similarities in the mythology and physical form of the Indrakhila and the Jewel, it is also evident that during the reign of King Tilok in Chiangmai the cult of the Holy Emerald Jewel received the same kind of veneration which had previously been given to the Indrakhila.[36] And, to cite another more recent case in point, it is apparent from Lingat's description that the ritual which was carried out in order to purify the city of Bangkok at the time of the great cholera epidemic (see above) was a typical Buddhist *paritta* ceremony in which the Holy Emerald Jewel had come to play the role usually assigned to an Indrakhila which had been specifically erected for the occasion.[37]

Though it is certainly the case that associations between the Holy Emerald Jewel and Indra are both numerous and multifaceted, the connections between the Jewel and the great Chakkavatti king are of even greater significance. Ac-

cording to the chroniclers' accounts of its origin, the Jewel, though it was obtained by Indra, was not his Jewel and did not come from the Tāvatimsa heaven
where he reigned; rather, it was a Jewel which was of the same essence as the
gem Jewel of the great Chakkavatti king, and it came from the place where that
gem Jewel was located — namely from Mt. Vibul. Moreover, the fact that the
fabulous gem Jewel of the Chakkavatti was well-known in the early Thai tradition can be demonstrated simply by pointing out that a significant section in
the well-known fourteenth century Thai text called the *Three Worlds According
to King Ruang* — a segment equal to two full book pages in English translation — was devoted to a vivid description of its glories and magnificence, as
well as its various magical powers.[38]

But over and above the Holy Emerald Jewel's association with the gem Jewel
on Mt. Vibul, it came to be identified with the Chakkavatti king himself or,
perhaps more accurately, with the Buddha in his Chakkavatti aspect. The role
which the Holy Emerald Buddha assumed as a manifestation of the Buddha-
Chakkavatti is, of course, suggested by the transformation of the raw Jewel
into an image of the Buddha and the subsequent incorporation of the seven
relics of the Buddha.[39] But it is even more specifically expressed by the custom,
which had already been adopted during the time when the Jewel was located in
Chiangmai, of fitting out the Jewel with full royal regalia. The association between the Buddha images which were decked out with such royal regalia and
the Buddha Chakkavatti has been brilliantly explicated by Paul Mus in his study
of the cultic practices which were carried on at the site of the Buddha's Enlightenment at Bodhgaya.[40] Moreover, the significance of Mus's study for our
purposes is enhanced when we recognize the strong possibility that the practice of fitting out the Holy Emerald Jewel with royal regalia was directly influenced by the Bodhgaya tradition which Mus describes and interprets. In
fact, the first evidence which we have of the practice in relation to the Holy
Emerald Jewel comes from the reign of King Tilok who sent a mission to Bodhgaya and who, upon its return, not only built a replica of the Bodhgaya
temple in Chiangmai but also fostered the casting of images in the style of the
central Bodhgaya image.[41] However, in northern Thailand this practice of
adornment was divested of the explicitly docetic and Mahayanist connotations
which it had acquired in the Indian setting and in the "Indianized" areas of
Southeast Asia; in this new Theravada context crowned images and other images representing the Buddha-Chakkavatti (including, presumably, the Holy
Emerald Jewel) were considered to represent a particular moment in the Buddha's life when he assumed the form of a Chakkavatti king in order to awe into
submission a powerful and prideful monarch named Jambupati.[42]

Thus the dimensions of sovereignty suggested by the Jewel hierophany itself, and accentuated through the various associations between the Jewel and
Indra, were expressed in their fullest and most complete form through the close
association which was made between the Jewel and Buddhism's royal figure par
excellence, the Buddha-Chakkavatti. Through the proper veneration of the
Jewel the king gained the support of sovereign power in its most potent and
beneficent form. And, on a deeper level the king's meditation on the Jewel imbued him with that power and thereby enabled him to exercise authority, to
establish order, and to guarantee the protection and prosperity for the kingdom. Moreover, it was this identification between the Jewel and the Buddha-

Chakkavatti which provided the ultimate justification for one of the most important functions associated with the Jewel in the Thai and Laotian kingdoms where it was venerated — namely, its role as the sovereign ruler before whom the various princes of the kingdom swore their fealty to the reigning monarch who possessed it.

During the course of its history in Thailand and Laos the basic symbolism of the Jewel as Buddhist sovereign was given a further and very important twist through the connection which came to be made between the Jewel and Mahāvessantara — the king whom the tradition identifies as the Bodhisatta in his last life prior to the one in which he attained Buddhahood. Though there are some references to the stories of the Buddha's previous lives in the chronicles, both the evidence for the association between the Jewel and Mahāvessantara and the key to its significance are to be found in the cult. At least from the time that the Jewel was located in Vientienne its adornments were changed twice a year, once at the beginning of the rainy season when it was fitted out with a monastic outfit, and once at the transition between the rainy season and the cool season when it was fitted out with full royal regalia (a third change was instituted during the nineteenth century when King Rama III provided a third royal outfit which was subsequently used to adorn the image during the dry season).[43] At least by the time of the Bangkok period this ritual of changing the Jewel's adornments had come to involve, as a central element, the chanting of the *Mahāvessantara Jātaka.*

In order to understand the significance of the association which was thus made between the Holy Emerald Jewel and the figure of Mahāvessantara it is necessary to take two different facts into account. The first is that through the changing of the outfit of the Jewel at the beginning and at the end of the rainy season the Theravadins expressed their conviction that the true Buddhist sovereign was a paradigmatic model for and of the traditional seasonal oscillation between the concentrated piety and renunciation appropriate for the four-month rainy season (the "Lenten" season in the Buddhist context) and the more normal "secular" life appropriate for the remaining eight months of the year. And, the second fact that needs to be taken into account is that the story of Mahāvessantara is one in which the royal protagonist exhibits these two modes of existence in their most impressive and dramatic forms. On the one hand, the great bulk of the Mahāvessantara story recounts the way in which Mahāvessantara perfected the virtue of giving by giving away his kingdom and all of his possessions (wife, children, and so on) and adopting a radically renunciatory mode of life. But, on the other hand, the story culminates in a miraculous restitution of all of the possessions which he had previously given away, and his return to his throne amid the joyous celebrations of all his subjects.[44] In other words, the association of the Jewel with the figure of Mahāvessantara reinforced and dramatized the same point which was made in the cultic performance as a whole — namely the intrinsic and intimate correlation between the two phases in the life of the Jewel (monastic or renunciatory and royal), the two phases in the rhythm of the cosmic cycle (rainy season and other seasons), and the two phases in the life of the community (the phase of concentrated piety and the phase of normal "secular" existence).

Having considered the way in which the symbolism of the Holy Emerald Jewel was both extended and given a specifically Buddhist and even more specifically Theravadin form through various associations which connected it with Indra, the Buddha-Chakkavatti and Mahāvessantara, we may now turn our attention to the last of the four associations which have been widely affirmed in the course of its history, that which relates it to the figure of Rāma. There is no reason to believe that this relationship was affirmed during the earlier periods of the Jewel's history, but its importance during the Bangkok era is demonstrated by the fact that in the Chapel of the Holy Emerald Jewel in Bangkok the galleries which surround the Jewel are literally covered with murals depicting scenes from the *Ramakien* in which Rāma is the great hero.

The fact that an identification between the Jewel and Rāma is intended is obvious, but its significance is not immediately apparent. To be sure, it is true that in Buddhist circles Rāma was sometimes recognized as a future Buddha, but this tradition is not strong and does not seem to be at all to the fore in this particular context. Rather, the key to the association is in the fact that at a very early point in its history the Chakri dynasty chose to identify itself with the figure of Rāma. When this crucial element in the situation is taken into account, it becomes self-evident that the very vivid and very public portrayal of the connection between the Jewel and Rāma is meant to convey to the people of the Bangkok kingdom the identity between the religious merit and sovereign power of the jewel and the religious merit and sovereign power of the reigning dynasty founded by King Rāma I and presently represented by his lineal descendant, King Rāma IX.

The Jewel and Other Legitimating Symbols

Thus far in our discussion we have focused on the symbolism of the Jewel itself, taking account both of its intrinsic power as a hierophany and of the more specifically Buddhist and royal meanings which came to be associated with it during the course of its history. However, in order to gain a more complete understanding of the role which the Jewel has played in legitimating the rule of Thai and Laotian kings, it is crucial to look more closely at the relationship between the Jewel and the sacred scriptures, and then to consider the relationship between the Jewel and the sacred mountain or stupa. As we proceed, we will also consider certain fascinating parallels between the Buddhist pattern of legitimation in which the Jewel played an important part, and other patterns of legitimation which preceded it in the Southeast Asian context.

In the chroniclers' accounts of the Holy Emerald Jewel the "theoretical" relationship between the Jewel and the sacred scriptures is suggested by the myth which deals with its origins, while the "historical" dimension is brought directly into the foreground in the legends of King Anawartha's activities. In recounting the Jewel's origin, the chronicles describe the fashioning of the raw Jewel into an image of the Buddha and the consecration of the image which occurs when the Thera Nāgasena invites the seven relics of the Buddha to enter into it; and in this way they establish the Jewel's character as the *rūpakāya* (material body or form body) of the Buddha which, according to the tradition, is the manifestation of the Buddha's continuing presence which must coexist with and supplement his *dhammakāya* (dhamma or scriptural body). On the "historical" level, the subsequent account of the chroniclers presupposes that the Jewel and the sacred scriptures coexisted with one another in Ceylon, but maintains that in Southeast Asia, due to the storm which diverted one of

Anawartha's boats and his later forgetfulness, the two became separated – the Jewel becoming established at Angkor, the scriptures in Pagan.

Though the details of the account are obviously mythical or legendary in character, there are good reasons to believe that the dénouement of the story concerning King Anawartha reflects an actual historical situation which existed in Southeast Asia early in the second millenium A.D. It is a firmly established historical fact that the Theravada scriptures were brought from Ceylon to Pagan during or shortly after King Anawartha's reign (late eleventh, early twelfth centuries A.D.) and that a Holy Jewel held an important cultic position in the Angkor court of about the same period (late eleventh century). Moreover, there is now considerable evidence which enables us to associate the Holy Jewel which was venerated at Angkor with the *devarāja* (divine king) cult practiced by the Khmer rulers [45] as well as a solid basis for affirming that this Angkor Jewel was – if not the Holy Emerald Jewel itself – at least a "model" which the Holy Emerald Jewel came to represent and whose sacrality it was believed to manifest.[46] In any event, the chroniclers recount that the Holy Emerald Jewel and the sacred scriptures became separated when the "pure" Theravada tradition was brought from Sri Lanka to Southeast Asia. But the chroniclers do not condone the separation, and therein lies the key to their purpose. The ideal which is implicit in their narrative is the reuniting of the Holy Jewel which was associated with the royal cult at Angkor and the sacred scriptures which King Anawartha had succeeded in bringing to Pagan. And, it is just this ideal which we know was actualized by King Tilok of Chiangmai, and then by the other kings who subsequently gained possession of the Jewel. King Tilok actualized this ideal in a most dramatic way – on the one hand, he acquired the Jewel, brought it to his capital, and established its cult; on the other hand, he sponsored a great Ecumenical Council (the eighth such Ecumenical Council according to the Thai reckoning) at which the monks were enjoined to reconstruct the sacred scriptures in their pristine purity. Since Tilok's time the Thai and Laotian kings who have possessed the Holy Emerald Jewel have kept a full copy of the most "orthodox" version of the Pāli canon in close proximity to it.[47] By bringing and keeping together these two forms of the "body" of the Buddha, these kings have symbolically reestablished the fullness and purity of the Buddhist religion; and in so doing they have proclaimed the legitimacy of their own rule.

From our discussion thus far it would appear that the pattern of Buddhist legitimation symbolism with which the Holy Emerald Jewel has been associated has involved two basic foci – namely the Jewel itself and the sacred scriptures. However, there is a third focus which is hinted at in the chroniclers' narratives and is very prominent, in a somewhat different form, in the actual historical patterns of legitimation in which the Holy Emerald Buddha has played an important role. In the chronicles, this third focus is suggested by the references which are made to Mt. Vibul and the gem Jewel of the Chakkavatti in the story of the Jewel's origins; in the Angkor context, this third focus is suggested by the role which isplayed by Mt. Mahendra and the linga which resides there; and, in the Thai and Laotian contexts, this third focus appears in its classical Buddhist form as the central stupa of the kingdom in which an especially sacred relic of the Buddha is encased.

In the context of the chronicles, the Holy Emerald Jewel was, as we have seen, a "substitute" for the Jewel par excellence – the gem Jewel of the

Chakkavatti king. This great gem Jewel remained in its original place on Mt. Vibul, while its power was manifested in the world through the presence of the Holy Emerald Jewel. In the case of Angkor (assuming that Herman Kulke's recent interpretation of the *devarāja* cult and my own closely correlated identification of the Holy Jewel as the *devarāja* itself are correct) was a movable embodiment of the power of the immobile linga which resided on Mt. Mahendra — the sacred mountain on which great founding king of the Khmer Empire was consecrated as Chakravartin. And finally, in the various Thai and Laotian capitals, the Jewel appeared as the palladium of the reigning king which embodied in a special way the same power which was also present in the relic encased in the stupa which served as the symbolic center of the kingdom. In the case of Chiangmai this stupa was the famous Chedi Luang which was built by King Tilok. In the case of Vientienne this stupa was the famous That Luang built by the Laotian king who had brought the Emerald Buddha from Chiangmai. In the case of Bangkok this stupa, which admittedly played a less prominent role than the Chedi Luang in Chiangmai or the That Luang in Vientienne, was the famous Golden Mount at Wat Saket.[48]

What seems to be involved in these various contexts are two manifestations of the *rūpakāya* of the Buddha whose functions directly parallel those of two different types of indigenous deities which dominated the "cadastral" religion of the Asia of the monsoons from very ancient times. The first of these two types was the so-called "public" god of the soil, and the second was a more personalized deity often associated with the ancestor of a local chieftain who was primarily responsible for its cult. In many cases these two types of deities were closely identified so that the second became a personalization of the first. This was, for example, the situation in the Cham cults which were the prime focus of Paul Mus's crucial study on the subject.[49] But in many other situations, particularly in societies with a more hierarchic social structure, (including, it would seem, many of the non-Buddhized Tai communities in northern Indochina), the two were clearly distinct.[50] In an excellent study of the ancient Mon tradition Harry Shorto has shown one way in which these two different types of indigenous cadastral deities were transposed into a specifically Theravada Buddhist form. In the Mon tradition, Shorto demonstrates, the public, territorial type of deity came to be represented by 32 stupas located in the 32 subdivisions of the kingdom (each one supposedly containing a portion of an especially sacred relic brought to the Mon area by Gavampati), while the more personalized deities which complemented them came to be represented by 32 "dewatau sotapan" (deities who have entered the Buddhist Path), whose presence was manifested in sacred trees located in the compound of the respective stupas.[51] In the Thai and Laotian cases with which we are concerned here the more personalized "ancestral" or "dynastic" deity has reappeared in a very different Theravada form — namely that of the Holy Emerald Jewel, whereas the reliquary stupa has once again served as the Theravada transformation of the more public deity of the soil.[52]

When we collate the two segments of our discussion of the Jewel and other Buddhist symbols of legitimation, what emerges is a pattern in which three elements play a crucial role. Within this pattern the legitimating presence of the *rūpakāya* of the Buddha is represented in two forms which parallel the two types of deities which existed in the pre-Buddhist, pre-Indianization cadastral religion of Southeast Asia and in the Brahmanic tradition of Angkor. The *first* of these forms is the Jewel itself which corresponds to the more personalized ancestral deity in the indigenous tradition and to the Khmer *devarāja*, adapting and extending the role of these earlier deities on the basis of the rich Buddhist symbolism which we have previously discussed. The *second* of these forms is the stupa which takes the place of the public god of the soil in the indigenous tradition and of Mt. Mahendra in the Khmer context, extending and adapting their role on the basis of the equally rich or perhaps even richer symbolism inherent in its profoundly cosmological structure and decor.[53] And finally, the *third* basic element which completes the triune pattern is the symbol of the *dhammakāya* of the Buddha, namely the sacred scriptures in their "pure" Pāli form. For almost half a millenium the Holy Emerald Jewel maintained its distinctive position within this triune pattern through which the kings of northern Thailand, Laos and central Thailand sought to legitimate their rule.

With the identification of this broader complex of legitimating symbols and of the role of the Holy Emerald Jewel within it, our study is now basically complete. However, as a kind of postscript, it may be of interest to point out that in the broader Thai-Laotian cultural area there is another especially sacred image which has played a role similar to that of the Holy Emerald Jewel within the same basic pattern of legitimating symbols. In an earlier study of cultic traditions in the old Laotian capital of Luang Prabang I pointed out the fact that the three major celebrations of the yearly ritual calendar reached their culmination in three distinct cultic actions — in the veneration of the Prabang image which served as the palladium of the reigning dynasty (as I noted earlier, the symbolic associations of the Prabang image are similar to those of the Holy Emerald Jewel, and the two images have often been considered as rivals); the veneration of the capital city's central stupa; and the veneration of the abbots of the four major temples which traditionally had responsibility for the four segments into which the sacred scriptures were divided.[54] In that earlier paper I argued that these three central actions involved the successive veneration of the Three Jewels in which all Buddhists take refuge — namely the Buddha, the Dhamma, and the Sangha. In the light of the research reported in this present paper, I am now convinced that these three objects of veneration may also and perhaps even more appropriately be identified with the three basic elements in the complex of legitimating symbols which were so persistently utilized in Chiangmai, Vientienne and Bangkok. In other words, it now seems apparent that the Prabang image and the central stupa serve to represent and to convey the *rūpakāya* of the Buddha in its more personalized (i.e., dynastic) and more public (i.e., communal and territorial) forms, while the monks serve to represent and to convey the ultimate legitimating presence — namely, that of the holy scriptures through which the *dhammakāya* of the Buddha is made accessible to the kingdom and its populace.

Notes

1. In addition to works referred to in the body of the paper, see Nancy C. Falk, "Wilderness and Kingship in Ancient South India," *History of Religions,* XIII, No. 1 (August, 1973), 1-15; H. L. Seneviratne, "The Natural History of a Buddhist Liturgy; Being a Study in the Nature and Transformation of a Kandyan Sinhalese Metropolitan Ritual" (Unpublished

doctoral dissertation, University of Rochester, 1972); Donald K. Swearer, *Wat Haripuñjaya. The Royal Temple of the Buddha Relic, Lamphun, Thailand*. AAR Studies in Religion, 10 (Missoula, Montana: The Scholars Press, 1976); and two articles by Charles Archaimbault, "La Fête du T'at à Luong Prabang," in *Essays Offered to G. H. Luce*, ed. by Ba Shin, Jean Boisselier and A. B. Griswold (*Artibus Asiae*, Supplement XXIII, Vol. I: Ascona, 1966), 5-47, and "La Fête du T'at à Sieng Khwang," in *Artibus Asiae*, XXIV, No. 3/4, 1967, 187-199.

2. *Barabadur: Esquisse d'une histoire du Bouddhisme fondée sur la critique archéologique des textes* (École Française d'Extrême-Orient: Hanoi, 1932). Though Barabadour is, of course, a Mahayana stupa, Mus devotes much attention to the early and Theravada forms of the tradition. Another more easily accessible source which deals with some of the same kind of material is Robert Heine-Geldern's well known essay on "Conceptions of State and Kingship in Southeast Asia" (Data Paper No. 18; Cornell University Southeast Asia Program: Ithaca, 1956).

3. This distinction is also highlighted in a more succinct way in his "Bouddhisme et monde occidental pour une nouvelle methode," which serves as the "Introduction" to René de Berval, ed., *Présence du Bouddhisme* (*France Asie*, Nos. 153-57: Saigon, 1956).

4. "Cultes indiens et indigènes au Champa," *Bulletin de L'École Française Extrême-Orient*, Vol. XXXIII (1933), pp. 367-410.

5. The three main texts are the *Ratanabimbavamsa*, which was probably written in Sukothai sometime after 1450; a chapter in the *Jinakālamāli*, which was written in Chiangmai in the early part of the sixteenth century; and the *Amarakatabuddharupinidāna*, which was probably written in Vientienne in the latter part of the sixteenth century. For discussions of these texts, see George Coedès, "Notes sur les ouvrages palis composés en pays thai," *Bulletin de l'École Française Extrême-Orient*, Vol. XV (1915), p. 8ff, and Robert Lingat, "Le Culte du Bouddha d'Émeraude," *Journal of the Siam Society*, Vol. XXVII, No. 1 (1934), pp. 9-38. The chapter of the *Jinakālamāli* has been translated by N. A. Jayawickrama (see *The Sheaf of Gardlands of the Epochs of the Conqueror*, which is No. 36 in the Translation Series of the Pali Text Society and was published in London by Luzac and Company in 1968, pp. 139-45); The *Amarakatabuddharupinidāna* has been translated by Camille Notton (see *The Cult of the Emerald Buddha* which was published in Bangkok in 1931). Beyond these basic texts, occasional references to the Holy Emerald Jewel and to its various powers and adventures occur in a number of other Thai and Laotian sources.

6. Sir John Bowring, in his work on *The Kingdom and People of Siam* (London: Parker, 1957), Vol. I, p. 316, records a letter from Mongkut himself on the subject. Reportedly, Mongkut read a more complete statement when the functionaries of the realm gathered to take their oath of allegiance before the image.

7. In his account of Ceylon Fa Hien, an early fifth century Chinese traveller, tells of the presence of an extremely impressive image of the Buddha made of green jasper. See *A Record of Buddhistic Kingdoms* by James Legge (New York: Paragon Reprints, Dover Publications, 1965), p. 102.

8. Lingat, *op. cit.* Also see Lawrence Briggs, *The Ancient Khmer Empire*, Transactions of the American Philosophical Society, Vol. 41, Part 1: Philadelphia, 1951, p. 151, where the inscription is given in English and the historical context sketched out.

9. It is true that both the flood legend and the legend of King Anawartha are included in the Cambodian chronicles (see Adhemard Leclerc, *Histoire du Cambodge*, published by Paul Guethner in Paris, 1917, p. 130). However, this is not really valid evidence, since the Cambodian chronicles are late works compiled on the basis of Thai sources (on this matter, see Coedès, "Documents . . . .," *op. cit.*, p. 114, note 2).

10. The consensus of modern writers who have touched on the subject (Giles, Le May, and Lingat) is that the stone comes from an area near Nan where smaller specimens of the same type of jewel have been found. This is not far from the area of Sarvanne where the aborigines discovered their "image."

11. The relevant portion of the chronicle is mentioned by Charles Archaimbault in "Une Cérémonie en l'Honneur des Génies de la Mine de Sel de Ban Bo (Moyen Laos)," *Bulletin de l'École Française Extrême-Orient*, Vol. XLVIII, Part 1 (1948), pp. 227-28, especially note 1, p. 228.

12. During the past couple years the more recent history of the image has become a matter of special public interest in Thailand and Laos. Following the Pathet Lao takeover in Vien-

tienne, the Laotians have begun to talk of demanding the return of the Emerald Buddha to their capital. The Thai, however, have responded by reminding the Laotians that they had previously "stolen" it from the Thai. This matter is reported and discussed in an article entitled "Lao Kae Phon Doi Duay Chatniyom" ("Overcoming Inferiority with Nationalism in Laos"), in the weekly Thai magazine *Prachachat*, July 31, 1975, p. 14.

13. Lingat, *op. cit.*

14. There are three images in Thailand today for which the Holy Emerald Jewel tradition is claimed. However, scholars who have studied the subject with any seriousness are agreed that the image presently located in the Royal Chapel in Bangkok is the authentic Jewel. The best description and pictures of this image are found in Notton, *The Cult of the Emerald Buddha, op. cit.*

15. Kunz, George F., *Magic of Jewels and Charms* (Philadelphia: J. B. Lippincott, 1915), p. 305.

16. *Ibid.*, p. 311.

17. *Ibid.*, p. 81.

18. *Ibid.*, p. 136. Kunz here refers to the Mexican emerald which bore the name of the "quetzal" bird. This bird had brilliant green plumes and was the symbol of sovereignty in the area.

19. *Ibid.*, p. 135.

20. *Ibid.*, p. 281.

21. Originally, Mani Mekhala appears in the Jātakas as a goddess of the seas and the protectress of navigators. Later on, in the Buddhist literature and cults of the Tamil country she takes on a more definite form. In addition to her place in the myth under consideration (which, so far as I can determine, is found in this form only in Indochina), she is also present in southern Thailand where she plays an important role as a helper in the elephant hunt. For a study of her very interesting career the following sources are important: Levi, "Manimekhala, divinité de la mer," *Extrait des Bulletins de la Classe des Lettres et des Sciences Morales et Politique*, Séance du 2 juin 1930, p. 293ff; Pascalis, "Manimekhala en Indochine," *Révue des Arts Asiatiques*, Vol. VII (1931-32, pp. 81-92); and Giles, "An Account of the Rites and Ceremonies Observed at the Elephant-Driving Operations in the Seaboard Province of Lang Suan," *Journal of the Siam Society*, Vol. XXV (1932), pp. 153-214, esp. pp. 198-201 where the author gives a short summary of the entire subject.

22. René Nicholas, "The Thai Ramayana," *Révue Indochinois-Extrême Asie*, N.S., Vol. 2 (1928), p. 301 (my translation).

23. For traditions concerning the local guardian *phi* in Chiangmai and the introduction of the Emerald Jewel as the preeminent guardian deity of the city, see especially the "Chronique du Mahathera Fa Bot," translated by Camille Notton in *Annals du Siam*, Vol. I (Paris: Charles Lavauzelle, 1926), pp. 44-68. For a broader study of guardian deities in which some references are made to Chiangmai traditions and to parallel Brahmanic rites in Cambodia, see Paul Levy, "La sacrifice du buffle et la prédiction du temps à Vientienne," *Bulletin de l'Institute Indochinois pour l'étude de l'homme*, No. 6 (1943), pp. 323-324.

24. "The History of Wat Mahathat," *Journal of the Siam Society*, Vol. XXIV (1931), pp. 1-29. Another special ceremony to which Lingat refers in his article specifically on the Jewel (*op. cit.*, p. 24) illustrates both the similarity of function between the "indigenous" city guardian and the Jewel, and the complete preeminence of the latter. He describes the grand ceremony which was held on the one hundred fiftieth anniversary of the founding of the Chakri dynasty, taking note of the fact that the Jewel was the focus of veneration and the recipient of the offerings; and then he goes on to point out that two days later the "indigenous" guardian deity was the center of a similar ritual which was performed on a greatly reduced scale, by low-ranking functionaries.

25. The account of the origins of the image can be found in Camille Notton, tr., *The Chronicle of the Buddha Sihing* (Bangkok, 1928). The reference to the nāga king's removal of the image to his underworld kingdom is found in Notton, "Chronique du Mahathera Fa Bot," *op. cit.*, p. 38.

26. *Ibid.*, p. 38. It is very interesting to note that in the local Laotian chronicle of Khun Borom it is stated that when the people speak of the *phi sua muang* or local guardian deity they in reality speak of Mani Mekhala whose emerald and celestial associations we have already noted *and* of Nan Thoroni, the goddess of the earth. (The passage is quoted

by Louis Finot in his "Récherches sur la Literature Laotian," *Bulletin de l'École Française Extrême-Orient*, Vol. XVII [1917], No. 5, p. 156). A very similar phenomenon – namely the marriage of stones with male and female associations – is reported by Kunz, *op. cit.*, passim.

27. It would be interesting to pursue the extent to which this kind of analysis could account for the great variety of affinities and antagonisms among especially potent images in Thailand and Laos; however, in order to do this, another paper would be required.

28. Anna Leonowens, *The English Governess at the Siamese Court* (Boston: Fields, Osgood, 1873), pp. 189-90. It is also worthy of mention that she reports the great consternation of the populace when it became known that the fire had gone out, and the great rejoicing which ensued when it was appropriately rekindled.

29. Lingat, *op. cit.*, p. 21 (my translation). For an interesting discussion of the fire cult associated with the Holy Jewel in the court of Angkor, along with a short discussion of the symbolism of the celestial fire, see F. D. K. Bosch, "Notes archéologiques VI – Le Temple d'Angkor Vat à La Procession du Feu Sacré," *Bulletin de l'École Française Extrême-Orient*, XXXII (1932), pp. 7-11.

30. Notton, "Chronique de Mahathera Fa Bot," *op. cit.*, p. 49.

31. The Pāli canon testifies to the fact that the Indrakhila existed in ancient India both as a post, stake or column located in front of the city gate, and also as a large slab of stone put into the ground at the entrance of a house (see the "Indrakhila" entry in the Pali Text Society's Pali-English Dictionary). There was also an Indrakhila cult in South India which was connected with a reference in the Mahābhārata, and it is perhaps significant that this cult was active around the ninth century A.D. (see H. Krishna Sastri, "The Sculptured Pillar of the Indrakhila Hill at Bexuwada," *Archaeological Survey of India*, Annual Report for 1915-16, pp. 95-100.) The primary sources which we have used as the basis for the following discussion of the Indrakhila cult in the early period of northern Thai history are the "Chronique de Suvanna Khamdeng" and the Chronique de Mahathera Fa Bot," in Notton, *Annals, op. cit.*

32. As Paul Mus indicated in his review of Notton's translation of the chronicles (*Bulletin de l'École Française Extrême-Orient*, Vol. XXX [1930] pp. 466-71), these early ascetics were Buddhist. They were almost certainly the Hinayana monks using Sanskrit as their sacred language to whom Prince Damrong Rachanubhab refers in his "Histoire du bouddhisme au Siam," in *Revue Indochinoise-Extrême Asie*, No. 13 (July 1927), N.S. Vol. 2, pp. 25-27.

33. Presumably the five precepts were the standard prohibitions against killing, stealing, lying, illicit sexual activity, and the consumption of intoxicants; the eight precepts included these five plus three more which devout Buddhists followed on special holy days.

34. "Chronique de Mahathera Fa Bot," *op. cit.*, pp. 43-44. The sexual overtones of this account are obvious and correlate closely with the local and cross-cultural parallels referred to in note 2.

35. "Chronique de Suvanna Khmadeng," *op. cit.*, p. 33. It is perhaps worth noting that the prize possession of the goddess Mani Mekhala seems to have originally been identified as a bowl or vase; only later, in Siam and Cambodia, did the bowl or vase become an emerald. On this matter, see Pascalis, *op. cit.*, pp. 89-90.

36. In Chiangmai the cult of the Indrakhila did not die out but has been continued right up to the present time. The present Indrakhila now resides in a special shelter in the compound of the Chedi Luang (central stupa) very close to the spot where, during the reign of Tilok and his immediate successors, the Holy Emerald Jewel was kept.

37. Lingat, *op. cit.* For a full description of the classical Paritta ceremonies and the role of the Indrakhila in them, see Peter Schalk, *Der Paritta-Dienst in Ceylon* (Lund: Bröderna Ekstrands Tryckeri AB, 1972), 152-166.

38. Frank and Mani Reynolds, tr., *Three Worlds According to King Ruang* (Stanford, California and Bangkok: Stanford University Press and the Siam Society, forthcoming 1978).

39. The association between the Buddha's relics and their cult on the one hand, and his Chakkavatti aspect has always been close. See, for example "Le Parinirvana et les funérailles du Bouddha," *Journal Asiatique*, 1918-20.

40. "Le Buddha Pare," *Bulletin de l'École Française Extrême-Orient*, Vol. XXVIII (1928) pp. 153-278. For a study of the adornment tradition in the Khmer context, see George Coedès,

Bronzes Khmers (Études et documents publiés par V. Goloubew; *Ars Asiatica*: Paris, 1923).

41. For a discussion of King Tilok's mission and its results, see Alexander Griswold, *Dated Buddha Images of Northern Siam (Artibus Asiae*, Supplement SVI: Ascona, 1957).

42. The interpretation of crowned images in northern Thailand is discussed by Griswold, *ibid.* A translation of the *Jambupati Sutta* is given by Louis Finot, *op. cit.*, pp. 66-69.

43. For a description of various aspects of the ceremony, see Lingat, *op. cit.*, pp. 26-27. In Notton, *Cult of the Emerald Buddha, op. cit.*, pictures are included, and in Bowring, *op. cit.*, there is a good reproduction of sketches of the three outfits made by King Mongkut.

44. This culmination of the story, which is often reenacted while the Mahāvessantara story is being chanted in the ceremonies marking the end of the rainy season in many areas of Thailand and Laos, helps to account for the promise that those who listen to the recitation will be reborn when the future Buddha Metteya comes to establish his reign on earth. It is also quite probable that this culmination explains the reason for a chronicler's report that when the Holy Emerald Jewel was brought to Chiangmai the procession was accompanied by the chanting of the Mahāvessantara story.

45. The basis for connecting the Angkor Jewel with the better known *devarāja* cult is provided in a recent article by Herman Kulke in *Saeculum*, XXV, Heft 1 (1974), pp. 24-55, in which he develops a very significant new interpretation of the *devarāja* and its meaning. However, Kulke argues, without adducing any specifically Khmer data to support it, that the actual object of the *devarāja* cult was a bronze image. It seems much more likely that given the close association which Kulke himself emphasizes between the function of the *devarāja* and the fire of the fire cult, and the direct connection which is made in an important inscription he himself quotes between the fire cult and the Holy Jewel (an English translation of this inscription is given in Briggs, *op. cit.*, p. 151), that it was the Holy Jewel which was venerated as *devarāja*. Moreover, it is perhaps not insignificant that this inscription, which provides the basic evidence for affirming the correlation between the *devarāja*, the fire cult and the Holy Jewel comes from the reign of King Sūryavarman I – a king whose Buddhist (albeit Mahayana) preferences are well established.

46. As we noted above (see p. 177), Robert Lingat has made the case for a direct, physical identity between the Angkor Jewel and the Holy Emerald Jewel. However, even if this physical identity is not accepted – and in the above discussion I have suggested that the issue is by no means settled – the basic "religious" identity between the two Jewels can still be affirmed. As Alexander Griswold has pointed out in his *Dated Buddha Images . . ., op. cit.*, an image which is made as a "copy" of another image (and presumably a Holy Jewel which is like another Jewel which it represents) is believed to possess the sacrality and power of the original.

47. See, for example, the diagram of the Chapel of the Emerald Buddha compound in J. J. Boeles, "Four Stone Images of the Jina Buddha in the Precincts of the Chapel Royal of the Emerald Buddha," *Felicitation Volumes of Southeast Asian Studies Presented to His Highness Prince Dhanivat*, Vol. II, (Bangkok: Siam 1965), pp. 186-87 (Drawing A).

48. In Chiangmai and Vientienne the Holy Emerald Jewel was kept in close proximity to the central stupa. However, when the Jewel was established in Bangkok, it was integrated directly into the symbolic structure of the royal palace which was located at some distance from the Golden Mount. In the layout of the palace grounds [see Karl Dohring's description which was originally included in his *Siam*, Vol. II (Darmstat, 1923), p. 13, and was quoted in Robert Heine Geldern's "Weltbild und Bauform in Sudostasien," in *Weiner Beitrag zur Kunst und Kulturgeschichte Asian*, (1930)], the Chapel of the Emerald Buddha was located at the point of greatest sacrality – namely the northeastern segment of the compound. For a discussion which highlights the importance of this position, see Pierre Paris, "L'importance rituelle du Nord-est et ses applications en Indochine," *Bulletin de l'École Française Extrême-Orient*, XLI (1941), pp. 303-33. In addition, a fascinating discussion of the significance of the northeast in the specific context of Thai kingship rituals is included in Koson Srisang, "Thai Dhammocracy: Social Ethics as a Hermeneutic of Dhamma" (unpublished Ph.D. dissertation, University of Chicago, 1973), pp. 216-18.

49. Mus, "Cultes indiens . . . .," *op. cit.*

50. For a discussion of the Tai traditions, see Henri Maspero, "La Société et les Religions des Chinois Anciens et celles des Tai Modernes," *Mélanges posthumes sur les religions et l'histoire de la Chine* (Civilizations du Sud; Paris: A.E.P., 1950).

51. See his article on "The 32 Myos in the Medieval Mon Kingdom," *Bulletin of the School of Oriental and African Studies*, Vol. XXVI, Part 3 (1963), pp. 572-91, and especially his subsequent article on "The Dewatau Sotapan: A Mon Prototype of the 37 Nats" in the same *Bulletin*, Vol. XXX, Part 1 (1967), pp. 127-41.

52. In the Bangkok period the ancestral associations of the Holy Emerald Jewel are explicitly expressed through the presence in the Chapel compound of the so-called "Pantheon" in which images of all of the Chakri kings are kept and where, on special occasions, they are venerated.

53. This symbolism of the stupa in the Theravada as well as the Mahayana tradition is exhaustively treated by Paul Mus in his *Barabadur . . ., op. cit.*

54. "Ritual and Social Hierarchy: An Aspect of Traditional Religion in Buddhist Laos," *History of Religions Journal*, Vol. 9, No. 1 (August, 1969), pp. 78-89. Reprinted in this collection.

Buddhism as Universal Religion and as Civic Religion: Some Observations on a Recent Tour of Buddhist Centers in Central Thailand

Frank E. Reynolds

EACH OF THE great world religions has involved universal and more particularistic elements. More specifically, each of these great religions has maintained a significant universalistic emphasis while, at the same time, it has become oriented to the more particularistic concerns of a number of different ethnic groups and nations. In the case of Buddhism, including the Theravada tradition, these two emphases have coexisted from a very early period. From the time of the Buddha himself, Buddhism has presented itself as a universal message directed to all men quite apart from their ethnic or national identities. It is also true that since the time of King Asoka (third century of the Buddhist era, third century B.C.), when Buddhism began to spread outside the confines of its original homeland in northeastern India, it has quite self-consciously taken on the role of a civic religion directed to the peoples of the particular lands where it has become established and prospered.

In the Theravada context (as in other Buddhist traditions) the universalistic emphasis has remained pre-eminent in the strictly doctrinal strand of the tradition. The Four Noble Truths and the Noble Eightfold Path are clearly universal in their intention and relevance. And the same is true of the central emphases on the co-dependent origination of all phenomena, the impermanence of all things, and the *anatta* or selfless character of all reality. Despite the slightly different interpretations which have been developed in various contexts, the universal thrust of the Dhammic and Abhidhammic teaching has remained basically intact.

However, the theoretical expressions of Theravada Buddhism are not limited to the strictly doctrinal or Abhidhammic modes. Quite the contrary, from the time of the Buddha himself until the present this universally oriented strand of the tradition has been closely correlated with a strong emphasis on Buddhology and cosmology.[1] Moreover, in these Buddhological and cosmological strands of the tradition in which various kinds of mythology and symbolism have played a prominent role, both a universal and a more particularistic style of expression have been prominent. In this paper I propose to focus attention on the Theravada tradition in Thailand, and to highlight some of the ways in which the mythology and the symbolism of the Buddhological and cos-

This paper was delivered at the Siam Society on 4 February 1974. Both the textual research and the field observations on which this paper is based were carried out jointly with Mani Reynolds. The field observations were made during a stay in Thailand made possible by a Fulbright-Hayes research fellowship and special grants from the American Philosophical Society and the University of Chicago. Originally published in *The Journal of the Siam Society*, January 1975, Vol. 63, Part I, pp. 28-43. Reprinted with permission.

mological traditions have expressed and nurtured Theravada universalism on the one hand, and Thai Buddhist particularism on the other. At the outset I will deal with the historical tradition, and will utilize primarily textual and pre-modern materials. And then, with this background in mind, I will report on a recent tour of four contemporary Buddhist centers in central Thailand.

At the level of Buddhology the emphasis on the universal and more particularistic thrusts of the historical Theravada tradition in Thailand are nicely illustrated by the two most important Buddhological texts which have been produced by Thai Buddhists. The first of these two texts is the *Pathamasambodhikathā* which was written in Bangkok in the first half of the nineteenth century by Prince Paramanuchitchinorot who, a few years after completing the text became the Sangharāja or highest ecclesiastical officer in the land.[2] The second is the biographically structured chronicle called the *Jinakālamālīpakaranam* or *Sheaf of Garlands of the Epochs of the Conqueror* which was written in Chiang Mai in the early sixteenth century by Ratanapañña Thera.[3]

The *Pathamasambodhikathā* is a classical type of sacred biograpny which continues and culminates the tradition of universally oriented biographies which began, insofar as the Theravada tradition is concerned, with the *Nidānakthā* which was included as the Introduction to the *Jātaka Commentary* in Sri Lanka in the fifth century A.D.[4] From one perspective the *Pathamasambodhikathā* is of great interest because it represents the most comprehensive, the richest, and the most literarily successful of the Theravada biographies of the classical type. Thus it brings together in one well-integrated and vividly written literary unit stories of the Buddha's previous lives and royal genealogy, an extended account of his life as Gotama from the time of his descent from the Tushita heaven (his birth) to his Parinibbāna (his death), and a comparatively short, but fascinating account of the fate of his relics. However, from the point of view of our present interest the primary importance of the *Pathamasambodhikathā* lies in the fact that it provides a prime example of the universalistic emphasis within the Thai Buddhological tradition. Thus the Prince's account of Gotama's life includes no specifically national references beyond India itself. And his account of the fate of the relics is similarly devoid of materials which relate Buddhism to any specific ethnic group or nation; rather, it describes the distribution of the Buddha's relics which took place immediately after his cremation; it describes the re-distribution of the relics during the reign of King Asoka; and it then moves directly into an account of the decline of the religion and the final events which will take place at the end of the present age when the Buddha's relics will come together, when his last sermon will be preached, and when his final *dhātu* or relic Nibbāna will be attained.

The other major Buddhological work produced in the Thai tradition — namely the *Jinakālamāli* of Ratanapañña Thera — continues and culminates a rather different tradition of more particularistically oriented biographical chronicles which first came to the fore through the writing of the *Mahāvamsa* in Sri Lanka in the fifth century A.D.[5] Like the *Pathamasambodhikathā*, the *Jinakālamāli* includes stories of the Buddha's previous lives, an account of his life as Gotama, and a series of accounts which deal with the fate of his relics. However, the *Jinakālamāli* differs from the *Pathamasambodhikathā* in at least two important respects. In Ratanapañña Thera's work less emphasis is placed on the account of Gotama's life, and much more attention is devoted to the accounts of the relics and other symbols of the Buddha's continuing power. And, what is more significant, both the account of Gotama's life and the stories of the relics are structured in a way which highlights the relationship between Theravada Buddhism and the history of particular national communities. The Thera's way of recounting the Buddha's life as Gotama puts into the foreground the stories of journeys and predictions which prefigure the establishment of Buddhism in Sri Lanka. And the chronicle-style accounts which relate the later "epochs of the Conqueror" describe the process through which Buddhist symbols and the Buddhist community became established in the island Kingdom. And they then go on to describe the way in which these holy objects and traditions were subsequently transmitted from Sri Lanka to the kingdom of Lannathai where, according to the test, they were enthusiastically received and supported by the reigning dynasty. Thus the *Jinakālamāli* reaches its climax not in the universalistic mode of the *Pathamasambodhikathā*, but rather in the establishment of the Theravada tradition as a basic element in the civic religion of northern Thailand.

In the sphere of cosmological thought and symbolism the same kind of polarity between universal and more particularistic elements in the Thai Buddhist tradition can be discerned, though in this case the polarity is manifested in a rather different way. In the cosmological context the contrast can be seen between the major textual forms of expression in which the universalistic element is pre-eminent, and the architectural, socio-religious forms of expression through which each particular Thai Kingdom sought to portray itself as a complete, localized embodiment of the classical cosmological structure.

The two most important and interesting Thai Buddhist texts which are essentially cosmological in character are, first of all, the *Trai Phum Phra Ruang* or *Three Worlds According to King Ruang*, and, secondly, the *Phra Malai Sutta*.[6] The *Trai Phum Phra Ruang*, which was written in the middle of the fourteenth century by Phya Lithai, who was then the heir-apparent to the throne of the great Thai kingdom of Sukothai, is a highly significant work because it achieves, for the first time in the history of the Theravada tradition (so far as we are able to determine from presently available sources), a truly comprehensive synthesis of the major Buddhist cosmological motifs. The *Trai Phum* quite systematically describes the conditions of beings in the eleven realms of the world of desire (*kāmabhūmi*), the sixteen celestial realms of the world with only a remnant of material qualities (*rūpabhūmi*), and the four highest celestial realms which make up the world without material qualities (*arūpabhūmi*). It then goes on to describe the traditional Buddhist cosmography which is organized around the central axis provided by Mt. Meru, as well as the periodic creation and destruction of the lower cosmic realms including all of those within the realm of desire. Finally, it concludes its thoroughly universalistic account of the three worlds with a description of the Path which all beings must follow if they are to free themselves from the ultimately unsatisfying cycle of death and rebirth, and to attain the highest goal of Nibbāna or Final Release. The *Phra Malai Sutta*, on the other hand, was written in Chiang Mai in the sixteenth century, and culminates quite a different tradition of Theravada cosmological and visionary literature.[7] The Sutta begins by recounting the visit of a famous Sinhalese monk named Phra Malai to the sub-human realms of woe. It then recounts his visit to the heaven of the thirty-three gods where he meets the great god Indra and the Future Buddha Sri Ariya Metteyya, and where he questions the latter concerning the time of his coming into the world. And it reaches its climax with the great Bodhisatta's admonition that those who wish to be reborn at the time of his coming should gain the necessary merit by listening to the chanting of the *Mahāvessantara Jātaka*. Thus the *Phra Malai Sutta* obviously differs from the *Trai Phum Phra Ruang* in terms of its comprehensiveness and its soteriological emphasis; however, what is of more importance to us is the fact that both texts present their cosmological descriptions and their soteriological messages in a thoroughly universalistic mode.

But in spite of the universalism of the major Thai cosmological texts, the more particularistic pole of the cosmological tradition also played a crucial role in the history of classical Thai Buddhism. As we have already suggested, this role can be most clearly discerned in the sphere of architecture and in socio-religious patterns. Thus the capitals of the various pre-modern Thai kingdoms were laid out around a central representation of Mt. Meru, often in the form of a stupa known as a Golden Mount. And in each kingdom the reigning monarch was symbolically and ritually associated with the various divine rulers in the heavenly realms, the court with the lesser *devatā* or heavenly beings, and the common people with ordinary human beings. In other words, important aspects of the universal cosmic symbolism were appropriated so as to provide a basic element in the civic religious orientation which undergirded the specific political and social structure in each particular Theravada kingdom.[8]

During the modern period of Thai Buddhist history new modes of thinking and new types of experience have brought about many changes in the Thai Buddhist tradition. And in the process both the Buddhological and the cosmological styles of expression have been adapted to changing conditions. But in spite of the changes which have taken place, both strands of the tradition continue to exert a powerful influence in Buddhist life, and both continue to be expressed in a universal and in a more particularistic mode. What is more, this continuing influence of the Buddhological and cosmological types of Buddhist mythology and symbolism, and the persisting polarity between the universalistic and the more particularistic orientations, are evident in many areas of contemporary Buddhist life.

The fact that these emphases continue to be expressed in the symbolic and ritual patterns which reach various segments of the population could be demonstrated in a number of different ways. However, I would like to illustrate the point by briefly describing four commonly visited Buddhist centers which I observed during a recent tour of central Thailand. In fact, these centers were not originally chosen because they fit the interpretative framework which I had previously developed through my more historically oriented studies of the Thai tradition. On the contrary, they were originally chosen as appropriate sites for family sightseeing, without any special scholarly purpose in mind. However, when the trip was completed, and I began to reflect on what we had observed in the context of our sightseeing, it became clear that these centers, taken together, vividly illustrated the continuing vitality of the Buddhological and cosmological themes on the one hand, and the continuing influence of the universal and more particularistic modes of expression on the other.

The first two centers – namely, Wat Phairongwua in Suphanburi province,

and the Phra Pathom Chedi at Nakorn Pathom – are basically Buddhological
in their structure. The former is a new center, still under construction, which
is being built up very rapidly through the influence of a charismatic monk
named Luang Paw Khom.[9] The second is the very large, very ancient, and very
famous *chedi* which some traditions identify as the center of the fabled kingdom of Suvannabhūmi where the Buddhist presence in Southeast Asia was
first established, perhaps as early as the third century B.C.

Though the center at Wat Phairongwua has gained considerable notoriety
because of some very vivid three-dimensional depictions of the grotesque and
often obscene conditions into which those who commit evil deeds are said to
be reborn, the basic structure of the very extensive exhibition which is presented in the *wat* compound is Buddhological in character.[10] In the eastern segment of the main exhibition area there is a very extensive display in which
scenes from the Buddha's life associated with his birthplace at Kapilavastu are
depicted. Towards the back is a "palace" which contains, on the top floor, a
room in which there is a representation of the Future Buddha in the Tushita
heaven prior to his birth as Gotama, and below that a room in which there is
a representation of a scene associated with the Buddha's birth. (Significantly,
this room also contains a plaque on which is inscribed the original vow taken
by Luang Paw Khom in which he committed himself to following the Path
throughout his entire life, to ridding himself of any desire for personal riches,
and to constructing images of the Buddha.) In front of the palace there are
three-dimensional representations of scenes from the Buddha's youth, and in
the foreground there is a very large display which portrays the Buddha's Great
Departure from Kapilavastu on the back of his fabulous horse Kanthaka. The
central section of the main exhibit (and actually the area as a whole) is dominated by a gigantic black image of the Buddha at the point of his Enlightenment; and in front of this great image is a fascinating representation of the
Wheel of the Dhamma being pulled and guided by monastic figures as it is
pushed from behind by figures who clearly represent ordinary working-class
laymen. Finally, the section of the compound directly to the west of the central image contains a variety of different buildings and displays which, at first
glance, seem to be a kind of random collection.

Through closer observation, however, a definite pattern can be discerned.
The rear portion of this western segment of the exhibition area is dominated
by a sala where Luang Paw Khom sits as he speaks with his devotees and visitors, where he distributes amulets, and where he receives offerings from the
faithful. Near the sala, in full view, is a large poster which proclaims that the
monk, whose original vow to practice the Path and to construct images had
already been correlated with the birth of the Buddha, has attained a spiritual
level which qualifies him as a man who is, at the same time, "truly Thai"
(*"Thai thae"*), "truly Chinese" (*"Chin thae"*), "truly European" (*farang thae"*),
and so forth. Moreover, a similar emphasis is reflected in the character and contents of the various buildings and other symbols which are situated in this western section of the compound. Those which have already been completed include
buildings and a variety of other symbolic expressions which are representative
of Thai Buddhism, of Chinese Buddhism, and of Buddhism in Japan. Quite
clearly then, what is being expressed and communicated in this area, both in
the interpretation of Luang Paw Khom's presence, and in the various exhibits,

is the extension of the Buddha's life through a tradition which makes universal men of those who practice it, and a tradition which is well on the way to universality at the level of its actual communal life.[11]

Unlike Wat Phairongwua, which only recently became a significant Buddhist center, the Phra Pathom Chedi at Nakorn Pathom has a long and illustrious tradition behind it. Both in the pre-Thai period and in the course of the history of the later Thai kingdoms, this famous *chedi* has been rebuilt and enlarged on a number of different occasions. It received basically its present form through the repair and reconstruction efforts encouraged by King Mongkut in the latter half of the nineteenth century, and from that time forward it has been one of the most sacred and visited shrines in all of Thailand.

As Paul Mus has long since demonstrated, a *chedi*, even in the Theravada context, is conceived not only as a form of cosmological architecture, but also as a symbol both of the Buddha's career which culminates in his Parinibbāna, and of the continuing efficacy of his power and message in the life of the Buddhist community.[12] Thus it is not surprising that this *chedi*, like many other similar Buddhist monuments, incorporates representations which evoke the stories of important events in the Founder's life and ministry. Typically, the eastern chapel of this great monument contains an image which represents the crucial moment of the Buddha's Great Awakening under the Bo tree at Bodh Gaya. The story is continued, as one proceeds in a clockwise direction around the monument, by the image in the southern chapel which portrays the Buddha as he preaches his first sermon in the Deer Park at Benares, and thereby "sets in motion the Wheel of the Dhamma." The third image which one confronts as he continues his clockwise circumambulation — that is to say, the one which is located in the western chapel — is, not unexpectedly, a great reclining Buddha which represents the Founder at the moment at which he attained his Parinibbāna. But what of the fourth and final image which one finds ensconced in the northern chapel? It is a standing Buddha figure which is important, and receives special veneration, but its significance in relation to the preceding three images is not immediately obvious.

The significance of this final image becomes clear, however, when three facts which are known to those who frequent the *chedi* are taken into account. The first of these facts is that this standing image which is located in the northern chapel bears the name of Phra Ruang Rochanarit, Phra Ruang being a popular designation for the famous line of monarchs of the Sukothai kingdom to whom the Thai have traditionally looked as national founders and pre-eminent supporters of Buddhism.[13] The second fact is that the head which was used in the casting of the present image was originally attached to an image of the Sukothai period which was quite possibly a portrait statue commissioned by one of the latter members of the Ruang dynasty in order to represent himself and the Buddha in a single image.[14] And the third important fact is that the statue now contains, in its base, the ashes of the king who commissioned it and had it placed in its present position — namely King Vajirawut (reigned, 1910-25) who is well-known as the pre-eminent formulator and exponent of modern Thai nationalism, and the place of Buddhism within it. When these various bits of information are taken together, it becomes evident that this image, which extends the Buddhological imagery beyond the Parinibbāna of the Founder, represents the continuation of the Buddha's life and work in the life and work of the Thai kings, and the establishment and the maintenance of the Buddhist faith as a basic element in the civic religion of the Thai nation.[15]

The other two contemporary Buddhist centers which I observed in the course of our tour of central Thailand — namely Wat Phutudom in Pathumthani province, and the complex of buildings in the royal palace area in Bangkok — utilize symbolic patterns which are basically cosmological in character. The former, which expresses the cosmological tradition in an essentially universalistic mode, is being built through the efforts of Phrakhru Udomphawanaphirat who was formerly a resident at Wat Mahathat in Bangkok. The center is still in the early stages of development; but in spite of the fact that much work obviously remains to be done before the building in the compound is completed, the basic structure of the main exhibition can be clearly discerned, and the *wat* has for several years been receiving a steady stream of visitors from Bangkok and from other sections of the country as well.[16] The area around the royal palace, where cosmological themes are expressed in a more particularistic mode, is exceptionally rich in traditional associations and, moreover, it is probably the most famous and visited site in Thailand, Buddhist or otherwise.

When the visitor reaches Wat Phutudom (like Wat Phairongwua, this *wat* is most accessible by boat), he finds that the main exhibit is in the northern half of the compound, the other half being occupied by an ordinary *vihan* and a gigantic metal elephant which serves as a kind of added attraction for visitors and especially for their children. In the important northern half of the temple area the foreground is taken up with a large artificial and revolving mango tree, and a similarly large and revolving "wheel of the Dhamma." These exhibits are designed to evoke the famous story of the Buddha's ascent into the heaven of the thirty-three gods which originated from a sacred mango tree in the city of Sāvatthi; they are designed to suggest the purpose of his ascent which was to preach the Dhamma to his mother; and they are especially designed to remind those viewing them of the related story of the great miracle of "opening the world" — that is to say, the miracle of making visible the conditions of the beings in every cosmic realm — which the Buddha is said to have performed at the time of his return to the earth. After the visitor passes by these exhibits, he proceeds into the main temple building where the great cosmic vision is portrayed for all to see. His tour begins in the dark recesses of the temple basement where he observes depictions of the various hells (*narok*), the realm of the suffering ghosts (*peta*), and the realm of the sub-human giants or *asura*, and where he is informed concerning the various kinds of sins which have caused beings to be reborn in these terrible places. On the main floor, where a great Buddha image is seated, he passes through and observes the realms of the animals and of men. And then, as he climbs through a series of upper rooms which are constructed one above the other and reach all the way to the temple roof, he passes through and observes the six heavenly realms of the *devatā* (divine beings who enjoy conditions of great sensual pleasure because of the merit which they have gained in their previous lives), the sixteen higher heavenly realms which can be attained through the practice of certain forms of jhānic meditation, and the four highest heavenly realms of meditation which are associated with other forms of jhānic attainment. Moreover, a fascinating twist is given to the visitor's tour of the thirty-one cosmic realms by the fact that the heavenly realms are depicted in nine sets (one set being depicted in each of the nine upper rooms), each of which is associated with a particular planet and with a particular segment of the week. Therefore, as the visitor climbs upward through the twenty-six realms which extend above the realm of men, he passes through the major astronomical segments of the celestial regions and, in addition, he passes through a full temporal cycle as represented by a calendric week.[17] Thus, by the time his journey is completed, the visitor has been provided with a visual and symbolic image of the structure of the cosmos in terms of both space and time; and, in addition, he has been vividly apprised of the opportunity which he shares with all men to improve, through the practice of proper morality and meditation, the status which he presently occupies in the universal cosmic hierarchy.

Whereas the symbolic patterns and imagery which have been utilized at Wat Phutudom emphasize aspects of the traditional Buddhist cosmology which concern each of the thirty-one realms and are basically universal in character, the symbolic patterns which are expressed in and around the royal palace in Bangkok focus more specifically on the Meru cosmography, and are more particularistic in their intention. Thus the Phukaothong or Golden Mount, which is situated nearby in the compound of Wat Saket, serves as a permanent representation of Mt. Meru in its role as the central axis of the present Thai kingdom. The buildings in the main royal palace compound are architecturally constructed so as to evoke the impression of the *devatā* realms associated with the Meru cosmography, and the compound itself is dotted with sites which bear the names of specific *devatā* heavens. And, to cite only one more specific example, the various gates which guard the entrance to the nearby Chitrlada palace, where the present king resides when he is in Bangkok, are explicitly associated with the abodes of the four guardian deities whose heavenly realm is situated on the four mountain peaks which surround the peak of Mt. Meru where the palace of the great royal deity is located.[18] In the modern era it is certainly true that these and similar symbolic patterns have lost much of the force which they had up until 1932 when a coup d'etat brought an end to the so-called "absolute" monarchy. But at the same time, they have persisted down to the present day; and what is more, they continue to enhance the aura of sacrality which surrounds the present Thai king, and to re-enforce the conception that the Thai nation continues to be structured as a microcosmic order organized in accordance with Buddhist principles.[19]

In the course of this present paper I have utilized categories and methods which have been developed within the discipline of the history of religions (Religionswissenschaft) in order to relate and to interpret a variety of expressions of Thai Buddhism, some classical and some contemporary. By way of summarizing and concluding the discussion, I would like to suggest some implications for further research which can be drawn from the approach which I have taken, and from the materials which I have chosen to highlight.

In the first and more textually-oriented segment of this paper I have focused attention on the fact that there are four specifically Thai Buddhist texts which extend and culminate two of the three major strands of theoretical expression within the Theravada tradition. At the level of Buddhology the Thai tradition has produced the *Pathamasambodhikathā*, which extends and culminates the classical tradition of Buddha biographies, as well as the *Jinakālamāli* which extends and culminates the equally important tradition of biographical chronicles. And at the level of cosmology the Thai tradition has produced the *Trai Phum Phra Ruang*, which is the most comprehensive and systematic of the Theravada treatises on the subject, as well as the *Phra Malai Sutta* which represents the highpoint of a significant genre of Theravada literature dealing with cosmic visions and journeys. The existence of these important and fascinating texts, quite apart from the very specific and limited use which I have made of them for the purposes of this particular study, strongly suggests that Theravada scholars must begin to give the same sort of careful attention to the later expressions of the Theravada literary and textual tradition which they have previously given to the canonical and commentarial texts which were produced in the earlier periods of Theravada history.[20]

In the process of interpreting these texts and related historical materials I have highlighted the fact that the classical expressions of Theravada Buddhism in Thailand reveal a dual focus. On the one hand, very important mythic and symbolic patterns, both at the Buddhological and cosmological levels, express a Theravada orientation which is explicitly and consistently universal in character. And, on the other side, equally important mythic and symbolic patterns which appear at both of these levels of the tradition express an orientation in which Theravada Buddhism is presented primarily as an element in the civic religious ethos of a particular Thai kingdom. The existence of this polarity in materials of this kind suggests that a further exploration of the more universal and more civic orientations, and of the actual dynamics of their interaction in the course of Thai history, would provide a fruitful subject for further historical research.[21]

Finally, the observations which I have made concerning contemporary Buddhist centers in central Thailand suggest that the persistence of traditional mythic and symbolic patterns, and the continuing interaction of the universal and more particularistic Buddhist perspectives, are interesting and important phenomena which deserve a great deal more attention from students of contemporary Thai religion and society.

Notes

1. For a discussion of the roots and development of the Buddhological tradition in Theravada Buddhism, see my paper on "The Many Lives of Buddha" which appeared in Reynolds and Capps, eds., *The Biographical Process: Essays in the History and Psychology of Religion (Religion and Reason Series*, XI; The Hague: Mouton, 1976). For a similar discussion of the roots and development of the cosmological tradition, see the introduction to Frank E. and Mani B. Reynolds, trs., *The Three Worlds According to King Ruang* (Stanford, Calif. and Bangkok: Stanford University Press and the Siam Society, forthcoming 1978).
2. Bangkok: Ministry of Education, 1962.
3. Translated by Jayawickrama of the Pali Text Society and published as No. 36 in the *Translation Series*. London: Luzac & Co., 1969.
4. T. W. Rhys-Davids, tr., *Buddhist Birth Stories*. Boston: Houghton and Mifflin, 1880.
5. Geiger, Wilhelm, tr., *Mahāvamsa* (Pali Text Society *Translation Series* No. 3: London, 1912).
6. *Trai Phum Phra Ruang* (Bangkok: National Teacher's Association, 1962). *Dika Malai Deva Sut* (Bangkok: Thambanakhan Press, 1971). For a translation of the former, see Mani B. and Frank E. Reynolds, *Three Worlds According to King Ruang, op. cit.*

7. For a discussion of this tradition see Eugene Denis, "L'Origine Cingalaise du Prăh Malăy," *Felicitation Volume of Southeast Asian Studies Presented to H. H. Prince Dhaninivat,* Vol. II (Bangkok: Siam Society, 1965), pp. 329-338.

8. For an excellent discussion of the ways in which the cosmological homologies were operative in various traditional kingdoms in Southeast Asia (including those with a Theravada orientation), see Robert Heine-Geldern, *Conceptions of State and Kingship in Southeast Asia* (Data Paper No. 18 of the Southeast Asia Program; Ithaca, N. Y.: Cornell, 1956).

9. According to a report in the daily newspaper (*Thai Rath,* Sept. 23, 1973, p. 16), more than $1,000,000 has already been spent in the construction of this center and present plans call for the expenditure of another $1,000,000 during the next several years.

10. The depictions of the various pleasurable heavens and the realms of woe are located in a second, quite distinct area lying behind the main segment of the *wat* compound which concerns us here.

11. In this connection it is interesting to note that in our conversation with Luang Paw Khom we were very quickly confronted with a strong Buddhist missionary message. His approach left no doubt in our minds that he understood his own vocation as a builder and teacher as an effort to further the spread of Buddhism and, by so doing, to further actualize the universality of the historical Buddhist community.

12. See especially his *Barabadur: Esquisse d'une histoire du Bouddhisme fondée sur la critique archéologique des textes* (Hanoi, Imp. d'Extrême-Orient, 1935).

13. Rochanarit is a descriptive term which refers to the glory and magic power which has traditionally been associated with the monarchs of this dynasty.

14. The fact that some of the later Sukothai images were of the portrait statue type has only recently been recognized. For some background and discussion, see Barbara Andaya, "Statecraft in the Reign of Lü Thai of Sukhodaya," *Cornell Journal of Social Relations,* Vol. 1, No. 6 (Special Issue on Southeast Asia), Spring, 1971, pp. 61-83. Reprinted in this collection.

15. Interesting variations on this same pattern are apparent in the symbolism which is utilized in other Buddhist *wats* and *chedi* in various sections of the country. For example, at the very famous Wat Doi Suthep in Chiang Mai, the image which completes the Buddhological symbolism dominating the most sacred portion of the *wat* compound has standing before it, as if to mediate its power and message to those who visit the site, two life-sized pictures. The one on the right side is a picture of King Phumipol, the reigning Thai monarch, while the one on the left is the great monk-hero of the Lannathai area who was responsible for building the road to the temple, Khruba Sriwichai.

16. In fact, our attention was originally drawn to this *wat* by an account of a journey there written up in a professional teachers' magazine. See Snguan Raktham, "Namtieo Wat Phutudom: Chom Prachao Poed Lok," *Suphasa,* October, 1971, pp. 49-55.

17. These various associations were pointed out to me by Phrakhru Udomphawanaphirat in a conversation at Wat Phutudom on Nov. 23, 1973.

18. For a detailed discussion of this whole topic, see Prince Dhani Niwat, "The Royal Palaces" (*Thai Culture Series,* No. 23; Bangkok Fine Arts Dept., 1957).

19. For a study which clearly describes this conception and portrays its actual sociopolitical operation, see Lucien Hanks "Merit and Power in the Thai Social Order," *American Anthropologist,* 54 (Dec. 1962), 1247-61.

20. The need for this kind of study is clearly demonstrated by the fact that, in contrast to the large number of canonical texts and the significant number of early commentaries which have been translated into western languages, only one of the four texts mentioned (the *Jinakālamālī*) is available in translation, and it is clearly evident from the introduction that even in this case the translator was not primarily interested in presenting the text from the point of view of its significance as an expression of Theravada religion (see *Jinakālamālī*).

21. I have treated a few limited aspects of this interaction in "Sasana khong phonlamuang nai prawatsat Thai," which appeared in the *Social Science Review* (Bangkok) in the Fall, 1971 issue.

Some Observations on the Dynamics of Traditions

S. N. Eisenstadt

Some Introductory Concepts

THIS PAPER is based on certain concepts about the nature of social and cultural order and traditions. We view social and cultural traditions, first, as the major ways of looking at the basic problems of social and cultural order, and of posing the major questions about them; second, as giving various possible answers to these problems; and, third, as the organization of institutional structures for implementing different types of solutions or answers to these problems.

We assume that the search for answers — symbolic and institutional alike — to some of the major problems about the nature of human destiny, of the nature of social, cosmic, and cultural orders, of the possibility of some ordered social life, is an important ingredient in man's universe of desiderata, although it is not necessarily the most important one. This entails a reformulation of certain of the basic assumptions of sociology regarding the nature of the individual's orientation to the social order. It also redefines the nature of institutional loci of this orientation and the relation of these loci to the political sphere. The focus of this reformation is the recognition of the fact that social order is not just given by certain external forces imposed in some way on individuals and on their own wishes. Nor is it just an outcome of rational premeditated selfish evaluation of their interests or of the exigencies of the social and economic division of labour engendered by these interests. Some quest for social order, not only in organizational but also in symbolic terms, is among people's basic egotistical wishes or orientations. In other words, the people seek the "good society," they want to participate in such an order. Their quest is a basic component in the whole panorama of social and cultural activities, orientations and goals. But it calls for rather special types of response, which tend to be located in distinct parts or aspects of the social structure.

This quest for some adequate symbolic or social order and for participation in it is very closely related to the quest for some relation or attachment to the charismatic, "the 'vital,' ultimately serious event of which divinity is one of many forms."[1] The crucial role of the charismatic dimension and symbols in

The author is indebted to Mrs. L. Aran for very detailed criticisms of a former draft of this paper; this version is abridged from the paper delivered at the innovation conference and served as a discussion paper at a conference on Tradition and Change, sponsored by the Rockefeller Foundation at Bellegia, Italy, July, 1968. This article was originally published in *Comparative Studies in Society and History: An International Quarterly*, Vol. 11 (1969), 451-475. Reprinted with permission of Cambridge University Press.

social order was, of course, first fully explored by Weber. Recently it has been taken up again by Shils, who had pointed out that the charismatic is not only, as it is usually represented in sociological literature, something extraordinary, but also has specific continuous institutional location within any social order, and in macro-societal order in particular. He has attempted to specify at least one of the institutional foci of the charismatic — in what he designates as the center of the society.[2] This tendency towards the institutional convergence of the charismatic in the center or centers of society is rooted in the fact that both the charismatic and the center are concerned with the provision and maintenance of some meaningful symbolic and institutional order.

But this close relation between the charismatic dimension and the centers does not imply their identity. It raises many new questions and problems. What is the structure of such centers and what are their structural relations to the periphery? How many centers embodying charismatic orientation are there in a society? Does it occur in other centers besides the political, cultural, religious, or ideological? What is the relation between the "ordering" and "meaning-giving" (i.e., charismatic) functions of such centers, on the one hand, and their more organizational and administrative activities, on the other? How can we distinguish between different types of centers? What are the paradigmatic premises of the symbolic frameworks of different types of centers?

It would be out of place to attempt here any extensive classification of social and cultural orders and centers, although some dimensions of such a classification will come out during our discussion. At this point it may only be worthwhile to point out one type of distinction — namely that between weak and strong centers.

A weak center is one which, while performing its own technical tasks (such as external political and administrative activities of the political center, or the ritual and theological activities of a religious center), has but few autonomous interrelationships with other centers or symbolic orders of social life, and little access to them or control over them. Such a center cannot derive strength and legitimation from the other centers or orders of social and cultural life, nor does it perform very adequately some of its potential charismatic ordering and legitimizing functions. Hence it also commands only minimal commitment beyond the limited sphere of these functions. Its relations with other centers or with broader social groups and strata are mostly either purely adaptive relations (as, for instance, in the case of many nomad conquerors in relation to the religious organizations of the conquered people) or it may symbolically and perhaps even organizationally totally submerge in them — as was the case, for instance, in some of the Southeast Asian religious centers, which were almost entirely submerged in the political ones.

In contrast to this a "strong" center is one which enjoys such access to other centers and can derive its legitimation from them, either by monopolizing and controlling them or by some more autonomous interdependence with them, and which can accordingly command some commitment both within and beyond their own specific spheres.

As has already been stressed above, the preceding emphasis on the charismatic dimension of social order does not necessarily mean that this is its only relevant dimension. But it is out of these indications that some of the distinctions between the charismatic and the ordinary can be brought out. Non-charis-

matic or ordinary activity seems to comprise those types of activity which are
oriented to various discrete, segregated goals directed mainly towards adaptation to any given natural or human (social) environment, to persistence and
survival within it, and not connected together in any great pattern or "grand
design." A very large part of the daily activities of human beings in society is
probably organized in such a way and oriented to such goals. The implementation of such goals calls for many specific organizations and structures which
tend to coalesce into varied institutional patterns. In a sense, it is they that
constitute the crux of the institutional nexus within any society. And yet, very
often all these goals and patterns tend also to become somehow related to a
broader, fundamental order, rooted in the charismatic and focused around
the different situations and centers in which the charismatic is more fully embedded and symbolized. These interrelations between the non-charismatic and
charismatic orientations of human activities, as well as the nature of these
orientations and their structural implication, tend to vary greatly between one
traditional society and another.

Some Characteristics of a Traditional Society and Patterns and Problems of Change in Traditional Societies

However different they may be, traditional societies all share in common
the acceptance of tradition, the givenness of some actual or symbolic past
event, order, or figure as the major focus of their collective identity; as the de-
lineator of the scope and nature of their social and cultural order, and as ultimate legitimator of change and of the limits of innovation. Tradition not only
serves as a symbol of continuity, it delineates the legitimate limits of creativity
and innovation and is the major criterion of their legitimacy. It is no matter
that the symbol of tradition may originally have been a great innovative creation which destroyed some earlier major symbol of the legitimate past.

While the content and scope of these past events or symbols naturally varied
greatly from one traditional society to another – and the most dramatic processes of change within them were indeed focused on changing this very content and scope – yet in traditional societies always some past event remained
the focal point and symbol of the social, political, and cultural orders. The essence of traditionality is in the cultural acceptance of these cultural definitions
of tradition as a basic criterion of social activity, as the basic referent of collective identity, and as defining the societal and cultural orders and the degrees
of variability among them.

These connotations of traditionality are not, however, confined to purely
cultural or symbolic spheres only; they have definite structural implications.
The most important of these is, first, that parts of the social structure and
groups are, or attempt to become, designated as the legitimate upholders, guardians, and manifestations of those collective symbols, as their legitimate bearers
and interpreters, and hence also as the legitimizers of any innovation or change.
In the more differentiated traditional societies these functions tended to become crystallized into the central foci of the political and cultural orders as distinct from the periphery. It is in the symbolic and structural distinctiveness of
the centers from the periphery that the basic structural and cultural implications of traditionality tend to meet together – and it is here that their implications for processes of change within traditional societies stand out most clearly.

The distinctiveness of the center in traditional societies is manifest in a three-fold symbolic and institutional limitation: the content of these centers is limited by reference to some past event; access to positions as legitimate interpreters of the scope of the traditions is limited; and the right of broader groups to participate in the centers is limited.

Even the greatest and most far-reaching cultural and religious innovations in traditional societies — the rise of the Great Universal Religions, which greatly changed the general level of rationality of the basic cultural symbols, their contents, and scope — did not change the basic threefold structural limitations. This is true even though in their initial charismatic phases they sometimes attempted to reduce them. It does not follow, however, that these societies were stationary or changeless. On the contrary they were continuously changing, either from one form of traditional society to another or in the direction of modernity. All of these processes of change impinged on existing patterns of social life and cultural traditions, undermining them and threatening their members' social and psychological security. At the same time they opened up new social and cultural horizons, vistas of participation in new institutional and cultural orders. But the degree to which existing patterns of social life and of cultural traditions were undermined, as well as the scope and nature of the new vistas, naturally varied greatly in different situations of change in these societies, as did also the "reactions" to these changes and the ways of solving the concomitant problems that the elites and the members of the society faced.

On the structural, institutional level we may roughly distinguish three degrees or types of change: small-scale or micro-societal changes; partial institutional changes; and over-all changes in the contours and frameworks of the society, especially in the structure and content of the centers. Small-scale changes concern only details of organization, roles, and membership in social groups and communities. Their effect is relatively slight even within the institutional field in which they occur. Partial institutional changes occur only in a limited institutional sphere, such as the economic or administrative, but they create new opportunities and new frameworks for certain groups. They are either isolated from the central institutional core of a society or constitute accepted secondary variations within this central sphere. The incorporation of new urban groups, such as merchants or administrative groups in patrimonial or imperial systems, often through immigration or colonization, or of various sects within universal religions, are among the commonest examples of partial institutional change within the range of traditional societies. Changes in the central institutional core affect the total society. Important illustrations are the establishment of city-states out of tribal federations or of great imperial centers in the place of city-states or patrimonial states. This far-reaching type of change in traditional societies was usually connected with the creation of new and broader political or religious frameworks, with the development of new levels of differentiation and social complexity, with the establishment of new societal centers and of new relations between these centers and the periphery, the broader strata of society.

Propensities to all three types of change have been inherent in all traditional societies but have varied greatly in strength. There has also been great variation in the extent to which the more "local" or partial processes and movements of change impinged on central institutional cores. Often such propensities to change were manifest mainly in momentary outbursts of protest, as for example in peasant rebellions, or were confined to religious sectarian movements that had few lasting or even short-time structural effects. Yet other movements of the kind could become foci of far-reaching structural changes creating new levels of differentiation or new political centers and centers of new Great Traditions. Change was more likely to be far-reaching when it was either initiated or taken over by secondary elites in fairly central positions. Successful far-reaching changes were also very often related to economic or political international forces. All such processes of structural change created possibilities of disorganization and for the elites and members of these groups posed the problem of how to organize new role-patterns, organizational structures, and institutional frameworks, and of how to find and to regulate access to new institutional links to the broader frameworks and centers.

These different structural aspects of change were usually very closely connected to patterns of change and of reaction to it in the sphere of cultural tradition, symbols, usages, and ways of life. Such processes of change in traditional ways of life could be of at least two types. One has been gradual, piecemeal replacement of one custom by another, in an almost imperceptible but cumulative process of change which could result in crystallization of different patterns and symbols in what have been called "Little Traditions." These types of cultural change were probably usually connected with the "small," and with some partial institutional structural changes, and much less with changes within the central institutional cores of a society. The other type was the more dramatic change of the central pattern of a society's cultural tradition. This usually entailed the creation of wider and more complex cultural units and of new cultural symbols. The result would be the elaboration of new symbols and centers of Great Traditions. Frequently these developments were connected with growing rationalization of the major traditional symbolic order. A primarily religious symbolic order would become more separate from the concrete details of daily life. Its relation to the secular society would cease to be unexamined and would become more and more distant and problematic, more logically coherent and abstract. All this tended to undermine many of the existing traditional usages, customs, ways of life, and symbols. Members of the society faced many problems on the cultural level that were similar to those they faced on the structural level, but were often more complex.

It is therefore worthwhile to analyze, in somewhat greater detail, some of the processes connected with the elaboration of such Great Traditions. Cultural traditions, symbols, artifacts, and organizations became, in the new situation, more elaborate and articulated, more rationally organized, more formalized, and different groups and individuals in a society acquired a greater awareness of them. Concomitantly there was a tendency for tradition to become differentiated in layers. Simple "given" usages or patterns of behavior could become quite distinct from more articulate and formalized symbols of cultural order such as great ritual centers and offices, theological codices, or special architectural edifices. These layers of tradition tended to vary also in the degree and nature of their prescriptive validity and in their relevance to different spheres of life. As most of these changes in elaboration of Great Traditions were usually connected with growing structural differentiation between the various spheres of social life, these spheres, economic, administrative, or political, could be associated in different ways with both old and new traditions. To put it the other way round, the old and new traditions and symbols could be perceived as more or less relevant to these spheres in terms of prescribing the proper modes of behavior within them, in defining their goals and in providing their over-all "meaning."

These processes were often related to a growing "partialization" and privatization of various traditions, especially of the older existing traditions. Even if the given, existing "old" customs and symbols did not become negated or "thrown out" they underwent far-reaching changes. What had been the "total" sanctioned pattern of life of any given community, society, or individual tended to become only a partial one, in several respects. It could persist as binding for only some members of a given society, or only in some spheres, and even the validity of its prescriptive power or of its use as the guiding symbolic templates in these spheres of life become greatly changed and differentiated.

Hence there always arose in such situations the problem, first, whether the old or the new traditions or symbols of traditions represented the true tradition of the new social political or religious community, and second, how far any given existing tradition could become incorporated into the new central patterns of culture and "tradition." In such situations, the validity of the traditional (existing) sanctions for the new symbols and organizations, of the scope and nature of the traditional sources of legitimacy of the new social, political or cultural order, and the extent to which it was possible to legitimize this order in terms of the existing traditions became uncertain.

In consequence, the several layers of tradition could differ in the extent to which they became foci of awareness and "problems" for different parts of the society. Sometimes, in such situations the very traditionality of the given social and cultural order tended to become a "problem," and in some cases these processes might give rise to the erosion of any traditional commitments and to concomitant tendencies of social and cultural disorganization. For people especially sensitive to such problems of symbolic templates, all these problems could become crucial from the point of view of their personal identity and its relation to the collective identity of their respective social and cultural orders. Both on the personal level and on the level of the more central symbols of tradition, there could arise, often as a reaction to the possibilities of erosion, the tendency known as traditionalism; there could then be a potential dichotomy between "tradition" and "traditionalism." Traditionalism is not to be confused with a "simple" or "natural" upkeep of a given tradition. It denotes an ideological mode and stance, a mode oriented against the new symbols, making some parts of the older tradition into the only legitimate symbols of the traditional order and upholding them as against "new" trends. It is especially opposed to the potentially rationalizing tendencies in the new Great Traditions. Through opposing these trends the "traditionalist" attitudes tend towards formalization, on both the symbolic and organizational levels.

The Major Types of Response to Change and the Major Modes of Persistence, Change, and Transformation of Traditional Symbols and Structures

Given the ubiquity of change in traditional societies there arise at least two major problems for analysis: which types of traditions tend to generate different types of change, and what are the directions of change inherent within such traditions; what are the different possible reactions to change that may develop within them? We shall deal mainly with the second question, touching only indirectly, in the latter part of the paper, on the first. In a sense we shall be taking for granted the existence of some change, without inquiring into its causes, but concentrating on the analysis of different reactions to change.

We may first distinguish between a generally positive as against a negative attitude to change, that is, between tendencies to accept or to resist it. A second question of great importance is whether or not a given society or sector thereof possesses the organizational and institutional capacity to deal with the problems created by changing situations.

A combination of these two major types of attitudes to change and of different levels of organizational capacity gives rise to various concrete types of response to change. Among these I would stress the following: (a) a totally passive, negative attitude often resulting in the disappearance or weakening of such resisting groups; (b) an active resistance to change through an organized "traditionalistic" response aiming to impose some, at least, of the older values on the new setting; (c) different types of adaptability to change; (d) the appearance of what may be called transformative capacity. This last is the capacity not only to adapt to new conditions but also to forge new general institutional frameworks and new centers. Transformative capacity may vary according to the extent of coercion which it evolves.

These various types of response to change become manifest in the ways in which different groups tend to retain, arrange, replace or transform existing traditional symbols and structures. The common denominator of all these processes of change in the pattern of tradition is, as we have seen above, the differentiation between layers of tradition, the privatization and particularization of various traditional symbols and usages and the tendency towards segregation between different symbols from the point of view of their relevance and validity for different spheres of life.

Hence the most general indicators for distinguishing between different types of response to change are first, the ways in which the people in question differentiate between layers of tradition and segregate various social spheres in their relevance for tradition; and second, the ways they attempt to find new common symbolic forms that may serve to link a given sphere with a given layer of tradition.

From these points of view it is possible to discern the most important differences in the mode of persistence of traditional symbols and frameworks between groups with high or low adaptability to change and those with high or low transformative capacities.

In groups or societies with a relatively high resistance to change (low adaptability) and/or with low transformative capacity, there may be a tendency to segregate "traditional" (ritual, religious) and non-traditional spheres of life without, however, developing any appropriate connective symbolic and organizational bonds between the two. In other words, new precepts or symbolic orientations that might serve as guides to the ways in which these different layers of tradition could become connected in some meaningful patterns, especially in their relevance to different spheres of life, do not readily develop. At the same time, however, strong predisposition or demand for some clear unifying principle tends to persist, and there may be a relatively high degree of uneasiness and insecurity when it is lacking. A tendency toward "ritualization" of symbols of traditional life, on personal and collective levels alike, may also appear. There may then be a continuous vacillation between withdrawal of these traditional symbols from the "impure," new, secular world on the one hand, and increasing attempts to impose them on this world in a relatively rigid, militant way, on the other hand. This mode of persistence of traditional patterns is usually connected with the strengthening of ritual status images and of intolerance of ambiguity on both personal and collective levels and with growing possibilities of apathy and of erosion of any normative commitments because of such apathy.

These orientations also may have distinct repercussions on interrelations between the personal identity of the individual participants in these groups and the new collective identity that emerges in the centers of new traditions. This interrelation tends to be either tenuous and ambivalent or very restricted and ritualistic. The new emerging symbols of the social or cultural order are perceived by the members of these groups as either negative or as external to their personal identity. They do not serve as their major collective referents, and they do not provide participation in the new social or cultural orders with adequate meaning; nor are they perceived by the members of those groups as able to regulate the new manifold organizational or institutional activities into which they are drawn.

A similar pattern tends to develop with regard to the relations between traditional symbols peculiar to "partial" groups — regional groups, ethnic, and occupational groups, or status-groups — and the emerging new central symbols of Great Traditions. These groups do not normally incorporate their various "primordial" symbols of local, ethnic caste or class groups into the new center of the society, and their reformulation on a new level of common identification does not take place. Rather, they constitute foci of separateness, of ritual traditionalism. A similar, but obverse, relation tends to develop between the more innovative groups or elites and a "traditionalistic" center or setting. This has greater disruptive potential, and we shall analyze some of the structural implications later.

These modes of persistence of traditional symbols and attitudes are closely connected with certain specific patterns of structural changes that may grow up among groups with a negative reaction to change. Internally, these groups generally display little readiness to undertake new tasks or roles, to reorganize their internal division of labor and structure of authority, or to encourage their members to participate in other, new groups and spheres of action. In their relations to other groups they tend to evince, and even to intensify, a very high degree of social and cultural "closeness" and self-centeredness, however great their dependence on other groups may have become. A purely external-instrumental attitude to the wider setting will then predominate, with little active solidary orientation to it or identification with it. This attitude may take two seemingly opposed yet often coalescing forms. In one form it is a relatively passive attitude to the wider social setting. One may observe this in many "traditional" rural and urban groups of lower and middle status. Closeness and passivity appear in the rigidity of their conception of the social order in general and of their own place within it in particular. There may be a clinging to very rigid, "ritual" status images which allow little flexibility of orientations to the wider society. People may have few aspirations beyond the traditional scope of occupations and very little interest in participating in political or social leadership or organization.[3] The second major way in which this external-instrumental attitude to the wider social setting can be manifest is in what may be called exaggerated, unlimited "openness" and "flexibility" of aspiration and status image. Attempts to obtain benefits, emoluments, and positions may be quite unrealistic.

Such resistance to change and the concomitant development of the external-instrumental attitudes may sometimes bring about the disappearance and obliteration of the groups in question. However, total disappearance of these groups, or their relegation to a very marginal place in the society, probably happens only in relatively rare cases. When it occurs it is most likely due to poor leadership or organizational ability; the leadership may be almost totally dissociated from the membership of the groups. Insofar as some leadership exists, and shares the attitudes of resistance to change with the membership of the group, then these groups tend to survive, but with rather specific relations to the broader social setting. They may become more or less segregated from the wider social setting, turning into what have been called "delinquent communities," that is, communities not oriented to the attainment of their manifest goals, economic, professional, or cultural, but simply to the maintenance of their members' vested status position within the existing setting. But more often they may restructure their relation to the new wider settings, on both organizational and symbolic levels, according to more traditional and less differentiated patterns and criteria of social action. Even more far-reaching may be the attempts of such groups to control the broader frameworks of the society, in order to bolster their own power and positions and to minimize the attempts of the new central institutions to construct viable solidarities at a higher level.

The patterns of transformation of tradition that are likely to develop among groups with a relatively positive orientation to change are markedly different. We might expect to observe a differentiation between various layers of tradition, segregation between traditional and non-traditional (religious and non-religious) spheres of life and of the relevance of different symbols and traditions for different spheres of life. But this segregation is of a rather different order from that found among groups or elites with relatively high resistance to change. It is less total and rigid. There tends to be more continuity between the different spheres, with greater overflow and overlapping between them, though this continuity does not ordinarily become fully formalized or ritualized. There is not usually any strong predisposition towards rigid unifying principles, and in this way greater tolerance of ambiguity and of cognitive dissonance is built up. Because of this, there is no oscillation between a total withdrawal of the more "traditional" or "religious" symbols from the new spheres of life, on the one hand, and attempts to impose various rigid religious principles on these spheres, on the other. Rather we find here a predisposition towards the growth of a more flexible or segregated new symbolic order, under which the various social spheres which have developed some degree of autonomy can be brought together and within which various previous symbols and traditions can be at least partially incorporated.

A predisposition toward a closer and more positive connection between the personal identity of the members of the group or society and symbols of the new political, social, and cultural order may develop. The members then accept the new symbols as the major collective referents of their personal identity. These symbols provide guiding templates for participation in the social and cultural order and lend meaning to many of the new types of institutional activity.

Closely related to those modes of persistence and transformation of traditional organizations and symbols are the characteristics of structural, organizational change which these groups often undergo. First, we find a much higher degree of internal differentiation and diversification of roles and tasks, a growing incorporation of such new roles into these groups, a greater readiness by their members to undertake new tasks outside their groups and to participate in various new groups. Second, these new roles, tasks, and patterns of participation tend to become interwoven in a variety of ways, according to more highly differentiated principles of integration, with a greater degree of what may be called "openness" towards new structural possibilities and towards new goals and symbols of collective identification. Third, a process of incorporation of symbols of both more traditional and more innovative groups in the new central symbols of social, political, or cultural order, with new organizational exigencies, may take place.

Elites with different orientations to change tend to develop organizational policies parallel to the structural consequences of different orientations to change formed in broader groups. Elites with a high resistance to change and with strong traditionalistic orientation were likely to develop, in the spheres of their influence, a ritualism, rigidity, and possible militancy parallel to that found among broader groups resisting change. The potential effects of this orientation among the elites were, however, much more far-reaching. In the more central institutional cores of a society such elites have tended to define the central symbols of their social, political, and cultural order, even though they may have been obliged to adapt to some changes at this level, in a way that de-emphasizes or negates innovation. They define them in a traditionalistic manner that minimizes the chance of integrating within them the new symbols or orientations favored by the more innovative groups. These ritualistic tendencies narrow the possibility of integrating central symbols as referents or ingredients in the personal identity of members of the more innovative groups. The less innovative groups themselves prefer a rather fixed, non-flexible relation between personal identity and the traditionalistic centers. In the organizational sphere these elites have preferred a strongly monolithic orientation. They attempt to control other groups and elites, to maintain them within traditional confines, to segregate them from one another, to minimize and control channels of mobility among them, and to limit their access to the cultural and political centers. Insofar as such elites have adapted to change, they have usually tried to segment the innovations, segregating them in fields they perceived as technical or "external." But they have not done so consistently. Rather, they have oscillated between repressive policies and *ad-hoc* submission to group pressures of various groups. Although they have not been guided by any clear principle in this, they yield more readily to pressure from traditionalistic groups.

On a macro-societal level their responses can lean in two general, often overlapping "ideal-typic" directions. One is that of a militant "traditionalism" on the central levels of the new societies, characterized mainly by conservative ideologies, coercive orientations and policies, and by an active ideological or symbolic closure of the new centers, with a strong traditionalistic emphasis on older symbols. The other may be called pure patrimonialism. The aim is simply to establish, or to preserve, new political and administrative central frameworks. Such symbolic orientation of a cultural and religious nature as exists is weak and non-committal, concerned mostly with the maintenance of the existing régime and of its *modus vivendi* with the major sub-elites and groups in the society. We might describe this as an external traditionalism, lacking any deep commitment to the tradition it purports to symbolize. Elites with a fairly positive "adaptive" orientation to change are those that have largely accepted new institutional goals and have favored participation in new cultural, social, and political orders. Elites of this kind, when they have appeared in the less central and more instrumental institutional spheres, such as the economic and the administrative spheres, have shown considerable ability in creating new *ad-hoc* organizations and new institutional patterns. Often, however, these are only at the same level of differentiation as existing structures, and the aim is mainly to optimize the position of the elites in the new situation.

In other cases, the new organizations may be more differentiated than the old and the new frameworks wider. Activity may be oriented to new sociocultural goals. But the extent to which these tendencies come to be actualized throughout the whole symbolic and institutional organization of any social sphere, especially in any central institutional sphere, has depended on the extent to which the groups and elites concerned are able to develop transformative as well as adaptive capacities.

Truly enough, given certain favorable international and internal conditions, conditions that have probably existed many times in human history, a society or polity can adjust itself to various changing situations and maintain its boundaries with the help of adaptive elites quite weak in over-all transformative capacity. Centers built up by such elites may be strong in coalition-building, but tend to be weak in producing any binding, common attributes of identity or in crystallizing collective goals.

Full realization of all the possibilities of developing new institutional frameworks and centers, of changing the patterns of participation in them, of incorporating new groups within them, of developing new symbolic orders and new efficient central institutions and symbols has been relatively rare in human history. It calls for a high level of transformative capacity within all the elites at the center, and among all that have access to and influence over it. The most dramatic examples of the creation of such new social and cultural orders, in the history of traditional, pre-modern society, are the Great Empires and the Great Religions.

A very important dimension of the activities of central elites seeking to alter the structure of society is that of coerciveness. This is apparent when central elites try to force their elites, and broader strata, into new social and political orders that are alien to them. Examples are found in the history of militant religious elites, whose methods in some cases resembled those of militant traditionalistic elites. More obvious examples are found among contemporary revolutionary elites, rationalistic or communistic. The basic orientations and the institutional implications have usually been a mixture of those of the "traditionalist" and the "transformative" elites. Coercive elites share the "traditionalist" elites' strong inclination to rigid control and regulation, their somewhat negative attitude to the possibility of allowing any degree of autonomy to groups whose symbols and traditions differ from their own, and their resistance to any independent innovation. These coercive orientations and policies have often led to the annihilation of other elites and of entire ethnic groups and social strata. Coercive elites resemble the flexible, non-alienated transformative elites in taking on the task of forging new goals, symbols, and centers, of attempting to establish new political and cultural orders with new ranges of institutional activities, and of widening at least symbolically, if not institutionally, the participation of broader strata in these orders.

Differences between the coercive and non-coercive innovative elites stand out most clearly in their attitudes with respect to regulating the relations between personal and collective identities. Coercive elites in ideological and educational fields attempt to submerge personal identities in the new collective identity. They minimize personal and subgroup autonomy, making collective symbols and their bearers the major controllers of the personal superego.

The more transformative, non-coercive elites, on the other hand, prefer to encourage or at least permit the development of a type of personal identity which has reference, but not a too rigid one, to the new collective identity. This personal identity is not entirely bound up with any one political system, state, or community. It has flexible openings to a variety of collectivities and communities. Yet it tends to generate a strong emphasis on personal commitment to do something for the community. It also entails a very strong connection between personal commitment, personal identity and several types of institutional activities. We may sum up the differences in the impact of different orientations and patterns of response to situations of change by reviewing the several ways in which they utilize the reservoirs of tradition available to them, and the several ways in which different forms of traditional life and symbols persist within the new settings. The reservoirs of tradition consist of the major ways of looking at the basic problems of social and cultural order and of conceiving solutions to them. They also identify the available structures through which the various solutions may be implemented.

A high degree of resistance to change implies inability to define such problems in a new way. There is often a militant emphasis on the necessity of holding exclusively to the old, given answers to these problems. If the possibility of new answers is admitted, it is limited to very partial, discrete, new answers to segregated aspects of the social order. These discrete answers may be subsumed under some of the broader of the older answers. In all these answers there is stress on the importance of defending the exclusiveness of the old problems. The defense may thus become a new problem. Resistance to change is also usually characterized by attempts to maintain the internal structure and the existing level of differentiation of existing social units and to minimize the scope of new and more differentiated groups.

The highly adaptable groups and elites, on the other hand, are characteristically willing to use existing tradition for posing and solving new problems of social and cultural order. Hence they distinguish between different layers of traditional commitments and motivations and try to draw on them all and on existing organizations, so far as possible, in the new tasks and activities. There are clearly two major foci of continuity of tradition among such groups. The first is the persistence, perhaps flexibly, of certain poles or basic modes of perception of the cosmic, cultural, and social order. The second lies in the persistence of autonomous symbols of the collective identities of major subgroups and collectivities, however great may be the concrete changes in their specific content.

Non-coercive transformative elites also utilize reservoirs of tradition, especially through differential use of the various layers of traditional commitments and motivation in new activities and organizations. They may also accept, or even encourage, continuity in the collective identities of many subgroups and strata. Yet there are several major differences between transformative and adaptive elites. The first, by their very nature, are obliged to redefine the major problems of social and cultural order and to enlarge the scope of available and permissible solutions. True, in doing so they usually stop short of rejecting the pre-existing symbols, preferring, as we have seen, to incorporate them in their own new symbolic order. Nevertheless, they do redefine the major problems of this order. Because of this, and especially because of their acceptance of a certain variety of answers to these problems, they tend also to facilitate or encourage the rise of new groups or collectivities, especially of more differentiated, specialized ones, committed to new institutional goals. Hence they may maintain continuity of tradition mostly on levels of commitment to central symbols of the social and cultural orders and of very general orientations to these orders. But they do not maintain commitment to the full content of these orders, which may continuously change.

With a coercive elite, the situation is more complex. On the one hand, if it is successful in attaining or seizing power, it is then in a position to destroy most of the concrete symbols and structures of existing traditions, strata, and organizations and to emphasize new content and new types of social organization. Yet at the same time it may preserve considerable continuity with regard to certain basic modes of symbolic and institutional orientations. Most coercive elites grow out of societies with a relatively low level of institutional and symbolic flexibility. They may as a result pose some of the basic problems of social and cultural order, and of their interrelations, in broad terms, for example, with emphasis on power, in much the same way as their predecessors did. However, the solutions and the manner in which they are worked out, for example, in the problem of how to establish a "strong" autocratic absolutist society as against a "strong" industrial one, would differ greatly from those of the preceding order. Coercive elites attempt to utilize many of the traditional orientations, but shorn of much of their concrete content and of their identification with and connection to the older order or to any parts of it. In other words, the basic attempt is to unleash and to control, in a new way, the primary motivational orientations inherent in the older systems, while at the same time changing their content and basic identity. A similar process occurs with regard to the incorporation of symbols of partial groups or even of some of the older central symbols, especially "patriotic" ones. On the one hand we find an almost total negation of these symbols; on the other hand, because the problems that have to be posed about the nature of the social order remain much the same, there may be parallel attempts to use or uphold these symbols, or similar general symbolic orientations, although in an altered context and with little or no autonomy.

Some Factors Influencing the Development of Different Patterns of Response to Change

We may now briefly examine some of the conditions that influence types of orientation and patterns of response to change, with special reference to traditional societies. Anthropological, sociological, and psychological research point to several sets of variables and their interrelations as being of chief importance.

Certain of these variables, for example the extent of rigidity or differentiation, so closely resemble some of the characteristics of different patterns of response to change that there may well be some circularity in the argument. Yet the claim that the more "flexible" social structures or traditions tend also to develop more "flexible" or positive patterns of response to change seems to us to be indeed true or at least feasible. But the correlation only partially accounts for the patterns of response to change. They fail to account for differences within the range of positive attitudes to change between "adaptive" and "transformative" response, or for the emergence of coercive elites. Again, many variations in the patterns of response to change seem to be related to other variables, not just to the degree of flexibility of the social structure.

The first set of these other variables seems to be the extent of the internal solidarity and cohesion within a group. A second set includes the rigidity and uniformity of the internal division of labor and of the social structure and cultural order, as evident especially in the degree of autonomy of their various components. It includes also the degree of openness of any given group towards other groups, towards the broader society, and towards the social and cultural orders in general.

Structural flexibility or rigidity can be measured first by the extent to which institutional tasks are differentiated and performed in specific situations, and second, by the extent to which each group, role, or situation, is governed by autonomous goals and values or is dominated by those of another such sphere.

The flexibility or rigidity of the symbolic orders of the cultural tradition of a society has to be measured first by the extent to which the content of the cosmic and cultural order, of the social collectivity and the social order, and of the socio-political centers, is closed, fixed, or relatively open. Second, it is to be measured by the degree to which participation in these orders is open to different groups, and third by the nature of their symbolic, organizational, and institutional interrelations and interdependence.

Here several possible constellations can be distinguished. Each such symbolic sphere may be seen as autonomous, but closely interrelated with the others, in the sense that participation in one gives access to another without, however, imposing its own criteria or orientations on it. Or each such order may be relatively closed, with purely "external" or "power" interrelations among them. Finally, one of these orders may predominate over the others, regulating access to them and imposing its own values and symbols on them.

The exact nature of such institutional and symbolic flexibility or rigidity necessarily differs greatly between different types of societies. Thus, in primitive societies rigidity is especially manifest in the close interdependence of units, such as clans and kinship groups, and in organizational and symbolic overlapping, or even identity, in the definition of these units. There is little differentiation between the symbols of belonging to one or another institutional sphere (political, economic, or ritual), and between the situations and roles in which they are enacted. In more complex societies with a much higher degree of organizational differentiation of institutional and symbolic spheres, flexibility or rigidity is especially evident in the institutional autonomy of the spheres, in terms of their specific goals, as against a relatively tight symbolic or institutional control of some central sphere over all the other spheres.

Beyond such interrelations, there is an additional set of variables in the content and organization of a cultural tradition. It is especially important to know the extent to which any given tradition entails active commitment to its values and symbols on the part of individuals and to know whether such commitment is relatively "open" or ritualistically closed or prescribed. The distinction introduced above between weak or strong centers is closely related to this.

These major sets of variables — the extent of solidarity of a social group or system, the extent of autonomy of different institutional and symbolic systems, and the weakness or strength of different centers — tend to influence the different orientations and patterns of response to change. It seems that the general orientation to change is influenced by some combination of two of these sets of variables, namely, by the scope of solidarity of a system and by the degree of its institutional flexibility.

Most available data show that the lower the solidarity and cohesion of any given social system, the lower also is its members' adaptability to change. Social and psychological research show that the maintenance of the cohesion of primary groups, and to some extent of their solidarity links to wider social settings, is of crucial importance if their members are to be free to face new, or adverse, conditions. Destruction of solidarity may greatly impair this ability. Most of these studies, however, have dealt with primary groups within larger formal organizations, mainly in the framework of modern societies. There arises, therefore, the problem of how these variables are related to variables in more formal aspects of micro- or macro-societal structures. It is here that the importance of institutional autonomy appears. In general, the adaptability of a social system to situations of change increases with the extent of the autonomy of its social, cultural, and political institutions and of its major symbolic orders.

Comparative research on this problem, here only beginning to be systematic, suggests that the chances of a society's orientation to change becoming positive depends on the strength of autonomous interrelations among its various symbolic orders, and on the extent to which the precepts of its traditions are non-ritualistic. Conversely, the degree of resistance to change depends on such autonomy being absent or slight, and on the social, cultural, and political orders being closely identified with one another.

Obviously there are many more permutations among these various elements of cultural traditions. Their influence on processes of change will have to be more fully and systematically analyzed in further research. Thus it may seem as if group cohesion and solidarity, on the one hand, and rigidity or flexibility of the social and cultural order, on the other hand, have a similar influence on adaptability and on transformative capacity, that they always tend to go together and seem to reinforce one another in their influence on processes of change. But closer examination of the data indicates that this need not always be the case. It may well be true that a very low degree of group solidarity and cohesiveness reduces adaptability and that high cohesiveness makes for positive orientations to change. But between the extremes the picture is not so simple. For example, a relatively high degree of group solidarity may be connected with a relatively rigid internal division of labour. In that case it need not denote lack of organizational adaptability to change; it may foster special kinds of adaptation.

In general, and in a very tentative way, one may say that the extent of the solidarity of a group or a structure tends to influence the degree to which individuals or groups with organizational ability will appear within it, and that the extent of flexibility in the social structure influences the nature of the general attitude to change within a society. What is important here is the relative focus of solidarity and cohesion of various groups and of their structural characteristics in relation to the social framework of the society. What matters above all is the possibility of carrying over this solidarity into new fields of instrumental activity, into patterns of participation in new social spheres. But neither of these sets of variables as yet explains the extent of a society's ability to crystallize new effective institutional frameworks of any given shape. The crucial variable seems to be the extent to which different types of entrepreneurial and/or charismatic elites and groups may emerge.

The process of social change or the undermining of existing patterns of life, social organization, and culture, accompanied as it often is by structural differentiation, gives rise, by its very impetus, to a great variety of new groups. These will display a new range of differences in basic organizational features. By their very nature most new occupational, religious, and political groups in new status categories or in elite groups undertake new tasks, new types of activities, and are oriented to new organizational settings. These tasks and activities vary greatly, of course, according to whether the emerging system is an empire with a predominantly agrarian base, or is some system with mercantile and factorial bases, or is a system of industrialism, possibly democratic. But these groups of elites also differ greatly in general organizational ability, in their adaptive, innovative or transformative capacities in their own direct sphere of activities, and in their relationships to the broader groups and to the more central institutions of their society.

What are, then, the conditions that influence such elites? We referred above to inherent tendencies, within patterns of tradition, to initiate certain kinds of change. Instead of dealing with this point directly, we shall concentrate on the third set of variables mentioned above, the set affecting the content of a cultural tradition and the strength or weakness of a center.

The strength or weakness of the major centers of any social or cultural order may have structural repercussions on the cohesion and orientations of its major elites in general and of the intellectual strata in particular. Weak centers tend to generate or to be connected with the emergence of new elites that are low in internal autonomy and cohesion, restricted in their social orientations, and inclined to be dissociated both from each other and from the broader strata of the society. Strong centers, on the other hand, generate, or are connected with, more cohesive elites and with intellectual strata that in general have fairly close interrelations. Whether these interrelations will be coercive, hierarchical, or autonomously interdependent and the nature of relations with broader groups and strata will depend largely on the exact structure and content of such centers, especially on their flexibility and on the openness of their symbolic content.

It is the interrelation among: (a) the degree of solidarity of different groups and strata, (b) the structural and symbolic autonomy of different social spheres, that is, the degree of rigidity or flexibility of these spheres, and (c) the strength or weakness of the major centers of the symbolic orders, that is, the social, political, and cultural (in case of traditional societies usually religious) centers, that can best explain, in a limited and preliminary way, the development within a given society of elites and groups with different degrees of organizational, innovative, and transformative capacities. In any society, but particularly in well differentiated societies, these relations are rather complex and heterogeneous. A complex society with a multiplicity of different traditions and groups necessarily gives rise, in situations of change, to a great variety of elites and groups that differ in organizational, innovative, and transformative capacity. These often compete strongly among themselves for relative predominance in the emerging social structure. It would be impossible here to go into all the possible variations; we shall present therefore only some general hypotheses in terms of very general tendencies. Further research will enable us to go beyond these very rough generalizations.

First, in a society, or parts thereof, that has high solidarity but low structural flexibility, new groups will be relatively traditionalistic but well organized. On the other hand, in a society, or parts thereof, that has a high level of flexibility but a relatively low level of solidarity, several new groups or strata may be fairly adaptable, but not very well organized. In a society that has high levels both in flexibility and in solidarity, we might expect groups or elites to appear that would be both fairly well organized and fairly adaptable.

But the extent to which such elite groups are able to influence broader institutional settings, and especially the more central institutional cores of the society, will mostly depend on the types of centers that exist, and on their relations to these centers. The capacity to affect the broader institutional settings will be smaller among elites that are relatively non-cohesive, that are alienated from other elites and from the broader groups and strata of the society, and that are either very distant from the existing center or succeed in monopolizing it, to the exclusion of other groups and elites. In terms of center-building such groups will probably emphasize the maintenance of some given attributes of collective identity, together with the regulation of internal and external force.

Still other societies, or parts thereof, are marked by high levels of rigidity in the social system and in the symbolic orders, displaying little symbolic distinction between their various social and cultural orders, and having relatively weak centers. This seems to have been the case in many Southeast Asian patrimonial régimes. Here the elites will be traditionalistic, and non-transformative. Yet they may show a certain organizational capacity and some predisposition for limited technical innovation. In the less cohesive sectors of such societies there may be a few other elites with some positive orientation to change. These will be new ideological, professional or political groups, capable of adapting to new ideologies or symbols but having little ability for continuous institutional activity, and therefore little transformative capacity. Both of these types of elite will tend to develop "closeness" in social and status perception, and to place a ritual emphasis on certain specific and very limited types of status orientations. They will then conceive their own legitimation in terms of maintaining these restricted ranges of status symbols.

Insofar as rigidity of the social and cultural orders and resistance to change coexist with a rather strong center, one might also expect to find militantly innovative elites with coercive orientations. They will be most likely to arise in groups not too distant from the center and enjoying some internal solidarity.

Where there is a high degree of structural and cultural autonomy and flexibility, and also high cohesion within social groups, elites may attain a realtively high level of adaptability to change, but without showing much transformative capacity.

Here, again, it is the symbolic and institutional structure of the centers and their strength or weakness that is of crucial importance. The combination of conditions of flexibility with strong centers, which would then almost by definition be open, seems to increase the likelihood that highly transformative elites will appear. Research in a number of micro- and macro-societal settings suggests that under these conditions transformative capacity occurs mainly among elites that are relatively cohesive and have a strong sense of self-identity. It is found mostly among secondary elites somewhat removed from the center. They may manage to function within relatively segregated institutional spheres. Or they may have positive solidary orientations to the center and maintain some relations with the older elites and with at least some of the broader groups of the society. Such elites tend also to develop simultaneous orientations to collective ideological transformation and to concrete tasks and problems in different "practical" fields. They perceive their own legitimation in terms of wide changes, not solely in terms of providing immediate benefits or status symbols to other groups.

Where high flexibility coexists with weak centers, the development of transformative elites is usually much impeded. Instead, one may expect to find a very great variety of elites, some of them traditionalistic and some highly adaptable, but each one with distinctive orientations. Insofar as no balance of power develops among them, their very multiplicity may jeopardize the successful institutionalization of any viable new institutional structure.

The preceding analysis of the conditions of development of different types of elites and of their center-building activities may seem to have been put in a rather deterministic way. This was, however, by no means our intention. As has already been pointed out, in every complex society there always exist rather heterogeneous conditions and a variety of sectors, each of which may produce different kinds of elites. Among such elites there usually develops a strong competition for predominance, and the emerging situation as well as the result of such competition are never fully predetermined.

The relative lack of predetermination emerges still more clearly if we bear in mind the importance of the international setting in the development of various elites, as has been stressed above. Throughout our discussion we have emphasized the crucial importance of various secondary elites or movements as potential bearers of socio-political transformation. But the structural location of these elites seems to differ greatly among the different types of political régimes, mainly according to the nature of the division of labor prevalent within a society on the one hand, and the relative placement of these elites within the internal system of the societies, or within the international settings of their respective societies, on the other.

In general, it seems that insofar as the division of labor within any given social system is either "mechanical" and/or based on a center focused mostly on regulation of force and/or on the upholding of symbols of common identity, then change-oriented or transformative cultural or political elites would more probably arise within international enclaves around the society than *within* it. The probability of any such transformative elite effecting change within the society would depend, however, either on the breakdown of its center because of some external or internal forces and/or on finding secondary internal groups or elites that would be willing, for ideological or interest reasons, to become its allies. On the other hand, insofar as a social system is characterized by a high degree of organic solidarity, then it is probable that a change-oriented elite, although it might be closely related to broader international settings and enclaves, would to some extent develop within the society.

The probability of its becoming effective would then depend more on the character of its relations with that society's centers and with its other elites, and with its broader groups, as has been briefly discussed above.

It is natural at this stage of the discussion to inquire whether the development of these different types of elite depends only on the "formal" structure of the social and cultural orders from within which they tend to develop, or also on its content, that is, on orientations and systems of beliefs.

It would be very important for our discussion to analyze how differences in the content of tradition influence the perception of change, adaptability to change, and the possibility of effecting cultural transformation, that is, to see how such content influences the basic paradigms of a cultural tradition. We cannot deal with this problem in detail here. However, it may be worthwhile to present some tentative conclusions derived from a re-examination of Weber's thesis regarding the Protestant Ethic.[4]

According to this analysis the central aspects of Protestant religious and value orientations, those that created, as it were, their transformative potential, were as follows. First of all was its strong combination of "this-worldliness" and transcendentalism, a combination orienting the behavior of the individual to activities within this world, without ritually sanctifying any of them, through a mystic union or through any ritual act, as the final point of religious consummation or worthiness. Second, was the strong emphasis on individual activism and responsibility. Third was the unmediated, direct relation of the individual to the sacred and to the sacred tradition. This attitude, while strongly emphasizing the importance and the direct relevance of the sacred and of tradition, yet minimized the extent to which the individual's relation to the sacred, and his individual commitment, can be mediated by any institution, organization, or textual exegesis. Hence it opened up the possibility of continuous redefinition and reformulation of the nature and scope of such tradition. Further, it enhanced this possibility by a transcendentalism so strong as to minimize the sacredness of any "here and now."

These Protestant orientations, especially strong among Calvinists, were not, however, confined to the realm of the sacred. They were closely related to and manifest in two major orientations inherent in most Protestant groups' conception of social reality and of their own place in it, that is, in what may be called their status images and orientations. Their "openness" towards the wider social structure was of crucial importance. It was rooted in their "this-worldly" orientation in the economic sphere and in other social fields. Second, they were characterized by a certain autonomy and self-sufficiency from the point of view of their status orientation. They displayed little dependence, from the point of view of the crystallization of their own status symbols and identity, on the existing political and religious centers.

A full comparative application of these insights to other religions is still to come, but some preliminary hypotheses can be offered. The effects of the transformative capacity of religious or ideological ideas and movements on the motivational level, that is, in producing strong motivation to undertake new types of non-religious roles, may be greater when the transcendental and this-worldly orientations of these religions or ideologies are strong and when they evince clear ideological autonomy with regard to any given social or communal order. Conversely, such transformative effects are reduced by the degree of strength of a this-worldly or an other-worldly orientation towards immanence, by the extent to which the religious groups are embedded in the existing political order and by the degree of apathy that negative attitudes to this order may entail.

The transformation of new central symbols and frameworks is, in its turn, greatly dependent on the extent to which the religious or ideological systems have shown a relatively high level of both ideological and organizational autonomy while at the same time being oriented to participation in the socio-political order. The more autonomous the religious organizations are, and the less they are identified with the existing political order, the more effective they can be in developing new types of central political and cultural symbols. Conversely, their ability in this direction is smaller when their autonomy is less and when their identification with the existing political order is great.

Again, the greater the extent to which a given polity and state constitute a basic referent of religious activity, the smaller is the extent to which internal movements and systems of reform oriented to the redefinition of the central spheres of the society can develop. Conversely, the stronger the universalistic and transcendental elements within these religious orientations the greater are the chances that such movements will arise.

Finally, the more the activist orientations within the religious value-system are other-worldly, the less likely it is that reform movements will direct themselves to recrystallization of the central spheres of the society. Conversely, the more these orientations have emphasized involvement in the secular world, and the stronger the specific ideological formulations of these orientations, the more likely it is that they will have far-reaching transformative effects.

Notes

1. See E. Shils, "Charisma, Order and Status," *American Sociological Review*, 30 (April, 1965), 199-213; and S. N. Eisenstadt, *Charisma and Institution Building*, in S. N. Eisenstadt, ed., *Max Weber on Charisma and Institution Building*. (Chicago: University of Chicago Press, Heritage of Sociology Series, 1968), pp. iv-lvi.
2. See E. Shils, "Centre and Periphery," in *The Logic of Personal Knowledge, Essays Presented to Michael Polanyi* (London: Routledge & Kegan Paul, 1961), pp. 117-31.
3. The great propensity for academic, professional, bureaucratic, white collar occupations as against more technical, business, occupations which is so widespread in many of the modernizing countries on all levels of the occupational scale is perhaps the clearest manifestation or indication of these trends.
4. A fuller exposition of these points can be found in S. N. Eisenstadt, "The Protestant Ethic Thesis in an Analytical and Comparative Framework," *The Protestant Ethic and Modernization, A Comparative View* (New York: Basic Books, 1968), pp. 3-46.

Contributors

BARBARA WATSON ANDAYA was born in Sydney, Australia in 1943 and graduated in 1963 from Sydney University with a Bachelor of Arts degree and a diploma in Education. After teaching high school for three years she received an East-West Center grant in 1966 and obtained a Master of Arts degree in Southeast Asian History from the University of Hawaii in 1969. In 1975 she obtained her doctorate in Southeast Asian History from Cornell University with a thesis entitled, "Perak, the Abode of Grace: A Study of an Eighteenth Century Malay State." This will be published shortly by Oxford in Asia. She has published several articles on Malay history in the *Journal of the Royal Asiatic Society, Malaysian Branch,* and the *Journal of Southeast Asian Studies.* She is working on a study of the Kingdom of Riau from 1899 to 1911, and later plans to collaborate with Dr. Virginia Matheson in an edited translation of the well-known Malay text, the *Tuhfat al-Nafis.* In October 1977 she became a Research Fellow in the Department of Pacific and Southeast Asian History, Australian National University, Canberra. She is married with one child.

JOHN W. BUTT is Instructor in the Department of Religious Studies at Macalester College, Saint Paul, Minnesota. He received his B.A. from Southwestern University at Memphis and his S.T.B. and S.T.M. from Harvard, where he is presently a candidate for the Th.D. degree. From 1963-66 he served with the United Presbyterian Church, U.S.A., as a Fraternal Worker in Thailand. He returned to Thailand in 1971 and spent fifteen months doing research for his doctoral thesis, which focuses on the nature and dynamics of contemporary Thai religious reform.

SHMUEL NOAH EISENSTADT, Rose Isaacs Professor of Sociology, Hebrew University. Born Warsaw, Poland, 1923; M.A., 1944, and Ph.D., 1947, Jerusalem. Visiting Member, 1958, London School of Economics and Political Science; Fellow, Center for Advanced Study in the Behavioral Sciences, Stanford, California, 1955-56; Visiting Professor, University of Oslo, 1958; University of Chicago, 1960 and 1971; Mass. Institute of Technology, 1962-63; Harvard University, 1966, 1968-69, 1975, 1976; and University of Michigan, 1970; Visiting Research Associate, University of Michigan, 1964; Harper Fellow, University of Chicago, 1969; Fellow, Netherlands Institute for Advanced Study, Wassenaar, 1973; McIver Award Lecturer, American Sociological Assn., 1964. His many publications include the following books: *The Absorption of Immigrants* (1954), *From Generation to Generation* (1956), *Essays on Sociological Aspects of Economical and Political Development* (1961), *The Political Systems of Empires* (1963), *Essays on Comparative Institutions* (1965), *Modernization, Protest and Change* (1966), *Israeli Society* (1968), *The Protestant Ethic and Modernization* (1968), *Comparative Perceptions on Social Change,* editor (1968), *Charisma and Institution Building: Selections from Max Weber,* editor (1968), *Tradition, Change, and Modernity* (1973), and *Socialism and Tradition,* co-editor (1975).

JOHN P. FERGUSON holds a doctorate in anthropology granted in 1975 from Cornell University. His field work on Theravada Buddhism was done in Chiang Mai, Thailand, and his thesis was on the symbolic relationship between Burmese monks and kings. He has taught the anthropology of Southeast Asia at the New York State University, the College at Oneonta. Before coming to

225

anthropology, he taught English at the secondary level and holds a B.A. in English from Williams College and an M.A. in literature from Columbia University. At present, he is the recipient of a fellowship from the American Council of Learned Societies for research on the iconography and cosmology of modern Theravada Buddhism in Burma and Thailand. He has edited *Sangha and State in Burma* (Cornell University Press, 1975) by E. M. Mendelson and has co-authored articles on the Thai Sangha and modern Buddhist murals in Northern Thailand.

CHARLES F. KEYES is Professor of Anthropology and a member of the Programs in Comparative Religion, Comparative Studies in Ethnicity and Nationality, and South Asian Studies at the University of Washington, Seattle. His B.A. is from the University of Nebraska (1959) and his Ph.D. from Cornell University (1967). He has taught at the University of Washington (Seattle) since 1965 and was a Visiting Lecturer, Faculty of the Social Sciences, Chiang Mai University, Thailand, 1972-74. He is the author of *Isan: Regionalism in Northeastern Thailand* (1967); *The Golden Peninsula: Culture and Adaptation in Mainland Southeast Asia* (1977); and numerous articles on Buddhism and society, on ethnic group relations, and on peasant society with particular reference to Thailand. He has also edited and contributed to *Ethnic Adaptation and Identity: The Karens of the Thai Frontier with Burma* (1977).

A. THOMAS KIRSCH is Associate Professor of Anthropology and Asian Studies at Cornell University. He did field research among the Phu Thai of Northeast Thailand during 1962-64, concentrating on religious syncretism and religious change. His publications include *The Human Direction: An Evolutionary Approach to Social and Cultural Anthropology* (Appleton-Century-Crofts, 1970), and *Feasting and Social Oscillation: A Working Paper on Religion and Society in Upland Southeast Asia* (Cornell University, Southeast Asia Program Data Paper No. 92, 1973). He is also co-editor of *Change and Persistence in Thai Society: Essays in Honor of Lauriston Sharp* (Cornell University Press, 1975).

SOMMAI PREMCHIT, M.A. in archaeology at the University of the Philippines, is an Acharn in the Department of Sociology/Anthropology and Director of the Northern Thai Research Center at Chiang Mai University, Chiang Mai, Thailand. He is currently completing a multi-volume catalogue of manuscripts in Chiang Mai monastery libraries and is the translator into Central Thai of the Northern Thai *sāstra, Mangrai Customary Law* (1975)

FRANK E. REYNOLDS received his doctorate from the University of Chicago in 1971 where he presently serves as Associate Professor of Buddhist Studies in the Department of South Asian Languages and Civilizations and as Chairman of the History of Religions Field in the Divinity School. He has lived in Thailand for three years where he has taught at Chulalongkorn University and done research on a Fulbright-Hayes Faculty Fellowship. He has served as Chairman of the Asian Religions/History of Religions Section of the American Academy of Religion (1972-75) and had appointments as a Visiting Professor at Stanford University (1971), John Carroll University (1973), Carleton College (1975), and Notre Dame University (1976). In addition to a variety of articles, he has completed (with Mani B. Reynolds) the translation of a Thai Buddhist cosmology, the *Three Worlds According to King Ruang*, which will be forthcoming from the Siam Society and the Stanford University Press, and has co-edited two books — *The Biographical Process* and *Religious Encounters with Death* — which will be released by the Mouton and Penn State University Presses in late 1976 and 1977 respectively.

MANUEL SARKISYANZ is Professor and Director of the Political Science Department of the South Asia Institute at the University of Heidelberg. He studied at the University of Teheran, receiving his M.A. from the Asia Institute, New York City, and his Ph.D. from the University of Chicago. In 1959 he did research in Burma as a Guggenheim Fellow. Among his books are: *Russland und der Messianismus des Orients* (J.C.B. Mohr, 1955); *Südostasien seit 1945* (Oldenbourg-Verlag, 1961); *Geschichte der Orientalischen Völker Russlands bis 1917* (Oldenbourg-Verlag, 1961); *Buddhist Backgrounds of the Burmese Revolution* (Martinus Nijhoff, 1965); "Religionen Kambodschas, Birmas, Laos, Thailands und Malaysias," in *Religionen der Menschheit* (edited by Cr. M. Schroeder), Vol. 23, pp. 384-560 (Kohlhammer, 1975); and *Modern History of Transcaucasian Armenia* (privately printed by E. J. Brill, 1976).

DONALD K. SWEARER, Ph.D., Princeton University (1967), is Professor of Asian and Comparative Religions at Swarthmore College where he has taught since 1970. From 1965-70 he was a member of the Department of Religion at Oberlin College. His publications include *Wat Haripuñjaya: The Royal Temple-Monastery of the Buddha's Relic in Lamphun, Thailand* (American Academy of Religion, 1976); *Secrets of the Lotus: Studies in Buddhist Meditation* (Macmillan, 1971), with Sobhana Dhammasudhi and Eshin Nishimura; *Buddhism in Transition* (Westminster, 1969); and the forthcoming *Confrontation or Dialogue? Christianity and Other Religions* (Westminster, 1977). This article is part of a more extensive study of Buddhism in Northern Thailand.

BARDWELL L. SMITH is the John W. Nason Professor of Asian Studies at Carleton College, Northfield, Minnesota. He also served as Dean of the College, 1967-72. He has received his B.A., B.D., M.A., and Ph.D. from Yale University and was a member of the Yale University Council, 1969-74. During 1972-73 he did research at the School of Oriental and African Studies, University of London, on a grant from the American Council of Learned Societies. He has edited a number of books, among them: *The Two Wheels of Dhamma: Essays on the Theravada Tradition in India and Ceylon* (American Academy of Religion, 1972); *Tradition and Change in Theravada Buddhism: Essays on Ceylon and Thailand in the 19th and 20th Centuries* (Leiden: E. J. Brill, 1973); *Unsui: A Diary of Zen Monastic Life* (Honolulu: University Press of Hawaii, 1973); *Hinduism: New Essays in the History of Religions* (Leiden: E. J. Brill, 1976); *Religion and Social Conflict in South Asia* (Leiden: E. J. Brill, 1976); and *Essays on T'ang Society: The Interplay of Social, Political and Economic Forces* (Leiden: E. J. Brill, 1976), co-edited with John Curtis Perry.

STANLEY J. TAMBIAH is Professor of Anthropology at Harvard University. Previously he was Professor at Chicago University (1973-1976), and Fellow of King's College and Lecturer in Anthropology in the University of Cambridge (1964-1972). He has done extensive fieldwork in his country of birth, Sri Lanka, and in Thailand. He is the author of *Buddhism and the Spirit Cults in Northeast Thailand* (1970), *World Conqueror and World Renouncer, A Study of Buddhism and Polity in Thailand Against a Historical Background* (1976), co-author of *Bridewealth and Dowry* (1973). He has published numerous papers on the ethnography of South and Southeast Asia, kinship, social classification, ritual, literacy, and modernization.

Index